Security Intelligence

A Practitioner's Guide to Solving Enterprise Security Challenges

Qing Li
Gregory Clark

WILEY

Security Intelligence: A Practitioner's Guide to Solving Enterprise Security Challenges

Published by
John Wiley & Sons, Inc.
10475 Crosspoint Boulevard
Indianapolis, IN 46256
www.wiley.com

Copyright © 2015 by John Wiley & Sons, Inc., Indianapolis, Indiana
Published simultaneously in Canada

ISBN: 978-1-118-89669-3
ISBN: 978-1-118-89667-9 (ebk)
ISBN: 978-1-118-89666-2 (ebk)

Manufactured in the United States of America

10 9 8 7 6 5 4 3

For general information on our other products and services please contact our Customer Care Department within the United States at (877) 762-2974, outside the United States at (317) 572-3993 or fax (317) 572-4002.

Wiley publishes in a variety of print and electronic formats and by print-on-demand. Some material included with standard print versions of this book may not be included in e-books or in print-on-demand. If this book refers to media such as a CD or DVD that is not included in the version you purchased, you may download this material at http://booksupport.wiley.com. For more information about Wiley products, visit www.wiley.com.

Library of Congress Control Number: 2015934208

To Huaying, Jane and Adalia;
in Him.

—Qing Li

To my parents, James and Mary Clark: thanks for providing guidance early in my
education and career.

—Greg Clark

To the cyber security researchers and professionals who are keeping us safe in the
digital world. We offer you our sincere admiration and gratitude for what you do.

—Qing Li and Greg Clark

Credits

Executive Editor
Carol Long

Project Editor
Rosemarie Graham

Technical Editor
Robert J. Shimonski

Production Editor
Rebecca Anderson

Copy Editor
Marylouise Wiack

Manager of Content Development and Assembly
Mary Beth Wakefield

Marketing Director
David Mayhew

Marketing Manager
Carrie Sherrill

Professional Technology & Strategy Director
Barry Pruett

Business Manager
Amy Knies

Associate Publisher
Jim Minatel

Project Coordinator, Cover
Brent Savage

Proofreader
Kim Wimpsett

Indexer
J&J Indexing

Cover Designer
Wiley

Cover Image
©iStock.com/a-r-t-i-s-t

About the Authors

Qing Li is the Chief Scientist and Vice President of Advanced Technologies at Blue Coat Systems, Inc. He is an industry veteran with over 20 years of experience. He has spent the past 11 years designing and developing industry-leading technologies and products at Blue Coat.

Qing is fully responsible for the IPv6 secure proxy, IPv6 WAN optimization technology, and product lines at Blue Coat. He produced the industry's first IPv6 Secure Web Gateway product in 2009 and received the IPv6 Application Solution Pioneer Award from the IPv6 Forum in 2010. Subsequently he produced the industry's first IPv6 WAN Optimization appliance in 2011, and he produced and released the industry's first IPv6 visibility solution in early 2012.

In 2013 Qing took over responsibility for the PacketShaper product. He reinvented the technology and in early 2014 introduced the new PacketShaper S-series appliances into the market place, which are Blue Coat's first 10 Gbps visibility and QoS solutions. The PacketShaper S-series appliance product line reinvigorated new product revenue growth for the first time since 2008, when Blue Coat acquired Packeteer.

In the past five years, Qing's research has concentrated on emerging technologies including advanced application classification algorithms, mobile security, SSL interception, malware detection, and data analytics. His innovations have transformed the Blue Coat technology and product landscape.

Prior to Blue Coat, Qing spent over eight years at Wind River Systems and was the Lead Architect of Wind River's Networking Group. He was responsible for both the pSOS+ and VxWorks networking systems. He led a large distributed team and, in a development partnership with Siemens, successfully delivered VxWorks 6.0 for Network Equipment in early 2003; this was the first VxWorks release that offered full IPv6 support.

Qing is a published author, most notably of a two-volume reference series on IPv6. Volume I, *IPv6 Core Protocols Implementation*, and Volume II, *IPv6 Advanced Protocols Implementation*, were published in 2006 and 2007, respectively, by Morgan Kaufmann Publishers. In 2003 Qing wrote the embedded systems development book *Real-Time Concepts for Embedded Systems*, which was published by CRC Press; it has served as a reference text in the industry as well as in universities. Qing was also a contributing author to *Handbook of Networked and Embedded Control Systems*, a first-of-its-kind book published in 2005 by Birkhäuser.

Qing holds 17 U.S. patents, with many more pending in the areas of networking and security. He has been an active speaker at industry and academic conferences and contributes to discussions of technological innovation and development across a wide range of media around the world.

Gregory Clark is currently the Chief Executive Officer and a member of the Board of Directors of Blue Coat Systems, Inc., a developer of products and services that secure enterprise infrastructure. Mr. Clark previously served as Chief Executive Officer of Mincom, a leading global provider of software and services to asset-intensive industries. Prior to Mincom, he served as Chief Technology Officer and subsequently became President and Chief Executive Officer of E2open, a leader in ERP-agnostic global supply chain integration.

Earlier in his career, Mr. Clark was the IBM Distinguished Engineer responsible for IBM's security technology and served as a vice president at IBM's Tivoli Systems, Inc. Before joining IBM, he founded the security software firm, Dascom, Inc., which was sold to IBM in 1999 and formed a critical element of IBM's security product line. Mr. Clark previously held senior roles with AT&T's UNIX System Laboratories. He is also a member of the Board of Directors of the Global Healthcare Exchange (GHX), Imperva (IMPV), and Emulex (ELX). Mr. Clark is also a Senior Operating Partner at Thoma Bravo. He has almost 30 years of experience in enterprise infrastructure and security and has been granted multiple patents in security technology and business process applications.

Acknowledgments

I want to thank my beautiful wife, Huaying, for replenishing my perseverance with her inexhaustible love and support and for being my best friend and a great mommy. I am blessed with two beautiful girls, Jane and Adalia; they are the joy of my life, my inspiration, and through them I see God's grace. I am also grateful that I can draw my strength from Philippians 4:13, "I am able to do all things in Him who empowers me."

I would like to thank Wenjing Wang and Min Hao Chen for being my research assistants. You guys are simply awesome!

I would also like to thank Chris Larsen, Ron Frederick, Tim van der Horst and Ryan W. Smith for their insightful thoughts. I would like to thank Liliya Bederov for helping with the graphics.

I would like to thank Carol A. Long for recognizing the value of, and being the executive acquisitions editor for, this book. I would also like to thank Rosemarie Graham for her tireless efforts at managing the editing and production phase of the book and for pushing it over the finish line.

—Qing Li

Contents

Foreword

It is difficult to unlearn something that was once considered fact; it's against human nature. But unlearning and then reimagining is where we find ourselves in the field of information security today. Think about the changes in how we use technology that have happened over the past decade: the unbounded mobility of workers, the adoption of cloud services, and the rise of nation-state hackers, hacktivists bent on destruction, and cyber-criminal organizations that are run like efficient corporations. These shifts are reshaping our profession daily and challenging yesterday's "best practices."

When I began teaching at Columbia University in the mid-2000s, the term *hacking* conjured up images of disaffected teenagers for most people. How quickly that association has changed. The professionalization of hacking has led to massive loss of intellectual property and the theft of countless personal records. It has destroyed companies, threatened nations, and thrust security into the consciousness of people who would otherwise not be concerned with technology.

So where does a modern security practitioner become grounded in the realities of today's security? This book is a great place to start. Qing Li and Greg Clark have both left a permanent stamp on the security industry and continue to help some of the biggest organizations in the world to protect themselves. This book is a great resource for security professionals and cyber warriors, as Qing and Greg share the knowledge they have accumulated from building products that protect more than eighty percent of the Fortune 500 corporations around the world.

As the chairman of the world's largest security conference, and an academic and practitioner, I can tell you there has never been a more important time for you to read this book. Think of it as a primer for security in modern times, against modern adversaries. What I have always admired about Qing and Greg is that they are grounded in the practical. This is a book that doesn't speak in absolutes—it respects the dynamic nature of information security. It tackles the hard topics like malnet detection, application intelligence, and retrospective analysis. It examines the design of a system that can protect modern *endpoints*, which can be anything from workstations, laptops, phones, and tablets to smart refrigerators, power meters, and yet-to-be-conceived devices in the Internet of Things. It also exposes the power of what is still one of the most important weapons we have in the fight against attackers: the security proxy.

If you are new to information security, this book is a terrific modern primer. If you have been in security for a while, you must approach this book with a simple truth in mind: our industry is having to reinvent itself in the face of modern attacks. Eight-character passwords and a defined network perimeter are a part of our industry's past, not its present or future. Come with an open mind and allow Qing and Greg to reintroduce you to tools you thought you knew in the context of today's sophisticated attacks.

In this new era of security, the authors will take you into the world of malware distribution networks and show you how they play a central role in attacks. You'll also learn how modern techniques like sandboxing, security analytics, and fine-grained application controls can be wielded to protect a modern enterprise.

Information sharing is essential for today's security professional. The content in this book can help invigorate thought on how to build better security solutions. It can also help you come up with more relevant questions to ask in areas where you want to attain clarity.

When security is done right, it is not about lockdown and fear. It is about opening possibilities and liberating business instead of stifling it. In that way, this is a very hopeful book, and I hope you will enjoy reading it as much as I have.

Hugh Thompson, Ph.D.
Los Gatos, CA
December 2014

Preface

The digitization of a prodigious amount of information is intensifying, from health care records and educational backgrounds, to employment history, credit reports, and financial statements. Words like *eBilling*, *eStatements*, and *paperless transactions* have become part of our everyday language. The ever-increasing ability to retrieve this digital information online, combined with both the unremitting compilation of such information to extrapolate personal traits and behavior and the explosion of convenient venues for accessing the Internet, should encourage questions in curious minds: "Just how vulnerable are we to threats against personal privacy?" and "Who is at liberty to scrutinize the vast amounts of private data?"

In recent years, the rapid growth of high-bandwidth network infrastructures accompanied by a dramatic reduction in storage costs serve as the catalysts in the construction and commercialization of various cloud-based services, which are offered to both institutions and individuals. These cloud-based services range from personal online backup storage, content-sharing, and collaboration tools to customer relations management (CRM). These services are easily attainable with affordable prices that will only invigorate adoption and proliferation. Naturally, for security-conscious minds, questions arise as to how penetrable these services are by nefarious entities and, when compromised, how limited in scope the resulting damages will be from a specific breach incurred on the cloud community as a whole.

Utility companies, power plants, air traffic control systems, public transit systems, and others are predominately under digital control. Media coverage of specific cyber-attacks that have targeted these critical infrastructures indicates that the frequency of the attacks is escalating and with rapidly evolving sophistication, and these attacks are incurring more severe damages on their targets. These stories may include enticing details that are suspenseful and entertaining; however, failure to detect, defend, and remediate these threats will effect monetary catastrophe and endanger the population with unimaginable consequences. So, what mechanisms have been contrived to entrap offenders before they assail us under a camouflage of bit streams?

Branches of government and the armed forces restrict information flow and closely inspect each individual's cyber activities. Similarly, organizations such as health care providers, insurance companies, and financial institutions must comply with certain industry rules and regulations. Many sumptuary laws require exhaustive access logging and retrospective analysis. Mining this voluminous data into a structured representation demands interdisciplinary expertise, through a process that sanitizes the raw data, sieves out the relevant subsets, transforms and normalizes the selection, and applies analytics to seek out patterns. Data mining and analytics are critical components of the security envelope. The flexibility and diversity of queries that can be issued against the extracted knowledge measure the quality of the data mining approach. In the security context, the length of time taken to excavate data determines how quickly active threats can be divulged, imminent attacks revealed, and felicitous resolutions conjured in response, instead of reacting with extemporary and ineffective countermeasures.

Security implementation and enforcement begins with us thinking in terms of the end goals. These goals must be expressible in plain language. For example, the thoughts of the CIO of a large enterprise may be as follows:

- When Bob accesses Dropbox, I want to prevent him from uploading any files but permit him to download content from his account between 8 a.m. and 5 p.m., at a rate of no more than 256 Kbps. Bob is not allowed to upload files because he is new to the company and is under a three-month probation period. However, he does have access to sensitive marketing information, and I want to prevent him from sharing such information externally. Bob has permission to download files from Dropbox because his manager utilizes Dropbox for file sharing across a distributed team. Because Dropbox is Bob's main online application, I want to limit Bob's network bandwidth utilization so that Dropbox does not over-consume available network resources.

- When Alice runs the Skype application, I want to log her text chat sessions because she works in a restricted financial environment. Due to SEC regulations and U.S. Treasury mandates, financial institutions must monitor employee transactions and online behavior in order to detect insider sabotage, data theft, or security breaches that originate externally. For these reasons, all of Alice's online activities must be logged and analyzed.

- When users visit websites during work hours, I want to disallow them from accessing sites that are categorized as adult entertainment. I want the content of each website to be analyzed in real-time for adult material, and if any is discovered, I want to terminate that user session immediately and send an alert to HR for coaching the user on company policies.

These security goals seem straightforward, yet a plethora of networking and security technologies is necessary to achieve the desired end results. For example, let us try to translate the first goal into an actual implementation and observe the various networking and security disciplines that are involved.

The prerequisite of implementing the first security goal, at a minimum, includes knowing which user initiated the network traffic, which application is associated with which traffic flows, and which specific application action generated the traffic.

When Bob initiates a Dropbox session to www.dropbox.com, the associated traffic that is observed on the network does not contain visible user information such as login name simply because the entire session is encrypted using TLSv1. One way to determine the user information is by examining the source IP address and then querying a directory service such as Active Directory for mapping information between the username and the IP address. This method is unreliable because multiple users could be running on the same host machine that is assigned a single IP address. In other words, if both Bob and Alice are using the same multi-user system for accessing Dropbox, then the IP address-to-username mapping approach will not produce accurate identification. Therefore, the most reliable way of extracting the user information is by examining the actual HTTPS payload.

Because the traffic is encrypted, it is impossible to decipher unless there is a way to plant a device in the communication path; this device would act as the man-in-the-middle (MITM) that can communicate with the user as if it were the server, while at the same time communicating with the server on behalf of the user. Even when the application does not utilize data encryption between its client and server, the art of application classification will be the key to associate data flows to user-initiated application actions, such as file download or file upload commands. The data rate must be measured constantly and must be adjusted according to the desired rate, assuming the data flow has been associated with a specific application command.

So, to summarize, this simple example involves technologies ranging from application classification and authentication protocol to encrypted traffic interception and quality of service management. Yet the example we have just presented is only one aspect of enterprise security, which relates to employee online access behavior and resource usage monitoring, followed by enforcement according to defined policies. Monitoring an employee's online activities involves more than just restricting recreational traffic for productivity gain; more importantly, an employee could be the source of various types of security breaches. For example, an employee could visit a well-known reputable website; however, if the site has been compromised by hackers who have installed malicious URLs to alluring content, the unsuspecting employee may follow a web link and download a malicious piece of code unintentionally, which then turns the employee's computer into a sensor for a malicious botnet.

Security tools that rely on a reputation-based rating system to evaluate the safety level of a website cannot protect users from new dynamic URLs that link to malicious content. The just-described scenario is occurring with increasing frequency due to the ever-growing and evolving lures that entice unsuspecting users into the dark corners of the Internet. The employee's personal information could be stolen. However, if, for example, the employee is a health care worker who may have access to millions of private records, then this private data could be compromised on a massive scale, inflicting unimaginable damages on families and individuals. Unfortunately, public disclosures of such incidents have been made at an alarming rate in recent years.

If a security breach has been detected, postmortem analysis of the various security compromises that encompass the breach is critical in constructing adequate and flexible defense mechanisms against similar attacks in the future. Depending on the severity and level of sophistication of the attack, the analysis process is typically comprised of inspecting terabytes, if not petabytes, of data that may include user transaction logs and raw packet captures. The essence of this *retrospective analysis* is data mining, and the goals are, at a minimum, to identify the victim or victims of the attack, the area of the initial penetration, and the speed of dispersion and propagation, and to analyze the threat DNA against the known attacks. The combination of real-time traffic analysis, correlation of events and response, and data recording and analytics, together with vulnerability management, are loosely termed Security Information (or Incident) and Event Management (SIEM). The maturity and sophistication of a security solution, therefore, can be demonstrated in its effectiveness at translating security requirements, articulated from natural language into actionable and enforceable security policies within that solution.

Our book is designed and written for CISOs, network administrators, solutions architects, sales engineers, security engineers who implement security solutions, and developers who are building new generations of security products. Similar to unraveling a math word problem, this book guides the reader through a deciphering process that translates each security goal into a set of security variables, substitutes each variable into a specific security technology domain, formulates the equation that is the deployment strategy, and then verifies the solution against the original problem by analyzing security incidents and divulging hidden breaches, ultimately refining the security formula iteratively in a perpetual cycle.

Fear not, you do not need a Ph.D. to read this book. We do assume that you have a basic understanding of the TCP/IP protocols, the HTTP protocol, and a high-level conceptualization of SSL/TLS technology.

The book is organized into nine chapters.

Chapter 1, "Fundamentals of Secure Proxies," dissects traditional defense technologies, such as firewalls and IDS and IPS systems, to illustrate the deficiencies in legacy security solutions. The *proxy* technology is described in detail from the developer's perspective. This chapter then demonstrates the power of proxies by diving into the specifics of how SSL interception is achieved.

Chapter 2, "Proxy Deployment Strategies and Challenges," provides definitions of the various types of proxies in terms of their deployment strategy, accompanied by their advantages and disadvantages. A proxy, being a stateful device, is confronted by various and unpredictable network infrastructure designs. This chapter enumerates the top deployment challenges and offers respective solutions in detail.

Chapter 3, "Proxy Policy Engine and Policy Enforcements," leverages the policy language of a real-world security product to illustrate the essential elements of an effective policy system and demonstrates how various components of a policy are implemented in various stages of the traffic processing path.

Chapter 4, "Malware and Malware Delivery Networks," provides an overview of the types of malware that are active in the wild. The ploys, lures, and schemes fashioned by the attacks are illuminated through actual incidents. Advanced persistent threats (APTs) and other sophisticated strategies such as Stuxnet and Flame have been employed as infiltration and cyber weapons to wage warfare among countries. This chapter sheds light on this topic.

Chapter 5, "Malnet Detection Techniques," describes the algorithms that are applied for detecting suspicious URLs and content that lead to malware infection. Techniques employed for trapping and analyzing malware and suspicious code are fully articulated in this chapter, along with a discussion of open-source analysis tools.

Chapter 6, "Writing Policies," offers meticulous detail on policy design for many common security objectives in enterprise environments.

Chapter 7, "The Art of Application Classification," examines the classification techniques for identifying applications accurately over live traffic in real-time. Knowing what traffic is associated with which application is the first step in applying intelligent control. This chapter elucidates the technical complexities behind this challenging class of security problems that are under active research.

Chapter 8, "Retrospective Analysis," discusses the algorithms and techniques for data logging, storage, management, and mining knowledge, all in the context of security intelligence.

Chapter 9, "Mobile Security," focuses on the new and fast-growing mobile computing world, where security is optional. This chapter discusses the various technical challenges that make designing and building mobile security solutions difficult. With millions of applications available for download, mobile application identification is a formidable challenge. This chapter offers a comprehensive overview of the current active research trends in this new discipline.

There are countless books on firewalls, malware and viruses, cryptography, IDS, IPS, data mining, and many related concepts. However, a book is needed that unifies these concepts, analyzes and compares the various solutions, digests the security problems into succinct requirements, and crystallizes the implementation strategies that correlate to specific technology and solution categories. This book is the missing manual that teaches you how to assemble all those parts into practical solutions that solve real-world enterprise security challenges.

At a minimum, we hope this book can assist you in turning some of those desultory conversations of acronyms into meaningful discussions on enterprise security.

Fundamentals of Secure Proxies

The evolution of the secure proxy is a reflection of the evolution of the web. The proxy began as a gateway that bridged content that was processed and managed by various information systems, and served that content to the open web during the early days of Internet web construction. The term *web proxy server* was given to this general intermediary to reflect its main duty at the time, namely, translating web requests from the Internet to representations that could be understood and fulfilled by different internal systems, and vice versa.

The web has evolved, expanded, and flourished from a content-centric, information-sharing system into an elaborate ecosystem for commerce, an acculturation establishment for Millennials, and a foundation for modern-day cloud computing. The web browser has become the instrument that unlocks all of the wealth the web offers. The fundamental web protocols and technology, such as HTTP, SSL, HTML, XML, Java, and JavaScript, have been amalgamated into a complex conduit, which faces relentless assaults from nefarious forces that try to subvert it for profit. However, private intellectual properties and confidential data hosted in private and protected networks are accessible through a browser over secure connections across the Internet. The web has also been adopted as a system of portals for managing critical infrastructures at municipal, state, and national levels. Consequently, the user and the browser have become attack vectors for breaching corporate as well as national security.

The web proxy has evolved from a content gateway into an essential security gateway that focuses on users, applications, and content. The security proxy differs from a generic web proxy in that the secure proxy can interpret and intercept more application protocols than just HTTP. Secure proxies, especially when deployed in enterprise environments, serve as both protectors and enablers so that their user community can benefit from the web while minimizing the risk of being victimized by malware delivery networks.

Security Must Protect and Empower Users

The rise of the Internet becoming the foundation of the new era in commerce, culture, communication, education, entertainment, and technology was invasive, with profound impact on our social behaviors. It is now ubiquitous and is an indispensable element of both professional and personal life. At the time of the Internet boom, even long before the advent of mobile computing, the line between work hours and personal time was indistinguishable. With the introduction and rapid adoption of smart phones and tablet computing, there is no longer a distinction between a personal and a work-related computing device. This situation is particularly true for employees who travel a great deal as part of their job functions. For this mobile workforce, a regular laptop computer is typically installed with both personal software and work-related applications. They work wherever and whenever they can while roaming through airports and hotels. The expansion of both the Internet and affordable residential broadband networks has enabled many employees to work from home. Similar to the mobile workforce, the home computer serves as both a personal entertainment and productivity platform and a professional instrument that performs corporate-related job functions. Both computing paradigms raise a dilemma: a well-formed physical perimeter that isolates and guards the enterprise network with traditional IT governance is nonexistent. This lack of separation of personal, private information from corporate intellectual property and data on the same storage device can be a liability for both the employee and the employer.

The Birth of Shadow IT

Business applications are migrating from locally hosted solutions within the enterprise to a cloud-hosted collaborative model. This transition means enterprise users are accessing business-critical applications through their web browser, over the standard web protocols, using a diverse range of computing devices that may not be owned or managed by the enterprise. Consequently, the traditional security practice of the allow-or-deny-all approach is inadequate in managing today's complex web-oriented computing paradigm.

In today's enterprises, users demand the ability to choose from a vast number of applications that they can utilize to maximize their productivity when performing their duties, while at the same time leveraging those same applications for personal objectives. Because enterprise IT and network access policies tend to be restrictive, many user-chosen applications may not be authorized for use in an enterprise network due to security risks, such as the type of information the application gathers and transmits to entities that are external to the enterprise. The servers that the application communicates with may also be easily compromised by attacks. For example, many organizations prevent users from running Dropbox for file sharing for fear that company-related confidential documents may be leaked as a result of unintentional but careless actions. Another typical restriction is that users are forbidden from running any application that participates in a peer-to-peer (P2P) network. This prohibition is likely the precipitant of the Digital Millennium Copyright Act that was signed into law in the United States in 1998. From an enterprise perspective, any copyright infringing material that is stored and that transits the enterprise network presents serious legal liabilities and ramifications. Application software may be produced by various publishers that range from large commercial vendors to independent software developers. An enterprise may exclude an application from its permissible list based on the publisher and its reputation.

One of the fundamental evolutions that have taken place in the enterprise IT environment is the emergence and growth of *shadow IT*. Employees' desire to circumvent IT restrictions led to the use of shadow IT. In the previous example, if Dropbox were blocked by IT policies, then employees would find alternative mechanisms and tools to share files, thus resulting in shadow IT usage. Consider the following example: sales engineers (SEs) travel constantly, and they need to share files with other SEs, employees, and their customers. E-mail systems implement file size limits such that large files cannot be transferred over e-mail. Because Dropbox has been blocked, these SEs may experiment exhaustively with Box.com, Wuala.com, Google Docs, Google Drive, TeamDrive, SugarSync, OneDrive, CloudMe, or Amazon Cloud Drive until they find a solution that is capable of penetrating the IT security net.

Internet of Things and Connected Consumer Appliances

The *Internet of Things* (IoT) refers to uniquely identifiable embedded devices that are networked, which are reachable and manageable through the Internet infrastructure. These embedded devices have proliferated and matured beyond just smart sensors to more intelligent applications such as smart building and home automation systems. Google's $3.2 billion acquisition of Nest in January 2014, followed by Samsung's acquisition of SmartThings in August 2014, offers a glimpse into market developments that are shaping the future of the IoT. Much of this IoT can now be accessed and controlled through applications on popular mobile devices such as the Apple iPhone and iPad and Google's Android-based gadgets. For example, a homeowner can use the ADT Pulse app on their iPad to activate or deactivate their ADT home alarm system, check motion sensors, and watch live video feeds from various video cameras that have been installed in their home. The Tesla Model S iPhone app allows a car owner to track their car's location or start and stop electrical charging of the vehicle.

The IoT has met little resistance as it has gradually become engrained into our daily lives, in what appears to be almost a seamless integration, because convenience and ease-of-use have replaced security at center stage. Securing the IoT is a complex problem. Two main aspects of defense include protecting the IoT device and securing the access channel. The access channel includes the communication between the device and its peer (commonly known as *machine-to-machine communications* [M2M]), and the communication between the device and its operator. Because it is embedded, the IoT device has limited computing power and resources, which limits the device's ability to run sophisticated software such as a virus scanner. Such an embedded device is typically powered by either a custom operating system (OS) or a special variant of a known OS. An embedded OS generally lacks security software that is commonly found in a desktop OS, for example, antivirus software. At the time of this writing, the popular Apple iOS has been on the market for over seven years, yet antivirus software for the iPhone and iPad is limited in both variety and functionality; more importantly, such antivirus software is rarely installed by iOS users. Considering the iPhone is by definition an embedded device, the prospect of antivirus and anti-malware software finding its way into the iPhone as a standard application seems impossible, at least for the next few years.

Running an embedded OS implies that software patches that fix security vulnerabilities may not be released at a regular interval, if such a practice exists at all. Even when such a firmware patch mechanism exists, in most cases the patch process relies on the user to be diligent in exercising security practices, and such a demand on the general population is simply unrealistic. Therefore, these factors indicate that IoT devices can become popular attack targets and can be compromised with relative ease. Once such an IoT device is hacked, user information may be retrieved and the device can in fact cause physical harm to its owner; for example, a hacker shutting off a smoke detector during a house fire can cause physical injury or damage. These IoT devices can also be turned into zombies and become part of a large botnet, which can be commandeered into participating in a planned distributed denial-of-service (DDoS) attack against another target.

Other types of consumer electronic appliances, such as the Sony PlayStation 4 (PS4) and Internet-ready HDTVs, are network-capable and face security threats similar to those faced by IoT devices. An Internet-ready HDTV may not allow its owner to browse and surf the web; however, it permits its owner to log in to Facebook and update their Facebook status through the built-in application. The Facebook account information could be stolen if the Internet-ready HDTV is hacked. The Sony PlayStation owner can purchase games at the PlayStation

Store. The PlayStation Network user account information includes the account holder's birthday and contains a stored credit card number. The user credential to log in to the PlayStation Network to play multi-player online games can be stolen by an attacker who has compromised the PS4, thus putting the account holder's privacy at great risk.

Conventional Security Solutions

The *security posture* of an organization refers to the role security plays in the organization's business planning and its business operation. The security posture encompasses the design and implementation of a well-defined security plan. The security plan is comprised of technical solutions including technology in terms of software, hardware, and services that can be implemented at end points and within the network. The security plan also includes non-technical aspects: employee education on the importance of security as an essential element of business operations; a definition of policies on employee conduct and behavior that conforms to corporate security governance; a definition of policies for achieving regulatory compliance; and a definition of procedures and guidelines on responding to security incidents, both internally and externally.

In essence, the security posture refers to how an organization views security: as a business enabler or as a hindrance and an inconvenience to its operational efficiency. An organization's security posture dictates its practices of security and determines the effectiveness of its security implementation. In today's information age, the availability and timely accessibility of information are important keys to an enterprise's success. Enterprises strive to foster innovation by harnessing the wealth of information capital available on the Internet, while at the same time maintaining an energized and engaged workforce.

Security should afford users the freedom to explore and harvest the riches of the Internet, and alleviate the fear of becoming victims of cyber threats. Existing threats change and new ones emerge as the web evolves; therefore, security postures cannot remain static for long and need regular assessment. It is essential to have an in-depth knowledge of available security solutions, and an understanding of the strengths and the weaknesses of each solution in order to perform assessments such as vulnerability testing, penetration testing, and standards-based auditing. Understanding security technologies is the key to implementing the layered defense that is now mandatory in securing users and enterprise networks.

Traditional Firewalls: What Are Their Main Deficiencies?

The firewall, the most commonly known and referenced security device, was once the motif of security-related conversations and continues to be an essential element of any network security design. The traditional firewall is still the first line of defense. However, the growing body of threats have long surpassed the capabilities of the traditional firewall. The security landscape is now cluttered with acronyms such as unified threat management (UTM), deep packet inspection (DPI), intrusion detection system (IDS), intrusion prevention system (IPS), secure web gateway (SWG), web application firewall (WAF), next-generation firewall (NGFW), application intelligence and control (AIC), and many more. These acronyms create the perception that perhaps the security threats are largely under control, yet in reality, adroit, menacing malware crafters flourish in the shadows, and security battles rage on with growing ferocity and intensity. The various technologies that are behind the acronyms add confusion and inundate the security implementers with over-lapping solutions. These overlapping solutions obscure the deficiencies in the core technologies, and this lack of clarity results in the construction and deployment of inadequate defenses.

The deficiencies of the traditional firewall lie in its inability to examine the packet payload, especially when content is encrypted. The traditional firewall examines layer-2 (L2) to layer-4 (L4) packet header information, such as source and destination IP addresses, L4 protocol type, and L4 source and destination port information, as depicted in Figure 1-1. A firewall rule can be written to compare any header field or bits against any specific values and can define instructions for the firewall to apply one or more actions accordingly. For example, a firewall rule can state, "If an incoming packet is a TCP connection initiation frame (i.e., the TCP header contains the SYN flag bit), then transmit a TCP RESET frame back to the sender." Basically, this firewall rule blocks all incoming TCP connection requests.

Here is another example of a firewall policy: "If the source IP address is 10.9.44.108, the protocol is TCP, and the destination port is 6881, then discard the packet." TCP port 6881 is commonly used by the BitTorrent program for P2P traffic. Enterprise firewalls block this port to prevent employees from downloading questionable content and consuming valuable network band-width. This firewall policy can be problematic in actual deployment. First, the popularity of BitTorrent has enabled its adoption by various organizations for legitimate use, for example, by communities that distribute open source soft-ware releases. In such cases, blocking TCP traffic on port 6881 would preclude users from permissible use of BitTorrent and, in some cases, would interrupt the only distribution channel for a specific open source project. Therefore, the content of a specific BitTorrent session, instead of simply the destina-tion port, should determine whether such a session is permitted. However, a traditional firewall does not have the ability to perform content analysis. Second, BitTorrent uses port 6881 when the port is available; otherwise, port 6882 and subsequent ports are tried until an unused port is found. As such, port 6881 can be occupied by traffic belonging to an admissible application. The firewall cannot determine which application originated the traffic to port 6881. Consequently, simply blocking port 6881 could disrupt a permissible application from its normal operation. Figure 1-2 illustrates the port-sharing dilemma that confuses a firewall.

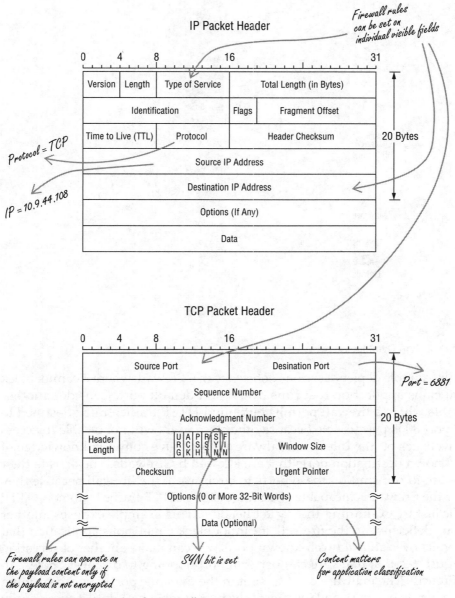

Figure 1-1: TCP/IP Headers for Firewall Processing

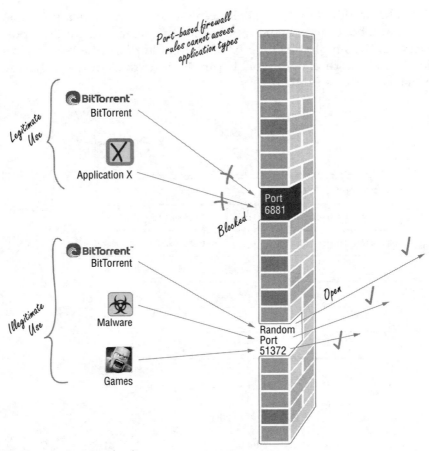

Figure 1-2: Port Overloading

This example depicts a serious deficiency in a firewall, where it cannot block a malicious application that runs over a non-default port. Consider another example where a firewall permits outbound HTTP traffic: traffic destined to TCP port 80 is permissible because otherwise users will not be able to access any websites on the Internet. Malware writers have common knowledge of well-known destination ports that are allowed by firewalls. They create their malware to transmit on these ports to circumvent the firewall because they know the firewall is incapable of distinguishing HTTP traffic from non-HTTP traffic just by examining the packet headers. This example exposes another serious deficiency in the firewall: it cannot block a malicious application that transmits over allowed well-known ports. We can make another observation in Figure 1-2, that malware can perform port hopping to discover "holes" in the firewall. The malware can transmit in the dynamic port range, beginning with a high-value port, and increment the port number by 1 until it successfully receives a response from its intended peer.

Every packet that passes through a firewall will match at least one firewall rule. The firewall understands the connection concept, whether it is a TCP connection or a UDP connection. A common firewall feature is that it keeps stateful information on TCP connections and UDP sessions. This stateful information cache, known as the *state table*, reduces the firewall workload and increases firewall scalability. For example, when the first packet of a TCP connection is seen by the firewall (in this case a TCP SYN packet), the firewall executes its rules against this TCP SYN packet, which results in a firewall action. This resulting action and the TCP connection information (connection 4-tuple and the TCP header) is then stored into the state table. Figure 1-3 shows an example of a firewall state table.

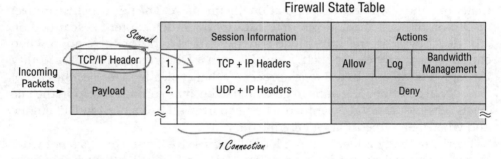

Figure 1-3: Firewall State Table

Instead of running through all of the rules repeatedly on the subsequent packets from that same TCP connection, the firewall can consult the state table directly and obtain the action quickly. This is the reason why the firewall is also known as the *stateful packet inspection* (or simply stateful inspection) firewall. Examples of firewall actions include allowing traffic to pass, denying traffic by silently dropping the packets, denying a TCP connection by generating a TCP RESET protocol packet, and generating connection logs. Each entry in the state table contains minimal information that represents a connection. Packets belonging to connections that are permitted by the firewall transit the firewall unmodified. In practice the firewall updates its state table entries using only information from the packet headers.

Firewall with DPI: A Better Solution?

A new breed of firewalls—let us call them the second-generation firewall (SGFW)—incorporated DPI technology to address the problem of identifying what application generated the traffic in question. With DPI, the packet payload is scanned for specific known patterns, also known as *signatures*, which can potentially identify applications. We say potentially identify because of the challenges of application identification using static patterns, which is a topic we cover in Chapter 7. These SGFWs enable administrators to specify and enforce policies that are based on application names and types, more than just IP addresses and port numbers. In addition, by integrating user authentication information that provides mapping between a user and a specific IP address, some of these SGFWs extend the policy coverage to enforce policies that are defined around individual users.

When an SGFW performs DPI to scan a flow for an application signature, as Chapter 7 covers, multiple packets may have passed through the firewall before an identification can be made. These leaked packets may have already provided the black hats with useful information to further their attacks. Because DPI relies on pattern matching, prevalent in the form of regular expression matching, the operation is computationally intensive. The performance impact of DPI on firewall throughput determines how much content is scanned on a per-packet basis and how much stateful data is kept for correlation when conducting analytics. As such, firewalls with a DPI engine obtain scalability through a hardware-based regex processor that typically increases the cost of the overall solution. Firewalls in general had become commoditized in the late 1990s. The cost factor determined whether a firewall had a built-in DPI engine and what capabilities that DPI engine offered.

There are many issues that render DPI ineffective. First, DPI does not work on an encrypted payload. An encrypted payload is indistinguishable from random byte streams and thus cannot match any known patterns. Other data obfuscation techniques, such as compression, encoding, and tunneling, can achieve the same effectiveness in defeating DPI.

Second, firewalls with DPI engines cannot modify the content even when malicious content has been identified: entire packets must be discarded that will impact the overall sessions. Here is the reason why: as Figure 1-1 illustrates, the firewall rules are formulated against the fields from the layer-3 and layer-4 headers, in this example, from the IP header and TCP header. Any alteration made to the packet can cause a TCP checksum error, unless the TCP checksum is recomputed by the firewall. Because TCP checksum covers all of the payload data, re-computing the TCP checksum is an expensive operation. The firewall may need to perform packet reassembly due to IP layer fragmentation, thus incurring additional processing overhead. Revising the TCP checksum is insufficient and will not work in cases where, for example, an Internet protocol security authentication header (IPSec AH) is employed to verify end-to-end message integrity; in other words, any modification of the original message by intermediate systems, in this case the firewall, would fail the AH integrity check at the final destination.

Although an SGFW can provide better visibility by recognizing certain unencrypted applications by means of DPI, its enforceable actions are still as limited as the traditional firewall. This coarse protection method can impede the usability of other defensive systems against sophisticated attacks.

IDS/IPS and Firewall

A firewall is the first line of defense, but it has limited visibility into the content while it makes traffic-filtering decisions. Because a firewall is commonly deployed at the ingress and egress points of a network, all traffic paths will converge and traverse through the firewall. Therefore, the performance and scalability of a firewall affects the network as a whole. For this reason, although some firewalls may incorporate a DPI engine, a firewall is designed to execute a limited set of actions against each packet, even when hardware acceleration is activated in the firewall. When an attack circumvents the firewall, an IDS extends the security coverage by inspecting the network and the end systems for evidence that corroborates whether some network events and security alerts were instigated by attacks or malicious infiltrations. An IDS generates alarms and reports to network management systems upon detecting abnormal or suspicious traffic.

An IDS examines packets for signatures that are associated with known viruses, malware, and other malicious traffic. In addition to pattern scanning within the packets, an IDS analyzes overall traffic patterns to detect anomalies and known attacks. Some examples of known attacks are denial-of-service (DoS), port scanners that search for vulnerable network services, buffer overflow exploits, and self-propagating worms. Examples of anomalies include malformed protocol packets and traffic patterns that deviate from the norm. An IDS is divided into two main categories: a network-based intrusion detection system (NIDS) and a host-based intrusion detection system (HIDS). NIDS and HIDS differ in where the IDS is deployed, which consequently dictates the types of data collected and analyzed by that specific type of IDS. Figure 1-4 illustrates an example deployment of IDS systems behind a firewall.

As shown in Figure 1-4, the NIDS is deployed inside the organization's internal networks, behind the firewall. A NIDS monitors the activities of the entire network and examines both intranet traffic and Internet-bound traffic. On the other hand, the firewall concentrates on traffic that flows into and out of the internal network to the Internet.

The traditional NIDS scans packets against a database of signatures of known attacks. Similar to the open source IDS tool Snort, each signature in the data is often implemented as a matching rule. This *signature-based IDS* runs the packets through these matching rules or signatures to detect attacks. Another approach is the *statistical-based* or *anomaly-based NIDS*, which is also known as the *behavior-based NIDS*. With a statistical-based NIDS, a profile of the network under protection is built over time, based on evolving historical data, which represents the norm of the network. Some examples of data collected and compiled into a profile that represents the network operating under normal conditions include the following: the number of new applications that are discovered per day on the network and the average traffic volume generated by each type of application; the average number of DNS queries transmitted from a specific IP address at a given time interval; the average overall aggregate throughput of the network; and the average number of HTTP transactions issued per minute from a specific IP address. Any deviation observed by the NIDS may be interpreted as anomalies or misuse that instigates responses as defined by corresponding security directives.

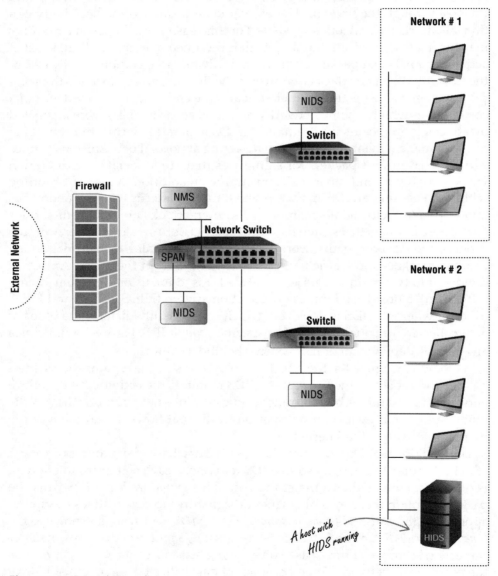

Figure 1-4: IDS and Firewall

The key to the success of a signature-based NIDS is the richness in the collection of the attack signatures. Identifying a unique and effective signature for a new attack, especially a complex attack, takes time to develop and evolve. As new attacks propagate across the networks and infrastructures, the signature-based NIDS is incapable of detecting these attacks while the new signatures are being implemented. The success of the statistical-based NIDS depends on the knowledge or heuristics of the network characteristics that are considered as normal and serve as the baseline. Establishing the boundaries of normal network behavior is challenging as the network fosters a wide range of protocols and applications and hosts a user base with a diverse spectrum of online behaviors that can trigger sporadic traffic patterns. A statistical-based NIDS can be effective against new attacks because new attacks can incite network behaviors that alarm the NIDS.

A host-based IDS (HIDS) is purposefully built, either for an operating system or for a specific application, and operates in individual end systems. The HIDS analyzes the operating system process identifier (PID), system calls, service listeners, I/O and file system operations, specific application runtime behavior, and system and application logs to identify evidence of an attack.

Firewalls are called active protection systems because a firewall is in the path of all traffic, known as inline deployment. This enables the firewall to examine live traffic, and when the firewall identifies an attack, it is capable of blocking that attack while it is in progress. In other words, upon detection, a firewall can prevent malicious traffic from reaching a targeted system.

Intrusion detection systems can be categorized as passive protection systems because an IDS is typically connected to a SPAN (Switched Port Analyzer) port on a network switch or to a network tap that duplicates packets for an entire link. While an IDS can also examine every packet, however, the packets under analysis have successfully passed through a firewall and cannot be filtered by the IDS; those packets may also have already reached the intended targets and enacted malicious activities. In other words, an IDS identifies an attack that may have already taken place, at which point the IDS begins to remediate the damage by executing countermeasures, for example, sending alerts and notifications to monitoring and management systems. The passive traffic-processing nature of an IDS implies the performance of an IDS does not have any impact on active live traffic. As such, an IDS can perform much more in-depth analysis, and correlate more data sets, than a firewall. A firewall fulfills a security role that prevents the firewall from being a replacement for an IDS.

DPI is also an integral part of the IDS. Using the open source Snort software, here is an example of a rule created by the Sourcefire Vulnerability Research Team. The rule scans for the signature of the Flashpack/Safe/CritX exploit kit that attempts to download a malicious file as part of the attack:

```
alert tcp $EXTERNAL_NET $HTTP_PORTS -> $HOME_NET any (msg:"EXPLOIT-KIT
Flashpack/Safe/CritX exploit kit jar file download";
```

```
flow:to_client,established; file_data; content:"filename="; http_header;
content:".jar"; within:4; distance:24;
pcre:"/filename\=[a-z0-9]{24}\.jar/H";
metadata:policy balanced-ips drop, policy security-ips drop,
   service http;
reference:url,
   www.malwaresigs.com/2013/06/06/flashpack-exploit-kit-safepack/;
classtype:trojan-activity; sid:26892; rev:2;)
```

This example illustrates that as the IDS scans for attack signatures, it suffers from the same inherent deficiencies in the DPI engines as those found in the firewall. Evasion techniques that are used against DPI engines are also effective in defeating the signature-based IDS engines. In this example, the code in bold face is a Perl Compatible Regular Expression (PCRE). The question is, what if the exploit kit uses HTTPS to download the payload, resulting in the payload being protected by the SSL encryption so that this rule cannot be applied at all?

Unlike the passive network monitoring of an IDS, an IPS takes the active role of performing mitigation actions in real-time once attacks are detected. An IPS possesses all of the capabilities of an IDS, but an IPS is deployed physically inline in the network, which enables the IPS to drop attack packets, reset TCP connections, or activate filters to block the source of the attack. An IPS can perform other functions such as configuring dynamic policies in security devices, such as a firewall, to interrupt the malevolent maneuvering and prevent further damage to the network.

Unified Threat Management and Next-Generation Firewall

The most significant limitations of the traditional firewall are its inability to perform payload inspection and to distinguish applications. The concept of Unified Threat Management (UTM) gained visibility and momentum in 2004 to address the security gaps in firewalls, and to offer a solution for the lack of unified policy management across the various security control technology products commonly deployed together in an enterprise network. The UTM strategy is to combine multiple security features such as a firewall, NIDS, IPS, gateway-based antivirus, and content filtering into a single platform or appliance to offer multiple layers of security protection with simplified management and ease of policy implementation. The security posture continued to increase its focus on users and their applications, as the transformation in UTM took place in parallel.

Then, Gartner Inc., an information technology research and advisory company, claimed to be the first to define the *Next-Generation Firewall (NGFW)*. In its NGFW definition, the three key attributes of an NGFW are its ability to detect application-specific attacks, to enforce application-specific security policies, and to intercept and decrypt SSL traffic. The NGFW includes all of the capabilities of the traditional firewall and incorporates the full functionality of a signature-based IPS. Another key characteristic of the NGFW is its inline deployment as a bump-in-the-wire. In addition, the NGFW can collaborate with external services to incorporate additional security-relevant data and feeds to enhance its enforcement capabilities.

The NGFW definition has a large overlap with that of the UTM. The articulated differences have limited technical merits, and the deviations are largely a result of verbiage manipulation. The NGFW concept seems to be a desired byproduct of combining the UTM with the unique features of the secure proxy. The conceptualization of the NGFW, with such a rich set of security features, processing network traffic at multi-gigabit wire speed, and without any performance degradation, would be the ultimate goal of security system design architects and developers. However, as we will illustrate in this book, firewall and proxy are fundamentally incompatible with respect to the policies each is designed to interpret and to enforce. The process and method of application classification collides with the operation of proxy interception.

Security Proxy: A Necessary Extension of the End Point

A firewall, even with UTM, performs primarily syntactical analysis of traffic that is largely signature driven and is capable of enforcing security with limited actions. Without the ability to decrypt content for analysis when encountering encrypted sessions, a firewall is confined to simply denying traffic in environments with restrictive enforcement policies. In enterprise networks, a legitimate but encrypted session could be blocked, causing discontinuity in both business and productivity. A security solution that can decrypt SSL cipher text, then feed the plain text into other security technologies, is a mandatory step to combat advanced and fast-evolving threats.

The secure proxy was invented long before NGFW was conceptualized. The demand for the secure proxy in enterprises in the financial sector, defense industry, and many others has flourished since 2002. Even the design for SSL interception was in full swing at that time. In essence, the secure proxy is the result of combining a secure web gateway with application proxies, operating with a complex and expressive policy engine at its core.

A *security proxy*, sometimes referred to as a *secure proxy* or simply a proxy unless stated otherwise, performs semantic analysis in the context of individual protocols, most importantly layer-5 to layer-7 application protocols. At the time of this writing, the majority of proxies have some capability to decrypt SSL traffic. A proxy is a security enforcement companion to a firewall, an IDS and IPS, an enterprise-grade virus scanning appliance, analytics engines, and many other security solutions. As illustrated in Figure 1-5, a proxy is the data hub that feeds decrypted traffic to any attached companion system that performs one or more dedicated security functions. Each companion system requires a different type of input. The proxy is capable of extracting mail attachments, web URLs, and executable files from the payload and feeding these inputs to its security attachments accordingly.

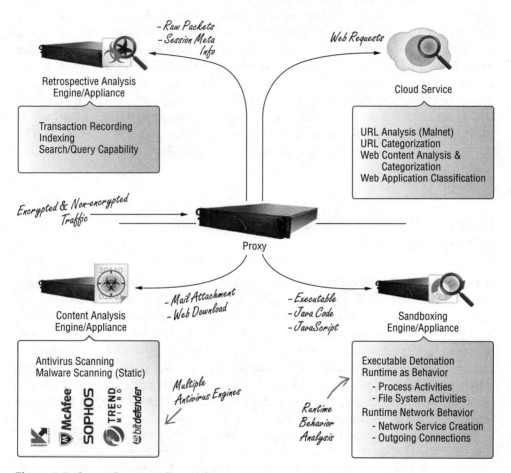

Figure 1-5: Secure Proxy as a Data Hub

A proxy is predominantly deployed inside a firewall-protected network. The secure proxy performs proxy functions beyond just analyzing the web traffic. We define web traffic as that which is carried over the HTTP or HTTPS protocols. The secure proxy can intercept more protocols than just HTTP. However, the proxy concept is best illustrated in Figure 1-6 using HTTP as an example.

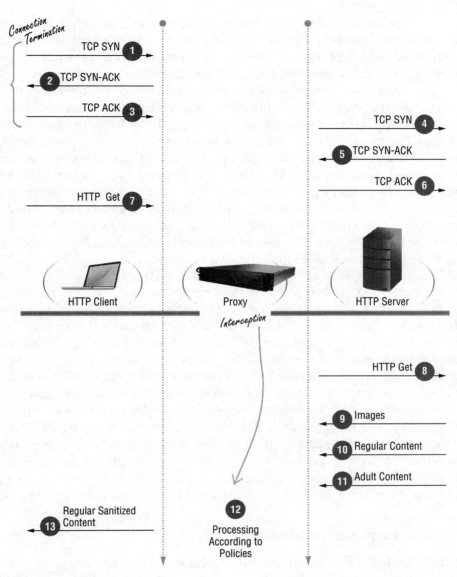

Figure 1-6: Proxy Concept

As shown in Figure 1-6, the first and most important action a proxy exerts on a connection is *interception*. Connection interception is achieved through connection *termination*. We will use the term *client* to refer to the initiator of the connection request, and the term *server* to refer to the original intended recipient of the connection request. In TCP, connection termination involves the proxy completing the TCP three-way handshake to establish the connection with the HTTP client. The next step in the interception process is for the proxy to establish another TCP connection with the server. In this example, the original destination is Google. Once both connections have been established successfully, the next act of the interception procedure is for the proxy to receive traffic from one connection and then inject that traffic, either unmodified or transformed, into the other connection. In other words, the proxy splices the traffic between these two TCP connections. Unlike a firewall, a proxy can modify any packet and manipulate any content exchanged in these connections. In the example shown in Figure 1-6, the proxy detects the presence of adult material in the returned content and strips away that material as part of the configured policy. The sanitized content is then transmitted back to the HTTP client. This example illustrates that a proxy performs intrusive maneuvering of communication exchanges that are visible to the proxy. The payload obfuscation techniques used to defeat a firewall are proven ineffective against the proxy. Because the proxy terminates the connection, the proxy will reassemble packets and decode the content type before subjecting the session to higher-layer processing.

A real-life example of a proxy in action is free WiFi access at airports. When you connect to a WiFi access point, your computer indicates it is connected and has obtained an IP address. Yet, without opening a web browser you are unsuccessful when you try to run any application that needs the Internet. This is because you have not agreed to the terms and conditions of use. When you open the browser for the very first time, a legal agreement web page displays, and you can proceed to use the Internet once you accept that agreement. This legal agreement page displays as long as you have not accepted that agreement, regardless of how many times you choose to close and reopen the web browser. This is called a *captive portal*, which impels a user to fulfill some action, such as responding to user authentication queries. A captive portal is also used by hotels that offer Internet access, where a web page prompts the user to review and agree to the charges on first use. A web proxy (or HTTP proxy) is one of many techniques and an effective approach in implementing a captive portal.

Transaction-Based Processing

A proxy also keeps state information on the connections it processes, but unlike a firewall, a proxy participates in the connection activities, exchanging packets as a communicating peer both to the originator of the connection and to the originally intended destination. As such, there are some notable differences when comparing the firewall state table against the proxy state table, as shown in Figure 1-7. Each entry in the firewall state table represents a single connection. As Figure 1-7 illustrates, the proxy must maintain the state information that correlates the two TCP connections with the two corresponding HTTP transactions as belonging to a single user transaction that was initiated from that specific HTTP client. When the firewall processes incoming packets, only the packet headers are applied when updating connection state information. In the proxy case, entire packets are processed and may be stored as part of the transaction state information. Remember, the proxy must receive traffic from the client-side connection and then transmit that traffic, either modified or verbatim, to the server-side connection, and vice versa.

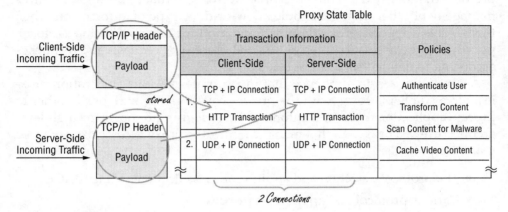

Figure 1-7: Proxy State Table

Some application-level protocols are carried over UDP. Because UDP is connectionless, the proxy must have the ability to track when a UDP-based transaction begins and ends. Similar to the TCP case, the proxy needs to create two UDP flows and update the state information according to the transaction. For example, a DNS proxy creates the UDP flow entry in its state table when it processes the DNS query message. The DNS proxy may modify the query message before sending it onward to the identified DNS server. The proxy must maintain this DNS transaction until the proxy receives the corresponding answer message, regardless of how the proxy may have processed the query content. The DNS proxy may change the time-to-live (TTL) of a particular entry in the DNS answer, or it may remove entries from the answer due to policy restrictions. The DNS proxy removes the transaction from the state table once it has transmitted the final DNS response to the client. In this example, the DNS proxy treats the DNS query and the subsequent response as the complete DNS transaction.

The Proxy Architecture

The DNS proxy example illustrates that a proxy must have in-depth knowledge about a specific application protocol and also about its structure and operational detail in order to perform proper interception. Depending on the protocol in question, examples of this knowledge may include the following: whether a centralized directory service is involved in locating a service or peer; how the connection is established between the communicating peers;

the type of authentication mechanism employed; the encryption methods that are available and the negotiation approach; the types of requests and the associated payloads; the types of responses and the associated payloads; and how the various content is encoded and transported. For every application protocol that may exist in an enterprise network, if that application requires management other than the simple allow-or-deny type of enforcement, then there exists a specific proxy designed and built for that application protocol, performing the necessary interception and processing requests and responses according to defined security policies.

A *secure proxy* is an appliance that incorporates various application proxies into a single platform, with the proxies collaborating with one another to process application traffic and enforce policies. Figure 1-8 shows the high-level architecture of a proxy. As shown in the figure, the proxy is comprised of three main components:

- The protocol detection and application classification engine (PACE)
- Various protocol and application proxies
- The policy engine

When the proxy receives a transaction for the first time, the PACE dispatches traffic to the proxy according to the default port designation. The PACE first terminates the connection and then transfers the established connection to a specific proxy. The connection transfer is done through a dispatcher that has the knowledge of the various well-known ports and the designated proxies. As shown in Figure 1-8, the ports table maps a proxy to a well-known port. For example, the DNS proxy is assigned to handle port 54, and the SSH proxy is assigned to port 22. Because malicious traffic attempts to evade the firewall by utilizing the well-known ports, a specific proxy must accurately detect if a given traffic flow is in fact from the protocol that the proxy is built to handle. For example, port 443 is used by HTTPS sessions. The first set of data packets exchanged on the established connection must be the SSL handshake traffic. Each proxy scans the payload for specific known signatures belonging to the protocol or application in question. In the HTTPS example, when the SSL proxy accepts the connection from the dispatcher, the SSL proxy expects to receive the SSL `ClientHello` record, which begins with the byte pattern: `0x16 0x03 0x01 0x02 0x00 0x01 0x00 0x01 0xfc 0x03 0x03`. The SSL proxy redirects the transaction back to the PACE to perform further protocol detection if it cannot interpret the payload as SSL traffic.

The keen reader will now oppugn some of the statements just made in the last paragraph: if a proxy scans the payload for specific known signatures, then how is the proxy different from a firewall or IDS system with a built-in DPI engine? How can the SSL proxy scan for a predefined byte stream in encrypted traffic? And how can a proxy scan encrypted content?

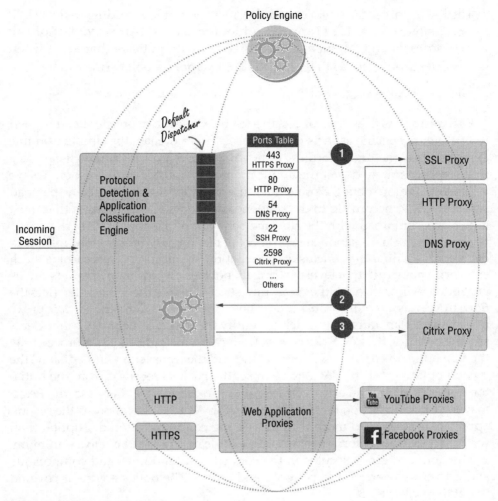

Figure 1-8: Proxy Architecture

The first question, asked differently, is: if the PACE has the ability to classify the traffic against specific protocols and applications, is the PACE duplicating work that is performed by the proxies? The answer is that there is no work duplication, and here is the reason why: The HTTP protocol is an ASCII protocol. The PACE parses the payload for keywords such as "HTTP/", "GET", "Content-type", "Content-length", "Accept:", and "<HTML>". Together these keywords provide a high probability that the payload belongs to an HTTP request. Therefore, the PACE forwards the transaction to the HTTP proxy. Once the HTTP proxy receives the transaction and encounters the keyword "GET", it interprets this keyword as a method and parses the subsequent bytes to look for the parameter (such as a filename) for this method.

The PACE parses the payload and classifies the traffic according to the HTTP *protocol syntax*. The HTTP proxy understands the full *semantics* of the HTTP protocol and, as such, can enforce security policies that are written specifically around the HTTP protocol. For example, a policy rule can be

```
Deny if (http.method == GET) and (Host == www.adserver.com)
```

Each proxy has its own nuances. In each proxy, security policies are designed to operate on specific aspects of a protocol. Therefore, as this simple example demonstrates, the proxy cannot apply any security policies unless it can, as a first step, accurately detect the application or the protocol in question. As we will show in more detail, a proxy identifies an application by specific payload signatures and according to the sequence of events and exchanges that must take place, combined with the runtime behavior of the application.

Application classification and protocol detection may require multiple packets before reaching the conclusion on what the application or protocol is. Each enterprise has a different level of stringent policies on how many packets can be permitted to flow through the proxy unrestricted before the proxy interrupts the flow and closes down the transaction. Therefore, the PACE and the specific proxy must work collaboratively to quickly identify the traffic. If the proxy cannot classify the protocol, the PACE can choose from two main options when proceeding: the first option is for the PACE to stop and end the transaction immediately; the second option is for the PACE to re-inject the packets received from the initiator connection into the other connection unmodified. In either case, the PACE may log this transaction for the administrator. A proxy that chooses the second approach is concerned more with preventing communication disruption than with strict security enforcement where packet leaks are to be kept to a minimum.

The policy engine executes in the context of all modules and components and across all layers between layer 2 and layer 7. The policy engine is covered in detail in Chapter 3.

The SSL messages transmitted at the early stages of the handshake exchange are not encrypted. These messages contain sufficient detail for an SSL proxy to determine if it will perform interception on a specific transaction. Other proxies rely on the SSL proxy to decrypt cipher text and offer these other proxies the plain text for further analysis and processing.

SSL Proxy and Interception

The remaining discussion in this chapter will focus on the HTTPS proxy because it depends on the SSL proxy. The SSL proxy is challenging to design, implement, and deploy not only because of privacy concerns but also because the SSL proxy performs identity emulation, and it must enforce authentication and the trust model, which are essential in secure communication. Figure 1-9 illustrates two main SSL interception scenarios. As shown in the figure, the proxy must masquerade as the server when communicating with the client. Similarly, the proxy must assume the identity of the client when it connects to the server. In essence, the proxy acts as the man-in-the-middle (MITM), and if the proxy does a good job, its presence remains undetected throughout its operational lifetime. The proxy can succeed in interception only if both the client and the server trust the proxy.

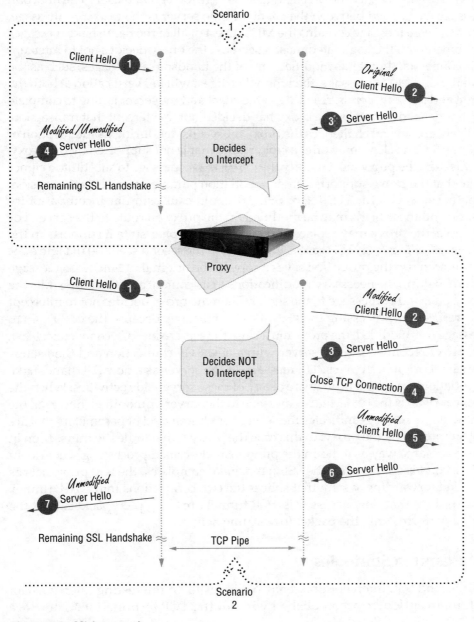

Figure 1-9: SSL Interception

In the first scenario, when the proxy receives the SSL ClientHello message at the beginning of the SSL handshake, the proxy forwards this ClientHello message to the server unmodified. When the corresponding ServerHello message reaches the proxy, the proxy makes the interception decision by applying the configured policies to the ServerHello message. At this point the proxy may modify the ServerHello message before transmitting it back to the client. The proxy does not modify the ClientHello message for a good reason. The final SSL message exchanged between the client and the server is the Finished message. The Finished message contains the MD5 digest of all of the handshake messages combined with the negotiated master secret. If the proxy decides not to intercept this connection but it has modified any of the handshake messages, such as the initial ClientHello message, then the MD5 digest will fail verification at both the client and the server ends, resulting in the client and the server failing to complete the handshake even after the proxy has decided not to intercept that transaction.

There are several challenges the proxy must consider during its interception of SSL traffic. The client may offer a cipher suite that is not supported by the proxy. In this case, the proxy must modify the ClientHello message to substitute a cipher suite that the proxy supports. Other negotiation parameters such as the version, whether it is TLS 1.1, TLS 1.2, or SSL 3.0, could cause similar incompatibility issues, and these fields may be modified by the proxy en route to the server. For example, the proxy may replace and substitute a cipher suite it supports in the ClientHello message. This case is illustrated in the second scenario in Figure 1-9. In this scenario the proxy first saves a copy of the original ClientHello message before making the necessary modifications to its content and then transmits the new ClientHello message to the server. Then the proxy decides not to intercept the traffic after processing the ServerHello message. Because the ClientHello message was modified, the proxy must close the server-side TCP connection. Next, the proxy reconnects to the server with a new TCP connection and then sends the saved original ClientHello message to the server as a new SSL handshake negotiation. The client is unaware of any of these server-side activities. When the proxy forwards the ClientHello message to the server unmodified, however, the ServerHello message indicates the server has chosen a set of parameters that are not supported by the proxy; in this case the proxy will handle the transaction in the exact same way as it did in the previously described processing scenario. In this second scenario, once the SSL handshake completes, the SSL proxy acts as a packet forwarding system that splices the two connections into a TCP tunnel. The packets that flow across this TCP tunnel are encrypted packets, and the proxy performs only the packet forwarding action.

Interception Strategies

The second SSL interception scenario alludes to an interesting question: can SSL interception be accomplished without the TCP termination? There are two main SSL interception strategies: one leverages the full TCP connection termination, while the other relies only on SSL encryption and decryption. The two SSL interception scenarios presented in Figure 1-9 can be summarized as the SSL interception strategy illustrated in Figure 1-10. This SSL interception strategy offers the most flexible and intrusive policy-driven processing of the content: content insertion, deletion, and transformation are all possible with this approach.

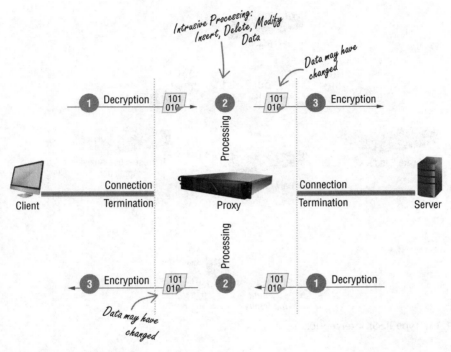

Figure 1-10: Type-I SSL Interception

Another SSL interception strategy is depicted in Figure 1-11. With this interception strategy, a single TCP connection is established between the client and server; in other words, the proxy does not terminate the TCP connection. The proxy has the ability to decrypt and encrypt the content within the SSL session, but the proxy cannot modify the content and must keep the content fully intact. Here is the reason why: SSL protects and transmits the data using a record protocol. The SSL record protocol is similar to the IP fragmentation and reassembly mechanism, where the data is divided into fragments and each fragment is independently encrypted and transmitted. On the receiving end, each encrypted payload is independently decrypted, verified, and reassembled back into the original data. Any modification applied to any of the SSL records would alter the original data and may render the data invalid.

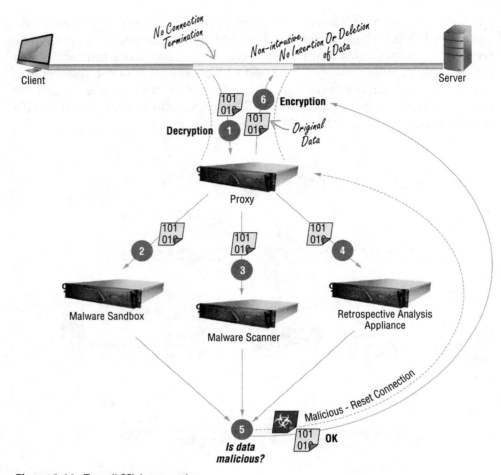

Figure 1-11: Type-II SSL Interception

Unlike the termination-based interception, the main course of action the proxy can enforce is to reset that single TCP connection, thus breaking the connectivity between the two end points. As depicted in Figure 1-11, the decision to break the TCP connection can come from a variety of sources. Once the encrypted payload has been transformed from cipher text into plain text, the SSL proxy can redirect the plain text to a diverse set of security devices to perform various in-depth content-centric analysis. For example, as shown in Figure 1-11, the content can be sent to a malware scanner first, and if something suspicious is discovered, the malware scanner returns an indication to the proxy. At that point, the proxy places the suspicious content into a malware sandbox to detonate the potential malware and investigate the outcome of the controlled execution. As soon as the malicious nature of the content is confirmed and the malware has been identified, the proxy begins retrospective analysis of the historical data to discover the earliest exposure to that vulnerability and begins the construction of countermeasures. In parallel, the proxy shuts down the TCP connection to prevent further damage.

The proxy communicates with the other security devices by utilizing regular TCP or UDP connections and transmitting the plain text over these standard communication channels to maximize interoperability, thus eliminating the need for these devices to make any software modifications.

Referring back to the proxy architecture illustrated in Figure 1-8, the concept of transaction handoff was discussed in the context of application recognition: the SSL proxy transfers the transaction to another proxy through the PACE when the transaction operates over a protocol on top of the SSL. Another purpose for the transaction handoff is when one or more proxies must work collaboratively to manage and manipulate a transaction. The transaction handoff concept is detailed in Figure 1-12.

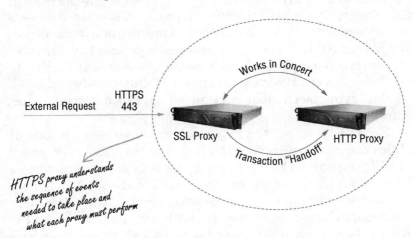

Figure 1-12: Transaction Handoff

As shown in Figure 1-12, the HTTPS proxy is conceptually comprised of two proxies: the SSL proxy and the HTTP proxy. In practice, the HTTP proxy is fully aware of the SSL processing detail when it handles the HTTPS request. Once the SSL handshake is complete, the SSL proxy must transfer this transaction to the HTTP proxy for HTTP-based proxy operation. Another example is the *stunnel proxy*, which is comprised of the SSL proxy and the TCP tunnel proxy. Therefore, the SSL proxy is typically implemented as a common proxy that provides services at the SSL layer to other proxies. Based on HTTP-specific policies, the HTTP proxy may instruct the SSL proxy to initiate certain operations, for example, performing a *rehandshake*, disallowing session resumption, or perhaps requiring client certificate authentication in future transactions with a specific client.

Certificates and Keys

One of the SSL design goals is to facilitate server authentication. For example, if you are making an online purchase at Amazon, your web browser must ascertain whether it is indeed communicating with an Amazon server before transmitting your credit card information to that server. An X.509 certificate binds a public key to a specific entity. A trusted third party, the *certificate authority* (CA), verifies the identity of the entity that owns the certificate and ensures the entity possesses the corresponding private key. At the completion of successful validation, the CA signs the certificate with its digital signature as proof of the certificate's authenticity. A CA-signed certificate guarantees the public key contained in the certificate belongs to the entity as claimed in that certificate. The CA's digital signature can be verified using the CA's public key.

The fact that an SSL proxy can perform traffic decryption and re-encryption after transaction interception implies that the SSL proxy possesses the server's private key if server authentication is mandatory. In practice and in the majority of cases, the SSL proxy will not have the server's private key. Can you imagine the SSL proxy having private keys from Google, Amazon, Facebook, Netflix, or any other commercial websites? Figure 1-13 illustrates how the SSL proxy achieves the keying mechanism necessary to perform decryption on intercepted traffic.

As shown in Figure 1-13, when the proxy receives the server certificate in Step 4, it modifies the certificate before sending it to the client. The proxy changes the certificate *issuer* to be the proxy itself. Because each certificate has a pair of keys—one public and one private—associated with it, the proxy replaces the original server's public key with its own public key. After making all of the necessary changes to the server certificate, the proxy signs the modified certificate using the private key of a preinstalled CA certificate and then replaces the *signature* field with the new signature value. The proxy transmits this newly transformed certificate to the client. How does the client respond when it receives this certificate from the proxy and begins server authentication?

The server certificate verification will complete successfully and uneventfully if the proxy is a legitimate intermediate CA holding certificate signing authority, and it is a part of a certificate chain that terminates at a client-trusted root CA. However, in most deployment situations the proxy will not have certificate signing authority. In this case, the client will neither trust nor accept the certificate fabricated by the proxy without user intervention. The common visual indication of a problematic certificate is a web browser pop-up window, similar to the one shown in Figure 1-14. In this example a proxy is deployed between the client and the Internet. When the user tries to access the Google website, the proxy modifies the Google certificate, subsequently triggering the browser pop-up window at the client end. As shown in Figure 1-14, the browser pop-up window states the server certificate cannot be verified as the reason for user notification.

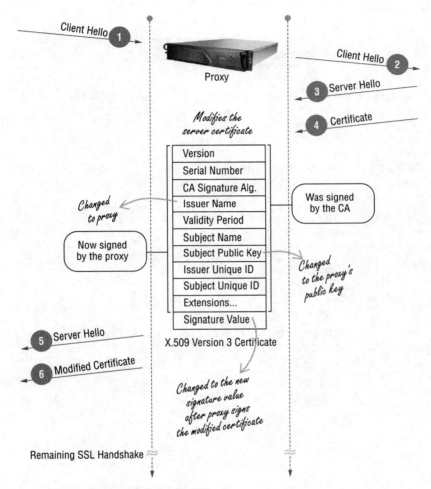

Figure 1-13: Server Certificate Modification

In the enterprise environment, such a browser pop-up window is a good indication that a corporate proxy is present in the network, which enforces the corporate use policy. Outside the corporate network, such an alert triggered by a non-verifiable certificate is strong evidence that a MITM attack may be taking place somewhere in the infrastructure.

SSL interception is confronted with another challenge when secure servers require client authentication. Client authentication may be necessary in situations where the client is granted access to restricted or highly confidential resources and services, such as military systems, only after the client authenticates successfully. The client certificate must be issued by an externally known and trusted CA. Client authentication is controlled by the server. The server that demands client authentication sends a certificate request to the client during the SSL handshake process.

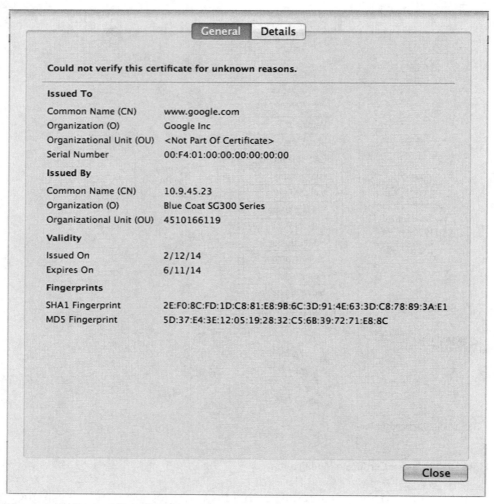

Figure 1-14: Browser Issued Warning about Proxy's Certificate

Installing an individual client certificate in the proxy so that the proxy can offer the right client certificate upon request by the server is a possible solution in enterprise networks. However, such a solution is neither scalable nor practical in any organization with a large number of users. One approach to solving the scalability problem is using a technique called *client certificate emulation*. Figure 1-15 illustrates an example of such a practice.

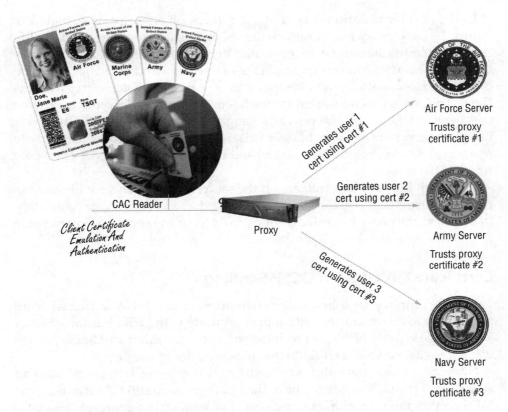

Figure 1-15: Client Certificate Emulation

The Common Access Card (CAC) serves as standard identification for military and DoD personnel. The CAC is a smart card that uniquely identifies an individual with that individual's private key embedded in it. In the fictitious scenario depicted in Figure 1-15, the same trusted CA is installed in the proxy and in the servers, and the proxy is given intermediate signing authority by this trusted CA. Once the proxy authenticates an individual, the proxy generates a certificate (possibly with a limited lifetime) that identifies this specific individual and the associated key pair and signs this certificate. When the server demands client authentication for that individual, the proxy offers the generated certificate to the server. The server can verify this certificate because the proxy has the signing authority issued by a CA that is also trusted by the server. As shown in Figure 1-15, instead of a single trusted CA, the proxy could install three different trusted CAs, one for the Air Force server, one for the Army server, and one for the Navy server. These CAs are trusted by each server, respectively.

In the non-termination–based SSL interception strategy, as depicted in Figure 1-11, the proxy must examine the SSL handshake exchange and modify the server certificate similar to the termination-based interception. The proxy transmits the modified server certificate to the client and uses that modified certificate along with its own key pairs to negotiate a master secret with the client. This master secret is used for traffic encryption and decryption between the client and the proxy. The proxy exchanges the master secret with the server using the server's original certificate. This master secret is used by the proxy to re-encrypt the decrypted client content and then transmit that newly encrypted traffic to the server.

With both interception strategies, if the server's private keys are installed in the proxy, then the proxy can avoid modifying the server certificate completely. In that case, the proxy has full capability to decrypt any content transmitted to the server using the server's private key.

Certificate Pinning and OCSP Stapling

Certificate pinning is a solution that attempts to solve a MITM attack when an entity tries to communicate with a peer securely using SSL, but the attacker assumes the identity of the peer by intercepting the certificate validation process using a rogue but valid certificate that masquerades as the peer.

How can a rogue but valid certificate be created in the first place? Such an attack was first made possible due to the fact there were still CAs that used the MD5 cryptographic hash function to generate certificate signatures. The MD5 hash function has known collision vulnerabilities that were discovered back in 1993; in a nutshell, it means that two different inputs to the same MD5 hash function can produce the same exact hash output. In 2005 researchers demonstrated a practical method to craft a pair of X.509 certificates, each having a different public key, to result in the same computed MD5 digest. The collision vulnerability attack against MD5 demonstrates that similar attacks could be made against other cryptographic hash functions, such as SHA-1, that are in use by CAs. Once an intermediate rogue CA certificate with certificate signing authority can be constructed, such a rogue CA certificate could be used to sign any fabricated certificate bearing the identity of any entity.

In recent years, there have been known incidents where CAs have issued questionable intermediate or subordinate root certificates. For example, in early 2012 Trustwave revoked a subordinate root certificate it issued to an unnamed company, which enabled that company to forge and issue unlimited certificates claiming the identities of any server or organization. The subordinate root certificate and the forged certificates it generated were all stored inside a hardware security module (HSM), and that specific certificate was issued for that company's internal use; however, such a certificate could have been misused, which warranted the revocation.

Another venue for attackers to gain access to rogue certificates is by breaching a CA and then obtaining rogue certificates through that CA. In late 2011 DigiNotar, a Dutch CA, was hacked and its certificate issuing servers were compromised by the hackers. Through DigiNotar, the hackers issued rogue certificates as well as signing rogue certificates. The breach came to light only after a third party made a public disclosure, and rogue certificates continued in circulation after the discovery and after DigiNotar claimed to have revoked all such rogue certificates.

With certificate pinning, the peer's certificate is included in the application when the application is built. For example, Google pins its certificates in its Chrome web browser, and when users download the Chrome browser, the Google certificates are already embedded inside the executable file. A peer's certificate can be manually inserted into a trusted certificate list after that certificate has been obtained through a secure and trusted channel. Certificate pinning eliminates the need to validate a certificate at runtime, during the secure connection establishment phase. Because the public key is the most important element of the certificate, pinning the public key instead of the certificate is another viable solution. There are no known workable solutions for an intercepting proxy to circumvent the certificate pinning mechanism other than holding the actual pinned certificate at the proxy.

A related identity validation concept is Online Certificate Status Protocol (OCSP) stapling, formally known as the Certificate Status Request TLS feature extension. OCSP stapling places the burden of identity verification on the peer, who must include an OCSP-signed and time-stamped response proving its certificate is valid during the TLS or SSL handshake. OCSP stapling also challenges the proxy's ability to perform transparent interception.

SSL Interception and Privacy

Privacy laws differ from country to country and region to region. Therefore, a proxy must sometimes obtain explicit consent from a user before intercepting any user traffic. When the proxy has intermediate certificate signing authority issued by a trusted root CA, any modified server certificate will not trigger a browser pop-up warning message because this modified certificate can be verified. In this case, how could the end user prevent proxy interception if the user has the right to choose the action?

Due to privacy concerns, Blue Coat Systems took the approach of utilizing the client authentication mechanism to determine if the client explicitly grants permission to allow for proxy interception. The proxy is programmed to parse two preformatted certificates, one that has the certificate common name "Yes Sir", and the other that has the common name "No Sir". The client installs two such certificates in its key ring, as shown in Figure 1-16.

Figure 1-16: Client Consent Certificate

Policies configured in the proxy would instruct the proxy to request client certificates for a pre-determined set of destinations that show up in client requests. Because the client has multiple certificates installed in its key ring, the browser prompts the user to select the certificate to return to the server. This process is shown in Figure 1-17.

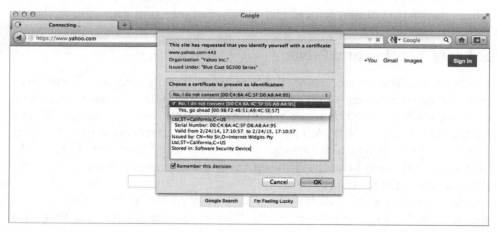

Figure 1-17: Client Consent Pop-up

Now the user has direct control over whether the proxy should intercept that particular session by selecting the right certificate. In other words, by choosing the "No Sir" certificate to transmit to the proxy, when the proxy parses this client certificate and sees the common name "No Sir", the proxy takes that as the cue and bypasses the session without SSL interception.

Summary

Firewalls are security devices that analyze traffic according to syntactical rules. The security policies enforced by a firewall are based on limited actions such as Allow or Deny. Firewalls provide the first level of traffic filtering. Intrusion detection systems perform traffic analysis based on historical data and heuristics and can scan for known threats. Both firewalls and intrusion detection systems become inoperable with encrypted traffic. This fundamental challenge is solved by proxies. Proxies are complex to design and implement. A proxy operates with deep knowledge of the semantics of an application or a protocol. The SSL proxy is a testament to just how sophisticated a proxy must be in order to successfully intercept and process various transactions. A significant part of this chapter was devoted to explaining the inner workings of the SSL proxy. The next chapter focuses on the various types of proxy deployments and discusses associated deployment challenges and solutions.

Proxy Deployment Strategies and Challenges

A proxy exerts its power and control on a network as an intelligent security device through its ability to perform deep traffic analysis in the context of an application and its users. One measure of the effectiveness of the proxy is its ability to intercept application traffic without interrupting the application or causing any side effects. An application being affected by a proxy can exhibit symptoms such as being unresponsive to user commands, engaging in transactions with sporadic data flows and unpredictable response times, and sometimes ceasing to function completely. Another metric that gauges the effectiveness of a proxy is its level of stealthiness while the proxy is active. When a proxy is stealthy, it can avoid being detected by both the application and its user.

After its successful incursion into a network, as part of its continued assailment, a sophisticated malicious application performs middle-box detection to avoid being discovered by the security proxies. Once a malicious application detects the presence of a proxy, it begins executing countermeasures such as changing its encryption methods, altering its communication patterns, masquerading as another victim, or sending a notification to its command-and-control server seeking further instructions. The proxy must hide itself from such applications so it can continue to surveil, pursue, and ultimately apprehend the malicious source.

The strategic physical placement of the proxy in the network determines the amount of network activity that may be subjected to proxy examination. The types of deployments demand that the proxy perform supporting network functions that are commonly found in a bridge or in a router. In this chapter we will discuss the various challenges of deploying a security proxy and describe the solutions that can either solve or alleviate these deployment issues.

Definitions of Proxy Types: Transparent Proxy and Explicit Proxy

A proxy's visibility to a user or to an application defines whether the proxy is a *transparent proxy* or an *explicit proxy*. The following example illustrates the characteristics of a transparent proxy. When Bob communicates with Alice through a peer-to-peer (P2P) application, such as an instant messaging (IM) application, once a transparent proxy intercepts this IM session, that transparent proxy masquerades as Bob when it speaks to Alice, and it masquerades as Alice when it speaks to Bob, all without either Bob or Alice knowing such an impersonation is taking place during that session. Also, no explicit configuration change is necessary in either Bob or Alice's IM application settings. The goal of the transparent proxy is to be as invisible as possible to both the client and the peers that the client communicates with. The application protocol operates normally and is completely unaware it is exchanging packets with a proxy. In this example, Bob and Alice did not give explicit consent to the interception of their session.

Unlike a transparent proxy, a user is aware of the presence of an explicit proxy. The application is explicitly configured to transmit certain types of traffic to the proxy for processing. For example, in the Firefox web browser, under the Advanced ➢ Network menu, various proxy configuration settings are available in the Connection Settings panel that specify how to access external networks through various proxies. As shown in Figure 2-1, the SSL proxy setting contains the IP address of the SSL proxy. When the user enters a URL that requires HTTPS transport, the browser will forward this request to the configured proxy. In the case of an explicit proxy, because a user has chosen to communicate through a proxy, the user gives explicit consent for the interception.

As shown in the Firefox Connection Settings panel, each explicit proxy is specified by an IP address and a port number, which means the following:

- An explicit proxy does not masquerade as the client or the server.

- An explicit proxy can be physically situated anywhere on the network as long as there is a routing path between the client and the explicit proxy, as depicted in Figure 2-2.

- Multiple explicit proxies can co-exist in the same infrastructure, each offering a different set of proxy services. Also, each proxy can be located on separate network segments. In Figure 2-2, the SSL proxy is directly connected on the same physical network segment as client A and client B.

The SOCKS proxy is one routing hop away from both clients, as is the HTTP proxy. Client A and client B can request proxy service from any of these explicit proxies.

- The IP address combined with the port number identifies the *service access point* where the proxy performs the connection interception. In this example the SSL proxy is located at IP address 10.9.45.3, and it is listening on port 443 for incoming interception requests to service.

- Because the explicit proxy can be located anywhere on the network, the proxy must use a source IP address that is different from the client's IP address when the proxy connects to the originally intended destination after intercepting the client-side request. We will discuss the types of source IP addresses that can be set for a proxy-initiated connection in more detail in a later section titled "Challenges of Transparent Interception".

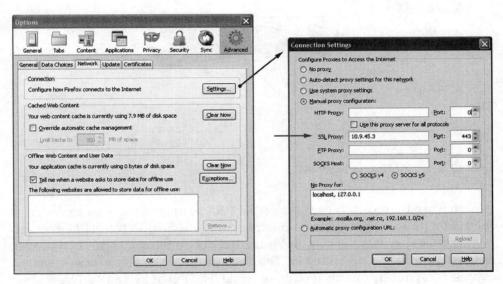

Figure 2-1: Configuring Proxy Settings in the Firefox Browser

If the client sends its request to the proxy or if the application connects explicitly to the proxy, how does the proxy know what the original intended destination is for a given transaction? An application protocol needs to contain enough destination information in its protocol requests in order for the explicit proxy to function properly. For example, for an HTTP transaction the web browser will issue a full URL in its HTTP request if the "HTTP proxy" setting is defined in the browser, as in

```
GET http://www.mywebsite.com/index.html HTTP/1.0.
```

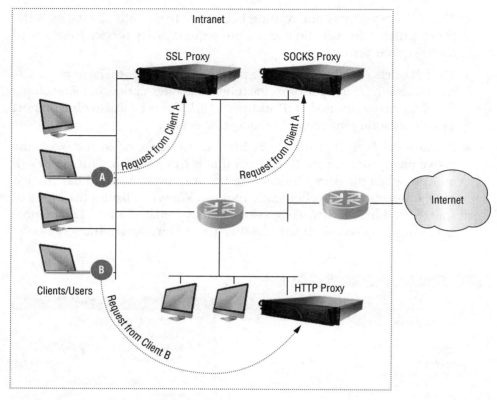

Figure 2-2: Explicit Proxy Deployment

Even when the browser sends the partial URL, as in `GET /index.html HTTP /1.0,` the HTTP protocol specification provides the *Host* field in the HTTP request header that specifies the original intended destination and can include an optional destination port number. The destination can be a server name that is expressed as a fully qualified domain name (FQDN) or by an IP address. The proxy extracts the destination from the Host field when it makes the outbound connection on behalf of the client. As this example illustrates, implementing an explicit proxy is possible only if an application protocol understands the concept of a proxy and provides a level of protocol support for operating with a proxy. However, the majority of application protocols are designed to run independently, without any proxy intervention. A transparent proxy is most likely the best method of deployment to intercept and process traffic from these types of applications or protocols. For the remainder of this book, we will use the terms *intercepted*, *proxied*, and *terminated* traffic interchangeably to describe traffic that is intercepted and processed by a proxy, either transparently or explicitly.

Inline Deployment of Transparent Proxy: Physical Inline and Virtual Inline

Transparent inline deployment offers the most flexibility to a proxy with respect to security policy enforcement, for the simple reason that the more traffic that is accessible to the proxy, the more traffic can be subjected to proxy examination and subjugated under policy control. The inline deployment can be categorized as either *physically inline* or *virtually inline*. All traffic on a network segment traverses the transparent proxy when that proxy is deployed physically inline. With virtual inline deployment, a configurable option is available to send either a selected subset or all of the network traffic to a transparent proxy.

Because network operations are commonly separate from security operations, network administrators, not being security engineers, are typically reluctant to deploy a proxy inline. The main reason is because network management is mostly concerned with optimal network resource assignment and utilization and maximization of network performance and uptime; ultimately network management is about attaining and maintaining the best end user experience. On the other hand, security operations generally focus on risk assessment, threat and vulnerability identification, and asset protection. Oftentimes security operations are viewed as a hindrance to network performance and an inconvenience for end users. Therefore, in addition to providing security capabilities and solutions, a proxy must strive to achieve scalability and stability, and equally as important from a network operation perspective, a proxy must minimize its effects on network traffic and "not break any applications".

Physical Inline Deployment

With physical inline deployment, a proxy is physically situated in a network as a *bump in the wire*, as shown in Figure 2-3. A transparent proxy typically installs in it a bypass network adapter for each network segment that it is attached to. A bypass network adapter, called a *bypass card* for short, is a special network device with built-in hardware circuitry that can be programmed to behave like a piece of wire after losing power or after the proxy stops activity (possibly due to a software crash) for a predetermined period of time from the software perspective. In the case of either hardware or software failure, this *fail-to-wire* feature is crucial to assure operational continuity in a production network. The network users must not be affected by the proxy outage or else lost productivity could be costly. At a minimum, the bypass card has two physical ports. It is this pair of ports that are connected by the special circuitry to become a wire during a system failure or loss of power.

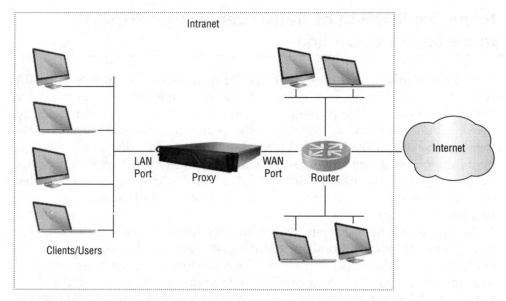

Figure 2-3: Physical Inline Deployment

The transparent proxy must provide various networking capabilities that are crucial to its normal operation with this physical inline deployment scenario. One of these networking capabilities is that the proxy must operate as a transparent learning bridge. As a bridge, all of the network interfaces run in the promiscuous mode to enable the proxy to receive all packets. Under normal conditions the bypass card operates as a regular network interface, and the proxy treats each port as a separate bridge port. The promiscuous mode of operation implies the transparent proxy must make the right decision on whether to intercept specific traffic flows. Consider the case where a transparent proxy intercepts a connection when both of its source and destination end points reside on the same physical network segment. Both the proxy and the destination will respond to the connection request, but the source will connect to the one that responds first. The communication will incur an unnecessary delay if the proxy responds first. Because the security policies implemented in the proxy are designed to provision traffic that takes place between entities that reside on different networks, the involvement of the proxy is unproductive and provides no security benefits in this scenario. With the learning bridge, the proxy compares the bridge ports where the source and the destination are known to reside on. Matching bridge ports indicate that the source and the destination end points are located on the same network segment, and as such the proxy will not perform interception.

The proxy translates policies such as "do not intercept any traffic from the CEO" or "do not intercept any banking transactions on the enterprise network" into explicit traffic bypass policies. The proxy must bridge any traffic that it does not intercept due to explicit bypass or because the traffic does not match any interception rules. Therefore, the proxy must learn the MAC addresses on all of the bridge ports and perform all the necessary bridging functions.

Another network capability designed into the proxy is the routing function. A sophisticated proxy can participate in the interior gateway protocol (IGP) by listening to the routing protocol exchanges. The proxy can extract the current routing infrastructure from the routing protocol exchanges and build a dynamic routing tree from routing protocols such as Open Shortest Path First (OSPF) or Routing Information Protocol version 2 (RIPv2). Doing so reduces the configuration requirement in the proxy and enables the proxy to enforce security policies without impacting existing traffic engineering practices. In addition, a proxy with routing capability can implement and enforce *policy-based routing* (PBR) for intercepted traffic.

One of the main challenges of physical inline deployment is performance and scalability. Unlike a switch or a router that processes L2 or L3 headers, a proxy performs much more complex operations such as TCP connection termination and L7 request parsing. Because an intelligent proxy needs to examine payload information beyond L4 headers, the so-called *fast-path processing* commonly found in traditional networking devices is not applicable to a proxy. Fast-path processing refers to hardware-assisted packet processing that relies on extracting bytes from packet headers, possibly from various offsets, and applying fixed logic to the packet based on pattern matching or value comparison. In other words, the proxy performs all of the networking functions in the software, including bridging and routing functions. For high-speed gigabit networks that are now common in large and small organizations, the proxy becomes a potential bottleneck: the higher the number of protocols and applications the proxy is capable of intercepting, the lower the network throughput that is achieved through the proxy.

Virtual Inline Deployment

With virtual inline deployment, a traffic redirector such as a router, a switch, or a load balancer sends the selected traffic to the proxy as illustrated in Figure 2-4. We will discuss traffic redirection shortly. The proxy returns the traffic, proxied or unmodified, to the traffic redirector, which then forwards the traffic towards the intended recipients, again according to either routing or traffic redirection policies. As such, with virtual inline deployment the proxy can be physically located anywhere in the network, as long as the traffic redirector can reach the proxy through normal routing.

An interesting characteristic of the virtual inline deployment scenario is that the proxy is physically placed out of the main network paths, as shown in Figure 2-4. There are two main advantages to this approach: increased scalability and improved reliability. Virtual inline deployment resolves the proxy scalability challenge by redirecting to the proxy only traffic that is intended for interception, while performing bridging and routing functions for the remaining traffic types on separate appliances, in most cases regular routers and switches. The second main advantage of virtual inline deployment is a reduction in the intrusiveness of introducing a proxy into the network. The administrator can gradually increase the number of applications for redirection to the proxy, according to the operational performance metrics of transparency, accuracy, and reliability of the interception obtained on the existing redirected traffic. This approach improves the overall network reliability and user experience, while enabling the administrator to discover the breaking points for the proxy in terms of performance or reliability with the mixture of applications and protocols. This method of redirecting more traffic incrementally also allows the administrator to enhance and calibrate the policies being enforced by the proxy with minimal user impacts. Another advantage of virtual inline deployment is that this approach does not require a network redesign and is more flexible in introducing additional supplemental solutions that collaborate with the proxy, such as a content inspection solution or a sandboxing solution.

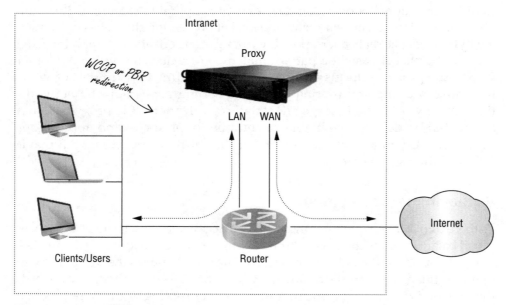

Figure 2-4: Virtual Inline Deployment

Traffic Redirection Methods: WCCP and PBR

In practice, there are two main methods of traffic redirection for implementing virtual inline proxy deployment: through *Web Cache Communication Protocol* (WCCP) or *policy-based routing* (PBR). WCCP is a Cisco proprietary protocol that was designed for traffic redirection, with built-in load-balancing and fault tolerance. The router that implements the WCCP protocol is called a WCCP router. The WCCP protocol exchange facilitates the automatic detection of a router or a proxy failure and enables a rediscovery and recovery process to take place automatically in order to resume normal operations quickly. A *service group* is established between one or more routers that perform the traffic redirection and one or more devices that receive and process the redirected traffic. The service group specifies the types of traffic to be redirected and helps the proxy to differentiate regular traffic from redirected traffic. Traffic selection can be based on source and destination IP addresses, source and destination ports, and the protocol type. The proxy describes the details of the service group to the WCCP router in a specific WCCP protocol packet.

When the WCCP router redirects the traffic to a proxy, the traffic can be encapsulated in a GRE tunnel or by means of an L2 destination MAC address rewrite. The WCCP protocol allows the WCCP router and the proxy to negotiate which redirection method to use. The advantage of using a GRE tunnel for encapsulating redirected traffic is that the WCCP router can be multiple routing hops away from the proxy. This is because the GRE packets are transmitted over IP packets, and the source and destination IP addresses can reside on different IP networks. The disadvantage of using a GRE tunnel is the possible overhead of packet fragmentation and reassembly. Adding a GRE header to the redirection packet may exceed the MTU, thus requiring packet fragmentation at the WCCP router and reassembly at the receiving proxy. Redirecting traffic by rewriting the L2 destination MAC address is simpler to deploy but requires the WCCP router and the proxy to be connected to the same physical network segment.

Because WCCP is a proprietary protocol, its implementation is vendor-specific, and each new release may create incompatibility with the existing third-party software that implements WCCP. PBR is a popular alternative to WCCP. PBR works similarly to WCCP L2 redirection, but it is even simpler to operate because PBR does not rely on a separate control protocol to negotiate a traffic redirection method. Once the physical network connectivity is established between the router and the proxy and the traffic selection or matching rules are defined in the router, simply configuring and installing the appropriate routing rules into the router enables PBR into action. There are several drawbacks with PBR. For example, it lacks automatic load balancing capability when multiple proxies are present. Also, although PBR can be used to redirect traffic to a proxy that is located multiple routing hops away, the routers along the path must be configured to perform the same redirection in order for this scenario to work. This is because PBR rewrites the destination MAC address of each packet to that of the redirection target. Therefore, each router on the path to the proxy must be explicitly configured with its respective next-hop router for the traffic types to be redirected. Another challenge with PBR is its difficulty in implementing an external bypass and failover solution.

When a proxy becomes unresponsive due to either a software or hardware malfunction, a bypass mechanism also exists with virtual inline deployment;

this bypass mechanism is called an *external bypass*. In the case of WCCP, the WCCP protocol enables the router to detect a non-responsive proxy. Assuming a single proxy is present in the service group, the WCCP router will consequently cease redirecting traffic to that unresponsive proxy until that proxy resumes participation in the WCCP protocol exchange. Traffic that was meant for redirection is simply routed according to exiting network routing policies during the proxy downtime. This bypass mechanism is initiated by the WCCP router and is performed automatically, and the physical bypass is external to the proxy. Obviously, the router will redirect the traffic to an alternative proxy if another proxy is present in the service group.

In PBR the detection of a non-responsive proxy is not an active process like that in WCCP. With PBR the routing paths are fixed. Although redundancy or failover may be an option, such a feature is implementation-dependent. For example, if the device implementing PBR is a Cisco router, then the automatic failover mechanism requires the deployment of a Cisco Discovery Protocol (CDP) to detect a failed proxy and then redirect traffic to an alternative one. In this case, the proxy must also implement the CDP in order to allow for the detection mechanism to work. As such, an external bypass may not be possible with PBR due to additional feature requirements.

LAN Port and WAN Port

There are typically two network interfaces (or more precisely two physical ports) installed in the proxy. These network interfaces can be either physical interfaces or *virtual interfaces*. A VLAN is a type of virtual interface. Referring back to Figure 2-3, with the physical inline deployment scenario there is a pair of physical ports belonging to a single special bypass network adapter, which connects the proxy on the physical link as a bump in the wire. A common practice is to connect one port towards the internal segments of the network and mark it as the *LAN port* and to connect the other port towards the network egress point and to mark it as the *WAN port*. In practice, the LAN port, also known as the *inside port*, has security and interception policies that are quite different from those designated for the WAN port, also known as the *outside port*. We will use the terms *LAN port* and *inside port* interchangeably. We will also use the terms *WAN port* and *outside port* interchangeably.

As we show in Figure 2-4, for a virtual inline deployment the proxy can be deployed using a single physical network interface that has a single physical port, which is allowable because a physical bypass is not a requirement. In this case multiple VLANs will be configured over this physical interface such that one VLAN interface is designated as the LAN port while another VLAN interface is designated as the WAN port. This configuration is mandatory for the WCCP and PBR redirection methods because the proxy must configure and enforce security policies differently for each port.

Forward Proxy and Reverse Proxy

The designations of LAN port and WAN port affect another categorization of proxies: forward proxy and reverse proxy. For a forward proxy, traffic interception takes place on the inside port but not on the outside port, while for a reverse proxy, traffic interception takes place on the outside port but not on the inside port. We need to give definitions for forward proxy and reverse proxy before we can explain the reasons and the types of policies that are set on the inside and outside ports. Figure 2-5 illustrates the concepts of forward and reverse proxies.

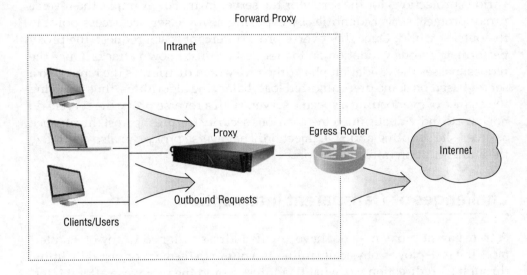

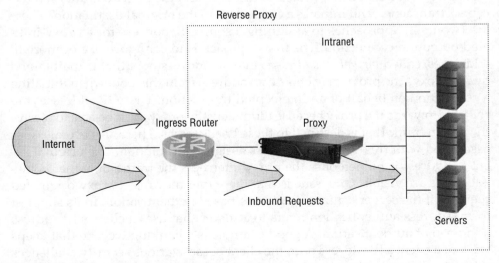

Figure 2-5: Forward Proxy versus Reverse Proxy

A *forward proxy* is deployed closest to the clients and users who actively seek access to network contents and resources and request services from servers that are located on either the intranet or the Internet. A forward proxy examines externally bound connection requests that are initiated from clients that are internal to the intranet. The goals of the forward proxy may include enforcing an organization's use policies, conducting content filtering, and providing access logging that tracks users and resources to meet compliance requirements.

A *reverse proxy* is deployed on the server side, which intercepts all incoming requests coming from the Internet. A reverse proxy is typically deployed in front of a group of servers, commonly known as a server farm, and offers various protections for the server or the server farm. For example, the reverse proxy protects server identities by exposing a single service access point to the outside world. Once the reverse proxy intercepts each request, the proxy performs rigorous validation on the request against known attacks. Once the request passes the validation phase, the proxy then distributes the request to a server based on some preconfigured load-balancing algorithms, thus reducing the chance of overloading a specific server. With a reverse proxy the servers do not have to individually implement various security features against threats such as cross-site scripting and SQL injection. The reverse proxy can also centralize the authentication implementation.

Challenges of Transparent Interception

A transparent proxy may not have any IP address assigned to any of its interfaces if it is deployed physically inline as a bump in the wire or virtually inline through L2 redirection. So, what IP address would the proxy use after it intercepts a transaction and initiates a connection to the original destination? There are two main approaches to assigning a source IP address for a proxy-initiated outbound connection. The first approach is to configure one or more IP addresses, called *virtual IP addresses,* into an address pool that is maintained by the proxy. The proxy may choose an address from this pool when initiating a connection on behalf of an intercepted transaction. These IP addresses are routable towards the proxy because ultimately the proxy must be able to receive the return traffic that is destined to these IP addresses. There are several issues associated with this source IP address assignment solution. The original client IP address is hidden once the proxy intercepts the traffic; only the proxy's addresses are visible. One issue is that the server may reject proxy-originated requests if the server utilizes IP address-based authentication. In its simplest form, address authentication refers to a server that uses a client's IP address as a form of authentication. A good example is a banking website that keeps track of a client's IP address once the client passes various security challenges interactively for the first time. When the client accesses the same service using a different IP address, the banking site will reissue those security challenges to revalidate the client's authenticity. In a more restricted environment, the client is prohibited from accessing a service unless the client is using a designated workstation that is locked to a specific IP address. In such cases the proxy will break the service and prevent the client from ever successfully establishing a connection with the server.

Another issue with using a virtual IP address is that the presence of a proxy may negatively impact IP address-based network bandwidth management solutions. As shown in Figure 2-6, a network appliance that enforces IP address-based QoS policies will become ineffective because the client IP addresses will have been replaced by the proxy's address. As depicted in the figure, the bandwidth management appliance has a QoS policy defined for each of the clients to restrict bandwidth usage. Because the proxy sets the source IP address for all server-bound packets to one of its virtual IP addresses, none of the QoS policies will match any of the client traffic. Therefore, all of the clients will have unrestricted bandwidth utilization, and the proxy essentially has defeated the QoS management objectives.

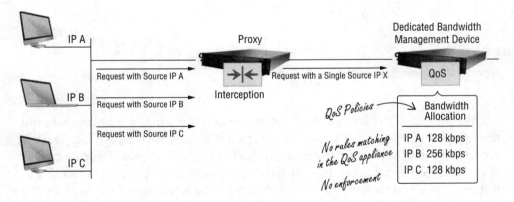

Figure 2-6: Transparent Interception with Virtual IP Negates QoS Policies

Therefore, a proxy may spoof the client IP address. Called *IP spoofing,* this is another source address assignment solution to solve the problems associated with virtual IP addresses. With IP spoofing the proxy uses the source IP address of packets from the original request as the source IP address for its outbound connection after it intercepts the client connection. This method comes with its own set of deployment challenges. For example, all of the routing paths to the client IP address must pass through the proxy. Consider the example depicted in Figure 2-7. The server responds to the proxy's request by sending the traffic to the client's IP address. In this case the return traffic is routed through a path that does not traverse the proxy, but instead reaches the client directly (③). This is an instance of *asymmetric routing* where the routing path taken in one direction is different from the routing path taken in the reverse direction. Because the client does not have a connection state for this particular traffic flow, the client resets the connection and causes the overall transaction to fail (④). The server-returned traffic can also reach the client directly when the proxy fails and its bypass adapter activates into the fail-to-wire mode.

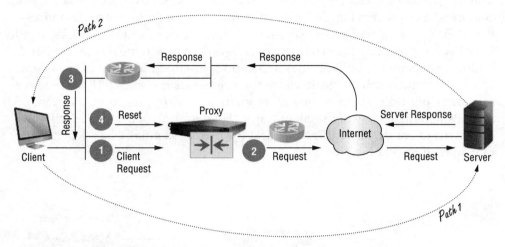

Figure 2-7: Asymmetric Routing Breaks Interception

One of the key challenges of virtual inline deployment is to ensure that both the forward direction traffic and the return traffic traverse the proxy, especially when the proxy is using the client's IP address as the source IP for its traffic. A common error found in the WCCP deployment is that the return traffic is not redirected to the proxy, thus creating asymmetric flows for intercepted connections.

Now, what happens if the client actually has a connection state that matches the returned traffic? A packet storm may ensue for a TCP-based transaction. This issue occurs more often than many believe. Consider the scenario depicted in Figure 2-8. The server is communicating with the client directly after the proxy has failed. From the server perspective, it is transmitting the TCP packets in sequence (①). From the client perspective, although the incoming connection is valid and is in the established state, the data packet received is not in the expected sequence number range. In this example the client is expecting a TCP packet with sequence number 10 but instead receives a packet with sequence number 25 (②). From the client's perspective there is a missing TCP segment. In this case the client's TCP implementation transmits a TCP ACK packet specifying the sequence number of the next expected data packet. The server's TCP implementation receives the client TCP ACK packet and treats it as a duplicate ACK packet, because the sequence number the client is asking for is in the past; that is, the data that the client is asking for has already been fully acknowledged and is no longer available (③). The server retransmits the TCP packets, and the client responds exactly the same way as before (④). Because the server continues to receive valid TCP ACK packets, it does not terminate the connection, even though it views the packets as duplicates. Similarly, the client keeps the connection open. At this point this ping-pong exchange with the exact same sequence of packets from the client and server repeats indefinitely and causes a rapid packet storm on the network.

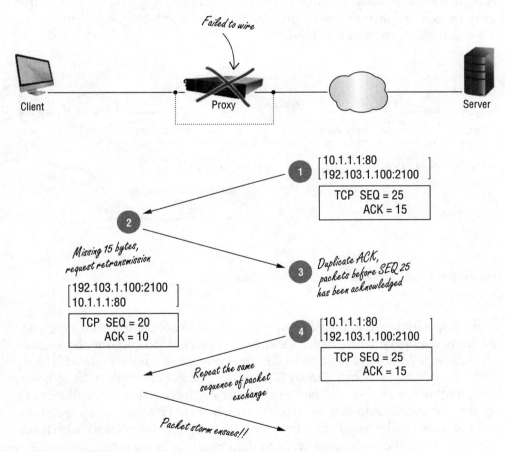

Figure 2-8: Packet Storm Caused by Failed-to-Wire Due to Proxy Failure

To solve the aforementioned packet storm problem, the proxy implements a source port selection process as a solution to reduce the chance of a collision in the client's connection space when the proxy performs transparent interception with client IP spoofing. The TCP port space is a 16-bit value for a total of 65,536 unique port numbers. However, out of this 64K port space,

- port range 0 to 1023 are well-known ports or reserved system ports;
- port range 1024 to 49151 are registered ports that are assigned by IANA to entities based on official port assignment requests; and
- port range 49152 to 65535 are dynamic ports, also called ephemeral ports; these ports can be used by any application for any purpose.

When the proxy initiates an outbound connection that is associated with an intercepted transaction, the destination IP address and the destination port remain the same as the original client's connection. The proxy picks a source port out of the ephemeral port range containing 16,384 unique port numbers. This concept is illustrated in Figure 2-9.

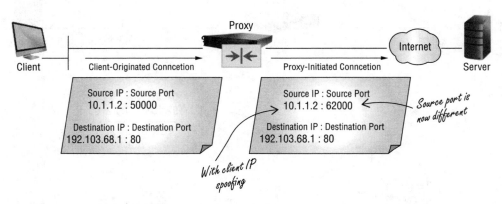

Figure 2-9: Connection with Proxy IP Address Spoofing

For a specific destination, when applying client IP spoofing for outgoing connections, the proxy needs to pick a source port that is different from the original client-selected port, but the port that is chosen must also not collide with other connections the proxy has already initiated on behalf of that client. In addition, the proxy needs to choose a port such that the selection does not collide with existing connections to that destination, which are not intercepted by the proxy but are managed by the client. In a typical large-enterprise network with thousands of users, the *connections-per-second* (CPS) rate is in the range of 100,000 to 180,000. The source port could deplete rapidly even if the interception rate is just 10 percent of the CPS rate. The packet storm problem caused by transparent interception with client IP spoofing is an NP-complete problem; in other words, no solution solves this problem completely. Instead, the proxy implements various strategies to reduce the possibility of such a problem occurring.

Directionality of Connections

A transparent proxy may process a connection in a specific way depending on the directionality of the TCP flow; for example, a policy may state, "intercept all traffic that is destined for IP address 100.1.2.3". The directionality of a TCP flow is defined by which end point transmitted the initial TCP SYN packet. The proxy cannot identify the directionality of a flow unless it has seen the SYN packet. Now consider the scenario where some failure has occurred within the proxy and it has begun operating in the bypass mode. The proxy does not perform any interception and does not keep any connection states while it is in the fail-to-wire mode. Clients continue to make service requests and initiate connections to destinations and servers on the Internet during the proxy outage period. At a later time after the proxy resumes its normal operation, any connection that has 100.1.2.3 as either the source or the destination IP address may match an interception policy; however, because the proxy did not process the SYN packet, it cannot resolve the ambiguity in directionality. Therefore, the proxy resets any such connection to force the client to reestablish that connection so that the proxy can then execute and apply the policy against those transactions appropriately. This conservative method of resetting a transaction to resolve ambiguity also applies when the policy changes, a topic that we discuss in detail in Chapter 3.

Consider another example where the proxy enforces the following policies:

- All traffic that is destined to TCP port 443 will be intercepted.
- All traffic coming from IP address 100.1.2.3 will be bypassed.

When the proxy receives a flow with source IP address 100.1.2.3 and source TCP port 443, the proxy does not know how to process this flow unless it knows the directionality of the connection. That is because this flow can match either policy, depending on the flow direction. If the initial TCP SYN packet has 100.1.2.3 as the destination address, then the flow matches the TCP port 443 interception policy; in this case the proxy will have intercepted that connection. However, if 100.1.2.3 transmits the TCP SYN packet, then the flow will match the bypass policy, and in that case the proxy will have bypassed that connection. This ambiguity cannot be resolved unless the proxy knows the flow direction; as such, the proxy will reset the connection for reasons explained previously.

Similarly, this flow directionality issue also affects interface-based interception rules. As discussed earlier, a proxy acting as a forward proxy performs traffic interception on the LAN port but not on the WAN port. If the proxy does not know the flow direction, it cannot apply the interface-based policies correctly.

Maintaining Traffic Paths

When a transparent proxy does not have an IP address assigned to any of its interfaces, there will not be any routing configuration in the proxy. So how does the proxy know on which interface to respond to the client request and on which interface to transmit the server-bound connection? There are situations where even when the proxy has IP addresses assigned and with a populated routing table, the proxy may still need to circumvent its own routing lookup and instead utilize the information contained in the client request to make transmission decisions. Consider the example illustrated in Figure 2-10.

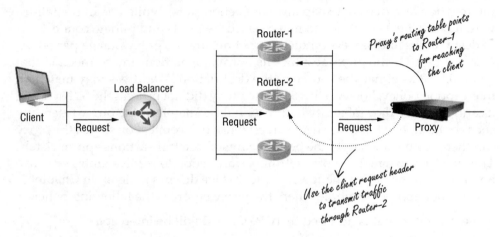

Figure 2-10: Use Source MAC to Take the Same Path Towards the Client

The client request first reaches a load balancer. The load balancer then distributes the traffic among three different routers. In this case the client request is forwarded through Router-2 to reach the proxy. If the proxy has a single default route installed and that route points to Router-1 as its default gateway, then the proxy's response to the client is transmitted through Router-1. Taking the path through Router-1 to reach the client negates the benefits brought by the load balancer. When responding to the client request, instead of performing a route lookup on the client, the proxy extracts the source MAC address from the client's request packet and uses that MAC address as the destination MAC address for the response packet. Doing so ensures the response packets will traverse Router-2 and reach the client through the same path as the incoming request packet because the source MAC address from the client's request packet belongs to the router interface that forwarded the client packet to the proxy.

The proxy may take a similar approach when transmitting a server-bound connection after intercepting the client request. Consider the example illustrated in Figure 2-11.

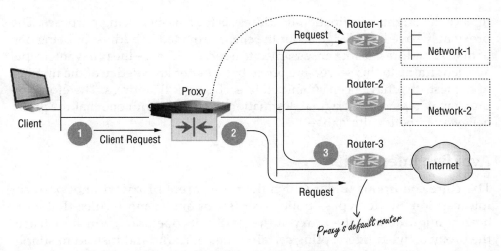

Figure 2-11: Use Destination MAC to Reach the Correct Next-Hop Router

In this example the client and the proxy are configured with different default gateways. Assume the client is connecting to a server that resides in Network-1. The client request traverses Router-1 without proxy interception. However, after the proxy intercepts the request, because Router-3 is configured in the proxy as its default gateway, the outbound request is sent to Router-3 (②). When Router-3 receives the request and performs a route lookup, Router-3 then forwards that request to Router-1 to reach the intended destination (③). In this case the request takes an extra routing segment unnecessarily. This routing overhead applies to all packets that are part of the proxy-initiated connection. One solution is to configure multiple specific routes into the proxy. A better solution is to utilize the information provided in the client's request. The client knows its request to Network-1 should be sent through Router-1. This knowledge is reflected in the client request packet's L2 packet header, which contains Router-1's L2 MAC address as the packet destination. Instead of performing a route lookup, the proxy can simply construct the outbound packets with the same destination MAC address as that of the original client request packet. Doing so allows the proxy-initiated packets to traverse the same path as that of the client's request packets without the interception.

The proxy can extract the destination IP address from the client request packet when it initiates a server-bound connection after interception. However, the proxy may perform DNS resolution if the hostname is known and uses its own DNS result instead of trusting the IP address from the client. This allows the proxy to offer an extra layer of validation against security issues such as pharming or DNS cache poisoning at the client end. Both pharming and DNS cache poisoning are discussed in detail in Chapter 4. Another reason for the proxy to replace the original destination IP address is for load-balancing purposes. The proxy may have knowledge about the client-provided IP address as being one of many IP addresses that are assigned to a server. Because the proxy intercepts all client traffic to this server, the proxy has a better knowledge of the number of requests that have been submitted to each server IP address. Therefore, the proxy may replace the original destination IP address with one that the proxy believes is a better alternative.

Avoiding Interception

There are conditions under which the transparent proxy will not perform interception. Static bypass policy consists of one or more rules that have been configured into the proxy at the start of its operation, which instructs the proxy to avoid intercepting certain types of traffic and instead to simply bridge or forward that traffic unmodified. For example, an enterprise must legally protect employee privacy if the employee's action does not violate corporate policies. An employee may conduct an online banking transaction during lunch hour. In this case the proxy is configured to bypass all banking sites during lunchtime. Another example is where a corporate attorney at a large enterprise is permanently exempt from being examined by a proxy. Legal material exchanged between the attorney and outside entities may be extremely sensitive, and therefore any network traffic that originates from or is destined to that attorney will never be stored or examined by any networking devices, including a proxy.

While processing an intercepted transaction, a proxy may decide to bypass such types of transactions in the future. For example, a user request to a destination may not match any banking sites, but the proxy may conclude the request constitutes a financial transaction after having analyzed the exchanged content. In this case, the proxy will install a bypass rule at runtime to avoid the interception of similar traffic in the future; this preemptive bypass action is termed a *dynamic bypass*.

A proxy typically has multiple interfaces installed in it. An interface that is dedicated to management traffic—such as connections that are established to access the web-based management console, or for receiving SNMP traffic for device management—will not be configured to intercept traffic. Interception will be disabled on an interface if it is known that intercepting inbound connections provides no security benefits.

Each organization has a network infrastructure design that must satisfy legal conformance and regulatory compliance requirements. The complexity of the network interconnect varies from enterprise to enterprise. An intelligent proxy must incorporate design logic that can recognize the traffic source and make an interception decision accordingly. One of the more challenging situations where interception must be avoided is when the proxy-initiated requests again traverse through that proxy due to a complex network infrastructure configuration or because of a temporary routing loop. It is critical for the proxy to detect self-originated traffic, after intercepting a transaction, and to avoid further interception of its own connections. Consider the example shown in Figure 2-12, which was taken from a real-world deployment at a large financial institution.

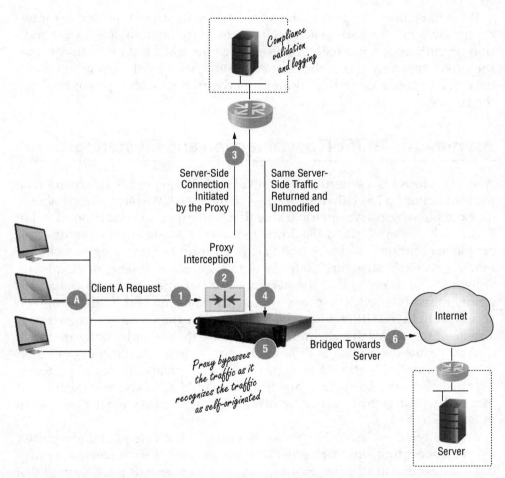

Figure 2-12: Recognizing and Bypassing Self-Originated Traffic

In this example, the client request reaches the proxy and is intercepted (①②). A purposefully configured route entry in the proxy causes the proxy to send the proxy-initiated server-bound connection towards a compliance validation service first (③). This service performs compliance validation on the request while at the same time logging the transaction. If the request is permissible, the compliance server forwards the original proxy-initiated connection, unmodified, back to the proxy (④). At this point, the proxy must recognize this connection as one that was initiated by itself and then bypasses this connection by bridging the connection onto its outside port (⑤). Without this ability to recognize self-originated connections, the proxy will intercept the same connection repeatedly in an infinite loop until its resources are completely exhausted.

What happens if the proxy intercepts a traffic flow and then decides interception was not the correct action? The proxy attempts to detect the condition of unintended interception as early as possible, but once discovered, the proxy typically resets the connection followed by the installation of a dynamic bypass rule so that it can properly process such types of traffic in the future.

Asymmetric Traffic Flow Detection and Clustering

A security proxy is a stateful device: it keeps connection state information on the transactions it has either intercepted or bypassed. We have already shown an example where asymmetric traffic flow can cause a transaction to fail in Figure 2-7. Asymmetric traffic flow can occur as a side effect of complex or erroneous routing policies or due to explicit traffic engineering or a change made in the infrastructure. Refer back to Figure 2-7; what is not explicitly shown in the figure is that the network in discussion has multiple access points to the Internet. The proxy-initiated connection is routed through an access point that is different from what is used by the server-returned traffic. The main reason for this asymmetry is because the server is configured with different routes according to different routing policies than those configured in the proxy. As illustrated in Figure 2-10, load balancers can also induce asymmetric traffic flows. One practical solution that has been implemented in a real-world security proxy involves building a proxy cluster, as shown in Figure 2-13.

As illustrated in Figure 2-13, Proxy A, Proxy B, and Proxy C build a cluster by interconnecting with each other in a *full mesh* topology where each proxy has a connection to all other proxies. Each proxy covers one possible path that can reach the client. Each proxy also exchanges its connection state information with all other peers of the same cluster. For each intercepted transaction, the proxy keeps track of both the client-side connection and the server-side connection. These connections are part of the state information that is exchanged with other peers. Bypassed transactions are also exchanged. The goal of this operating cluster is to form a virtual proxy that covers the entire infrastructure. Consider the example illustrated in Figure 2-14.

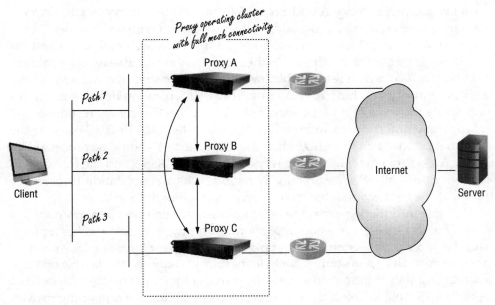

Figure 2-13: Full Mesh Clustering of Proxies

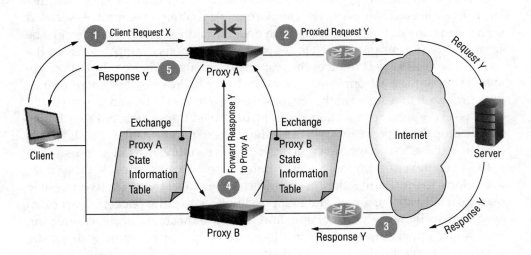

Connection	Owner
X	Proxy A
Y	Proxy A
Z	Proxy B

Synchronized information maintained by both Proxy A and Proxy B

Figure 2-14: Exchanging State Information and Processing Asymmetric Traffic Flows

In this example, Proxy A and Proxy B form a cluster. Proxy A and Proxy B exchange their respective processing state information with one another. At the conclusion of this information exchange, both proxies will maintain identical combined information databases. In these information databases, each connection is identified with a responsible owner proxy. Consider the example where a client request X reaches Proxy A (①), and after interception Proxy A generates and sends the request Y to the server (②). The respective server response to Y takes an asymmetric path and reaches Proxy B instead (③). Proxy B consults the information base and recognizes that the response to Y should be processed by Proxy A. So Proxy B forwards the response to Proxy A (④), and the transaction proceeds normally (⑤). Essentially Proxy B acts as an application-level router for all of the connections that have been processed by Proxy A.

The state information exchange taking place between Proxy A and Proxy B is a continuous process, not a one-time effort. Each time a request reaches a proxy, and the subsequent action that is applied to the request by that proxy must be announced to all its peers immediately, in the form of connection state table updates. Exchanging state information among the proxies requires a custom protocol that must also be able to detect unresponsive peers, enabling the remaining proxies to take appropriate actions on the orphaned connections. One other aspect of this custom protocol is to facilitate packet forwarding from one proxy to another. Because the forwarded packets are encapsulated in a custom protocol, the distance between each pair of proxies can be multiple routing hops apart. Associated with this distance is the communication delay, in milliseconds, and this must be accounted for in this proxy cluster design. In the previous example, consider the scenario where Proxy B receives the response to request Y before the announcement about request Y from Proxy A reaches Proxy B. Proxy B does not recognize the response, it may forward the response onward to the client, and the client will likely reset the server connection, resulting in a failed transaction; or Proxy B may silently drop the response that will cause the server to retransmit the packets, and in rare cases the server connection will timeout, also resulting in a failed transaction.

In the context of a proxy cluster, when a proxy receives a packet that does not belong to any connection in the information base, there are two possible reasons for this occurrence. The first possibility is that the packet is part of an asymmetrically routed connection, and the announcement of the connection owning that packet is en route. In this situation the proxy must wait for the maximum known delay between itself and its peers. Once the wait time has elapsed, it should then resume its normal processing of that packet accordingly. The second possibility is that the packet is asymmetrically routed and the path is not covered by the proxy cluster. In this case, when the wait time is over, the packet will be either routed normally or dropped by the receiving proxy.

If constructing a proxy cluster is not an option or there exists a single proxy in operation, then the proxy must have the ability to detect asymmetric routing conditions and act in the interest of ensuring a good user experience. Consider the example shown in Figure 2-15. The proxied server connection uses the client IP as the source address but has the proxy-selected port that replaces the original client port (②). The server response has taken a different network path and reaches the client directly due to client IP spoofing (③). The client resets the proxied server connection when it receives the asymmetrically routed server response (④). When the proxy receives the TCP RESET packet, it recognizes that the connection is one that was originated by itself. This is an indication that asymmetric routing has occurred between the client and the server. In this case the proxy will install a dynamic bypass rule that states all traffic from or to these two end points will be bypassed (⑤). The next time the client reissues the request, the proxy consults its bypass rules and discovers the client request should be bypassed; this time the proxy forwards the client request towards the server unmodified (⑥). Although the server response reaches the client asymmetrically (⑦), because the original request was not intercepted, the client will match the server response to its original request and respond accordingly to proceed with the transaction successfully (⑧).

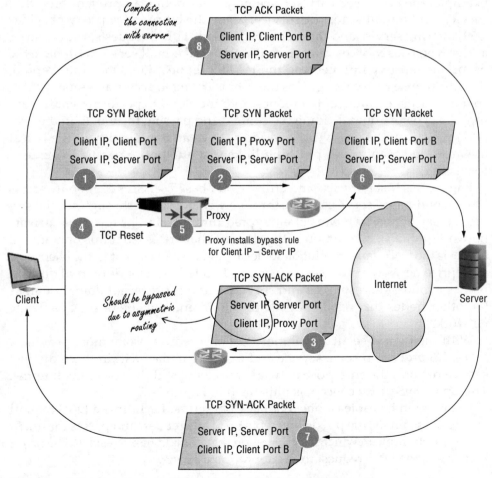

Figure 2-15: Dynamic Bypass to Handle Asymmetrically Routed Transactions

Proxy Chaining

One or more proxies can work in conjunction and process a request collaboratively. The proxy that receives the request may forward that request to another proxy to process fully, or the receiving proxy may process the request first and then forward that partially processed request to another proxy for further processing. When one or more proxies collaborate in such a fashion, these proxies form a *proxy hierarchy*, also known as *proxy chaining* with respect to a request processing. The proxy chaining concept is illustrated in Figure 2-16. The on-premise proxy is sometimes referred to as the *downstream proxy*, while its counterpart in the cloud is referred to as the *upstream proxy*.

What is illustrated in Figure 2-16 is known as a *hybrid security solution*, where an on-premise proxy works in concert with a cloud-based security service to collaboratively provide security services to the enterprise. For example, the cloud security service may offer data leak prevention (DLP) service, and e-mail scanning service, while the on-premise proxy provides URL filtering service and intercepts HTTP and HTTPS requests. For example, a user who tries to access an external web-based e-mail service will have the on-premise proxy intercepting the HTTPS request (①). Once intercepted, the on-premise proxy recognizes the user is trying to access an e-mail portal, so it forwards the intercepted request into the cloud to perform e-mail scanning (②③) before downloading the content and passing the e-mail to the user (④⑤). This way the user will have access to clean e-mail without the threat of embedded malware or phishing links that attempt to persuade the user to click.

Enterprises that purchase and utilize cloud-based services commonly access those cloud-based services either through web portals or through special service access points by means of encrypted tunnels, similar to virtual private networks (VPNs). A common network issue that arises from this operational model is the DNS name resolution for local domain names (that is, the client-side enterprise network resources, servers, and nodes), for cloud-internal domain names (cloud-side resources and services), and for external domain names (all other nodes that reside outside the cloud and outside of the client-side networks).

With the hybrid security solution, the on-premise proxy must provide a *split-DNS proxy* to resolve service and resource names within three distinct service regions: the enterprise network, the cloud, and the rest of the Internet. This split-DNS proxy concept is illustrated in Figure 2-17.

Each region has at least one distinct DNS server. Each time a DNS request arrives at the proxy, the proxy intercepts that DNS request and parses the query name to determine in which service region that domain name resides. The proxy then sends the DNS request to the appropriate server.

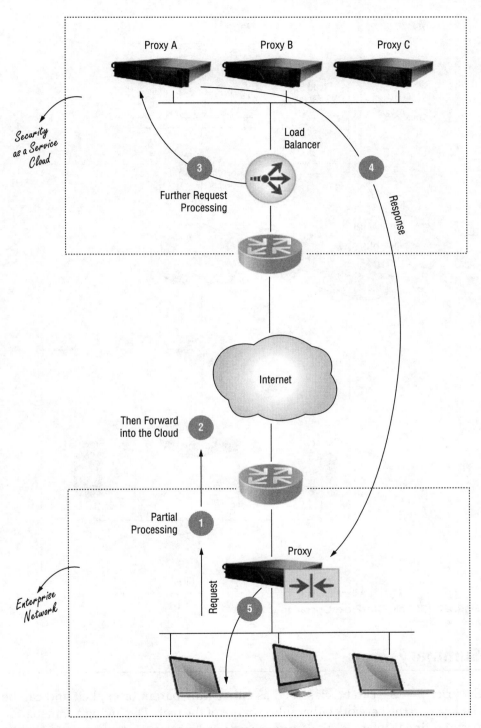

Figure 2-16: Proxy Chaining—A Hybrid Security Service Model

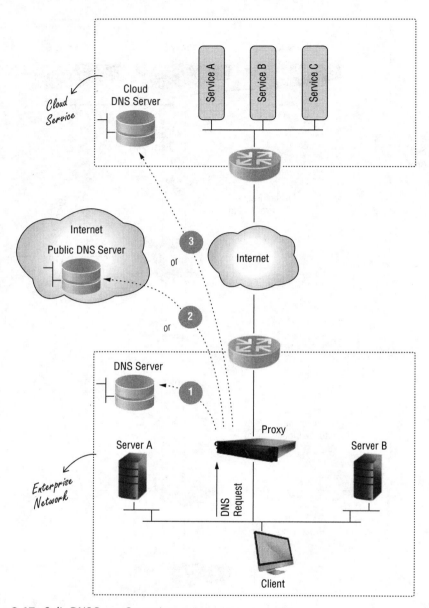

Figure 2-17: Split-DNS Proxy Operation

Summary

Security proxies can be classified as either transparent or explicit and can be deployed in the network either inline or out of the path. Deploying a transparent proxy inline is the most challenging scenario because the proxy must have the intelligence to make decisions on when to intercept a traffic flow and account for traffic engineering design embedded in the infrastructure, while at the same time performing networking operations such as bridging and routing functions. Asymmetric routing, which often occurs in a network, can induce complexity in operating a transparent proxy, and an intelligent security proxy must have the ability to recognize asymmetrically routed traffic and take the appropriate actions. In this chapter, we gave an example of how the split-DNS proxy operates, and in Chapter 6 we continue the discussion on specific proxies.

Proxy Policy Engine and Policy Enforcements

The expressiveness of a policy language is indicative of the maturity and sophistication level of a policy engine. The policy engine epitomizes a security proxy's ability to manage users and applications and to perform desired policy enforcement duties on the network. Chapter 1 explains the fundamental differences between a firewall and a security proxy. One of the key differences is in the expression of a policy. A firewall rule implements simple logic that examines information at the packet level, such as L2 to L4 packet headers, but not the actual packet payload.

The firewall rule concept is illustrated in Figure 3-1. When the firewall engine executes a rule in the context of a UDP flow or in the context of a TCP connection, the engine performs one or more actions that are specified by the firewall rule on the matching connections. For example, a firewall rule may instruct the firewall to reset a TCP connection if the connection has been idle for a specified period of time. The firewall must keep track of the TCP connection state, for example, by maintaining the current TCP sequence number and acknowledgment number in order for the firewall to generate a valid TCP reset packet.

Unlike the firewall rules, a proxy policy is highly expressive; this is evident in its formulation through flexible logical expressions that may encompass layer-2 (L2) to layer-4 (L4) packet header information, layer-7 (L7) application protocol content and its payload data, and session context such as authentication and authorization details. A proxy's policy engine can execute its policies in the L7 transaction context as well as enforce policies at all layers of the protocol stack.

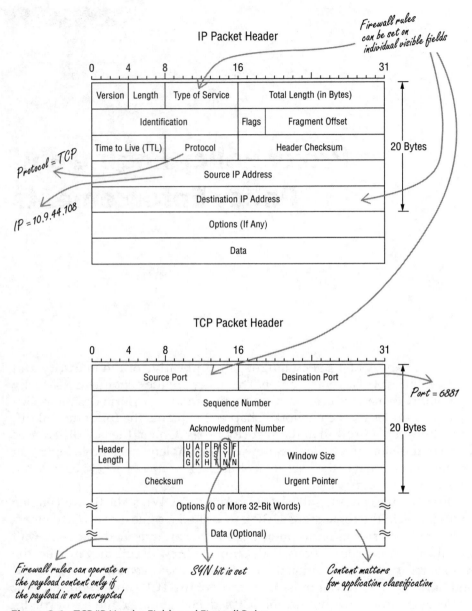

Figure 3-1: TCP/IP Header Fields and Firewall Rules

Understanding the internals of a policy engine and its implementation is essential to writing semantically correct policies. In other words, knowing what policies can be enforced under which conditions, then composing the security goals in the given policy language correctly, is the essential approach to ensure that the desired security outcomes can be achieved successfully.

Policy System Overview

In the context of a security proxy, a policy system is mainly comprised of the following:

- A policy specification language that can be used to express security policies, where security policies refer to a set of enforceable rules that orchestrate access to networked resources

- A policy compiler that translates the policy specification language into system configurations, operational settings, and actionable code

- A policy engine that executes compiled policy-actionable code within a context such as an application, a user, or a network environment

- A set of policy-aware proxies that provide the policy engine with an execution context and that invoke the policy engine at various points in the data processing path, thus enabling the proxies to subsequently obtain decisions regarding the necessary actions to be taken to achieve security objectives

The policy engine is not one monolithic entity that has full comprehension in all of the known applications, protocols, and user-related concepts. Rather, the policy engine provides the basic policy evaluation subsystem to the policy-aware proxies that interpret users' access requests against desired security goals and perform security enforcement actions accordingly. The policy compiler can identify conflicting decisions that are present in the policy rules at the semantics level and resolve those conflicts automatically when possible. Evaluating or executing the policy rules follows an execution order, and the rules can be prioritized.

In this chapter we will write example policies using a *pseudo Content Policy Language* (CPL) from the ProxySG product created by Blue Coat Systems. We will use this CPL for several reasons: the CPL is similar to a declarative programming language and is extensible for creating custom and complex policy gestures; the CPL is intuitive; and the ProxySG product is an industry-leading security proxy with over 12 years of widespread adoption, with the CPL proving to be an expressive policy language in those years. We use what we call a pseudo CPL, because we will create additional artificial keywords such as "and", "or", "not", "if", and "then" as logic operators when writing example policies for better readability and more clarity; however, these keywords do not exist in the actual CPL. Some of the gestures that are presented in the example policies may not exist in the CPL in that exact form. Again, these gestures are introduced to offer clarity. We will use the terms *policy*, *policy rule*, and *rule* interchangeably to refer to proxy policy rule from this point on.

Conditions and Properties

Policy evaluation achieves a policy decision concerning user authentication requirements, authorization rights, access restrictions, compliance verification demand, and access logging details. A proxy may examine data and information from all seven layers of the communication stack before making decisions on, for example, whether to intercept a request and whether to perform certain types of content transformation before serving the responses to the clients. As shown in Figure 3-2, the proxy extracts header and payload data from the networking layers all the way to the application context inclusively and incorporates each piece of information when consulting its policies on how to service a request.

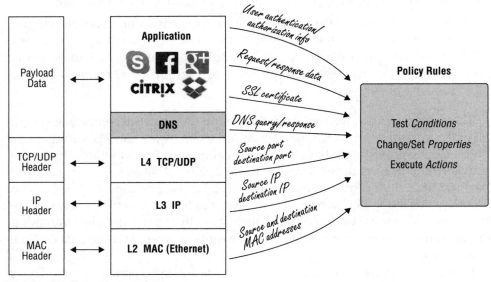

Figure 3-2: Policy System Overview

Consider the following policy rules block that is written to achieve the security goal "If a user is connecting from the engineering network (10.25.198.0/24), going to Dropbox, then authenticate the user to see if the user is Alice. If so, log the entire transaction for further analysis, and do not cache the response content".

```
if (client.address = 10.25.198.0/24) and
   (server.certificate.hostname = *.dropbox.com) then
   authenticate(NTLM)
   if (user = alice) then
       access_log.dropbox_log(yes) and
       cache(no)
   end
end
```

In this example, "client.address" is the L3 IP address of the client. The L3 IP address is extracted from the IP header of a packet. The code "server.certificate. hostname" is an attribute in the server certificate. The server exchanges the certificate information with the proxy only after the server has established a TCP connection with the proxy. The SSL certificate exchange phase occurs in the application context. As illustrated in Figure 3-2 and demonstrated in this CPL policy example, the proxy relies on information that is available from all layers of the protocol stack to make policy decisions and to enforce the desired outcome. This policy example introduces a set of terminologies and concepts that deserve further elaboration.

In this example, "client.address", "server.certificate.hostname", and "user", are each called a *policy condition* or *condition variable*. A policy rule tests each condition variable against a specific value, and if a match is found, then the condition becomes *true*; otherwise, the condition is said to be *false*. The code "cache" and "authenticate" are called *properties* of a transaction. One or more conditions guard a single or multiple properties. When the guarding condition is true, associated properties are set to desired values. Each property is a setting that controls how the proxy processes a client request. In this example, when the user is Alice and the server is identified as Dropbox, the "cache" property is set to "no"; subsequently, the proxy will not cache any content received from Dropbox for any of Alice's transactions. Setting the "authenticate" property to the "NTLM" value triggers the proxy to perform the user authentication action inside a preconfigured Microsoft NTLM (NT LAN Manager) authentication realm. In this example, "authenticate the user in the Windows NTLM realm" and "log the Dropbox transaction" are the policy actions.

As this example demonstrates, a policy rule consists of one or more conditions that are combined into a logical expression that guards binding properties and actions. Therefore, in essence, *policy enforcement* is the act of performing evaluation of conditions against a transaction, modifying one or more binding properties when the overall logical expression evaluates to true, and executing the associated binding actions.

Policy Transaction

So what is a transaction? A *transaction* or *transaction object* as defined by a proxy is an encapsulation of client-side and server-side connection states, client request and server response, policy evaluation states, and policy decisions. Figure 3-3 visualizes the high-level transaction concept. A transaction presents to the policy engine a centralized collection of all necessary data that is harvested from the client's request and from the server's response to assist the policy engine in making policy decisions (①). A proxy creates a transaction when it decides to intercept a client connection. A transaction is active and remains in existence for the duration from when the client issues a request to the time when the server delivers the response. More precisely, a transaction has a lifetime that is at least as long as the client-side connection.

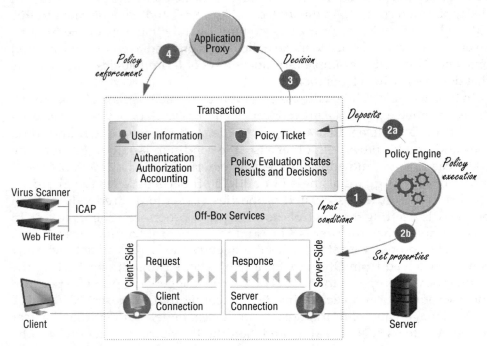

Figure 3-3: Overview of a Policy Transaction

Policy decisions that have been reached after executing policies against the client request and the server response are stored in the transaction object. The relevant policy properties are set to specific values once the policy decisions have been made. The policy engine consults the transaction object when applying policy actions on each and every packet that is part of the client-side or the server-side connections.

A client request may activate services that are external to the proxy, such as a virus scanning service or web filtering service that are running on external devices and are accessible through the Internet Content Adaptation Protocol (ICAP). In this case a policy decision depends on the returned service results, which are sometimes referred to as *external policy decisions*. For example, the virus scanning service may return a positive response indicating the given content is infected, which results in a "discard content" policy decision. Therefore, it is also necessary for the transaction to maintain processing states for the off-box services.

Policy Ticket

As illustrated in Figure 3-3, the policy engine deposits its processing states and its decisions inside the *policy ticket* within a transaction (②a) because policy evaluation and enforcement takes place throughout the lifetime of a transaction. The policy ticket is a key component of the transaction object. The application proxy examines the policy ticket to retrieve policy decisions (③) and performs enforcement (④) of those decisions on the transaction in question. A policy system may have hundreds of conditions and properties. The policy engine does not apply each and every condition to every transaction. The more conditions the policy engine evaluates, the less scalable the engine becomes in relation to performance. Conceptually the policy ticket selects the relevant conditions and properties in the context of a specific application or protocol, and these conditions and properties are then applied during the policy evaluation against a given transaction.

As a simple illustration, when a user connects to YouTube, the proxy will build a transaction and populate the policy ticket with conditions and properties that are relevant to the SSL protocol, the HTTP protocol, and the Real Time Messaging Protocol (RTMP). These protocols are relevant because the SSL and HTTP protocols facilitate a secure login to the YouTube account, and the RTMP protocol is the delivery mechanism for YouTube videos. The policy ticket will exclude conditions and properties that relate to the Skype application because Skype has no relevance to the YouTube sessions.

This example suggests that the proxy needs to qualify the transaction into a specific category at the transaction creation time. However, such a determination is impossible for most of the transactions. This is because when a proxy decides to intercept a client request, the proxy terminates the L4 connection and builds the transaction object at that time. Because the client has yet to issue the application-level request, the proxy lacks sufficient information to categorize the transaction. (Refer to the discussion on transaction handoff in Chapter 1, where the proxy makes a best-effort classification for a flow initially, and then refines its verdict as the proxy receives more flow data.) Eventually the proxy becomes more accurate in identifying the application, and the corresponding transaction type evolves accordingly. As the transaction may evolve from one category to another, so will the policy ticket as conditions and properties may be added or removed appropriately.

As the policy engine *compiles* the policy rules into internal executable representation, the policy engine has the knowledge on which condition is relevant for which types of transactions. So when a policy ticket is created or is being updated, any relevant condition must be marked for evaluation if that condition is present in the policy or is implied by a policy rule. Figure 3-4 illustrates the policy ticket concept.

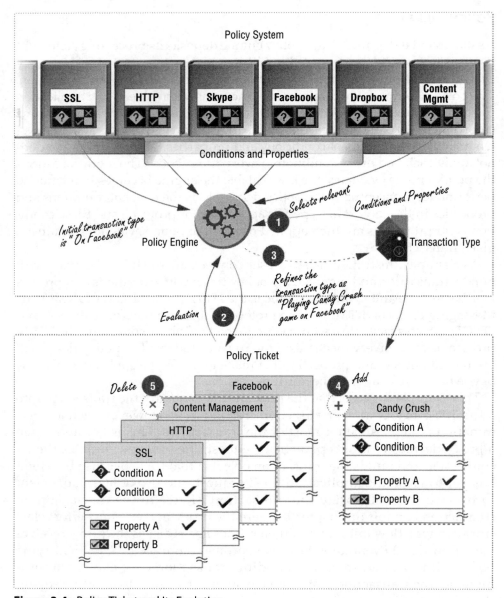

Figure 3-4: Policy Ticket and Its Evolution

The policy engine treats the transaction type as the filter to select the relevant conditions and properties for the transaction. As Figure 3-4 shows, a transaction may involve multiple protocols and applications. For example, when Mary uses secure HTTPS to log in to her Facebook account, the transaction is "Mary is on the Facebook web portal", so the policy engine creates a transaction object and populates it initially with conditions and properties that are relevant to SSL and HTTP (①). After browsing through her friends' Facebook postings, Mary begins to play the Facebook game Candy Crush. As the policy engine continues its evaluation, it refines the transaction type (②). Therefore if the overall transaction changes to "Mary is playing Facebook game Candy Crush", then the conditions and properties that are relevant to SSL, HTTP, Facebook, and Candy Crush will be selected into the policy ticket (③, ④).

Content management-related conditions and properties such as caching are typically selected into HTTP transactions. However, as the user navigates Facebook conducting various activities, the policy ticket is populated with different conditions and properties at different times as the transaction progresses. The content management conditions might be removed because caching is not an option for gaming (⑤). Even though many conditions are relevant to an HTTP transaction, however, the compiled policy marks only those conditions that are relevant and appear in the rules, which will be evaluated for a given transaction. Figure 3-5 shows an example policy ticket progression of executing the policy of "Log Mary's Facebook access and gaming activities".

When Mary begins the login to her Facebook account, a TCP connection is initiated towards the IP address of one of the Facebook servers, with TCP destination port 443 (①). The proxy intercepts this TCP connection (②) and subsequently creates a transaction object for this session (③). The SSL exchange takes place between Mary's workstation and the proxy after the TCP connection is established (④). The SSL exchange modifies the transaction type to an SSL transaction and allows the policy engine to place the SSL-related conditions and properties into the policy ticket (⑤). Then after the SSL exchange completes, the HTTP request to the `www.facebook.com` URL (⑥) causes HTTP- and Facebook-related conditions and properties to be added into that same policy ticket (⑦). While Mary visits her friends' pages, the transaction is categorized as a Facebook application. Finally, when Mary clicks the "Games" button and then selects the "Play Now" option for "Candy Crush", the policy engine detects this action after observing the HTTPS request to `https://apps.facebook.com/candycrush` (⑧); thereafter, the policy engine deposits additional conditions and properties for the "Candy Crush" game into the policy ticket (⑨).

The policy ticket also carries user authentication information. Each authenticated user has an associated set of authorized capabilities and permissions for accessing the resources on the network, where the network can be either an organization's internal network or the Internet in general. The purpose of evaluating authentication policies is to confirm the user's identity and to obtain the set of capabilities that are authorized and can be applied to satisfy the current user request. An *eager evaluation* refers to the policy engine evaluating and retrieving all capabilities associated with a user, even though not all capabilities are applicable to the current request. Similar to the concept of limiting the conditions and properties and selecting only relevant ones for a transaction, the more scalable approach is to perform a *lazy evaluation*, where the policy engine evaluates and retrieves only applicable capabilities that are necessary for the current request. A user is typically a member of a group. Authorization assigned to the group may either expand or limit the credentials of an individual user. Therefore, policy evaluation incorporates user group membership during user authentication. Lazy evaluation typically becomes mandatory in the cloud-based security solution that we will discuss shortly.

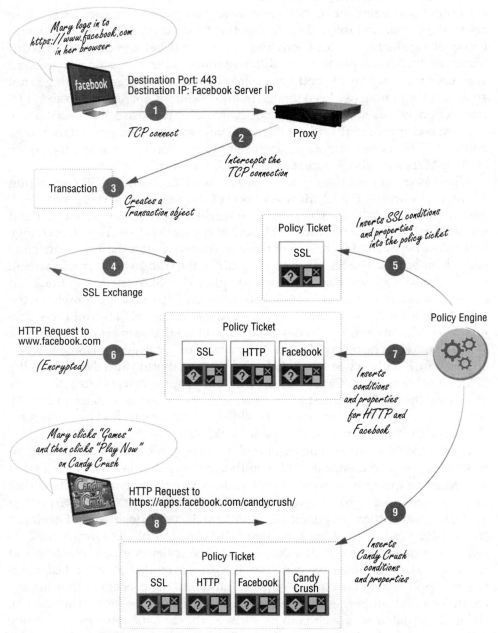

Figure 3-5: Progression of a Policy Ticket as the Transaction Evolves

Policy Updates and Versioning System

Another piece of information stored in the policy ticket is the policy version number. Policies that apply in a proxy may be written by various administrators or authors. Policies may also be imported from other proxies. Therefore, there is a need for a *policy manager* to collect and compile these policies originated from different sources into a single set and to apply a versioning system to each policy set. Adding policies into or removing policies from the set results in the creation of a new policy set that is assigned a new version number. Similarly, modifying a policy in a set will also cause a new policy set to be created with a different version number. The policy manager maintains the various sets of policies in a *policy repository*. This policy set versioning system is important in guaranteeing consistency in policy evaluation and enforcement during the lifetime of a transaction.

The policy engine refers to and applies the most recent policy set at the time when a proxy first begins to process a transaction. The policies may change while the transaction is pending on a response. The policy version system ensures that when the response becomes available, it will be evaluated against the same version of policies that were applied to the request. Otherwise, the inconsistency can produce an unpredictable outcome. Consider the example illustrated in Figure 3-6.

In this example, multiple authors contributed various policies, and these are compiled by the policy manager into a policy set with version A. The policy manager deposits this policy set into the repository and delivers this set to the policy engine. The proxy applies policy set version A against the request in Transaction X (①). A policy author then modifies the policy while Transaction X waits for the response to arrive (②). This modification triggers the creation of a new policy set with version B (③), and it is delivered to the policy engine as the new active policy set (④). Then when a new transaction arrives (⑤), the policy engine applies this new policy set version B to the arriving Transaction Y (⑥). When the response arrives for Transaction X (⑦), the policy engine must reapply the policy set with version A on the response (⑧). As you can see from this example, policy versioning requires the policy engine to store the version of the policy that is currently in effect for a transaction into the policy ticket.

Security Implications

Policy consistency is important because when the policy changes, so does the security goal. For example, at the time when user Mary generated Transaction X, the security policy version A allowed Mary the access rights to a video resource Z and permitted caching of that video resource but only for Mary.

By the time the server delivers the requested video, the policy has changed to version B, which disallows all users from accessing video resource Z but permits caching of all video content. If the policy engine evaluates policy version B against the response, then the video resource Z will be cached and marked as accessible by all users, and that is a clear violation of policy version A. The keen reader will ask the question: Why would applying policy version B against the response allow for the caching of resource Z? This example policy is comprised of two conditions: 1) disallow access to video resource Z by all users and 2) allow caching for all video content. The *order of evaluation* specifies that the first condition is evaluated before the evaluation of the second condition. This order of evaluation ensures that the request is denied immediately by the first condition if the user is asking for video resource Z; that is, the request will not be issued to the server. Therefore, when the response arrives, the policy engine applies only the remaining rule, and the only policy decision made should be about whether to cache the returned content.

One approach to solving the consistency issue is for the policy engine to *reevaluate* the request against the new policy version B, which will result in the request being denied and consequently the retrieved video resource being discarded. However, a valid argument exists that when Mary made the request, if the response became available before the policy changed, then Mary would have received the video resource. As such, the other option to ensure policy consistency is to reapply policy version A against the response. In this case Mary will obtain the video resource Z, and the video resource will also be cached. Unfortunately, this option still results in a policy violation. Because policy version B is the representation of the most current security goals to be enforced, video resource Z should not be cached.

This example presents a dilemma where either solution produces an undesirable outcome that violates the security objective. A security proxy has a restrictive nature when it comes to policy enforcement; that is, the proxy blocks more traffic than it permits to flow through. When ambiguity exists in a policy decision, a common practice is for the proxy to halt and abort the Transaction X without delivering any response to user Mary. One implication is that the proxy has a set of configurations and settings that control how the proxy behaves by default, when specific policies have been neither written nor committed. A firewall is typically configured right out of the box to deny and to drop all packets from all incoming and outgoing traffic. This default firewall behavior guarantees that when the firewall is brought online for the first time, and while the administrator is in the process of setting up specific rules, potential incoming attack traffic will be denied entrance, while any outgoing traffic that may create a potential security breach will also be blocked. Similarly, a proxy intercepts and then denies all transactions by default. This "deny-all" setting is a system-wide configuration.

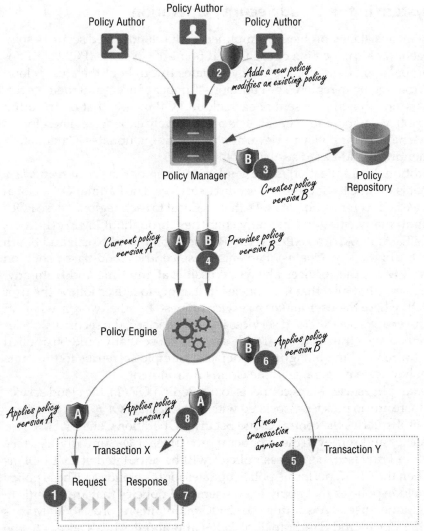

Figure 3-6: Policy Versioning and Its Effect on Policy Engine Operation

Policy execution and enforcement depends on a proxy's system-wide configurations and settings. The result of a policy evaluation may modify one or more proxy settings and can affect the proxy's actions. In the previous example, when the policy changes to version B, the proxy must examine its system-wide content cache and flush all of the existing cached video resource Z. In other words, a policy change may affect all operating components within a proxy. Another important point about policy change is that such a change can affect active transactions. Therefore, that change must be reflected and propagated throughout the entire system immediately to avoid negative side effects.

Policy System in the Cloud Security Operation

The policy inconsistency problem is amplified in the cloud-based security solution. The geographical location of each cloud point-of-presence (POP) signifies that the propagation delays of the policy updates throughout the entire cloud may vary from region to region. The enormous number of users and their respective transactions that are present at each cloud POP means that distributing the entire policy database to every POP is prohibitively expensive. Therefore, a scalable mechanism for policy retrieval and for providing updates is mandatory in implementing cloud-based security solutions.

One additional complication is the implementation of the *policy everywhere* concept that is unique to cloud-based security services. The hallmark of a global cloud service is its composition of POPs that are local to each region. These POPs are present in many cities and in many countries throughout EMEA (Europe, the Middle East and Africa), APAC (Asia-Pacific region), and North and South America. One of the key benefits of an enterprise-centric cloud-based solution is that not only are the services always accessible at any time and from anywhere the user is but also that the policies that apply to a user follow the user at every POP where the user makes a service request. In other words, when an enterprise user accesses the cloud services in San Francisco, the security policies applied to the user's transactions are the same as those that would be applied if the user were in Munich. Figure 3-7 depicts example scenarios to illustrate how the policy system operates in the cloud environment.

In this example, as user Mary connects to the Berlin POP (①), the cloud service discovers there are no policies associated with Mary at that POP (②). At this point the Berlin POP queries the central Cloud Security Operation Center (CSOC) for Mary's policies and retrieves these policies proactively (③). Similarly, as Mary travels to San Francisco, her access policies will be populated at that POP as well (④). Then the CSOC performs policy updates for the cloud (⑤). These policy updates include policies that apply to all users and policies that are specific to individual named users. Assuming the CSOC maintains records about Mary's access to the Berlin and San Francisco POPs and about Alice's access to the Singapore POP, then the CSOC will transmit the updates for Mary and Alice at the Berlin, San Francisco, and Singapore POPs, respectively (⑥, ⑦).

Unfortunately, the updates sent to the Singapore POP for user Alice failed to reach that POP, perhaps due to network outages (⑧). In the meantime, Alice continues to issue service requests into the cloud while the obsolete policies remain in effect (⑨). As we discussed previously, policy changes can affect an active in-progress transaction. A solution to this policy update problem is to give each policy ticket a *lifetime* that begins to count down when all of the decisions have been made for a transaction. Having a policy ticket lifetime ensures, especially for a long-lived transaction, that there is a limit on how long stale policies will remain active. When the policy ticket lifetime expires, the POP will revalidate the user policies with the CSOC directly and take actions accordingly (⑩).

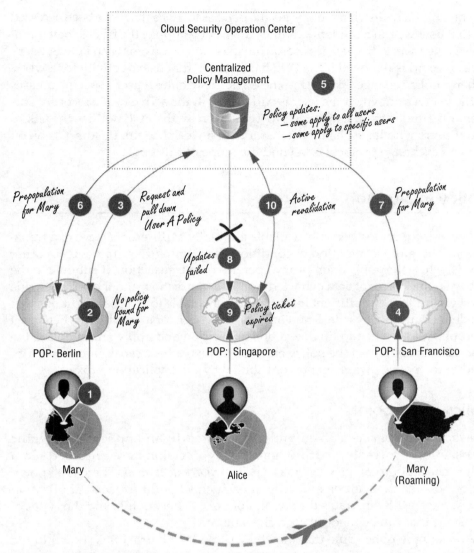

Figure 3-7: Operation of Policy System in a Cloud Environment

From this discussion we can make several observations. Each POP retains a *policy cache* as the POP services more and more users. The policy cache includes default policies that apply to all users and policies that must be enforced only at that POP. A policy database synchronization mechanism exists between the CSOC and each POP. At a minimum, the synchronization process should reliably distribute cloud-wide policies. However, the subject of policy database synchronization in a distributed environment is beyond the scope of this book.

The cloud will distribute user-specific policies to POPs that have been accessed by that user within a predefined timeframe. For example, the CSOC may maintain a user in an active usage records database for a week for each POP. A user's access record is removed if the POP has not seen that user's activity for a week. When a policy change takes place, the CSOC distributes a user's specific policies to those POPs on which the user is still visible in the active usage records. This scenario alludes to an exchange protocol whereby the POP notifies the CSOC about users who have been inactive for over a week. Again, the discussion on such an exchange protocol is beyond the scope of this book.

Policy Evaluation

Pieces of information become available gradually at different stages of a transaction. Therefore, evaluation of conditions has timing requirements. In other words, while the application proxy operates on a transaction, it submits to the policy engine pieces of data extracted from the transaction, and the policy engine must identify when sufficient information is available to test the conditions that are defined in a policy rule. Knowing when to check for a condition, when to set a property, and when to finalize a policy decision and apply an action are the essential capabilities of the policy engine. However, these capabilities are attributed to the policy-aware agents contributed by the application proxies.

Policy Checkpoint

A *policy checkpoint* is a fixed and known step in an application-specific transaction-processing path where policy decisions are enforced. So a policy checkpoint can be viewed as a *policy enforcement point*. There is a known set of policies that can be enforced at each checkpoint for each application proxy. Figure 3-8 illustrates the concept of policy checkpoints and the types of decisions that can be made at each checkpoint.

An example policy rule that may be written for Figure 3-8 is shown in the following pseudo policy code:

```
if client.address = 10.9.44.1 then
    intercept(yes)          // ①
    reflect_ip(client)      // ④
    rewrite(url, "http://www.original.com",
                 "http://www.different.com") // ⑦
    http.server.accept_encoding(client)  // ⑧
    response.icap_service(icap-server-1) // ⑨ - ⑪
    bypass_cache(yes)   // ⑨ - ⑪
    transform_active_content(how-to-definition)   // ⑫
end
```

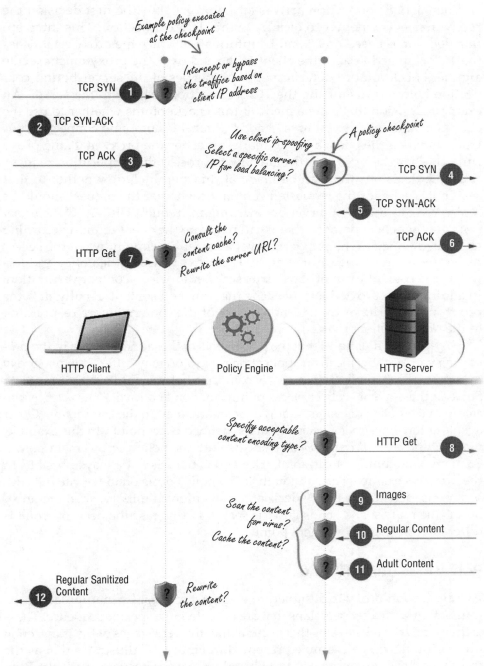

Figure 3-8: Policy Checkpoints in Transaction Processing

When a TCP connection arrives at the proxy at ①, the first decision the proxy makes is whether to terminate this TCP connection. This interception decision is based on L3 and L4 information. Once the proxy establishes the TCP connection with the client at the end of ③, the proxy must execute another checkpoint to determine the properties of the server-bound connection before transmitting the TCP connection request to the server. An example decision that can be made at this checkpoint is whether to use the client's IP address as the source IP address for this outbound connection (④). Later on when the client's HTTP request reaches the proxy at ⑦, the proxy runs another checkpoint to decide how to process this application request. Example decisions that can be made at this step include whether to first search its cache for the requested content or whether the request should be redirected to a different server by rewriting the request URL. At ⑧ the proxy runs another checkpoint so that it can re-create the client request according to defined policies. The proxy runs yet another checkpoint when the server responses are received (⑨ or ⑩ or ⑪). The proxy consults the policy and forwards the content to an off-box virus scanner for clean content verification. In addition, the proxy does not cache the returned content. Finally, at ⑫ the proxy may rewrite or transform a subset of the content before responding to the original client request.

This example illustrates that the placements of these checkpoints in the processing path are specific to an application proxy and may differ from one proxy to another. Each application proxy is comprised of various *policy-aware agents*. Some of these agents collect pieces of information and invoke the *policy evaluator* to make policy decisions that will be maintained in the transaction. Other agents enforce the policy decisions at the defined checkpoints. In this example, many of the *policy decision points* coincide with the policy enforcement points. Such an overlapping of different roles and actions is not always possible. In the previous example rule, although at ⑦ a policy decision to rewrite the URL has been reached, this policy decision is not enforced until ⑧ when the proxy builds the request and sends it to the server. In this case the decision point is different from the enforcement point.

Policy Execution Timing

An application proxy is designed to engage a request by manipulating the transaction with a set of actions that are executed in a specific sequence. These actions are driven by events that occur at the different stages of the transaction processing flow. The example presented in Figure 3-5 illustrates that as the transaction evolves, more conditions and properties become available. Each condition in a policy rule may be evaluated at a different time and at a different processing step compared to other conditions that are part of the same rule. For example, HTTP-related conditions cannot be evaluated at ④ because the

HTTP request has not been issued; thus, HTTP conditions are not yet available at that processing stage. Similarly, evaluation of conditions related to Facebook games cannot be done at ⑥ but instead can be performed at ⑧. Figure 3-9 depicts the policy execution timing concept. In Figure 3-9, ①a, ①b, ②a, and ②b mark the high-level checkpoints of a transaction.

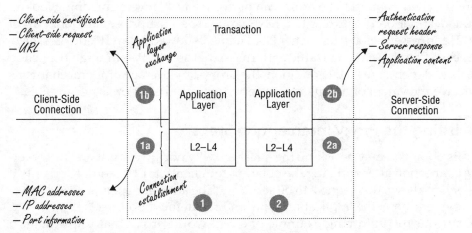

Figure 3-9: Transaction Checkpoints and Timing Constraints

Consider the following pseudo policy rule:

```
if (client.address = 10.9.44.1) and (server.authenticate(RADIUS)) then
    intercept(no)
end
```

This policy rule states that if the client is coming from IP address 10.9.44.1 and the server authenticates the user through the RADIUS authentication realm, then the proxy must not intercept the client traffic. This rule has a *timing violation* called "late condition guards early action" problem. The proxy tries to determine if it should intercept the client connection at checkpoint ①a; however, the authentication condition will become available only after the proxy connects to the server and has issued the server-side application request. The action of "intercept" must be executed at checkpoint ①a because the proxy must either terminate the TCP connection or bypass the connection completely. However, this action depends on a condition that cannot be evaluated at ①a, but at a later time at ②b, which results in a semantics error.

This example illustrates another key point: a decision must be made at a certain checkpoint because a policy enforcement action must be executed at that checkpoint to ensure security compliance. What happens when transaction processing reaches a checkpoint but a decision has not arrived? There may be such possibilities; however, the policy checkpoints are designed and created to avoid such ambiguity. The policy compiler must be able to identify such conflicts and raise errors against offending written policy rules.

Consider the checkpoint at ④ in Figure 3-8. The action "select a specific server IP for load balancing" seems problematic. How does the proxy know what other IP addresses belong to the same server as that of the destination IP address from the client request? The proxy can perform a DNS reverse mapping lookup of the destination IP address to a DNS name. Then the proxy can query all of the IP addresses belonging to that DNS name, followed by an IP address selection based on the existing traffic patterns to that server. So although the action seems to depend on a later condition, the proxy can leverage other mechanisms to derive the value for a dependent property; thus, the action is permissible.

Revisiting the Proxy Interception Steps

At this point you may be asking the question, why not always initiate the server-side connection after applying the policy to the client's HTTP request and only if the policy allows this request to be serviced? The answer depends on the proxy deployment type, the application type, and the defined policies.

Consider the following example of a real-world proxy that implements a feature called *delayed interception*. The typical proxy interception involves the proxy first terminating the client request by establishing a TCP connection with the client. Then the proxy processes the application-level transaction, executes the necessary policies, and, if permissible, initiates the connection with the server. In this scenario, if the proxy operates in the transparent mode, the client will perceive the server as being available once the client establishes the TCP connection with the proxy. Then the client will begin issuing its requests. Chapter 2 describes the transparent proxy and its mode of operation in detail.

At this point, the real server that the client tries to connect with may be temporarily unavailable, unwilling to service further requests due to overload, or have been taken offline permanently. If the proxy intercepts the client-side connection successfully and then discovers the server is unavailable, the proxy will close the client-side connection, but this action could have undesirable consequences for the overall communication and impact the application executing on the client. For example, because the client had successfully established a connection with the proxy previously, the client application may continue to attempt connecting to the server and consuming proxy resources unnecessarily. The solution to this problem is to emulate the server behavior, as illustrated in Figure 3-10.

As shown in Figure 3-10, the proxy suspends the client-to-proxy TCP handshake immediately after receiving the client's TCP SYN packet (①). The proxy delays the completion of the client-side connection until it can verify the server's availability and how the proxy will proceed with the client also depends on the server's response and behavior. In the first scenario, the server responds and completes the TCP connection with the proxy normally (②, ③, ④). The proxy then resumes the client-side TCP handshake and completes that TCP connection (⑤, ⑥). The client then submits its application request, and the proxy processes the request according to the defined policies (⑦, ⑧).

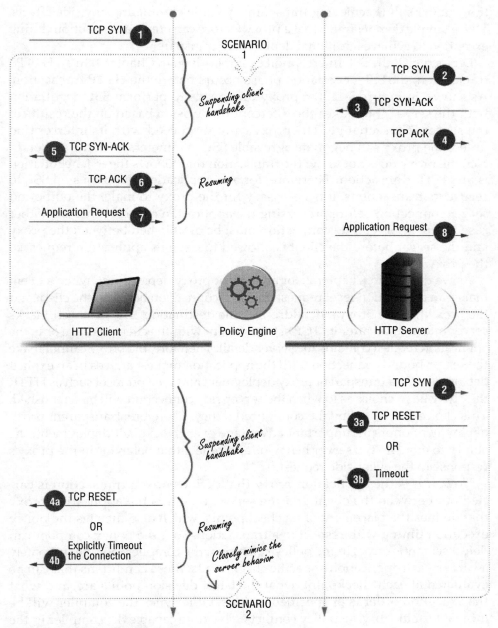

Figure 3-10: Delayed Interception

In the second scenario, either the server sends the TCP RESET that indicates the server is not accepting service requests (③a) or the proxy-to-server TCP connection request simply times out (③b), which indicates the server is simply not available. The proxy then emulates the exact behavior towards the client: resetting the client-side TCP connection (④a) or simply letting the connection timeout (④b), thus achieving transparency while eliminating any side effects. This example demonstrates that a proxy feature can create an execution timing exception to achieve additional deployment transparency.

Let us revisit the SSL interception example given in Chapter 1. In an HTTPS transaction, the SSL negotiation phase occurs before the HTTP transaction. As shown in Figure 3-11, the proxy first needs to perform SSL negotiation with the server and makes the interception decision based on the results of the server SSL exchange. The proxy cannot proceed with its interception unless the proxy can negotiate agreeable SSL parameters with the server. In fact, the proxy does not know the transaction that follows the SSL negotiation is an HTTP transaction. Therefore, for any application that relies on SSL to secure its transactions, it is necessary for the proxy to make the outbound server connection before processing the application request. This is another case where a server-side connection must be established between the proxy and the server before the client is allowed to issue its application request to the proxy.

As we discuss in Chapter 2, for an explicit proxy deployment, when a client makes an application-level request, the TCP connection between the client and the proxy has the proxy's IP address as the destination. The proxy still lacks server information after its TCP establishment with the client because only the application request contains the server detail. Therefore, the proxy cannot make the server-bound connection until the application request arrives in an explicit deployment. In a transparent proxy deployment and for a protocol such as HTTP, the proxy has a choice as to when the server-side connection will be established. This choice is dictated by the configured policy. Therefore, transparent proxy deployment offers an important advantage over the explicit deployment: the ability to emulate the server behavior and reflect that behavior in the proxy's response to the client-side request.

Now, if it is the application proxy that defines how a transaction is carried out between the client and the server, then it is the application proxy that defines the placement of its checkpoints, which also dictates the policy execution timing with respect to a transaction. So if the policy compiler can detect semantic errors in the policy rules, then the compiler must be intimately aware of each application's specific checkpoints, those conditions that can be evaluated at each checkpoint, what the latest decision points are, and what the execution order is of specified actions. Otherwise, the compiler will be incapable of identifying policy conflicts. The more capable the compiler is, the more expressive the policy language can be. Moreover, the policy language must be constructed with application-specific gestures. The earlier discussion emphasizes a key point that we made at the beginning of this chapter: a sophisticated policy language is a reflection of the capability and maturity of a security proxy.

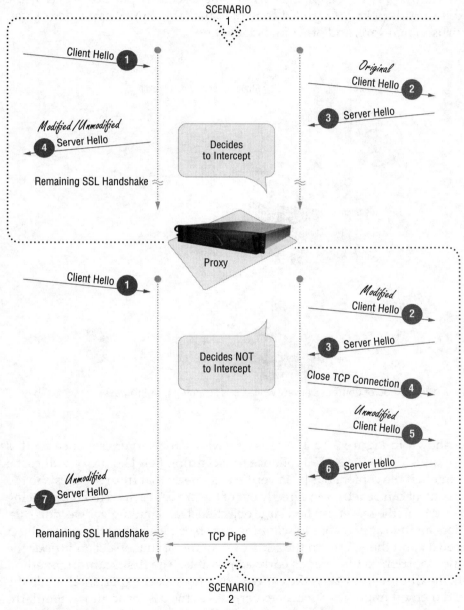

Figure 3-11: SSL Interception as Performed by a Proxy

Enforcing External Policy Decisions

Delegating a policy decision to an off-box device, such as an external virus scanner, and subsequently enforcing an external policy decision, can be rather challenging. Figure 3-12 illustrates a scenario where a security proxy collaborates with an antivirus (A/V) appliance to implement security policies, whereby the proxy forwards policy-controlled content to the off-box A/V appliance to scan for viruses, malware, and other malicious code.

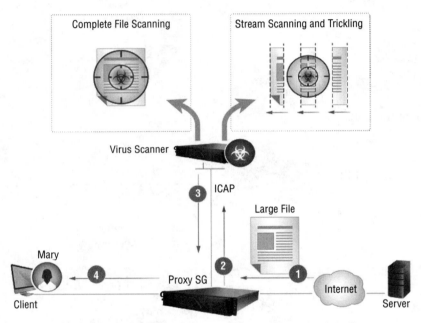

Figure 3-12: Method of Content Delivery while Virus Scanning is In-Progress

As shown in Figure 3-12, the proxy forwards the server response, in this case a large file, to the A/V appliance for scanning (②). The proxy will cache the content if the content has been verified as safe so that future requests to the same content can be retrieved directly out of the proxy's cache. The content being retrieved from the server can be a large object, such as a multi-gigabyte video file.

There are two approaches to scanning the object: wait until the entire object is received and then perform the scan, or scan the partial object and *trickle* the scanned portion to the user as early as possible. The first scanning method offers maximum security at the expense of a poor user experience, while the second method improves the user experience at the cost of accuracy. Similarly, the proxy can wait until the entire object has been received from the server and then forward the entire object to the A/V scanner, or the proxy can forward the partially received content to the A/V scanner as early as possible.

An industry practice is for the proxy to receive the entire object and then trickle the data to the client while the A/V engine performs the scanning. With the *trickle-from-start* method, the proxy sends the data from the beginning at a low data rate during scanning, for example, 1 byte per second, until the A/V scanning is complete. Once the scan is complete and if the content is safe, the proxy transmits the remaining data to the client at the normal data rate. With the *trickle-at-the-end* method, the proxy sends the data from the beginning at the normal rate up to a configured percentage, for example, at 80 percent of the entire object size. Then the proxy begins to trickle the data at a low rate, until the A/V scanning is complete. At that time the proxy will again transmit the remaining object to the client at the normal data rate. The trickle-from-start method is safer than the trickle-at-the-end method because a lower number of bytes are leaked if the content proves to be malicious. The trickle-at-the-end method provides a better user experience because most of the object is delivered to the user and only the last small portion needs to be delayed.

The challenges illustrated by this example are as follows:

- The proxy needs to be aware of the A/V engine's capabilities and its current workload so that the proxy can choose the trickle method to balance between performance and security.

- The off-box A/V engine is viewed as an external policy decision point, and the proxy is the policy enforcement point. The proxy must implement additional policies and actions to safeguard against a situation where the policy decision point is inaccessible. For example, if the compiled policies demand that all objects received from a specific server must be scanned for malicious content, and the A/V engine is offline, then the proxy must detect this abnormal situation and revert to another set of policies or operating parameters to process the returned content from that server.

In Chapter 6 we discuss other external policy enforcement systems such as the Data Leak Prevention appliance and technology.

Summary

A comprehensive policy system is comprised of an expressive policy language containing application-specific gestures, a compiler that is constructed with the deep knowledge of application proxies, and a policy engine that can execute policy rules and enforce policy-defined actions effectively at the various checkpoints along the transaction-processing path. The transaction object maintains the processing states for the client request and associated server response. The policy ticket selects the necessary conditions and properties that are applicable for a transaction. The policy engine operates on the policy ticket to make decisions that are subsequently tracked by the policy ticket. Policy-aware application proxy agents then consult the policy ticket to enforce those decisions by executing the binding actions. As policy rules change over time, those updates must be propagated to every system component that either participates in the policy decision-making process or acts as the policy enforcer. Understanding the policy execution timing is critical in writing semantically correct policy rules. Knowing when a policy condition can be evaluated against a transaction and when a decision must be enforced is the key to achieving the desired security objectives.

CHAPTER 4

Malware and Malware Delivery Networks

Firewalls have evolved over the years and have been effective in defending against threats that attempt to infiltrate through the open service ports from outside of a protected infrastructure. The ubiquitous presence of Network Address Translator (NAT) at the ingress points makes it nearly impossible to obtain any meaningful results when host scanning from outside the perimeters of an organization. Although distributed denial of service (DDoS) attacks are still as prevalent today as they were a decade ago, modern variations of traditional brute-force attacks against an infrastructure bring temporary network outages that can be remediated quickly. The existing defensive solutions also can be fortified to recognize these attacks easily, thus becoming capable of fending off similar assaults in the future. More importantly, these attacks inflict limited negative economic impacts on an organization.

Contemporary security attacks begin with an internal security breach, which results when an internal user is lured into creating outbound connections and reaching malware delivery networks where all kinds of malicious executable such as keyloggers, Trojans, rootkits, and ransomware are hosted for download. The security compromise is now coming from the inside. Hackers, black hats, threat actors—no matter what we call them, these individuals are intelligent, inventive, and capable of creating ingenious exploits. They are motivated by money or driven by political beliefs. Those who are sponsored by governments have inexhaustible resources at their disposal, making them formidable adversaries.

Instead of focusing on a host-based solution such as virus identification, memory forensics, malware executable analysis, and rootkit fundamentals, in this book we choose to focus on subjects that are relevant to key common operations that are carried out by the majority of exploits after a successful infiltration, namely, communication with the command and control (C2) center (or "phone home") and the exfiltration of valuable data.

Cyber Warfare and Targeted Attacks

Modern-day attacks are stealthy and target individuals as well as organizations for maximum economic gain. The Internet, and especially Web 2.0, has facilitated the rapid growth of an illicit shadow economy with hundreds of millions if not billions of dollars in exchange. Modern attacks on organizations have caused tremendous financial damage with far-reaching impacts beyond the victimized institutions. Classified materials that are crucial to national security have been compromised in cyber-attacks. Cyber warfare launched against countries can bring devastation that may be described and measured only with war terminology.

Espionage and Sabotage in Cyberspace

Moonlight Maze was a two-year-long cyber espionage operation carried out by a foreign country, suspected to be Russia, against the computer systems within the Pentagon, NASA, the Department of Energy, and various leading U.S. research institutions and universities between 1998 and 2000. Moonlight Maze stole a large volume of information regarding U.S. military installations and military hardware blueprints.

Titan Rain was the FBI designation for cyber-attacks that were uncovered by an employee at Sandia National Laboratories in 2004. The infiltration carried out by attackers targeted highly sensitive computer systems within Lockheed Martin and Sandia National Laboratories, along with possible targets such as NASA and other defense contractors. It was estimated to have been active for over three years and was believed to be sponsored by the Chinese government. Titan Rain was one of the most damaging cyber espionage attacks to be undertaken to steal military intelligence and classified data. Titan Rain was based on advanced persistent threats. *Advanced persistent threats,* or APTs, are sophisticated cyber attacks that are extremely covert in nature and developed by highly skilled personnel who may be subject experts with a full spectrum of intelligence-gathering and cyber penetration tools at their disposal. An APT avoids detection by siphoning the data gradually over an extended period of time. APTs are discussed further in Chapter 8.

Three years after Titan Rain, a second major cyber assault on an independent country became part of cyber warfare history. The cyberspace incursion into Estonia by attackers was allegedly funded and managed by the Russian government, which paralyzed the Estonian information infrastructures that covered government ministries, financial sectors, and media publications and broadcasters.

No sabotage campaign in the cyber war theater has played out as significantly as the *Stuxnet* attack on the Iranian nuclear fusion plant at Natanz. Stuxnet malware was discovered in 2010 and was purportedly jointly developed by the United States National Security Agency (NSA), the CIA, and the Israeli intelligence service to sabotage and prevent the progress of the Iranian nuclear fuel enrichment program. The development of Stuxnet spanned two U.S. presidential administrations. Stuxnet was designed to reprogram the programmable logic controllers (PLCs) that are common components in industrial control systems. In fact, Stuxnet contained the first known PLC rootkit to date. Stuxnet is comprised of zero-day exploits and a Windows rootkit, as well as techniques for evading behavior-based analysis by antivirus engines and for performing advanced process injection. It can propagate through a network or through removable drives. A *zero-day exploit* is an attack on a new vulnerability that is known only to the attacker.

Stuxnet breaks the centrifuge by altering the motor speed in a meticulous fashion to avoid detection: it increases the centrifuge speed for 15 minutes, then resumes normal operation, hibernates for 27 days, then lowers the centrifuge speed for 50 minutes before returning control; it then repeats this sequence after hibernating for another 27 days. During each attack sequence, the Stuxnet malware disables the relevant warning and safety controls so as to prevent the system from alerting the operators during the speed change. Stuxnet damaged approximately 1,000 IR-1 type centrifuges representing roughly 10 percent of the installation during the plant's peak operation. Stuxnet demonstrated that industrial sabotage can cause critical infrastructure failure, resulting in national emergencies. Stuxnet offered strong evidence that its creators had full access to the relevant industrial control systems and the centrifuge in order to develop and qualify the code. Only a state-sponsored organization could have facilitated such an operation.

In 2012, *Flame*, also known as *Skywiper*, was uncovered by multiple organizations and was reported as the most sophisticated malware ever encountered; it was expected to take years to unravel. Similar to Stuxnet, Flame appeared to be another joint effort between the United States and Israel that was five years in the making and served as a cyber espionage weapon to gather and exfiltrate intelligence from multiple targets inside Iran.

In 2013, *Operation Hangover* was exposed as a series of attacks that originated from India and that scoured entities in Pakistan to steal information that was of importance to India's national interests. Operation Hangover is another example of APT attacks, and although it ultimately failed in achieving its objectives, it was in operation for over two years before being exposed to the public.

These momentous state-sponsored cyber-attack events have forever changed and solidified the significance of cyberspace to the status of the "fifth domain" of war, as a new addition to the domains of land, sea, air, and space. The concept of cyber warfare has been transformed from abstract theorizations into formalized doctrines in preparation for actual deployment in military combat theaters. Information systems are treated as military assets that must be defended against enemy attacks, utilized to gather foreign intelligence, and deployed in offensive attacks against adversaries.

Weaponized malware is now part of the offensive capabilities in military arsenals because cyber warfare can inflict physical damage on targets that is comparable to conventional weapons. Cyber warfare can be launched against both military and civilian targets. Critical infrastructures such as smart power grids, nuclear power plants, water treatment systems, air traffic management and control systems, oil and gas pipelines, food and beverage supply chain management systems, and financial trading systems are all connected online and accessible through the network, making them desirable targets. Sabotaging these critical infrastructures can have detrimental effects, causing economic collapse of the financial system and massive loss of life and creating widespread panic and chaos across the country that is under the assaults. Cyber warfare can be launched from thousands of miles away, without a physical presence, and active military field equipment such as tanks, combat aircraft, and missile systems are all subjected to interference and destruction.

Industrial Espionage

A dramatic increase in industrial espionage is evident in many targeted attacks in recent years, with examples illuminating the fact that impenetrable security is nonexistent and insidious APTs constitute a grievous threat to any organization. A targeted attack implies there is a specific target that possesses data that is desired by the attackers, who will persist in their attacks until they have acquired the objective. Therefore, such a potential target must concentrate on continuous attack detection and eradication solutions to fend off APTs and incorporate a mentality that the attack is constant and may have been successful, instead of focusing on just attack prevention.

Operation Aurora

In January 2010, Google publicly disclosed that its operation in China, Google.cn, was subjected to an APT attack. *Operation Aurora* was a targeted attack on Google China that was carried out by an organization called Elderwood Group, based in Beijing. It was largely believed the attack began when targeted Google employees received an e-mail or an instant message that was forged to appear as if it came from a trusted source. In one case, the e-mail contained a link. The link led the employee to a website in Taiwan, and this website hosted malicious JavaScript. The employee's Windows Internet Explorer browser then automatically downloaded this JavaScript, which ran and exploited the zero-day vulnerability in the browser. Once the JavaScript executed, it downloaded another malicious payload that was disguised as an image file; this payload then created a back-door and connected the malware to its C2 server. At this point the attackers had gained full access to Google's internal systems.

In another case, the e-mail came with a malicious PDF file attachment that exploited a vulnerability in the Adobe Reader program. Once opened, the embedded malware inside the PDF file allowed the attacker to remotely control the system for further penetration. Regardless of the infiltration method, the malware went after source code repositories and tried to access Google e-mail accounts of Chinese political activists. More than 30 high-profile technology and defense companies were targets of the same espionage campaign. State sponsorship was evident in the sophisticated nature of the malware and the orchestrated manner of the attacks.

One disturbing fact about Operation Aurora is that, until Google discovered the attack in December 2009, many, if not all, of the victimized corporations were completely unaware of the fact they were being infiltrated and that their confidential intellectual properties were being exfiltrated by the attackers.

Microsoft had known about this zero-day vulnerability that allowed the attackers to perform remote code execution since September 2009. The patch to fix that Internet Explorer browser bug was scheduled for release in February 2010. Adobe had known about its vulnerability in December 2009, and the bug was not fixed until January 2010, after the Google disclosure. All users of these software programs were exposed to potential attacks while the vendors were working on the fix. In the meantime, the black hats were hard at work trying to maximize exploitation of these vulnerabilities. A crucial question for the security industry to address is what the general public can do to protect itself or to alleviate the threats during the vulnerable time before a solution becomes available.

Since the attackers gained access to the source code repositories, Operation Aurora unveiled a frightening new threat: after stealing the source code, the attackers could have modified the source code by implementing a new exploit or backdoor to be leveraged in the future against the entire user base of the product built from that source code tree. The code modification could be com-mitted into the original source tree either by masquerading as a legitimate user or by exploiting software bugs that may be present in the underlying source code control systems. The stolen source code will surely be subjected to elaborate vulnerability analysis for creating future exploits.

In Operation Aurora, the multi-layer security defense failed: the victims' anti-spam defenses failed to catch the malicious e-mails; their web filtering solution permitted users to connect to the websites that were hosting the exploits; their antivirus engines did not detect the malware download, possibly due to the zero-day nature of the exploits; their IDS and IPS systems failed to recognize any abnormal patterns during the intrusion; and their DLP systems did not block any data exfiltration.

Watering Hole Attack

We have witnessed in the animal kingdom the dramatic scene of a predator chasing down its prey, twirling with high velocity, and pursuing it with immense concentration while the prey foils the hunter with its mighty sprints. The intensity of the prey's struggle to survive is unimaginable, with death only a few feet away. Sometimes the prey escapes and the hunter limps away, salivating in discouragement.

Then there is another hunting approach often seen in the Serengeti, where the predator lurks by a watering hole, patiently waiting for its prey to approach the precious pond, and while it drinks avariciously, the predator dashes forward for a surprise ambush.

In cyberspace, attacking individual users requires the black hats to penetrate the first layer of defense, namely, a fortified firewall, which can be detected quickly. The *watering hole attack* is a type of targeted attack that, instead of focusing on an individual, is aimed at a specific group based on the group's interests and behavior. In August 2014, a watering hole malware campaign was launched on the website of a software company that produces simulation and systems engineering software for various industries. The website was known to be frequented by engineers who worked in the automotive, aerospace, and manufacturing industries. The attackers planted a Microsoft Internet Explorer zero-day exploit into the compromised website. This exploit leveraged out-of-bounds memory vulnerability to perform remote code injection and execution of multi-stage shellcode through the visitor's Internet Explorer browser. The exploit performed reconnaissance operations: it probed for various pieces of information on the visitor, logged the visitor's key strokes, and encrypted and then transmitted the collected data to its C2 server.

This exploit is unique in that it performs code injection without committing a copy of itself to disk. This behavior may be an indication that the attackers have high confidence in the exploit to infect the visitors on each of their visits. We can only speculate that the intention of the attackers is to harvest potential visitor information, correlate the user behavior according to what they entered, and then subsequently launch targeted attacks against the visitor or the visitor's employer to gain industrial secrets.

Malware exploits typically consist of two components: the decryption module and the encrypted code payload, as illustrated in Figure 4-1. *Shellcode* is a small piece of code that is the payload delivered by an exploit. The decryption module runs first to transform the payload into the shellcode by either decryption or some type of de-obfuscation algorithm (②). The control is then transferred to the newly formed shellcode where the execution resumes (③). The shellcode begins its subversion operations by spawning a system command interpreter, commonly known as a command shell (thus the reason for its name); then from within this command shell, it performs code injection and execution to methodically take control and commandeer the system. The shellcode is written as machine-independent code, meaning the shellcode can be loaded into any memory location for execution.

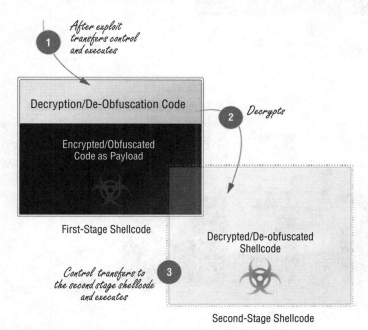

Figure 4-1: Shellcode

Code injection refers to the mechanism by which malicious software inserts code fragments into memory and then implants control transfer logic to intercept and manipulate the execution flow. Figure 4-2 depicts the concept of a watering hole attack.

As shown in Figure 4-2, when a user visits a compromised website (①), the watering hole exploit remotely injects a code payload directly into the Internet Explorer browser's running process in memory (②). From there, the first-stage shellcode then launches a standard Windows process, called *rundll32*, which is responsible for loading Windows dynamic link libraries (DLLs) and placing the functions (additional code) implemented by the DLLs into memory (③). After launching rundll32, the first-stage shellcode injects the second-stage shellcode into the rundll32 process (④) and then transfers execution control to it (⑤). At this point the exploit essentially has fully compromised the system.

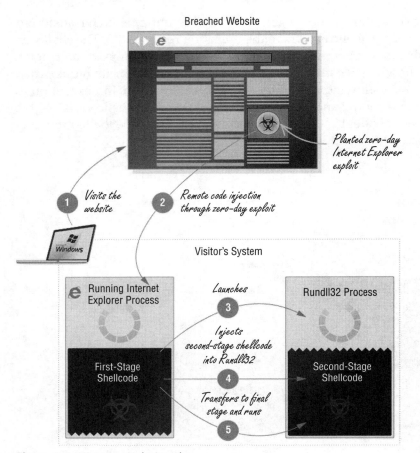

Figure 4-2: Watering Hole Attack

Breaching the Trusted Third Party

In February 2013, Bit9 was breached by hackers, and one of its digital code-signing certificates was stolen. Bit9 is best known for its whitelisting solution that certifies known safe applications. Its agent software intercepts and blocks any application that is not in the approved whitelist. Attackers used Bit9's signing certificate to sign malicious applications that subsequently circumvented Bit9-based defensive solutions. Bit9's customers discovered that malware and notified Bit9 because the certificate pointed to Bit9 as its owner. The irony was that Bit9 advocated its solution as the industry leader to offer non-traditional security solutions to enterprises, yet part of Bit9's network was not protected by its own solutions. Instead of launching direct assaults on the Bit9 security solution, the attackers made a strategic decision to breach the source of the solution, effectively neutralizing the defense system by falsifying the attacks as benign using the legitimate credentials of the system creator.

There are known cases where certificates that were issued to hardware manufacturers have been stolen because these manufacturers produced not only the hardware components and modules but also the companion drivers to run in popular operating systems such as Microsoft Windows. These drivers must be digitally signed by valid certificates before the driver binaries can be certified to run within the Windows kernel at privileged execution levels. Stealing code-signing certificates and then signing malicious code pretending to be system drivers can easily gain user and system acceptance.

The Korean gaming industry, especially the massive multiplayer online games, has had numerous breach incidents in the past few years. In each publicized case, malware bearing valid game publishers' digital signatures was installed through the game update process and infected millions of online players. The various malware have stolen subscribers' account information, seized in-game assets, installed in-game cheats, or pirated game source code.

Casting the Lures

So how is a user led to download a piece of malware and fall victim to its creator? It all begins with a wide variety of lures as colorful as the human imagination, with the majority rooted in social engineering to entice a potential victim. In the majority of attacks, the bait was conveyed through e-mail.

Social networks continue to be an effective attack vector. Although we like to avoid making general statements, incidents have proven time and again that most people on social networks tend to be less knowledgeable about computer security. A lot of them are relative newbies when it comes to Internet safe use practices. This population is always connected to the Internet through their smart mobile devices on fast 4G and LTE networks. They have become more impatient due to constant distractions coming from various mobile applications: Twitter, Snapchat, Skype, and text messages. They are constantly multitasking, participating in simultaneous online conversations, and they are much more willing to talk with strangers online. This changing user behavior subjects them to greater exposure to cyber threats and makes them easy prey to online scams and perpetrators.

The explosive growth of the user base that is energized by visual stimulants and always seeking out instant gratification propels social networking service providers to deliver more and more cool and easy-to-use features. Security becomes an afterthought, often left out of the application design, and is perceived as a hindrance to maintaining higher growth. The continuous addition of features to the infrastructure of social networks means that the code remains in a state of flux and security analysis is always incomplete. The interminable relationships developed among millions of users within these social networks serve as rapid infection paths with a broad reach.

Spear Phishing

Spear phishing is a black hat e-mail scam technique that—unlike regular phishing, which spams indiscriminately to all potential victims—targets specific individuals or organizations. With a spear phishing campaign against a well-known organization, the black hat first conducts a background investigation of the targeted organization and then forges a spear phishing e-mail directed at specific individuals in that organization. The e-mail header masquerades as if it were originating from someone within that company. The e-mail content contains information pertaining to a specific event that is taking place at the company or discusses a subject that is familiar to the potential victim.

For example, the e-mail may purport to seek help from the victim in reviewing a customer document, and the hyperlink to the document actually points to an exploit that is hosted on a malicious website. Or the e-mail may come with a malicious executable disguised as a PDF file attachment. In either case, once the victim takes the bait and executes the exploit that is obtained either directly or through a drive-by download, the exploit compromises the victim's system and takes a foothold in that corporation's network. The effectiveness of spear phishing credits its success to the deceptive social engineering tactic that breaks down the victim's suspicions because the e-mail came from a credible source, so the anecdotal warning "don't take candy from a stranger" need not apply.

Pharming

Pharming refers to an attack that leads visitors away from a legitimate website and redirects them to a forged site. The fake site is under black hat control and resembles the original legitimate site in almost every way to deceive the visitor. This forgery, when done successfully, persuades the visitor to think he has reached the right site (for example, a banking site), thus inducing the visitor to enter his user credentials to sign in to his account. After acquiring the user credentials, a typical action performed by the pharming code is to forward these credentials onward to the real site, essentially acting as a proxy without the user taking notice. The web browser must issue a DNS query to resolve the site's IP address before making the connection. As such, one type of pharming attack can be accomplished by exploiting DNS vulnerabilities so that the IP address returned from the DNS query is replaced by one that points to the fake site. Examples of DNS vulnerability exploitation include *DNS hijacking, domain hijacking, DNS cache poisoning*, and *DNS spoofing*.

There are different methods of *DNS hijacking*. In one method the system configuration is manipulated by malicious code that changes the DNS server to a rogue DNS server under black hat control. The rogue DNS server always returns IP addresses that connect to websites that masquerade as the respective legitimate ones. Similarly the malicious code can change the local DNS configuration file, typically called the *host* file, which directly maps a DNS name to an IP address.

Domain hijacking occurs when the owner of an established domain is changed to a different registrant without the knowledge of the original owner. Because a registered domain name has an expiration date, this change can occur due to a lapse in renewal by the original owner, resulting in the domain name being purchased by someone else. Another tactic is through impersonation, possibly by means of identity theft and deploying social engineering to modify the domain ownership. Related to domain hijacking, there is an attack vector where the black hat registers multiple domain names, with each being one possible misspelling of the targeted domain name. A visitor is redirected to a fake site when they misspell the domain name to one that has a valid registration having the black hat as the owner.

In *DNS cache poisoning*, a compromised system inside a managed network is induced by the attacker to query a domain name that is under the attacker's control. The attacker's domain name is resolved by a rogue DNS server that acts as the authoritative name server for that domain name. When the rogue DNS server returns the query result, it includes response entries for the domains the attacker wants to hijack. Obviously, the IP addresses associated with these legitimate domain names link to forged websites. Once the DNS server that resides in the managed network receives these DNS responses, it will cache these entries. Future DNS responses that contain valid entries for those legitimate domain names will not be accepted until the cached fake entries have expired.

Similar to DNS cache poisoning, in a *DNS spoofing* attack, the attacker leverages a compromised system to transmit specially crafted DNS responses for domain names to be hijacked. The goal is to insert a response into the DNS server cache with a fake entry so that the valid entry can be rejected.

An attacker can launch a pharming attack through a phishing e-mail. For example, the attacker can craft and forge an e-mail that appears to come from a well-known bank, asking the recipient to log into the banking site to validate their address information. If the recipient is an unsuspecting user who promptly clicks the link embedded in the e-mail, that user is led to a landing page that appears to be exactly the same as the banking site, but underneath it is a fake site whose only purpose is to harvest user credentials.

Cross-Site Scripting

Spear phishing is an essential component of a *cross-site scripting (XSS) attack*. An XSS attack is the exploitation of a type of vulnerability that has been discovered in web-based applications. This vulnerability enables an attacker to inject scripts that will execute on the client side to hijack an active client session using stolen session credentials. The XSS attack circumvents the basic *same-origin* web application security policy. The same-origin policy restricts the browser such that the browser disallows the content that was received from one website to read or write content that was received from a different site. There are various types of XSS attacks: reflected (or non-persistent) attacks, persistent (or stored) attacks, and Document Object Model (DOM) vulnerability-based attacks.

A reflected XSS attack describes the scenario where a web-based application extracts and includes a portion of the client's input verbatim in its response to the client. The goal of the attacker is to steal the session token, which may be in the form of a browser cookie, and hijack that client session. The session cookie is issued by the web application server; therefore, any dynamic JavaScript code that wants to retrieve the session cookie must come from that same web server. So the attacker attempts to explore the XSS vulnerability to own the session cookie. The assumption is that the attacker has deep knowledge of the web application under attack. It is a common practice for the black hat to first map out as much of the web application as possible and then to probe each operation within the application to expose one or more vulnerabilities. The prerequisite for a successful attack is that the attacker has discovered an application behavior, called an XSS vulnerability, where an operation is known to take a portion of the user input and include that input unmodified in the result of that operation. This discovery enables the attacker to create special input that targets the known XSS vulnerability. This attack scenario is depicted in Figure 4-3.

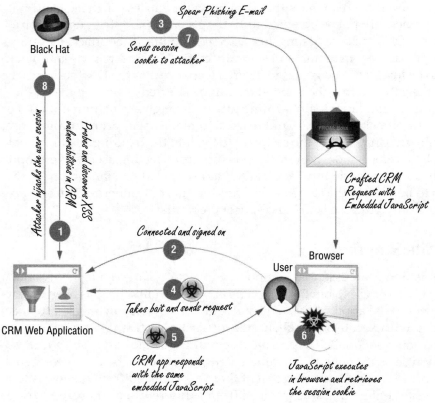

Figure 4-3: Cross-Site Scripting Attack

In this example, a black hat has discovered vulnerabilities in a customer relationship management (CRM) application, which may be exploited to launch XSS attacks against its users (①). Now a user has established a connection to this CRM application, and the user has successfully logged into his or her account (②). For example, the user may be a salesperson who needs to be logged into the CRM throughout the entire workday. So the attacker meticulously crafts a request targeting that CRM system and embeds in that application request a piece of obfuscated JavaScript code. The function to be performed by the JavaScript code is to retrieve the session cookie and send it to a designated web location. Then the attacker leverages spear phishing to send the user a spear phishing e-mail, with a subject title "please help validate customer contact info" (③). The attacker forges an HTML e-mail to appear as if it were sent from the user's supervisor. In this bogus e-mail is the customized request in hyperlink form with a link title that reads "Customer Bob's contact information". The user takes the bait and clicks the hyperlink, which sends the specially crafted request to the web application (④). The CRM system returns that exact JavaScript back to the user due to the XSS vulnerability (⑤). This time the user's browser executes the JavaScript (⑥) and transmits the session cookie to the attacker (⑦). Now the attacker can easily hijack and take over the user session (⑧).

The web has evolved from a repository of static content to an exciting, interactive web where participants of the so-called Web 2.0 can browse static web pages as well as publish dynamic content. For example, anyone can visit a social forum where he or she can view ongoing discussions in real-time. In many cases the forum allows both subscribers and anonymous visitors to contribute to that discussion by posting their comments and opinions. This interactive forum facilitates a persistent or stored XSS attack.

With a stored XSS attack, an attacker can post content with crafted JavaScript that will execute in the browser of whoever is reading that posting. Similar to a reflected XSS attack, the malicious code executes in the visitor's browser and sends the visitor's session cookie to the attacker. If the visitor is in fact a registered forum member, then this stored XSS attack will help the attack to eventually compromise that user's account. A stored XSS attack is more damaging than a reflected XSS attack.

A reflected XSS attack targets a single victim, but a stored XSS attack targets anyone who can view the maliciously crafted content. In a reflected XSS attack, when the attacker sends a spear phishing e-mail or any other kind of lure to the user, the user must have a session that is active with the web application in question when the user clicks the crafted request. In comparison, in a stored XSS attack, the user who is viewing a crafted posting will be doing so in an active session already, thereby eliminating the timing issue that is a prerequisite to a reflected XSS attack.

In addition to stored and reflected attacks, a third XSS attack method is called a DOM-based XSS attack. The DOM-based XSS vulnerability is a side effect of a website that attempts to improve the user experience by customizing content according to a given visitor. For a given web page constructed in HTML or XML format, there exists a DOM that describes the structures of that page and how that page is accessed and manipulated from the browser's perspective. When the browser renders the page, a DOM object such as the `document.URL` object may be fed a URL that contains an embedded and obfuscated malicious script that exploits the vulnerability similar to a reflected XSS attack.

Search Engine Poisoning

One method of luring potential victims to malware delivery servers is by *search engine poisoning* (SEP). The main goal of SEP is for the black hats to inject links that point to their malicious servers in the top search results for any popular search engine. Links that are part of the top search results have the highest potential of being clicked by the user who issued the search. Therefore, the more poisoned links in the search results, the better chance for the black hats to victimize users. This is why the process of deceiving a search engine to return malicious links in its search results is called search engine poisoning.

Black hats execute a series of steps to poison search engines. First, the black hat creates bait pages that contain popular search keywords and phrases. These keywords and phrases are repeated in a bait page but interleaved with random words, phrases, and sentences, and combined with random images to make the page appear more legitimate to a web bot or crawler. Then the black hat launches mass e-mail spam to advertise links to these bait pages. He also posts those links to various social forums and compromised websites and distributes those links through online advertising networks or ad networks. Link farms are also set up to broaden the reach. A *link farm* is a coterie of websites where each website cross-references every other site within the group through hyperlinks. A site may build a directory of web pages that serve as links. A link farm is another black hat venue for search engine optimization (SEO) that increases the relevancy of a website rating by a search engine algorithm that assigns weights or values to the hyperlinks.

The goal of the bait page is to lead potential victims to the malware delivery server. How is the malware delivered if and when the victim reaches the harmless bait page? The victim actually never sees the bait page. The trick is in how the malware server processes each HTTP request and what content is returned to fulfill the request. First, the malware server needs to know where the request is coming from, that is, who or what entity is issuing the request, before deciding which content should be returned. The *User-Agent field* in the HTTP request header discloses whether the entity is a search engine crawler or a web browser, as shown in Figure 4-4.

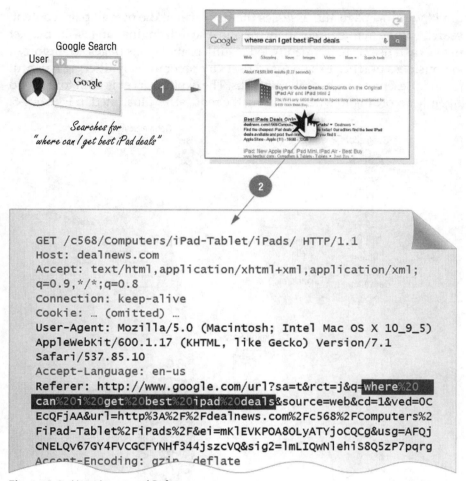

Figure 4-4: User-Agent and Referrer

For example, the Google web-crawling bot named *Googlebot* is identified by the following User-Agent string:

```
User-Agent: Mozilla/5.0 (compatible; Googlebot/2.1;
+http://www.google.com/bot.html)
```

In this example, a regular user running a Firefox browser on the Mac OS X operating system has the following User-Agent signature:

```
User-Agent: Mozilla/5.0 (Macintosh; Intel Mac OS X 10_9_5)
AppleWebKit/600.1.17 (KHTML, like Gecko)
Version/7.1 Safari/537.85.10
```

Besides computing the relevance of a web page, the modern search engine indexer has built-in detection algorithms to identify potential malware scripts contained within a page and assesses the risk level of the overall page content. The search engine market is competitive, and a search engine can lose its market share quickly if users are frequently led to junk or malicious pages. Therefore, it is good business practice to safeguard users by preemptively filtering harmful results and presenting them with safe links. The exploit server is built to respond intelligently according to who is making the request, as illustrated in Figure 4-5.

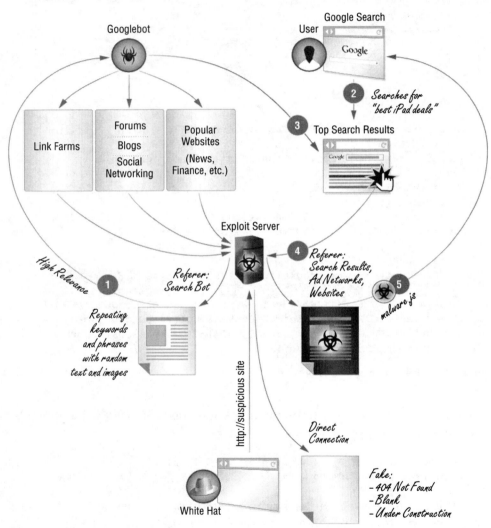

Figure 4-5: Search Engine Poisoning

As shown in Figure 4-5, when a malware server detects a search engine crawler is paying it a visit, the server presents a carefully constructed, innocuous bait page to the search engine bot to index (①). When the malware server detects that an HTTP request was directly entered into a browser to reach the malware site, the malware server presents a *snooper page* in return. The snooper page typically shows the site is under construction or the site is completely blank, thus offering no content to the visitor. The snooper page is a lame strategy put in place to keep a low profile and turn white hats away from examining the site. Sometimes the malware server simply redirects a prying visitor to a well-known site. Now, as soon as the malware server detects that the request originates from a search engine results page (②, ③, ④), this is when it returns the actual intended malicious content because it knows a user has taken the bait and clicked a poisoned link (⑤). The *Referrer* field in the HTTP request header contains evidence of the search engine results. Figure 4-4 illustrates an example where the user has entered "where can I get best iPad deals" in the Google search engine. When the user selects the top search result and follows the link, the Referrer field shows http://www.google.com. In addition, the words from the search phrase entered by the user are shown as a URL parameter, which is leveraged by the black hats to enhance the available keywords and phrases contained in the bait pages, thus improving the potency of those bait pages in poisoning the search engine.

The mainstream media has created a myth about SEP being a significant threat vector during newsworthy events. Research into the data that has been generated by Blue Coat's 75 million WebPulse users indicated a disparity between the compiled results and the press reports. In past significant events, between the years 2008 and 2013, which include natural disasters, sports finals, financial market meltdowns, deaths of celebrities, and so on, less than 0.01 percent of malicious links were activated due to SEP. This surprising find may be attributed to the following factors:

- Significant events are covered by all news organizations, which causes a search engine "clutter" effect. In other words, there is so much relevant and clean content (articles, commentaries, blogs) that is distributed across a large number of legitimate websites—reputable news media sites such as CNN, NPR, and BBC—that it causes the search engine to produce real content as top search results.

- People are now drawn to social networking sites such as Facebook and Twitter to obtain their information. Therefore, the attack vectors are chiefly phishing e-mails and malicious postings on well-known online social media sites.

- Search engines continue to improve their detection algorithms to sanitize search results.

Drive-by Downloads and the Invisible Iframe

As a result of SEP, *drive-by downloads* are a scheme that black hats employ to induce the download of malicious code from a crafted attack page, when a user visits a compromised or purposely built malicious website. The goal of a drive-by download is to inject malicious code into the user's system. In one approach, the black hats use social engineering to lure a user to consent and accept an offer and then manually download and run the malicious code that is behind the offer. A common bait to entice a user is through various offerings of digital material relating to A-list celebrities, such as a leaked nude video that requires the user to download and install a "missing" video codec or to upgrade an existing version of a player program in order to view the movie. Figure 4-6 shows a fake Adobe Flash Player upgrade scheme that we downloaded.

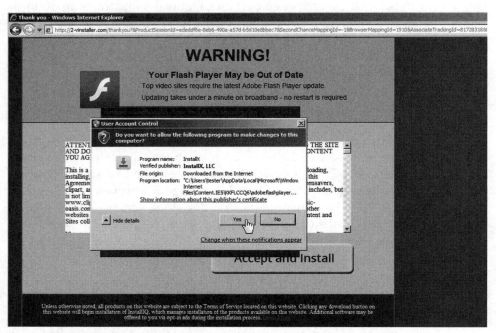

Figure 4-6: Fake Video Player Update

First of all, you may notice the displayed warning message is really just a web page that tries to simulate an Adobe update pop-up window. This should have raised an alarm. Second, there is the URL, "2-vinstaller.com", which means this website is not affiliated with Adobe. Below the big yellow Accept and Install button, the text in small print reads, "Clicking any download button on this website will begin installation of InstallIQ, which manages installation of the products available on this website." In other words, this is a fake warning message, and the executable has nothing to do with the Adobe Flash program. Clicking the Install button means the user agrees to install an unknown program that is published by an unknown software company that calls itself "InstallX, LLC" but it names its software "adobeflashplayer.exe". In this example, after completing the download step, we uploaded the binary onto VirusTotal; it scored 24 out of 54 hits as Trojan adware.

Another common ploy is to instigate fear in the user to act without hesitation, for example, displaying an animation that falsifies evidence of malicious activities that appear to already exist in the user's system. The user is urged to download and install antivirus software immediately to remove the virus and sterilize the system. Obviously the real malware is packaged as the fake antivirus software, and once installed, it causes serious havoc in the user's system. Figure 4-7 shows fake antivirus scan results that prompt a user to act immediately to clean up their system.

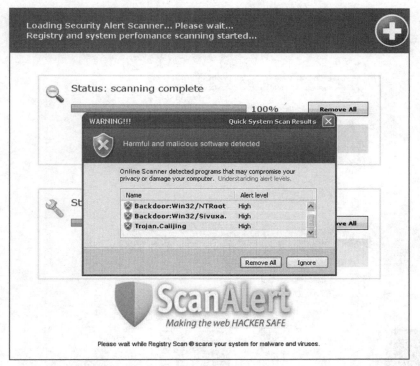

Figure 4-7: Fake Antivirus Scanning

This malicious web page used an animated image ploy that pretends to perform a virus scan on the visitor's system. In this case, we were actually running on a Unix system, not on Microsoft Windows. The fake "Windows Security Alert" pop-up prompts the user to click the Remove All button, but clicking anywhere on the web page will trigger a download and the installation of a Trojan virus.

Social engineering may be one attack vector, but another tactic is more dangerous and completely evades the user through an insidious automatic background download and execution of malicious code to infect the user's system. In other words, the download process does not require user interaction at all. When a user visits a compromised website, the user's browser is redirected to an attack page, possibly through multiple layers of deflection using techniques such as HTTP redirection, an invisible iframe, or JavaScript execution within a browser. Figure 4-8 illustrates a common iframe-based drive-by download scheme.

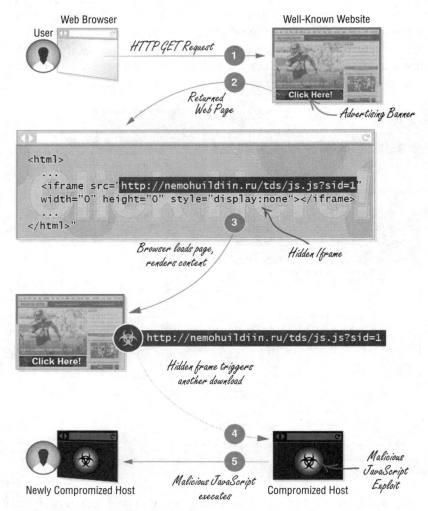

Figure 4-8: Invisible Iframe

In this example, the user visits a well-known but compromised website (①), and the page displayed to the user has an ad banner. Inside this ad banner is an invisible iframe; it is invisible because, as shown in the figure, it has 0 dimensions and the hidden display style (②). The source of the iframe points to a piece of JavaScript "js.js" that is hosted on a malicious site in Russia (③). The browser automatically downloads js.js when processing the embedded iframe directive in the page (④). Once downloaded, this JavaScript executes in the browser and exploits a browser vulnerability to compromise the visitor's machine (⑤).

So how are malicious ads placed on a well-known website if the website has not been compromised by hackers?

Tangled Malvertising Networks

In online advertising, websites, e-mails, RSS feeds, instant messaging, and other similar assets, together with online ads or ad banners, all are considered to be online inventories. An ad exchange connects owners of online real estate such as websites with ad providers to facilitate real-time trading of those online inventories and assets. An online advertising network, or *ad network*, is an ad distribution network that transfers the ads and displays those banners on the negotiated ad space.

Malicious advertising, also known as *malvertising*, refers to black hats leveraging ad networks to inject and distribute malware. Because ad networks cover virtually the entire Internet, malware can propagate quickly to infect large online user populations. Malvertising is an effective tool for black hats due to the nature of ad networks. The black hats only need to compromise a limited number of ad servers or well-known reputable websites to begin a malvertising campaign. As demonstrated by the previous iframe example, a modern malvertising attack can infect a user by the simple act of automatically displaying banner ads inside a browser, which is made possible by modern ad URLs that deliver JavaScripts instead of static images. These ad JavaScripts are often obfuscated to prevent the disclosure of information pertaining to ad server technology and platforms in addition to reducing ad frauds. The obfuscation makes scanning for known malware patterns in the end systems difficult if not impossible.

An online ad network is a complex world of ad servers, exchanges, buyers, partners, affiliates, and subordinate providers. One ad provider outsourcing its advertisement and ad spaces to other ad providers is a common practice to reduce operational costs and also to leverage multiple ad networks to reach as broad a population as possible. This complex web of advertising relations is an incubation ground for malvertising outbreaks. In fact, black hats launching attacks across a large region of ad networks have become alarmingly common occurrences. Figure 4-9 illustrates an example of how an ad network can be leveraged for malware distribution.

On a website, an ad banner area can rotate ads and display ads that are sourced from different ad providers. As shown in this example, websites trust their immediate large ad providers such as Google and Yahoo! However, large ad providers are just part of the ad syndication. The layers of advertisement outsourcing and subcontracted ad campaigns may result in a rogue ad provider injecting itself into the chain. The process of establishing a trust relationship between two ad providers varies dramatically from region to region, and an industry-wide, rigorous methodology is yet to be standardized. The trust relationship is not transitive from one layer to another. Therefore, a malicious ad can easily propagate throughout the ad network and reach a large audience.

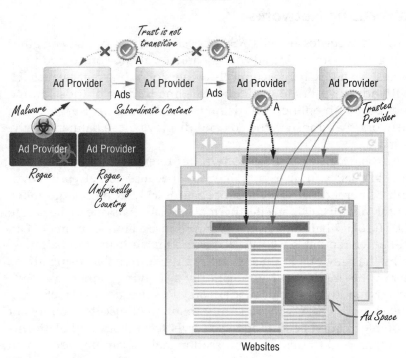

Figure 4-9: Ad Network

Once an ad server has been identified as having served links to malware, the challenge is to determine whether the ad server has been compromised by black hats or is itself truly malicious. Another possibility exists, where there may be some kind of compromise in the ad supply chain. Further analysis of the ad server in question can reveal compelling evidence in reaching a conclusion. An ad server having a recent and anonymous registration is suspicious. An ad server that distributes only its own ads is suspicious. An ad server that runs a single ad is suspicious. In Chapter 5, we discuss general rating strategies on websites.

Malware Delivery Networks

The modern web page is decorated with a colorful array of graphics and ad banners and embedded with links to entertainment news, articles, famous blogs, up-to-the-minute breaking news, real-time stock quotes, and auto-playing, embedded video clips. Even though these pieces of content are presented to the user in a single view, each piece may be sourced from different origins. The web page has become a valuable commodity, where every inch can be sold to a content provider for both tangible and intangible profit. Malware delivery networks (MDNs), or *malnets*, are born out of this complex content delivery network that we call Web 2.0. The malvertising network is a subnet of general malnets.

As the earlier drive-by-download example illustrates, the end of the browser redirection is some kind of exploit kit that is to be retrieved automatically by the browser. Typically the initial download is a *dropper*, and once activated, it scans the victim's system for the presence of known versions (and thus known vulnerabilities) of various software programs, for example, Java, Adobe Reader, Flash Media Player, and the web browser and browser plug-ins. The dropper then "phones home" by contacting its C2 servers to download and install one or more exploit kits that target each program appropriately. Figure 4-10 illustrates the concept of this multi-layer redirection technique.

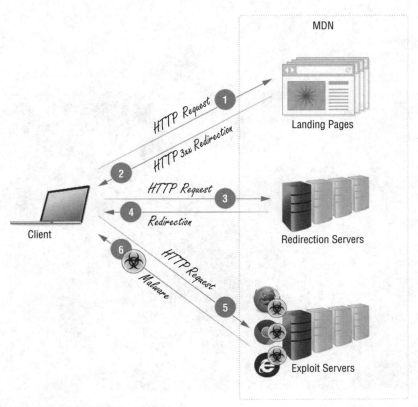

Figure 4-10: Redirection to Malnet

A landing page is usually the first destination in the malnet. A user can reach the landing page via search engine results, by clicking an embedded link inside a phishing e-mail, or by clicking an iframe link (①). The main purpose of the landing page is to perform a first-level referral that sends the visitor to another website using simple HTTP status code 3xx for URL redirection (②). Another approach is to feed the visitor's browser a JavaScript that generates a dynamic URL linking to a destination. As we will discuss in the next section, in most cases, these layers of intermediate destinations serve as either front-end proxies or redirectors that route the visitors deep into the malnet. In practice, three to five layers of redirection are common (③, ④). Finally the visitor reaches the real malware-hosting servers that will return an exploit to the user (⑤, ⑥). Figure 4-11 is a visualization graphic that was constructed out of real-world malnet data sets that have been collected by the Blue Coat WebPulse cloud security solution.

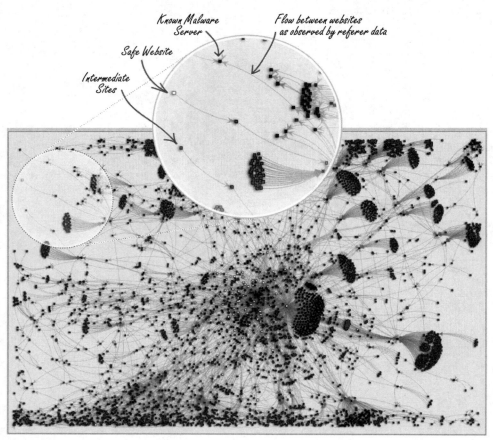

Figure 4-11: Visualization of Malnets

In Figure 4-11, each white square represents a safe website, the gray squares represent intermediate sites that perform request redirections, and the black squares represent known malware servers. Figure 4-11 illustrates the enormity of the malnet and that the threats it casts on the Internet are both deep and wide. This massive interconnection of landing sites, intermediate redirectors, and referrers is the result of malware evasion techniques.

Fast-Flux Networks

Botnets and MDNs employ the fast-flux technique to evade eradication of the actual servers that host malware. The core idea of fast-flux is to map different IP addresses to the same DNS name rapidly, often within a few minutes. These IP addresses belong to compromised systems that are called *bots* or *zombies*, and they are controlled by the black hats through C2 channels. Typically the black hats take possession of tens of thousands of IP addresses before putting the MDNs into operation. These hijacked IP addresses are cycled through quickly, and newly commandeered IP addresses are added continuously into the pool. The MDNs that operate in this manner are called *fast-flux networks*. The DNS records implemented to support an MDN operation may look like this:

```
webantivirusav.nl.     300   IN   A   64.251.21.188
webantivirusav.nl.     300   IN   A   64.251.21.222
webantivirusav.nl.     300   IN   A   65.111.184.227
webantivirusav.nl.     300   IN   A   65.111.184.229
webantivirusav.nl.     300   IN   A   69.60.98.234

webantivirusav.nl.     1800  IN   NS  ns1.webvirusdefence.nl
webantivirusav.nl.     1800  IN   NS  ns2.webvirusdefence.nl

ns1.webvirusdefence.nl 864000 IN A 5.61.32.183
ns2.webvirusdefence.nl 864000 IN A 192.241.81.86
```

A *single fast-flux network* describes MDNs with rapidly changing DNS address records for the domain name. In the given example, there are five A-records associated with the webantivirusav.nl domain, and these A-records have a five-minute lifetime. At expiration, new IP addresses replace the old ones for these A-records. A *double fast-flux network* refers to MDNs that also constantly change the IP addresses of the authoritative name servers. In this example, the A-records for the name servers ns1.webvirusdefence.nl and ns2.webvirusdefence.nl are also remapped at high frequency. Figure 4-12 illustrates the operations of a fast-flux network.

Figure 4-12 shows what happens when a user has been enticed to click a malicious link that points to some malware hosted on webantivirusav.nl. The user's browser needs to resolve the IP address of that DNS name before connecting to the site. The DNS query is sent to one of the bots that is part of the fast-flux network and that is identified by the DNS system as the resolver for that hostname (①). In actuality the bot does not perform the name resolution when it receives the DNS query. Unlike a regular DNS query process where an intermediate resolver will refer the query issuer to another name server through a DNS referral response, the bot never sends a referral but instead proxies the query and forwards it to the backend server (②). It is common for this backend server to run both DNS and HTTP services. The backend server runs load balancing algorithms to perform load distribution according to bot availability, bot reachability and health check statistics, bandwidth utilization level, service lifetime, and other attributes. Once the backend server reaches a decision, the DNS result is returned to the proxy bot (③), which then forwards that answer back to the query issuer (④). Subsequently the user sends the content request to the resolved IP address at 10.1.2.3 (⑤). This bot proxies the HTTP request to the backend server and retrieves the content to fulfill the user request (⑥, ⑦). In this example, the bot that serves the malware to the user is different from the bot that serviced the DNS query, which is located at 200.18.39.177.

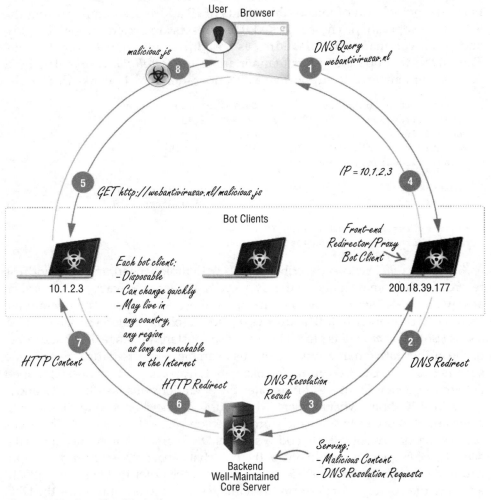

Figure 4-12: Fast-Flux Network

As shown in Figure 4-12, the bot clients are disposable because they are typically discovered by experienced white hats and are decommissioned within hours. Either the bot client knows the identity of the backend server through the C2 channels, or the infecting malware contains hardcoded logic to locate the backend server. Because each bot in the fast-flux network may reside in any region around the world, this, combined with the fast remapping to new IP addresses, makes the discovery of the backend server a difficult task. Blocking the IP addresses will only decommission the intermediate fast-flux bots or zombies, which is exactly what the fast-flux technique was designed to solve, thus shielding and prolonging the backend core servers to continue their operations with minimal interruption.

The fast-flux networks illustrate a common MDN strategy to sustain the malware servers and evade detection: creating multiple layers of dynamic redirections that can span various domains and countries, traversing web pages constructed with different languages, all for the purpose of deterring the white hats from building meaningful correlations to detect the malware-serving root hosts.

It may seem that the fast-flux network can be defeated by blocking the `webantivirusav.nl` domain. Filtering and blacklisting the domain is a viable solution if the `webantivirusav.nl` domain can be classified as the root of a fast-flux network. However, this discovery is not so trivial. First of all, the domain name must be seen as being contacted by the malware, correlated by evidence the domain name resolves to a large number of IP addresses rapidly. Secondly, a domain name can be hidden through dynamic name generation techniques.

Explosion of Domain Names

Black hats implement domain generation algorithms (DGAs) inside their malware to prevent a domain name from being identified as the contact point. A malware executable contains visible strings of domain names if those domain names are predefined and are compiled into the executable. The white hats can perform binary analysis by using tools such as a disassembler and a low-level machine debugger to uncover the domain names and insert them into their filtering lists. By performing DGA in real-time, the malware can generate tens of thousands of domain names in a day, with each domain name being a random string of characters. There are known cases where the malware generates up to 50,000 unique names in a day. Out of the generated names, the malware performs a selection algorithm to choose a subset of domain names to contact as C2 servers. Example domain names produced by a DGA may look like these: `uftfesnodnjflwta.inf`, `vxagtvsyqxtrfcm.com`.

The black hats register a small subset of those DGA-created domain names using the same selection algorithm. Registering unique domain names, even for a ".com" domain, can cost as little as $10 a year. The black hats have plenty of stolen credit cards at their disposal for purchasing new domains. Free domain provider freenom.com offers country code top-level domains (ccTLDs) free of charge for .cf (Central African Republic), .ga (Gabon), .ml (Mali), and .tk (Tokelau). Free subdomains are also abundantly available for the taking.

Address mapping detection of a fast-flux server requires selecting the candidates from hundreds of thousands of domain names that are in operation, then performing active DNS monitoring for an extended period of time, and finally aggregating the data collection to conduct analysis. Such an operation is impractical due to the sheer volume of collected samples. In addition, multiple domain names can share a single IP address, thus further complicating the discovery process.

Dynamic DNS (DynDNS) is another mechanism used by malicious content providers. The black hats register subdomain names within the DynDNS domains. For a specific DynDNS domain, the main domain resolver will resolve all of the names under that specific DynDNS domain. For each registered subdomain name, the black hats can change the IP address at will using an update tool. The IP addresses can be located anywhere on the Internet. In this category, the IP addresses that were hijacked by the black hats belong to dynamic IP addresses commonly found on broadband networks designed for residential homes.

Abandoned Sites and Domain Names

A lot of websites either are poorly maintained or have been neglected because they were built for some kind of experimentation by their respective owners. Oftentimes these sites are simply abandoned once the learning experience is over, but they are still connected and reachable. A great number of them have since been converted into malware hosting servers, unbeknownst to their owners.

Some domains were allowed to expire for one reason or another. Abandoned domains that were assigned to legitimate sites or hosts, which were used for conducting business on the Internet with either clean or reputable histories, are highly desirable. The past history of these domains gives legitimacy to whatever websites are put up by the black hats to host content once the black hats take ownership of the abandoned domains.

There is a set of challenges in preventing the circulation of malicious content using reputation-based solutions. Allowing all content from a reputable website indiscriminately will accelerate malware distribution. For example, a site such as CNN may be an innocuous, valuable doorway to legitimate web content, but the *dynamic links* inside each page served by the site could be composed from different sources, and some may be malicious. A reputable website can also be hacked to host malicious content. On the other hand, if a host has been compromised in the past and has been recorded as being a participant in an MDN, then this information may be stored for a long time. A simple reputation-based blacklist will render this innocent but victimized host permanently invisible. We discuss intelligent filtering solutions in Chapter 5.

Antivirus Software and End-Point Solutions: The Losing Battle

Zero-day exploits are still rare occurrences and are limited in number in the wild because creating zero-day exploits demands uncommon experience and skill sets possessed by a limited number of individuals, and they require elaborate efforts to discover new vulnerabilities. In the meantime, attackers continue to explore new ways to distribute and spread existing malware and exploits, knowing that not all users are diligent at patching their systems and updating their antivirus software or virus signature database. End-point solutions such as antivirus software continue to play an important role in identifying known viruses and malware and are an essential component in a multi-layered security defense.

However, traditional antivirus companies have conceded that modern antivirus engines have low malware detection rates. The detection rates of antivirus engines have been a debated subject in many RSA conferences over the years. The detection rate seemed to vary depending on the entity that performed the analysis. The data set used in the studies was another variable that also affected the results. The disparity seemed significant at times.

These signature-based solutions are ineffective against *polymorphic code*. Polymorphic code is code that changes itself each time the code executes, but the original functionality remains the same. Polymorphic malware possesses the runtime characteristics of polymorphic code. In addition, similar to shellcode, discussed in the previous section, the executable is packaged with a decryption function having the actual functional code being encrypted as the payload. When the malware executes, the decryption function decrypts the payload and then runs the actual code. A malicious executable that is downloaded from a malware site changes with each download. Antivirus engines have low recognition rates for polymorphic malware. We have seen typical identification rates between 0 to 2 hits out of more than 50 antivirus engines in VirusTotal after each download of the malware. Compounding the polymorphic payload problem is the challenge of recognizing the exploit that the payload delivers against a specific application or system module. The exploit can be detected only by examining its runtime behaviors.

Days, if not weeks, elapse after an attack surfaces before the major antivirus engines are updated to recognize a new threat. However, by then, private and confidential information may have been stolen, and valuable intellectual properties may have been lost. Antivirus engines are ineffective in battling zero-day attacks.

If a free service such as VirusTotal provides free scanning of uploaded files against more than 50 antivirus engines in parallel, then black hats can model this approach to antivirus-proof their new creation by subjecting the new malware to all known antivirus engines; they can evolve the new malware if necessary and then finally release the beast to the wild, knowing in advance that none of the existing antivirus engines will detect its presence.

Once a breach has occurred, the task in the aftermath is damage control; but the damage has already been inflicted. So why not shift the defense into a preemptive prevention strategy? In the next chapter, we focus on techniques that attempt to detect and prevent malware infection at each stage of the content retrieval process, from URL analysis at the beginning to content analysis at the end.

Summary

The push model of delivering malware from outside of an organization's fortified perimeter, by means of exhaustively exploiting and attacking possible vulnerabilities in a trial-and-error fashion, has become much less capable of achieving success. The black hats have focused their strategies on creating and posting bait on the web and having the population infect itself simply by visiting the compromised websites. Online users are lured into the dark web by phishing and SEP and have been victimized by drive-by downloads. The era of relying on just end-point solutions such as antivirus engines is coming to an end because these solutions are no longer effective in combating modern malware. In Chapter 5, we present the solutions that solve the malware challenge by focusing on detecting and then interrupting C2 and exfiltration channels.

Malnet Detection Techniques

A malware distribution network (MDN) or malnet is comprised of three main components: the landing pages, intermediate redirection servers, and malware exploit distribution servers. As discussed in Chapter 4, a typical infection process begins with a lure that leads the user to a malicious landing page; once there, the user's web browser is induced to download a piece of shellcode. In order to avoid detection, the web browser is redirected through multiple layers of intermediate nodes before getting to the initial exploit code. After the shellcode executes, it downloads the main malware payload from yet another server. Finally, the shellcode launches the malware to compromise the end system completely. More sophisticated shellcode may first fingerprint the user system, followed by the transmission of the collected information to its command and control (C2) server, which will subsequently provide further instructions to the shellcode on the location from where to download a targeted executable suitable for the user's system.

Some landing pages may be manually crafted by the attackers. However, other landing pages are part of legitimate websites. There are numerous known incidents where legitimate websites and web servers were hacked and the attackers planted malicious links to infect visitors. A more pervasive approach is to compromise the third-party content provider, which could result in many non-malicious landing pages to contain third-party content that could lead to exploited servers. For example, a dynamic advertisement banner may contain JavaScript that creates a hidden iframe that sources its content from another server. In such cases the website hosting the landing page should not be marked as a malicious site simply because the third-party advertisement it holds contains malnet redirection links.

Adding to the complexity of the landing page classification problem, a large number of ads are dynamically generated and are targeted to specific users or browsers or both. These dynamic ads may not always contain the malnet redirection links. Therefore, the aim of detecting malicious landing pages is to analyze the page contents and evaluate the embedded URLs so that if one of the URLs eventually leads to a malnet exploit server, that URL can be marked and tracked as a malicious URL rather than the URL that points to the landing page.

Identifying malware distribution servers is a part of the solution to disrupt a malnet. The identification technique must have the ability to differentiate between malicious and benign downloads. In addition, although the intermediate servers play a role in the MDN, these intermediate servers are disposable and are easily replaced. Blocking the distribution servers forces the malnet to migrate the hosting service to new endpoints and is the most effective venue in preventing malicious downloads while new servers are put into service. Therefore, the focus is on the actual distribution servers; once they are identified, implementing the blacklist can be done easily in the egress firewalls.

This chapter will describe the algorithms that are applied to rate the URLs and the web pages and also explore methods of exposing malware distribution servers. It will also describe open-source tools, called *honeyclients*, which are often used for malware and MDN analysis.

Automated URL Reputation System

A URL is the first linkage to a malware infection. A URL that leads to a malicious drive-by download should be recognized and blocked as early as possible, thus preventing the attack by blocking the download of the first piece of exploit code. Malicious URLs that lead to the same malware change quickly to avoid detection. A *web reputation* or *URL reputation system* analyzes a given URL in real-time to assess its trustworthiness, which concludes in a rating. The rating system is typically a scale that ranges from benign through good, cautious, unwanted, potentially dangerous, and finally, to malicious. However, the rating system is largely implementation-dependent.

A considerable amount of resources and time must be devoted to collect and rate URLs that exist on the web today. The sheer number of URLs requires a machine-assisted automatic solution to process and rate the URLs. In addition, the URL reputation system incorporates input from the user community when possible. A *learning machine* is essential in constructing a scalable system, which at a minimum performs high-level sorting of the URLs into a rating category, known as *classification*, followed by further granular analysis to remove false positives from each category.

In machine learning terminology, a *classifier* is a classification algorithm that maps input to a category. In its simplest form, a learning machine implements one or more classifiers. *Supervised learning* refers to feeding the learning machine a preselected data set with known categories and training the machine to reach the same classification results. A *feature* refers to a measurable heuristic property of the subject, or a characteristic of an observed event that is being classified. The more distinct and independent a feature is, the more quality the feature possesses in contributing to the accuracy of classification.

Building a learning machine-based URL reputation system begins with a collection of URLs that are known and pre-classified as either malicious or benign. Then, features are extracted from these URLs. In the context of URL classification, distinct features can be the number of characters in the second level domain (SLD) name, the number of subdomains in the URL, the number of non-alphabetical characters in the URL, and so on. The collection of the extracted features from a single URL forms a *feature set*. For example, with URL `ju2sd.d8ufv.uitsmake.ru`, the feature set containing the feature-value pairs is < length:8, subdomains:2, non-alphabet:0> because there are eight characters in the SLD name "uitsmake", there are two subdomains ("d8ufv" and "uitsmake"), and the URL does not contain any non-alphabetical characters. We will revisit the feature set in the next subsection in more detail.

The URL collection is fed into the classifier together with the pre-classified results. The classifier correlates each of the extracted features with the final result. After processing each of the URLs, the classifier tunes its formula to better match the pre-classified result. This process is called *classifier training*, and the URLs used in the training are called a *training set*. The classifier has a higher probability to be trained with higher precision if the training set is sufficiently large. Often times, another set of pre-classified URLs is prepared as a *test set*. Similar to constructing the training set, the test set consists of URLs that have been rated by other means, such as manual rating, and each URL has an ascertained rating. The test set is used to verify the accuracy of the automated reputation system by comparing the classification results with the pre-classified ratings, but neither enhancing the training set nor tuning the algorithms in the learning machine.

Creating URL Training Sets

Several free resources are available for collecting a list of URLs that are known to be benign and malicious. Alexa (`www.alexa.com/topsites`) composes a list of the most popular and frequently visited websites that are generally regarded as benign. Online databases such as PhishTank and EmergingThreats.net provide useful datasets on malicious URLs. In addition, the Google Safe Browsing API is available to check whether a URL has been identified by Google as suspicious or malicious. The URL training set is not static because the reputation of a URL can change over time. As discussed in Chapter 4, a website may initially be benign and then after being abandoned by its owner, it may be hijacked by black hats to distribute malicious content at a later time. This means that over time the reputation of the URL may have changed. Hence, a training set, whether a malicious set or a benign one, must be updated, and the classifier must be re-trained, either periodically or during real-time transaction evaluation, to reflect the dynamics in URL reputation.

Extracting URL Feature Sets

A URL is a string of text that may or may not have meaning semantically. Performing *lexical analysis*, that is, breaking the URL string into a series of tokens, allows for the extraction of desired features. One useful feature is the string length of the SLD name. In the fictitious domain `mydomain.com`, the SLD is `mydomain`. As discussed in Chapter 4, to distribute malware while avoiding detection, malware authors deploy domain generation algorithms (DGAs) to generate domain names in a batch and then algorithmically select a subset of the generated domain names to register for the malware distribution servers. DGAs tend to create longer SLD names to reduce the probability of name collisions. Therefore, the length of the SLD can be extracted as a feature to infer if the URL belongs to an MDN.

There are exceptions to long SLD names being malicious. Some legitimate subdomains are constructed using self-explanatory words to advertise the nature of the business of the website owner. For example, `www.stevenscreekchryslerjeepdodge.net` is a legitimate auto dealer website that has 30 characters in the subdomain name. Another reason for legitimate long domain names is because legitimate website owners tend to use lexical words for easy memorization while MDN creators have no such concerns. Having a short domain name does not imply the URL is less malicious. For example, the eight-letter SLD `qpqduqud.com` belonged to the second-largest spam botnet (named Srizbi) that was discovered in 2008.

A related feature to domain name length is whether the domain name consists of lexical words or is just a concatenation of random characters. A domain name composed of random characters is likely to be suspicious. However, the opposite of having a meaningful domain name is not a strong indicator of a benign domain. We know that black hats have created domain names out of the most frequently searched keywords, such as well-known events, breaking news, popular merchandise, and famous celebrities, all in the hope of getting the search engines to give the URL a preferential score that puts it in the top search results. For example, the botnet Torpig may call a Twitter API to use one of the popular trending topics in real-time in Twitter as the seed to generate domain names.

This discussion raises a number of important points about feature extraction:

- A feature may be useful only when it is applied in conjunction with other features.

- A feature may not be unique enough to be useful; that is, if there are too many exceptions to the rule, then the feature becomes irrelevant.

- A feature may evolve and transform into something else entirely different from the original intent.

- One feature may help in the development of another feature.

The reputation of a top-level domain (TLD) or of the country code TLD (ccTLD) may be selected as a feature. Dynamic DNS domains and free subdomains are known to be utilized heavily by MDNs. Certain countries are notorious in providing *bulletproof hosting*: .ru, .cc, and .cn continue to be the top ccTLDs that host malicious, illegal, and spam-related domains. The ratio of numeric to alphabetical characters and the number of subdomains in the URL can also serve as features for the URL reputation classifier.

The features that we have discussed thus far are static features; that is, these features are derived from static analysis of the URL. We can further explore the origin and formation of the URL to elicit additional features. In particular, we can collect the WHOIS information of a domain to extract features such as the age of the domain (the initial registration date of the domain), the registrar of the domain (registrar name and country), the domain's lease period (how long the domain is registered for, for example, three months versus one year), and whether the domain is automatically renewed at the end of the lease. These features, which are derived from WHOIS domain information, are relevant because legitimate websites do not usually choose to hide their registrant information, while questionable domains often perform anonymous registration.

Each feature is given a value once the feature selection is complete. The type of value assigned to a feature may differ from feature to feature. For example, the value type is an integer for features such as *length of SLD name, number of subdomains, age of the domain,* and *domain lease period*. The string value type is given to the *TLD domain name* feature. The Boolean value type is given to the *domain name consists of lexical words* feature, and the fraction value type is given to the *ratio of numeric to alphabetical characters* feature. In the following text, when we refer to a URL feature, we mean that the URL has the feature F with a value equal to f.

It is worth noting that the value for a feature may be a range instead of an exact number. For example, the *length of SLD name* feature can have multiple values ranging from 1 to 253. With that many possible feature values, it may be more meaningful to partition and assign a value range according to subjective and empirical insights regarding a feature. Continuing with the *length of SLD name* feature example, based on observation it may be possible to divide the values into three groups, that is, length value greater than 15 characters, between 15 and 8 characters, and less than 8 characters. We can use 0, 1, and 2 to represent each of the groups so that the *length of SLD name* feature will have only three different values for all the URLs in the training set.

Classifier Training

There are many classifiers that can be used to rate URLs. In this section, we show a straightforward example of how classifier training works using the Naïve Bayesian classifier. Our focus here is on how to prepare and present the data to the classifier for input classification.

The *Naïve Bayesian classifier* is an application of *Bayes' theorem*, which relates conditional probabilities with prior beliefs. In its basic form, $P(A)$ and $P(B)$ are the probability of event A occurring and the probability of event B occurring, respectively. $P(A|B)$ is the probability that A occurs given event B has occurred. The theorem states that the probability that event B occurs given that event A has occurred can be derived as

$$P(B|A) = \frac{P(B)P(A|B)}{P(A)}$$

In the context of a URL classifier, let us denote $P(m)$ as the probability of malicious URLs occurring in the training set. To get $P(m)$, we can count the number of malicious URLs and divide that value by the total number of URLs in the training set. Let F denote an extracted feature that represents *length of the SLD name greater than 10 characters*. $P(F)$, by definition, is the probability of F occurring in the training set. We can get this value by processing and counting the URLs that have more than 10 characters in the SLD name. The conditional probability $P(F|m)$ means the probability that the length of the domain name is greater than 10 characters given that the URL is malicious. We count the total number of malicious URLs in the training set and let A denote that sum. Within the malicious URLs, we count the number of URLs that have more than 10 characters in the SLD name and use B to denote that sum. By taking the ratio of (A/B) we obtain the value for $P(F|m)$. Applying Bayes' theorem, we can obtain the conditional probability $P(m|F)$ that the URL is malicious, given it has more than 10 characters in the SLD name, as

$$P(m|F) = \frac{P(m)P(F|m)}{P(F)}.$$

Similarly, let $P(!m)$ denote the probability of benign URLs in the training set. Using the same analysis and approach, we have the conditional probability of a URL being benign, given feature F, as

$$P(!m|F) = \frac{P(!m)P(F|!m)}{P(F)}.$$

Now, considering two independent features F_1 and F_2, we would like to obtain the probability of a malicious URL given F_1 and F_2. Applying Bayes' theorem, we can write the probability as

$$P(m|F_1,F_2) = \frac{P(F_1|m,F_2)P(m,F_2)}{P(F_1,F_2)} = \frac{P(F_1|m)P(F_2|m)P(m)}{P(F_1)P(F_2)}$$

Note in the preceding equations, because F_1 and F_2 are independent, $P(F_1,F_2) = P(F_1)P(F_2)$. Also, the conditional probability of $P(F_1|m,F_2)$ does not depend on F_2 and can be written as $P(F_1|m)$.

Expanding the two-feature analysis into a feature set with j independent features, the conditional probability of a URL being malicious given the independent feature set $<F_1,...,F_j>$ becomes

$$P(m|F_1,...,F_j) = \frac{P(F_1|m,F_2)P(m,F_2)}{P(F_1,...,F_j)} = \frac{P(F_1|m)...P(F_j|m)P(m)}{P(F_1)...P(F_j)}$$

$$= \frac{P(m)\prod_{i=1}^{j}P(F_i|m)}{\prod_{i=1}^{j}P(F_i)},$$

where $\prod_{i=1}^{j}P(F_i)$ and $\prod_{i=1}^{j}P(F_i|m)$ are the products of $P(F_i)$ and $P(F_i|m)$ from 1 to j respectively. In the preceding single feature example, we have shown how to calculate $P(m)$, $P(F_i|m)$, and $P(F_i)$; therefore, from the training set, we know every term in the equation, and we can calculate $P(m|F_1,...,F_j)$.

Similarly, we can also calculate the conditional probability of a URL being benign given feature set $<F_1...F_j>$, and we already know the value of each of the terms.

$$P(!m|F_1,...,F_j) = \frac{P(!m)\prod_{i=1}^{j}P(F_i|!m)}{\prod_{i=1}^{j}P(F_i)}$$

Finally, the Naïve Bayesian classifier classifies a URL with j features by comparing the probabilities of $P(m|F_1,...,F_j)$ and $P(!m|F_1,...,F_j)$. If the former is greater, the URL is malicious; otherwise, the URL is benign. If those two probabilities are the same, the URL can be either malicious or benign; however, such a case is very rare with a large set of features and quality training URLs.

The Naïve Bayesian Classification is merely an example showing how pre-collected data can be used to train the classifier in the context of classifying malicious URLs. Such a classifier that takes the labeled input training data and infers the label of unseen samples is a typical approach of supervised learning. Besides the Naïve Bayesian classifier, the approaches and algorithms in the general category of supervised learning include decision trees, linear regression, support vector machines, and so on. Each of the approaches can be used to design a classifier, and it is not always obvious which method is better than the other. A common practice is to apply multiple classifiers using different algorithms in parallel inside a single URL reputation system to improve accuracy. The final output of the URL rating is based on the combined weighted ratings from all the classifiers and can be represented as a reputation score. Further, the rating score can be translated to multiple levels other than just a binary value of malicious or benign. Those score and rating levels can reflect the confidence level of the classifiers' output; for example, based on the calculation, the ratings can be malicious, unwanted, regular, and trusted with the decreasing probability that the URL is malicious.

Many off-the-shelf data mining software applications are available that have already implemented the aforementioned classifiers. For example, the Naïve Bayesian classifier is available in Apache Mahout, and a comprehensive data-mining tool called Weka implements a wide range of classifiers, including the supervised learning classifiers we mentioned earlier. The off-the-shelf software can apply data-mining models to the extracted features, but not the URLs. As such we need to implement pre-processing functions to extract the features from the URLs and then feed the features to the data-mining software.

Another possible addition to the feature set is the *human tagged domain reputation*. Although manual rating of individual URLs is not a scalable solution, there are situations where it is useful for security analysts to examine domain names and assign trustworthiness ratings to them manually. In the aforementioned example, a domain may have had a good reputation but was hijacked to participate in an MDN campaign, and over a brief period of time the URL continues to surface in a redirection chain leading to malware. In such a case, the reputation of this domain should be adjusted to a much lower rating until that domain is removed from the MDN chain. In addition, security analysts can apply their expertise and heuristics to label potential malicious domain names with a threat severity level. For example, a domain that is constantly associated with a ransomware campaign is of a higher level of threat severity than a domain that merely distributes adware.

An interesting question to discuss is the size of the feature set. There is no universal answer to how large the feature set should be in order to give accurate ratings, as the outcome is highly dependent on the quality of the features, that is, how indicative those features are. Instead, we can focus on evaluating how important each of the features is to the classification result. We need to conduct a series of controlled tests to evaluate the importance of a specific feature. In an iterative approach, we run the classifier with all j features included against the training set and obtain a classification accuracy rating of X. In the next test, we rerun the classifier on the same training set, but with only j-1 features, and get an accuracy rating of Y. If $X > Y$, then the excluded feature helps to improve the classification accuracy. The larger the difference in X and Y, the more important that particular feature is. However, if $X \leq Y$, it indicates that the classifier is better off or indifferent without the excluded feature, and we can remove it from the feature set. There is also no definitive guideline on either the size of the training set or the size of the test set. However, a good training set should be able to train the classifier to reach over 99 percent accuracy in the similar-sized test set. In most cases, 20,000 URLs is a good starting point to build the URL reputation system.

At the time of this writing, a few free online URL reputation services were available. The most eminent ones are Blue Coat WebPulse Site Review and McAfee TrustedSource. Both products offer categorization results and allow users to submit revisions to the results if they feel the classification is inaccurate. The TrustedSource service lists reputation in a separate column in addition to the categorization. The reputations are Minimal Risk, Unverified Risk, Medium Risk, and High Risk. The WebPulse Site Review service combines the ratings with the descriptive categorization names; for example, a malicious URL can fall into the categories of Malicious Outbound Data/Botnets, Malicious Sources/Malnets, Suspicious, Potentially Unwanted Software, and so on. In addition, Google provides a safe browsing service that allows applications to check a URL against Google's own collection of suspicious and malicious pages through an API call. The responses from Google Safe Browsing servers are "phishing", "malware", "both phishing and malware", and "ok".

A URL reputation system can be deployed to detect and filter malicious URLs. However, this system has a few limitations:

- Not all redirection links are URLs with domain names. Sometimes the redirection link contains hardcoded IP addresses.

- The accuracy of the URL rating is highly dependent on the extracted feature set, the learning algorithm, and the quality of the training set.

To alleviate the first limitation, we can extend the URL rating to include IP address blacklists. Similar to intermediate redirection servers, the collected IP addresses are highly likely to be disposable. Newly seized IP addresses need to be constantly added to the blacklists, while stale entries must be verified and removed, thus rendering blacklists either ineffective or not scalable. The second limitation is much more difficult to address. Although advances in machine learning can be incorporated to enhance the effectiveness of learning and detection, extracting the URL feature set is quite subjective, and may not adapt well with the characteristics of an evolving MDN.

Dynamic Webpage Content Rating

A *webpage content analysis and categorization system* complements the URL reputation systems. A web content categorization system takes a webpage as its input, dynamically scans and analyzes the webpage content, and then generates a category for that page based on its evaluation. Entertainment, Adult/Mature, News/Media, Pornography, and Social Networking are just some example categories for a webpage. These categories are referred to as web categories for the remainder of this book. In the context of detecting malicious URLs, some content categories have high risk levels because they can lead to malware. For example, many lures are placed on porn sites that trap users into download-ing fake video players that are actually malware. Therefore, a user should be warned of the danger that lurks behind a webpage if the URL points to one that is classified as pornographic.

A webpage categorization system is a multi-dimensional engine that ana-lyzes the content from different perspectives using various algorithms, and the combined results determine the category. Analyzing the webpage content types and their respective layouts within the page is one dimension. Analyzing the advertised types of merchandise and services, as well as brand names, to derive the targeted demographics is yet another dimension. In the following section we will discuss one analysis dimension that extracts keywords from a webpage and then uses these keywords to derive a category for that page. This categorization system must be capable of extracting the most relevant keywords from a webpage and then have the ability to search, compare, and match for the most befitting category.

Keyword Extraction for Category Construction

The first step in keyword-based content categorization is to create categories of interest. Associated with each category is a set of keywords that, when com-bined together, form the most representative characteristics of that category. As a simple example, the keywords representing a Sports category may be "athlete, touchdown, inning, home run, quarterback, mixed martial arts". Although cer-tain webpages list keywords in their page titles, these keywords are subjective to the author's intentions and may not truly reflect what the real content of the webpage is. Therefore, the full text in each given webpage is analyzed, parsed, and condensed into a small set of words during the category construction phase.

At the beginning, a large volume of webpages are collected and compiled to form the basis of the categories. Human analysts are typically involved in this initial construction phase. An analyst applies heuristics to sort each collected webpage into a category that the analyst believes to best describe that page. Once all of the webpages are sorted into the corresponding categories, the collection of webpages in each category is then compiled through one or more algorithms to extract the keywords to represent the category. In the early stages, each category may contain a large number of keywords, and the keywords may overlap across the categories. Then, through a perpetual iterative cycle, the keywords in the categories are refined as new webpages are examined and processed by the categorization system. Refining a category implies possibly changing the number of keywords in the category, and some keywords may be replaced by new ones.

Term frequency-inverse document frequency (TF-IDF) is a well-known and widely adopted approach to evaluate how important a word is to a document in a collection of documents, or corpus. Many search engines use TF-IDF as the base algorithm to relate pages to given user queries. We will illustrate the concept of TF-IDF before you see a demonstration of how this algorithm can be used to extract relevant keywords for a category.

Let us assume we have a collection of English articles and we need to find out which article is most relevant to the topic of "Windows antivirus scan". Intuitively, "Windows", "antivirus", and "scan" are the three keywords or terms we want to search for in the articles. So, we start reviewing the articles and eliminate the ones that do not contain all those three terms. In each of the remaining articles, we count the occurrences of each term and sum those occurrences together. A larger value means more occurrences of the terms and hence greater potential to be more relevant. However, this method has drawbacks, such as in the case where the collection of articles is exclusively about Microsoft Windows. In such a case, "Windows" is a common word in all articles and is not a good term for distinguishing relevant and non-relevant articles. Therefore, we need some mechanism to offset the weight of common terms (in this example, "Windows") and to emphasize the importance of the unique terms (in this example, "antivirus" and "scan").

The preceding example infers that a good keyword representing a document should appear more often in that document while occurring less often in other documents. This is the basic concept of the TF-IDF algorithm. The algorithm has two parts: TF and IDF. TF is the function to evaluate the term frequency within a document. The frequency function can be simply the raw word frequency, for example, x occurrences among a total of y words. The frequency function may also be a function derived from the raw word frequency, for example, a logarithm function with the raw word frequency as a parameter, as in $\log(1+x/y)$.

IDF measures how important the word is to the document collection. Oftentimes, the IDF is the function $\log_{10}(N/n)$, where N is the total number of documents in a collection, n is the number of documents that the particular keyword appears in, and $\log_{10}$ is the 10-based logarithm. The product of TF and IDF is the score of the keyword, and we can write it as $S_{\text{TF-IDF}} = \frac{x}{y}\log_{10}\frac{N}{n}$. A larger score means the keyword better represents the page. Applying the document concept to a single category and mapping the corpus to all categories of interest, we can see the TF-IDF algorithm can be directly applied in keyword extraction out of the webpages that belong to the same category.

Table 5-1 shows the results of a scan we did on 100 webpages. For a particular page, we list the top five most frequently occurring words with their occurrence count in the single page and in the overall 100-page collection.

Table 5-1: Example of TF-IDF Calculation

KEYWORD	OCCURRENCE IN SINGLE PAGE (WORD COUNT)	OCCURRENCES IN COLLECTION (PAGE COUNT)	TF-IDF SCORE
Windows	50	10	50
Free	100	30	52.3
Antivirus	**100**	**5**	**130.1**
Scan	10	3	15.2
Explorer	5	50	1.5

Take "antivirus" as an example. To calculate the TF-IDF score, we first take the 10-based logarithm of total pages in the collection (100) over collection occurrences (5), which is $\log_{10}(100/5)=1.301$. We then multiply the number by the occurrences in a single page (100) and get 100 x 1.3 = 130.1. From the table, we can observe that although the words "free" and "antivirus" both appeared 100 times in the sample webpage, the TF-IDF score for "antivirus" is much higher than the score for "free", which indicates that "antivirus" is a better keyword than "free" in representing the webpage. Repeating this same process, we can compile additional top relevant keywords out of the remaining 99 webpages. Together, these keywords would represent the category these 100 pages have been sorted into.

There is almost always a need to sanitize a webpage and select a subset of contents within the page prior to applying the TF-IDF algorithm. Consider the scenario where a malicious webpage is populated with a large number of keywords that would classify the page to a benign category; however, in this case, these crafted keywords are made invisible to webpage visitors through display tricks, such as using a tiny font-size, or using coloration such as setting the font color to white while displaying the content on a white background. The descriptive lures are prominently visible to visitors, thus achieving the goal of leading the visitors down to a malnet, although the words that make up the lures have the smallest number of occurrences within that page.

Applying the TF-IDF algorithm to such a page will result in the extraction of keywords from the large volume of hidden text, which causes the classification algorithm to treat the webpage as benign and does not represent the true malicious intent of the webpage. A TF-IDF-based categorization system cannot circumvent the display rendering techniques to derive the right category for such a malicious webpage. Therefore, parsing the HTML code of a webpage to identify and eliminate hidden content that is aimed at poisoning the keyword extraction algorithm would be a necessary pre-processing step.

Building a collection of webpages for the IDF function is a perpetual process. The initial set of webpages may be manually collected and categorized first, but as the classification system is deployed to rate new webpages, these new pages are added to the collection, and periodically the TF-IDF algorithm is re-run to refine the keywords for each category.

Keyword Categorization

Let's assume there are C web categories and each web category c has a number of associated keywords. There is a set s containing a number of unique keywords extracted from a webpage. For each c, we test each of the keywords in s against each of the keywords in c. The categorization problem becomes a searching problem of finding the category c that contains the highest number of keywords from s. In other words, the matching is not a precise one-to-one matching. Therefore, categorizing a webpage is about identifying the most likely category instead of reaching an absolute answer.

A *bloom filter* is a memory-efficient data structure that enables the implementation of membership testing. A bloom filter is an example of a *probabilistic data structure*, which is a data structure having some probabilistic components. In the context of a bloom filter, the probabilistic component refers to the fact that a membership test gives a probabilistic answer, not a definitive result. In particular, with a bloom filter the test can determine whether an element is "definitely not" in the set, or the element "may be in" the set, but the test cannot conclude whether an element is "definitely in" the set. In other words, a bloom filter can give a *false positive* answer of "the element is a member of the set" when in fact the element is not in the set, but a bloom filter cannot give a *false negative* answer of "the element is not a member of a set" when the member is in fact part of the set.

The bloom filter concept was first introduced in 1970 to solve the problem of implementing a membership testing method using an error-free hash function on a large amount of source data. Due to the amount of the source data, an impractically large amount of memory is required to accommodate the hash area. The bloom filter method reduces the hash area in memory by allowing a small fraction of error in the membership test results.

The general idea of a bloom filter is to use a bit array to represent a set. Assuming a set has n elements, then at the start the bloom filter is a bit array of n slots, where each slot has a bit value 0. Each element in the set will be an input to a number of hash functions. Applying each hash function to an element will give a slot number, and then the bit value in that slot will change to value 1. To test for a set membership, the element to be tested is fed into the same hash functions, and the resulting bit array is compared against the bit array that was created for the set. The construction method for a bloom filter allows for new element insertion into the filter but cannot remove an element from it.

In the context of our webpage categorization problem domain, each bloom filter represents a web category. The filter is constructed as an array of m bits. We choose k independent hash functions. Each function will map a keyword to an array element in the range of 1 to m. The reason for choosing k independent hash functions is to reduce collision. It is possible for a single hash function to hash two different keywords into the same slot (or bit position) and cause a collision. In such a case, the bit cannot represent a unique keyword. However, with more than one hash function, a keyword is represented as a set of bits and thus greatly reduces the probability of collisions. In popular bloom filter implementations, the commonly used hash functions include Jenkins hash, Murmur hash, Fowler-Noll-Vo (FNV) series of hashes, and MD5 hash. Figure 5-1 illustrates the construction of a bloom filter for a web category that contains four keywords and three independent hash functions.

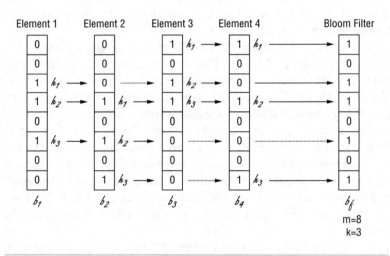

Step 1. Apply $h_1()$, $h_2()$, $h_3()$ on elements and get bit arrays ($b_1..b_4$).

Step 2. Bitwise *OR* of the element bit arrays to get the bit array of the bloom filter (b_f).

Figure 5-1: Bloom Filter Construction

The bloom filter for a web category is initialized by applying each of the k hash functions on each of the keywords in the category, resulting in k hash values. Each of the k hash values is an index into the array, and the value at that array slot is set to value 1. As shown in Figure 5-1, the three hash functions are applied to each keyword to obtain the bit arrays b_1, b_2, b_3, and b_4, respectively. Then these intermediate bit arrays are combined to form the bloom filter for the category. To test for membership, the same number of hash functions is applied to a given element to obtain an intermediate bit array, which is then compared against the bloom filter using a bitwise XOR operation. Figure 5-2 shows an example of a membership test.

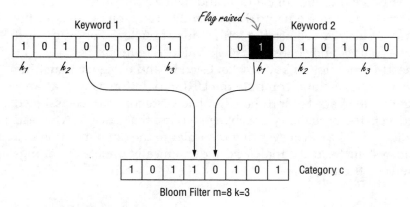

Figure 5-2: Bloom Filter Matching

This example illustrates the process of testing two keywords against a bloom filter of 8 bits built using three hash functions (h_1, h_2, h_3). When applying the hash functions to keyword 1, 3 bits are set in its array. The array is then compared with the bloom filter using bitwise XOR, resulting in a value 0, which means keyword 1 is in category c. For keyword 2, hash function h_1 sets the second bit that is not in the bloom filter, so the XOR operation results in a non-0 value, implying keyword 2 is not in category c.

In the context of content category classification, assume a category c-1 has five keywords (A, B, C, D, E), and a category c-2 has five keywords (B, C, D, F, G). If the harvested keywords from a webpage are (B, C, D), then the webpage will match both categories because (B, C, D) are in sets c-1 and c-2. If category c-3 has (A, C, D, I, J), then the webpage has a 75 percent match against c-3. Therefore, a webpage can match multiple categories due to overlapping keywords, which can be useful if the percentage of matching for a category is presented as part of the result so as to enable a security analyst to conduct further, more focused, analysis.

As mentioned earlier, one of the properties of a bloom filter is that it can never return a false negative answer, but it can give a false positive answer. That is to say, when an element (for example, keyword 2) is tested and the test shows the element is not in the bloom filter, the test is 100 percent accurate. However, we cannot be absolutely sure when a bloom filter test (for example, keyword 1) passes. This probability of a false positive (p) is a function of the values of k, m, and n as $p = (1 - e^{-\frac{kn}{m}})^k$, where k is the number of hash functions, m is the size of the bit array, and n is the number of elements in the bloom filter.

We can derive from the equation that the value of p grows with n. This means that as more elements are added to the bloom filter, the probability of false positives increases in tandem. Choosing the optimal value of the hash function number k as (m/n) ln2 can minimize the probability p. When designing a bloom filter, we first set the value of n and m, and then we calculate the optimal k value. Those three values are put into the probability function to calculate the false positive rate, which can be used to refine the parameters. For example, if p is too large, we go back and choose a large m value to reduce p.

Through the aforementioned keyword extraction and category matching techniques, we can process and compute the URL reputation as well as analyze and categorize the page behind the URL. Each category can be assigned a rating that reflects the probability a webpage having that category can lead to malicious infection. The category rating is similar to the domain rating in a URL reputation system. Security analysts can dynamically update the ratings to address emerging threats.

Detecting Malicious Web Infrastructure

Detecting malicious landing pages and redirection servers is the first tier of defense against an MDN. Despite efforts at detecting and avoiding malicious URLs and landing pages, some malicious ones will evade detection and lure users into a malnet. When reputable websites and legitimate servers have been compromised to host malicious content, reputation-based detection may fail to identify malicious downloads. In such cases, content-based analysis not only can offer protection for the end system but also record the host that served the malware.

Identifying each of the malware distribution points and taking them down one by one is an effective approach to defending against an MDN. However, individual malware distribution points are just the tip of the iceberg. There are malicious web infrastructures that orchestrate the MDNs. These MDN infrastructures are well hidden and cannot be easily accessed from the legitimate side of the web. Understanding their structures and the way they operate is critical in creating multi-layered defenses.

Detecting Exploit Servers through Content Analysis

One commonly deployed approach to detecting malware distribution points and exploit servers is to perform content analysis of downloaded files. The server that hosts a downloaded file, typically an executable file of some form, which is found to be malicious, is marked as either an exploit server or a suspicious host. The executable file must first be extracted from the download session and then scanned by a *content analysis system* for known exploits and malware signatures. Common components of a content analysis system include multiple antivirus engines and a *sandbox*. A sandbox is a controlled and restricted execution environment in which a suspicious executable file is placed and executed, a process often known as *malware denotation*. The runtime behavior of the executable is recorded and analyzed for identification of maliciousness.

The extraction of the executable content from a download session can be done with the help of a secure proxy. A secure proxy can hold and examine the connection between an exploit server and the user's browser. For example, with the HTTP proxy, if the `Content-Disposition` value in the HTTP header is "attachment", the HTTP proxy can get the filename from the `filename` parameter. Furthermore, the proxy extracts the HTTP payload as the content of the file and reconstructs the downloaded file with the extracted filename. The reconstructed file can then be sent to the content analysis system for a malware scan. The file transfer between the HTTP proxy and the content analysis system can be carried over the Internet Content Adaptation Protocol (ICAP). The HTTP proxy will serve the content to the user session if the content analysis system finds the file to be clean. However, if malware is detected, the HTTP proxy will record this connection with the exploit server IP address and hostname if possible. The proxy will also block the content, and the browser may be served with a warning page.

Once the proxy obtains a list of exploit server IP addresses and hostnames, this list can be added into a proxy policy to block future connections to these exploit servers. An HTTPS proxy is mandatory if the session is carried over an HTTPS session. HTTPS-based malware distribution is less common than HTTP-based distribution, mainly due to the fact that modern browsers will warn a user of non-CA (Certificate Authority) signed certificates and explicitly ask the user to confirm the acceptance of such non-authenticated certificates before proceeding with that HTTPS connection. In order to silence the browser warning, a malware distributor will need to obtain a valid certificate, which is both difficult and costly, in addition to being easily traceable. Some MDNs have been observed to host malware on well-trusted cloud storage providers such as Dropbox, Google Drive, and SkyDrive. However, such cases are rare because reputable cloud storage providers constantly monitor their servers for abuse and for malware infection and are known to quickly block access to the malware as soon as it is identified.

The major challenge of using a content analysis system to detect malware exploit servers is that most antivirus engines scan for particular patterns or signatures of known viruses and malware. The pattern-based scanning technique is prone to signature evasion. Even after the signature of malware is captured and incorporated by an antivirus engine, the malware authors can easily repackage or obfuscate the malware through encryption to result in a different signature. The repackaged and redistributed malware is most likely to evade the antivirus engines, although the major attack vectors remain the same. A sandbox is an essential part of the content analysis system because a sandbox detects malware through the analysis of runtime behavior instead of static signatures. Let us look at a few examples of runtime analysis of JavaScripts that can be done in a sandbox.

In order to analyze the webpage content, it is essential to understand what the malware is intending to achieve in different environments. Because most web-based attacks exploit the vulnerabilities of a web browser, it is logical to simply analyze the webpage contents, for example, HTML and JavaScript, by executing these contents in the browser. However, due to environment finger-printing techniques used by most malware, a single piece of malicious JavaScript may follow different execution paths depending on the particular browser version and system configuration, leading to completely opposite result states. It is time-consuming to create each specific browser and system configuration and therefore impractical to test the malware on all possible configurations.

Rozzle, a JavaScript multi-execution virtual machine, was designed specifically to explore these multiple execution paths and bypass environment checks in one pass. The key concept of execution-path exploration is to visit every control-flow branch. For example, when an if/else block is processed, both the if and the else code paths are executed. In the case of try/catch blocks, these are treated as virtual if/else branches and the code in the catch block is executed as well. Still, there are certain limitations with this approach. Malware can use a server-client structure to fingerprint the browser and detect the presence of multi-execution techniques. To do so, the malware client could sample a few code paths and send reports about the execution results to its C2 server. The C2 server could then return different content to render based on the sample execution results. In addition, there are some browser-dependent behaviors that cannot be captured by control-flow branches. For example, the expression (0 * window.innerWidth + 1) will return 1 in Firefox and Chrome but will return a NAN error in Internet Explorer. This expression can be coded as the key to trigger an attack in Firefox and Chrome, and such an attack is not visible when the code is executed on Internet Explorer.

Another challenge in content analysis is code obfuscation. Because malware extensively uses eval() or document.write() functions to dynamically create JavaScript at the time of execution, content analysis is not always strictly static analysis. Therefore, the analyzer needs to collect and process the JavaScript code at runtime. Fortunately, such tools are available to intercept the "unpacked" code that's dynamically generated in the JavaScript engine as the malicious code is being executed. When using the *Detours* tool, for example, it is possible to obtain the JavaScript code at each level of unpacking, such as each time it executes eval().

With the de-obfuscated JavaScript code, JavaScript analysis tools can be used to classify whether the code fragment is malicious or benign. *Zozzle* is an in-browser JavaScript malware detection tool. Zozzle generates an Abstract Syntax Tree (AST) from the JavaScript and then abstracts a set of features from the expression and variable declaration nodes in the resulting AST. An AST is a tree representation of the syntactic structure of a program that is written in a specific programming language; in this discussion the programming language is JavaScript. Figure 5-3 illustrates an example AST of a code fragment written in C. Each feature contains a context word and the AST text string.

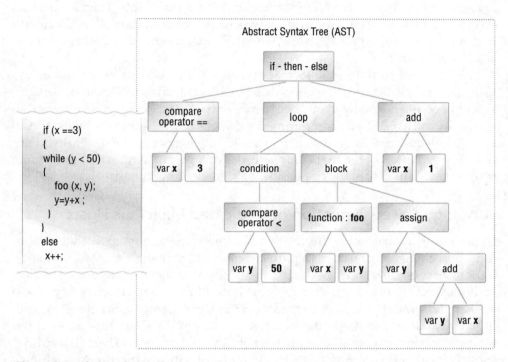

Figure 5-3: Abstract Syntax Tree

Zozzle is a direct application of the Bayes theorem. Zozzle excludes features that are statistically dependent. Its goal is to calculate the conditional probability that the JavaScript is malicious given a set of independent features that have been extracted from the JavaScript code fragment. Experiments show that Zozzle is surprisingly effective, with less than one false positive in a quarter-million samples. Integrating Zozzle into popular browsers does not show significant performance degradation. Nonetheless, such feature-based learning needs a large dataset to train the classifier, which makes distributed collection and classification at the end user's browser inefficient. In addition, malware authors can quickly restructure their JavaScript to obsolete the selected features. Code variations in the collected malware samples require continuous retraining of the classifier, which is also inefficient at the end user's system.

To address the code variation challenge, *Revolver* has been proposed with the attempt to understand the semantics of different variations of exploit code, particularly in drive-by-download attacks. Revolver requires honeyclients to collect the malicious code on the web despite the evasion attempts. (Honeyclients are described in the section "Detecting Malicious Servers with a Honeyclient".) The collected scripts can be generally categorized as either malicious or benign using honeyclients as well as other off-the-shelf antivirus scanners. Revolver analyzes the scripts by first constructing an AST for the scripts. Then it runs the scripts in a browser emulator to track which code path in the AST is executed. It also tracks scripts that lead to network I/O operations, such as those generated by an iframe.

The ASTs are stored in the format of a *normalized node sequence* in an array using pre-order traversal. In addition, each AST is tagged as malicious or benign. Working on the normalized node sequence of the ASTs, Revolver can check the similarity of two ASTs by computing the directed edit distance between those two node sequences. In the case of two malicious sequences, the similarity identifies the evolution of the malicious scripts. For a pair of benign and malicious scripts, the similarity shows a possible hidden evasion attempt.

Topology-Based Detection of Dedicated Malicious Hosts

In malnet infrastructures, there exist dedicated malicious hosts that have a high percentage of presence in paths of multiple malnets that lead to distribution servers. Instead of analyzing the types of malicious content served or activities taking place at each such host individually, one effective approach is to analyze the topology of the malnets these prevalent hosts belong to. The topological detection method examines the malnet infrastructure holistically to identify common nodes that are part of different malnets. Then, disrupting these critical and common hosts in the malicious infrastructure can achieve high negative impacts on the malnet's operations. We know malnet owners deploy DDNS (Dynamic DNS) and fast-flux to evade detection by registering a large number of domain names and mapping these domain names to a set of IP addresses. In these mapping tactics, multiple domain names can map to a single IP address, and a single domain name can have multiple IP addresses. So the malnets relate to one another through hostnames and IP addresses that appear in URLs and in web requests. Therefore, the Hostname-IP Cluster (HIC) data structure is utilized to compute the maximum overlapping. Each HIC is represented as HIC={H, I}, where H is the list of hosts and I is the list of IP addresses, essentially representing a group of malnet hostnames that are associated with a set of IP addresses.

Sufficient data collection is necessary before constructing the HIC. The first step in data collection is to gather a large number of URLs. The URLs are partitioned into known malicious URLs and known legitimate URLs. The URL data set typically numbers in the millions once it is finalized, and each

URL is crawled, possibly through multiple redirections of various techniques ranging from HTTP status code to JavaScript, to obtain the entire path to the malware. After processing the URLs, the HICs are built through an iterative process: first identifying the unique hostname (h_i) followed by identifying all of the IP addresses that have been resolved for that hostname h_i, resulting in the single-host HIC in the form of $HIC_i = \{h_i, (IP_1, IP_2, IP_n)\}$. These single-host HICs are then processed to determine if they can be merged with each other to form a larger multi-host HIC. This process repeats until none of the HICs can be merged with other HICs.

A pair of HICs can be merged if they are closely related, which is measured by the clustering coefficient r, or the Jaccard index. The *Jaccard index* is also known as the *Jaccard similarity coefficient* and measures the similarity between two data sets by dividing the size of their intersection by the size of their union. So the coefficient r is calculated as the number of shared IP addresses divided by the total number of unique IP addresses in HIC_i and HIC_j. As a percentage value, r falls between 0 and 1, with 0 indicating the two HICs are independent. The pair of HICs is merged if coefficient r is above a certain threshold value that is typically set to 0.5. The merge process is performed repeatedly on all HICs until no two HICs can be merged. In the context of a topology-based detection approach, an additional merge criterion is the similarity in the registrar information. By looking up the WHOIS database, we can obtain the registrar name from the domain name. Because malnets utilize free domains and dynamic DNS providers extensively, the registrar serves as a good indicator to determine whether a domain name is legitimate. Consequently, the HIC merging criterion is revised as $r >= 0.5$ and the hostnames share the same registrar. Figure 5-4 illustrates the HIC merge process.

Once the HIC merge process is complete, the final set of HICs contains both malicious and legitimate HICs. The *PageRank* algorithm is then applied to identify the malicious HICs. The PageRank algorithm was designed to compute the importance of a webpage or its *rank* by the number and quality of links pointing to the webpage. A rank propagates across the hyperlinks, and the rank of a page depends on the ranks of the pages that link to it. The idea behind applying the PageRank algorithm to the HICs to discover the malicious ones is that a malicious HIC will have a high rank in the malicious infrastructure; that is, a malicious HIC has high references from other malicious HICs, while at the same time receiving a low rank from the legitimate benign web infrastructure. This topological relationship in the malicious infrastructure enables this approach to identify new pervasive and dedicated malicious hosts, as well as uncovering new malicious URLs. In addition, this topology-based detection method is agnostic to the nature of the attacks that leverage the infrastructure, and taking down these dedicated pervasive hosts can disrupt many types of attack campaigns.

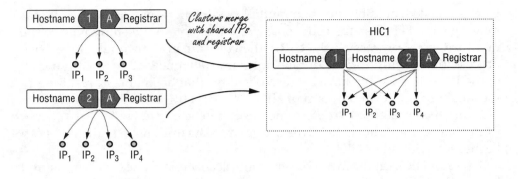

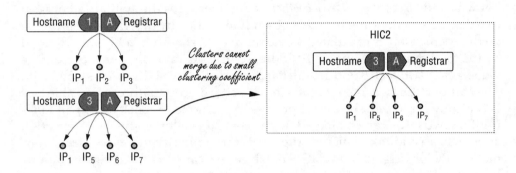

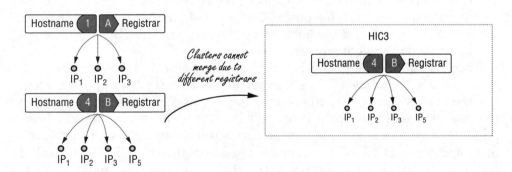

Figure 5-4: HIC Merge Process

Detecting C2 Servers

One type of resilience designed into the MDN is the separation of the C2 channel from the malware distribution or download channel, as shown in Figure 5-5. Unlike exploit servers, the C2 servers do not distribute the malware but rather are the command center to orchestrate the malnet operation. In particular, through the C2 channel, the malware downloader may obtain a list of URLs that specify where to retrieve the actual malware payload, to report the malnet download status to the C2 servers, to upload fingerprints of the host and the browser environment, and to receive further attack instructions. Because C2 servers are not associated with malware downloads, they do not generate a large volume of traffic in the C2 channels, thus making them difficult to detect. In particular, the challenges lie in the following aspects:

- The C2 servers and the malware bots can implement private communication protocols that are dynamic and can change at any time. It takes a great amount of effort to reverse-engineer those protocols.

- A C2 channel can be encrypted or obfuscated, making deciphering the C2 channel an extremely arduous process.

- Some C2 servers leverage the distributed P2P infrastructure, making their presence highly dynamic and live identification difficult.

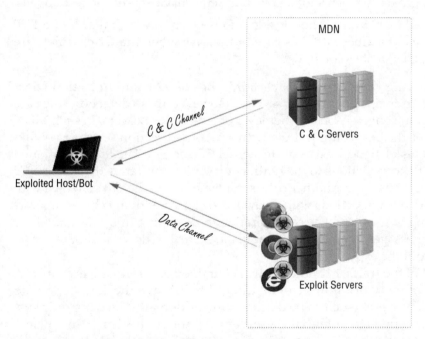

Figure 5-5: Separation of C2 and Download Channels

One approach to detect C2 servers is to create a contained environment, for example, by using honeyclients, and run malware inside it. The assumption is that the malware will infect the contained system and try to contact the C2 servers for further attack instructions or to download the malware payload. The goal is to set custom network policies to deceive the malware by blocking communications from the malware bot to one of the C2 servers so that the malware bot will enumerate the C2 servers it knows. In this way, the bot further reveals its full list of C2 servers. By deploying the contained test environment behind a proxy, we can enforce the desired behavior by adding the following rules on the proxy:

- Respond with "Name Error" when a DNS request is received. This rule is based on the observations that some malware bots have a hardcoded list of hostnames or URLs to connect to the C2 servers. The bot needs to resolve the C2 server's IP address before initiating the connection. The rule is to trick a malware bot to explore all of its known hostnames or domain names for the C2 servers.

- Reply "TCP RST" to all "TCP SYN" requests. This rule is to block TCP connections to C2 servers in case a C2 server is hardcoded with IP addresses. If a bot has an embedded list of pre-defined C2 server IP addresses, then the bot might try to reach another one if the current C2 server connection fails.

- Drop all UDP traffic. The consideration of this rule is similar to the TCP rule just described. It takes care of the case when the C2 channels are using UDP instead of TCP.

The preceding rules can detect certain types of C2 communication when the bots themselves know the C2 servers. However, these detection rules are ineffective if the bots rely on another layer of redirection servers. In such MDN deployments, the bots communicate with a set of redirection servers to obtain the hostnames or IP addresses of the actual C2 servers. The aforementioned rules block the connections to the redirection servers, and thus the de facto C2 servers are not revealed. Another rule is implemented in the proxy to deal with such cases: drop connections with a payload size greater than m bytes, in practice, choosing m to be 4K. The consideration in designing this rule is to allow C2 control messages to go through but to block further download of malware payloads from the exploit servers.

When all of the traffic to and from this contained environment is captured, the identified network flows can be filtered to remove the connections to well-known websites (such as the Alexa top 100K domains), leaving only suspicious connections to potential C2 servers. Although this is not an efficient strategy to decode the C2 communication protocol, nonetheless those suspicious connections can be used to extract and analyze potential C2 requests and responses.

Although advanced anti-detection mechanisms have been adopted by malware authors to hide the C2 servers, some features and patterns can be observed from uncovered malware campaigns to extract heuristics that will aid in detection design. For example, C2 servers usually have redundant deployments where there are multiple active and backup C2 servers. In addition, to avoid takedowns, those C2 servers span a diverse set of Top Level Domains (TLDs) across multiple Autonomous Systems (ASes). The domains are registered through geographically distributed registrars on multiple continents. Applying this property, if we observe a chain of connections each having small payloads to a diverse set of servers fitting such a property, then those servers are potentially C2 servers. As another example, C2 server domains and exploit server domains are often distinct from each other to avoid domain filtering. However, to reduce costs, MDNs usually choose the same service provider to host multiple malicious servers, including both exploit and C2 servers. In other words, both malicious domains map into the same provider prefixes. Therefore, applying the HIC and redirection graph approach that we discussed in the previous section, we can correlate and sort these into C2 servers that are less connected in an HIC and the exploit servers that are the most connected in an HIC.

Detection Based on Download Similarities

This detection method works by inspecting TCP/IP headers, HTTP headers, HTTP responses, and a preconfigured number of bytes in the payload. Once the HTTP response is identified as containing a download file that is not in a configured white-list, the flow information is recorded along with the request URI and a computed hash of a k-byte block from the payload. These metadata records are collected over live networks for a predetermined period of time, typically in days.

After the metadata extraction phase, different analysis techniques are applied to separate the potential malicious requests into a set of URIs. The first analysis aims to detect file mutation, also known as *server-side polymorphism*. Malware authors use file mutation in their attempt to defeat signature-based detection engines. The same malware file may be modified slightly each time it is served so that it has a different hash digest. A single URI that points to different files (according to different hash digests), and in a short time span, is a strong indication of active file mutation taking place on a distribution server.

The second analysis aims to detect fast-flux. From the metadata, domains that host at least one identical file (again according to the file digest) are grouped together into a cluster. When multiple domains in the cluster map into the same provider prefix, this is a sign of domain fluxing. The goal of a legitimate content delivery network (CDN) is to provide a reliable distributed content delivery infrastructure. The reliability stems from the fact that the same content is made available on different provider networks, in different physical locations, and on different physical servers to offer resiliency. Hosting multiple domains on a single IP address or on one provider prefix violates one of the basic CDN goals and does not seem to have any legitimate reason except for being a symptom of fast-flux.

Domains that host the same files and belong to the same legitimate CDN tend to have the exact same structured directory layout. This characteristic is missing from the malicious domain cluster. A legitimate CDN is likely to host a variety of contents, and therefore a large number of URIs would be associated with a legitimate domain, while a malicious domain would have a small number of URIs because each malicious domain usually hosts a small number of malware files. Similarly, the file types hosted by a regular CDN will show a wide variety while the file diversity in malicious domains is poor.

The third analysis aims to identify domains and IP addresses that participate mainly in the download of a single executable file. This is typically a symptom of domains and IP addresses that are active only in an attack campaign.

The fourth analysis aims to detect drive-by download domains that are triggered by second-stage shellcode. This analysis is based on the observation that some drive-by downloads are initiated by the shellcode and result in the HTTP header having a `User-Agent` that is different from the HTTP header generated by the user's web browser. Therefore, when multiple HTTP requests originate from the same IP address and go to the same destination but the requests have different `User-Agent` values, this is a sign of a malicious download, and the destination is potentially malicious.

What remains at the end of these analyses is a set of URIs that are highly suspicious. These URIs are then further analyzed using the techniques described previously.

Crawlers

The detection methods described in the previous sections are all activated by real-time traffic generated from user-initiated activities. The necessity for actively probing for an MDN in the web infrastructure is motivated by two aspects. First, active probing is intended to discover MDNs at large, and traffic from those MDNs is not available on premise. In addition, active probing can discover new MDNs or those that are in hibernation so that zero-day or even negative-day protections can be afforded. Second, active probing provides fresh training sets to refine classifiers or other machine learning-based systems. For a rapidly evolving malnet, certain indicative features, properties, and components can change over time. Compiling the up-to-date collection of malnet samples also helps us to better understand the new evolution trends taking place in an MDN.

Web crawlers are great tools for collecting malicious URLs and webpages as they traverse the web in a systematic way. Typically, web crawlers follow hyperlinks to land on as many webpages as possible. The key in designing the crawler is efficiency: with numerous pages on the web, the crawler needs to proactively filter the non-malicious links it encounters and focus only on the potentially malicious pages. Given the fact that popular search engines also crawl the web continuously, an efficient crawler can leverage the existing search engine infrastructure and use it to its advantage to locate the malicious pages of interest. The general concept is that the malicious pages share some common searchable features, and if the crawler can identify such features from known malicious pages, then it can utilize search engines to locate more pages with the same features. Those pages in the search results have high probability being potentially malicious pages. The more pages the crawler collects, the clearer a picture it gets of how malnets structure those pages.

The web crawler starts with a set of known malicious URLs as samples. As we discussed in previous sections, lists of such URLs are available from malware databases online. The web crawler first needs to visit those URLs and obtain a copy of the pages behind the URLs for processing. It is worth noting that the crawler extracts common features that are indicators of malicious webpages, which is a different approach from the dynamic content rating system we discussed earlier. In the latter case, the rating is based on the analysis of textual content that is visible to the end user, while in the former case, the processing covers more elements on the webpages, for example, the embedded links.

An easy-to-understand example of an extracted feature is "shared links". The web crawler first processes each of the sample pages and extracts the embedded URLs. A link is recorded as a shared link if the link is found on more than one page. At the end of this process you have a compiled list of shared links within those sample pages, which is an indicator of common malicious features. The crawler chooses the most highly referenced URLs (for example, top 10 URLs) from the shared-links list and submits them to the search engines. The search results will list other pages indexed by the search engines that have the same link. The crawler examines the retrieved pages and excludes the ones that are already in the sample pages. The remaining pages in the search results are the new pages that have the same malicious feature, that is, the shared links discovered by the crawler. The final step is to add the newly crawled pages into the set of sample pages. As the sample page count grows, the crawler will periodically process the sample set to try to discover possible new shared links.

There are two particular challenges in implementing the detection crawler. The first challenge is server-side polymorphism. As discussed in Chapter 4, a malware page can conceal itself from a crawler by returning benign or legitimate content while returning a whole different set of malicious content when it is visited by an exploited browser. By employing *server-side cloaking*, the exploited websites can respond to a crawler by traffic redirection to other benign or legitimate websites. In this regard, server-side cloaking is another malicious feature. Server-side cloaking is detected if the crawler eventually lands at two different TLDs when appearing to be a crawler or browser. Although a legitimate website can also deliver targeted contents based on users and exhibits certain levels of server-side polymorphism, it is unlikely that the targeted contents are served from different TLDs. The crawler implements server-side cloaking detection by visiting a candidate URL multiple times, each time using a handcrafted

HTTP header, in particular, with specific values in the `User-Agent` and `Referer` fields. For example, the crawler simulates a click from a Google search result by setting `User-Agent` as a regular browser, such as Internet Explorer or Chrome, and `Referer` as a Google search query URL. Then the crawler may simulate a Google crawler by setting `User-Agent` to Googlebot or Googlebot-News, which may experience a chain of redirections before reaching the final page. The crawler compares the TLDs in both cases and identifies server-side cloaking if the TLDs are different.

The second challenge in implementing a detection crawler is to collect the malicious URL samples. Free online databases are good sources, but due to the short lifetimes of malicious domains, a good portion of the URLs listed in those sources are outdated and are no longer valid when they are made available online because the hosts were either taken down or abandoned. Therefore, a key aspect in crawler implementation is to find live MDN campaigns that control and distribute malicious URLs. Search engines provide tools to show the up-to-date statistics and live trends of popular keywords, such as Google Hot Trends, Twitter hot hash tags, and so on. The same tools are also used by SEO and SEP campaigns to attract traffic onto malicious landing pages. Therefore, the keywords in the live trends are *potential* malicious features. In this case, the crawler searches the keywords through search engines and returns with links to a list of pages in which there are potential MDN landing pages. The crawler then leverages other techniques (for example, server-side cloaking detection) to evaluate whether those links are malicious.

A detection crawler is best deployed together with other MDN detection systems. On one hand, other detection systems can further filter the crawling results and hence improve crawling efficiency and quality. In particular, a URL reputation system can help to shorten the list of potential malicious URLs, and a content analysis system can provide high-accuracy detection on contents behind those URLs if the links eventually lead to file downloads. On the other hand, the crawler can be utilized as an exploration tool to probe for MDN infrastructures. For example, one important property of MDN infrastructure is that the dedicated malicious HICs are highly intertwined and highly connected with one another. Applying this property, the crawler, when encountering the hosts in the malicious HICs, can then try to explore all of the links that originate from that host because those links most likely point to other hosts in the same or related HICs that serve as the backbone of the malicious infrastructures.

Detecting Malicious Servers with a Honeyclient

A *honeyclient*, also called a *client honeypot*, detects attacks and malware by simulating a vulnerable client application and actively interacting with remote servers. This client-side approach is different from traditional honeypots, which simulate vulnerable server applications and then wait passively for incoming attacks. Although the concept of a honeyclient can be extended to any type of client application the power and popularity of browser-based attacks have made web browser honeyclients by far the most common type of honeyclient. Web browser honeyclients mimic a user browsing a list of websites and then analyze the activity to identify websites that exploit vulnerable web browsers or browser plugins. This section will provide an overview of browser honeyclients, discuss the design trade-offs using popular honeyclient implementations as examples, and conclude with some of the challenges and alternative analysis techniques.

High Interaction versus Low Interaction

Similar to other types of honeypots, honeyclients can be divided into two main categories: high interaction and low interaction. The major difference between the two is that high-interaction honeyclients use real applications, on a real operating system, and sometimes even on real hardware, while low-interaction honeyclients use software to simulate the vulnerable client applications. For example, in the original *honeyclient* implementation, the honeyclient drives a real Internet Explorer browser running on a Windows host to visit the malware websites and closely monitors memory, files, and Windows registry entries in real-time. In such cases where unexpected modifications and changes are observed, a malware attack is recorded, and the web page is flagged. On the other hand, low-interaction honeyclients simulate only the critical parts of the browser and operating system required to detect the types of attacks they're looking for and are often run on a different operating system than the vulnerable systems they are simulating. Because low-interaction honeyclients do not require the full application or operating system to be running, they are lightweight in nature and are typically easier to deploy.

Although high-interaction honeyclients generally give better detection rates and lower false positives, they are more difficult to implement on a large scale due to the amount of resources it takes to deploy a single full system and the exploding combinations of deploying each possible browser type with various configurations. On the other hand, low-interaction honeyclients are generally simpler to deploy on a large scale due to their lower resource overhead and ease of creating different configurations, but they have lower fidelity because they are only implementing a subset of the possible client capabilities. In an attempt to close this gap, hybrid honeyclient implementations have been proposed to gain the advantages of both high-interaction and low-interaction honeyclients. The challenge faced by such hybrid systems is usually in the complexity of combining multiple approaches.

In the following section, we give two examples that show how honeyclients work in detail. Note that although the particular honeyclients we discuss are designed with certain unique features, they reflect many of the common design elements shared by other honeyclient implementations.

Capture-HPC: A High-Interaction Honeyclient

Capture-HPC is a popular open-source implementation of a high-interaction honeyclient. It uses a dedicated virtual machine running Windows and Internet Explorer to interact with suspected malware webpages and monitors the system for unauthorized state changes to detect attacks. There is no other user activity occurring on the virtual machine, so activities that are not typical of normal web browsing behavior—such as sensitive file system changes or modification of registry key entries—can be flagged as strong indications of malware exploiting the web browser.

Capture-HPC is implemented using client-server architecture. The Capture-HPC clients are specially instrumented Windows executables and reside inside the guest operating systems to drive the browser and detect activity. A VMware ESXi server is used to host a number of Capture-HPC clients and is managed by the Capture-HPC server, which runs on a separate host. The Capture-HPC server communicates with both the VMware servers and the Capture-HPC clients via TCP using XML messages. For example, the Capture-HPC server can instruct a client to open a specific browser and visit a particular website. The server can also request the client to send activity data back to it for further processing. Capture-HPC uses the VMware APIs to communicate with the VMware server to control each of the guest VM instances, such as starting and stopping a VM instance. In the event that a Capture-HPC client detects and reports malware, the guest operating system is then considered infected, and the Capture-HPC server will instruct the VMware server to restore the guest VM to a clean snapshot before dispatching further tasks to that Capture-HPC client. Figure 5-6 illustrates the structure of the Capture-HPC system.

The Capture-HPC client detects malware by monitoring changes on the file system, the Windows registry, and the running processes. To do so, special kernel drivers are installed on the guest operating system. These kernel drivers implement a set of kernel callback functions, which are invoked when certain events occur during execution. In Capture-HPC's implementation, four callback functions are provided to monitor the system state: `CmRegistryCallback`, `FilterLoad`, `FltRegisterFilter`, and `PsSetCreateProcessNotifyRoutine`. When the Capture-HPC client program starts, it loads the kernel drivers together with a user space buffer. When a monitored event is received, the drivers invoke the callback functions and copy the actual event information to the buffer so that the client program can process it in user space. It is possible that certain events are received as a result of legitimate operations such as writing to the browser's cache, and therefore the events are compared with a whitelist of events and "normal" events are ignored. In addition to communicating with the specialized kernel drivers, the Capture-HPC client also monitors network I/O on the guest VM. It stores the network activity as packet capture files and sends them to the server when malware is detected. Capture-HPC is capable of driving multiple browser instances inside a single VM concurrently in order to parallelize execution and speed up the detection process.

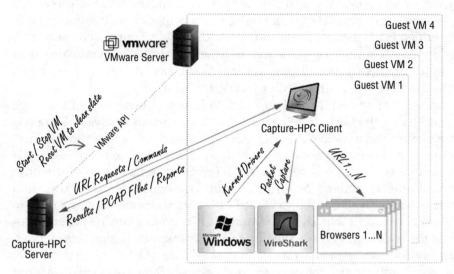

Figure 5-6: Capture-HPC Server/Client VMware Structure

Capture-HPC presents a good example of some of the key design concepts in high-interaction honeyclients:

- High-interaction honeyclients are typically virtual machines-based. This approach makes it easier to start and stop the honeyclients and revert them to a clean state when the system is infected.

- High-interaction honeyclients are instrumented to monitor sensitive system events in order to detect possible evidence of malware infections. Besides the kernel drivers approach seen in Capture-HPC, it is possible to intercept system calls using hooks in the System Service Dispatch Table (SSDT) or to directly hook in Windows API calls inside the browser process. Newer methods of event monitoring, known as *VM introspection*, can even monitor events without modifying the guest operating system at all. These methods achieve event-monitoring goals by instrumenting the virtual machine and inspecting raw CPU instructions, memory, and hard drive to detect sensitive events. By leaving the guest operating system unmodified, VM introspection is harder to detect by malware but requires significantly more effort to detect and understand the context of the events.

Thug: A Low-Interaction Honeyclient

Thug is a popular low-interaction honeyclient implemented in Python. It does not use actual browsers for its analysis but instead mimics the behavior of vulnerable web browsers. In other words, Thug only simulates the core functionality of a web browser without relying on features from the underlying operating system.

Thug works very efficiently using Python to collect and analyze malicious web pages. To emulate different browser configurations in an HTTP request, Thug sends modified HTTP header fields and uses individually configured "personality" components to mimic a specific web browser. The browser personality may also be configured with specific plugin versions such as Java, Flash, or Acrobat, as well as modifying certain DOM or JavaScript behaviors.

A webpage is analyzed using Thug's DOM interpreter when that webpage is retrieved using the URL. It is then prepared for further analysis. Thug has specialized modules to detect exploits for plugins such as Acrobat, Java, Flash, and ActiveX, and can also analyze arbitrary JavaScript code to inspect it for malicious activity. Thug uses the Google V8 JavaScript engine to perform both static and dynamic analysis on all JavaScript code encountered. In this dual approach, static analysis is used to identify high-value locations in the code to insert breakpoints, and then dynamic analysis is used to examine the environment once the code has been executed up to each breakpoint. Using this method, they can perform complex analysis, such as shellcode or heap spray detection, without significantly impacting performance. Because Thug uses a full JavaScript engine and DOM interpreter, it is capable of detecting and handling various types of obfuscation and can construct the page for additional analysis. The parse results usually contain more URLs to be analyzed, which can then be used to gradually crawl the web until an exploit is detected or a depth limit is reached.

Due to the lightweight implementation of Thug, it is possible to further emulate specific vulnerabilities to pinpoint the attack vectors that are otherwise harder to configure using a high-interaction honeyclient. For example, if browser vulnerability is exploited only with certain Windows language packs, it requires a high-interaction honeyclient to load such language packs one by one, which is time consuming. However, with Thug, because the browser is simulated, this requires only a few lines to be changed in the personality profiles.

Designing honeyclients to detect malware has drawn the attention of researchers from all over the globe, and there are many additional implementations not discussed in this chapter. For more information, visit The Honeynet Project website, which maintains a list of historical and ongoing honeyclient projects.

Evading Honeyclients

Honeyclients face many challenges when deployed to combat malware. In particular, they are prone to detection and evasion. Malware can adopt certain evasion techniques to detect whether a honeyclient is running and then modify its behavior to avoid detection, such as attacking only if the malware cannot detect the presence of the honeyclient.

VMware ESXi server has become a key ingredient in the migration to cloud computing. Because the majority of high-interaction honeyclients run on virtual machines, VMware ESXi makes a perfect virtualization environment to facilitate honeyclient implementations. Although cloud-based applications are likely running on an ESXi-based virtual machine, however, regular end users running the browser are likely to be in a non-virtualized environment. The malware tries to detect the presence of VMware ESXi before deciding whether to attack.

Although the JavaScript and HTML provided by the malware cannot directly access the file system, it is nonetheless possible to exploit certain dated browsers or new browser vulnerability to check the existence of certain files. In the ESXi case, one file to check for is `C:\Program Files\VMware\VMware Tools\vmtoolsd.exe`. To perform such a check, the malware page simply tries to load the VMware file as a source script. If the file does not exist, JavaScript throws a runtime error; otherwise, the file is found and loaded. Obviously, although JavaScript cannot load the binary file because of incorrect file format, it nonetheless offers a viable way to detect if the system is running on top of VMware ESXi. Because no actual attack is launched, this type of file existence check is usually overlooked. To avoid browser caching, some random data, such as current time, is appended to the filename of the checked file. The JavaScript snippet is listed as follows:

```
var is_esxi = 1;
var el = document.createElement('script');
el.id = "111";
el.type = "text/Javascript";
el.src = "res://C:\\Program%20Files\\VMware%20Tools\\vmtoolsd.exe";
el.src += "?"+new Date().getTime()+Math.floor(Math.random()*1000000);
el.onerror=function(){if (el.onerror) is_exsi = 0;};
document.getElementByTagName("head")[0].appendChild(el);
```

Using the preceding concept, the malware page can also detect whether a honeyclient is installed on the system. For example, in Capture-HPC, the executable file of the honeyclient is located at `C:\Program Files\Capture\CaptureClient.exe`. Similarly, if the honeyclient requires certain DLL files, the malware page can check for their existence as well. Honeyclients will not have enough protection from this type of file existence detection without dynamically naming their required files and moving them around.

More advanced VM detection mechanisms enable a browser to intelligently determine if it is running on a VM. *Red pills* refer to code that is designed specifically for detecting if it is running inside a VM or a CPU emulator. Browser-based red pills monitor the timing difference in I/O operations, thread operations including thread creation and inter-thread communication, and graphics rendering. When the same operation is performed repeatedly over thousands of times, completion time variations start to emerge, depending on whether the browser is running on a native physical host or on a virtual machine. Browser-based red pills are easily coded using JavaScript and can be used by malware pages to detect the existence of the underlying VM. The honeyclient would need to be able to first evaluate the JavaScript content of the webpage in order to detect the presence of browser-based red pills.

Various countermeasures have been proposed and put into practice in honeyclients to avoid malware evasion and detection against virtual machines. A hypervisor is a combination of software and firmware that together facilitates the creation and execution of virtual machines. A Type-1 hypervisor, also known as a bare-metal hypervisor, runs directly on top of the hardware and manages the hardware directly to facilitate the execution of a guest operating system. The guest operating system accesses the underlying hardware through the hypervisor. VMware ESXi server is a typical example of a Type-1 hypervisor. A Type-2 hypervisor is one that runs inside a conventional operating system. The regular operating system owns and manages the underlying hardware. With a Type-2 hypervisor the guest operating system accesses the underlying hardware first through the hypervisor, followed by the hypervisor accessing the hardware through the hosting OS. VMware client is a representative example of a Type-2 hypervisor.

To avoid malware detection against Type-2 hypervisors, *transparent* analysis systems are proposed to run the honeyclients directly on bare-metal hardware. Because the transparent systems do not have in-guest monitoring components, detection is done by comparing the disk-level statistics with the initial clean state. Such comparison and analysis is non-trivial and difficult to perform in real-time. In addition, user activities are difficult to simulate on transparent systems, which can sometimes be used by malware to detect the honeyclients.

Cloaking is another common approach malware employs to avoid detection by a honeyclient. By cloaking, the malware pages do not launch attacks and act as if they are benign if some conditions are met. For example, the malware page may match the User-Agent type in the HTTP header to a list of exploitable browsers and only choose to launch a drive-by download attack if the User-Agent matches one on the list. In addition, the Referer value in the HTTP header indicates where the URL link comes from. A malware campaign may keep a list of domains and host names where the malicious links are hosted on and check the HTTP Referer value on the requests from the honeyclient. If they do not match the expected Referer values, then the attack is not launched. Oftentimes in a honeyclient implementation, the malicious URLs are compiled by an external database and fed to the browser instances for an exploitation check. Although it is feasible to program certain HTTP header values, such as the User-Agent, it is not always possible to do so for every possible combination. After all, the honeyclient cannot set certain fields in the header, such as the referer, if it does not know what the expected values are.

The following code snippet is an exploit, found in the wild, which avoids the honeyclients. The code issues a load of an ActiveX control object, called *yutian*, which simply is known to be nonexistent. When the browser loading fails, that exception is caught by the wrapper code that subsequently executes the obfuscated true malicious code. Such honeyclient avoidance techniques can easily defeat a low-interaction honeyclient because the honeyclient itself usually emulates the library API calls of ActiveX and does not catch exceptions; thus, the malware remains dormant within the honeyclients.

```
try {
  new ActiveXObject("yutian");
} catch (e) {
var nop="%uyt9yt2yt9yt2";
var nop=(nop.replace(/yt/g,""));
var sc0="%ud5db%uc9c9%u87cd...";
var sc1="%"+"yutianu"+"ByutianD"+ ...;
var sc1=(sc1.replace(/yutian/g,""));
var sc2="%"+"u"+"54"+"FF"+...+"8"+"E"+"E";
var sc2=(sc2.replace(/yutian/g,""));
var sc=unescape(nop+sc0+sc1+sc2);
}
```

There are numerous other evasion techniques that malware uses to invalidate or cripple the honeyclient. In one interesting trick, the malware hibernates until the mouseover event to trigger the attack. This works because real users almost certainly move the mouse around when browsing, while honeyclients do not. Moreover, a technique called *Reflective DLL injection* can remotely load a malicious library from the shellcode and create a thread attached to the running browser. Because no new process is spawned, the additional thread is created unnoticed. The newly created thread can then potentially participate in a botnet until the browser process is terminated. This type of evasion does not access the file system or modify the running processes and thus can defeat many high-interaction honeyclients like Capture-HPC. The evasion is further complemented by *browser cache poisoning*, in which the cached JavaScript files are edited and appended with a code snippet that redirects the browser to fetch the injection library. This evasion will succeed even after browser restarts or even reboots.

Code obfuscation is one of the most common techniques to evade malware detection. By adding code obfuscation, the malicious piece of code is hidden in a chunk of scrambled scripts. The obfuscated code is still executable but is much harder for a human to read, understand, and reverse-engineer.

Summary

The malnet detection methodologies and approaches we have discussed in this chapter are fundamental knowledge in building malware and malnet defense systems. In practice, no single solution is capable of detecting all types and variations of malwares or malnets. Therefore, building a multi-layered detection and defense system that is comprised of different techniques, as depicted in Figure 5-7, is essential in combating today's threats.

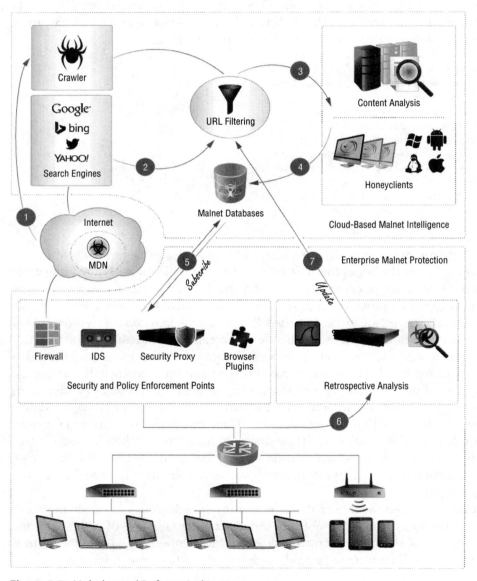

Figure 5-7: Multi-layered Defense Architecture

In the example solution system of malnet intelligence, crawlers constantly crawl (①) the web for malicious URLs that lead to an MDN. The URLs are filtered and fed into search engines to explore other related malicious URLs (②). With the captured list of malicious URL candidates, content analysis systems and other detection systems (③) are employed to detect malware and probe malnets. The results are composed in a database (④). The processes repeat perpetually and these components become the cornerstones of the cloud-based malnet intelligence. Enterprises are ideal subscribers of this cloud-based malnet intelligence (⑤) service. Security and privacy enforcement points—such as firewalls, secure proxies and web gateways, IDS, browser plugins, and so on—that either are located inside the perimeters of the enterprise network or reside in the end user hosts can obtain real-time updates from the malnet intelligence service to constantly protect enterprise users from malware attacks. On the other hand, the enterprises are contributors to building better and more comprehensive malnet intelligence. The on-premise malware retrospective analysis systems mine the enterprise network traffic (⑥) and proactively collaborate with (⑦) the malnet intelligence cloud to identify new threats. We discuss retrospective analysis systems in Chapter 8.

Writing Policies

A secure proxy possesses detailed knowledge about specific protocols and applications. This knowledge enables a proxy to examine network traffic thoroughly, conduct deep content analysis, perform data transformation, and manipulate connections and transactions, essentially applying every technique at its disposal to enforce defined security policies. A proxy is deployed at a vantage point that enables it to filter undesirable payloads, alert network administrators and security teams of policy violations, log user activities, and prevent confidential information leakage.

A proxy is commonly deployed collaboratively with other security solutions such as a data loss prevention solution, antivirus engine, and sandbox malware analyzer, and with systems that are essential to enterprise network operations such as an authentication server and a mail server. Together, these solutions offer a unified and layered security defense infrastructure against modern-day cyber threats conjured by black hats.

Chapter 3 examines the inner workings of a secure proxy's policy engine and discusses the general concepts behind a policy system, its policy language, and the intricacies of policy execution against transactions. In this chapter, we will provide example scenarios with specific security goals and explain how to implement those security goals using a real-world secure policy system.

Overview of the ProxySG Policy Language

In this chapter, we use the Blue Coat ProxySG policy language as our primary reference for discussing the constructs of a policy language. Examples that are shown in normal font are available in the ProxySG policy language, while examples that are shown in *italics* are conceptual policies that are not found in ProxySG. Let us first define the important terms that we will use frequently throughout this chapter:

- *Transaction* – A *transaction* is an *information container* that encapsulates the client request, server response, transaction processing states, policy decisions, and variables that provide runtime information that is gathered from the client-request and the server-response for the purpose of policy evaluation and enforcement. The transaction object is created when the proxy first intercepts a client request, and a set of default policy decisions are set in the transaction.

- *Condition* – A *condition* is a logical expression that tests one or more variables against specific values. If a match is found, then the logical expression evaluates to true; otherwise, it evaluates to false. The variable is called a *condition variable*. Examples of condition variables are "user login time" (user.login.time), "virus detected" (virus_detected), and "content category of the request URL" (server_url.category).

- *Property* – A *property* is a setting that controls how the proxy processes a transaction. Examples of properties are "authenticate user in a specified realm" (authenticate(yes)) and "request client certificate during SSL negotiation" (client.certificate.require(yes)). The value of a property is set when its associated condition evaluates to true. For example, this policy states that "if the user is Bob" (testing condition "user" against value "Bob"), then require the client to include its certificate during the SSL negotiation phase.

- *Rule* – A *rule* contains a set of conditions and properties. All of the properties are set if all the conditions in this rule evaluate to true. The order of the conditions and properties in a rule is irrelevant, but rules are executed sequentially.

- *Layer* – A *policy layer* is a logical container that groups a set of rules, where one decision will be made out of all the rules in the same layer. A layer starts with a layer name enclosed in < >, and it is named according to the policy engine component that executes the rules in that layer. For example, a <proxy> layer contains policy rules that control the transaction, and an <admin> layer contains policy rules that apply to management of the proxy device. Because a layer stops processing once a decision can be made, the order of the rules in a layer is important. The more specific rules should come before the less specific rules.

▪ *Definition* – A *definition* is a collection of conditions, policies, or other policy-related objects, which is customized to provide clarity and context so that this definition can be referenced in a policy rule by its alias in order to simplify the syntax and to facilitate *code reuse*. For example, if a condition matches an IP address against a list of predefined IP addresses, then it is generally a good idea to separately define this list of IP addresses as a definition and appropriately name the list as "IP Addresses in Building A" or "Finance Department".

A policy can be generalized to have the following format, where N is the number of conditions in a rule, and M is the number of properties in this rule:

```
<layer-1>
condition1.1 condition1.2 … condition1.N
property1.1 property1.2 … property1.M
condition2.1 condition2.2 … condition2.N
property2.1 property2.2 … property2.M
```

All of the conditions and properties in the same rule are implied to be logically connected by an AND relationship, while all of the rules in the same layer are implied to be logically connected by an OR relationship. Therefore, each layer can reach only one decision, even though a decision can consist of multiple properties. Semantically, the policy layer just shown can be interpreted as follows:

```
<layer-1>
    condition1.1 AND condition1.2 … AND condition1.N
    property1.1 AND property1.2 … AND property1.M
OR condition2.1 AND condition2.2 … AND condition2.N
    property2.1 AND property2.2 … AND property2.M
```

Another way to state these rules in the layer is as follows:

```
<layer-1>
    If (condition1.1 is True) AND
       (condition1.2 is True) AND …
       (condition1.N is True)
          Then
              (set property1.1 to value A) AND
              (set property1.2 to value B) AND …
              (set property1.M to value M)
    Else If (condition2.1 is True) AND
           (condition2.2 is True) AND
           (condition2.N is True)
          Then
              (set property2.1 to value A) AND
              (set property2.2 to value B) AND …
              (set property2.M to value M)
```

From this example it is clear that when the number of conditions is large, the policy rule becomes difficult to read and maintain. This is where policy definition becomes useful to bind these conditions into a single set that can be referenced as a whole, as in the following example:

```
define condition CONDITION_GROUP_1
    condition1.1
    condition1.2
    condition1.3
    ...
    condition1.N
end

<layer-1>
condition=CONDITION_GROUP_1 property1.1 property1.2 ... property1.M
```

It is also possible to apply a condition to a layer so that every rule in this layer is subject to the evaluation result of this condition. This is called a *layer guard*. The layer guard is a condition that is written on the layer line right after the end of the angle bracket:

```
<layer-1> condition=LAYER_GUARD_CONDITION
condition=CONDITION_GROUP_1 property1.1 property1.2 ... property1.M
```

This is semantically equivalent to applying `condition=LAYER_GUARD_CONDITION` to every rule inside this layer, but the policy engine can typically optimize its execution by skipping the layer entirely when the layer guard condition does not match.

Scenarios and Policy Implementation

Every enterprise defines network usage and Internet web access policies as part of its security posture. These policies govern the online behavior of each enterprise user. For example, they restrict user access to content and websites that are not relevant to employees' job duties or that may be legal liabilities to the enterprise, and they dictate the actions that are executed by the proxy to enforce the defined policies. We will begin with the most basic security policies and gradually evolve the examples into more complicated scenarios as new policy concepts are introduced.

Web Access

In the first example, an enterprise states in its web access policies that employees must not be allowed to access websites that are classified as adult websites because they contain adult content or are gambling sites. The IT security team implements this guideline by first defining the required policies into the proxy as shown in the following policy rules. Note that we include the line numbers in the policy examples so that the annotation can reference the specific rule that is under discussion. These line numbers would not be present in an actual policy file.

```
1 <proxy>
2 url.category="Adult Content" deny
3 url.category="Gambling" deny
4 allow
```

The first two rules (lines ② and ③) state that any transaction that is intercepted by the proxy, which requests web access to a URL that is categorized as either Adult Content or Gambling, must be denied, while all other types of transactions are allowed. If a user tries to access a site that contains adult material, he will get an error page in the browser that indicates that access has been denied. Typically the error page, commonly known as a *coaching page*, contains the reason for denial and advises the user to consult the corporate policies regarding online activities and behaviors. The last rule (line ④) is unconditional; that is, there is no associated condition, and therefore it is always executed by the policy engine. This is known as a *catch-all* statement that acts as the default policy for transactions that do not match a specific rule.

The way this policy is written to broadly allow transactions that do not explicitly match the forbidden categories is user friendly; however, it may introduce security loopholes. A secure proxy should be paranoid about what it does not know and what it cannot see. Having a default *allow* policy is subject to content leakage and may create unintentional access exceptions due to poorly written rules or to simple coding errors in the logics. A more conservative and restrictive security practice, however, is to use *deny-all* as the default statement and explicitly state only those specific activities and content that are permissible.

Now assume the Human Resources (HR) department has enhanced corporate policy to comply with privacy laws without compromising the existing security policies. The HR department demands that anyone who attempts to access inappropriate content should be notified first that this enforcement is in place, and their network activities, when not compliant with company policy, will be logged and reported to HR. Anyone who knowingly continues after having been coached about acting appropriately as an employee constitutes an explicit consent to be monitored because that employee is exhibiting a willingness to violate corporate policies.

```
1 <proxy>
2 service.name=HTTP exception(coaching_page)
3
```

```
4 <proxy>
5 url.category="Adult Content"
     exception(inappropriate_warning_page)
     access_log(inappropriate_log)
6 url.category="Gambling"
     exception(inappropriate_warning_page)
     access_log(inappropriate_log)
7 allow access_log(main_log)
```

The policy now contains two layers: the first layer (the first occurrence of <proxy>) is responsible for presenting the coaching page when any user browses the web; the second layer (the second occurrence of <proxy>) denies access to inappropriate URLs and logs both the URL and the IP address from where the request was issued. In this example, we introduce two new elements of the policy system: multiple layers and the property parameter. In the policy rule on line ②, exception() is a property, and coaching_page is the property parameter. A property parameter such as coaching_page allows a customized web page that contains more information regarding the transaction to be displayed to the end user.

Recall that a layer is a logical group that binds multiple policy statements within a context, and only the first statement with matching conditions is executed. In this case the first required action to be applied after intercepting a web connection is to present a coaching page to inform the user that accessing inappropriate content will be logged. The coaching page should give each user an opportunity to review the privacy agreement and decide whether to accept the terms. Policy layers enhance the structure of the policy design by facilitating a clear logical separation of the different conditions and actions that should be applied to different stages of a transaction. For example, the coaching page is presented to the user at the very beginning of the transaction, at the connection establishment phase. Upon intercepting an HTTP connection, instead of directly contacting the server, the proxy interrupts the transaction by serving an *exception page* (line ②). An exception page is essentially a web page that is generated and served by the proxy to inform the user of why it is unable to fulfill a request. The same mechanism is used to inform the user that a monitoring device is put in place, and the "Yes" and "No" buttons for "Accept terms and conditions" are embedded inside the exception page for the user to choose from.

The policy statement on line ⑤ contains one condition and two actions. A simple *deny* action is now replaced by an action to "generate an exception page", and the parameter for this action specifies that the content for the exception page comes from inappropriate_warning_page. The parameter tells the policy engine to deny web access by presenting a warning page, whereas the previous deny action simply closes the connection. This exception page in the second policy layer is not interactive, and the user request is terminated once the exception page is served to the user's browser. The second action in this policy rule records the user request to the access log file named "inappropriate_log", which is a separate log file intended to contain only users who have attempted to access inappropriate content. Any other web access is permitted and is logged in the main access log as defined on line ⑦.

Line ⑤ and line ⑥ are essentially the same policy except for the matching category. The number of URL categories can quickly become too large to manage this way. A better approach is to combine these rules and create a *combined condition* such as this:

```
define condition inappropriate
    url.category="Adult Content"
    url.category="Gambling"
end
```

The combined condition can transform the rules on line ⑤ and line ⑥ into a single statement:

```
condition=inappropriate
    deny(inappropriate_warning_page)
    access_log(inappropriate_log)
```

Access Logging

The proxy access log is an important data repository containing the history of transactions, on which analysis can be performed to derive user activities and behaviors. The proxy administrator specifies which pieces of information from the transaction are written to the access log at the end of each transaction.

An access log has a structured format. The *Extended Log File Format* (ELFF) is widely adopted by various types of security devices including ProxySG. With an ELFF-formatted access log, each log line corresponds to a transaction. Each log line contains a list of *field identifiers*, or just *fields*, with each field corresponding to a transaction variable. For example, the following access log tracks the client IP address, time of the request, and server URI:

```
#Fields: time c-ip s-uri
00:01:23 192.168.1.10 /login.html
```

In this log, time, c-ip, and s-uri are referred to as the transaction variables, namely, the time when a transaction began, the client's IP address, and the requested URI. Every field consists of a prefix, such as c or s, and an identifier, such as ip or uri, connected by a hyphen (-). The prefix c indicates that the field belongs to the client side of the transaction, while the prefix s indicates that the field belongs to the server side of the transaction. Although all of the possible prefixes are given in the following list, the number of possible combinations of prefix and identifier is too large to enumerate here. Always refer to the ProxySG product manual for a complete listing of fields that are suitable for capturing the desired information.

- c refers to the client.
- s refers to the server from the client's perspective; the physical endpoint for s could be the proxy.
- r refers to the server (remote destination) from the proxy's perspective; this is the original destination of the client's request.
- cs is client to server, from the client's perspective.
- sc is server to client, from the client's perspective.
- rs is remote destination to proxy, from the proxy's perspective.
- sr is proxy to remote destination, from the proxy's perspective.
- x is the custom identifier.

Notice that there are two prefixes that refer to the destination: s for server, and r for remote. The *server prefix* refers to the server (or destination) part of the incoming connection that is originated from the client; the *remote prefix* refers to the server (or destination) part of the outbound connection that is originated from the proxy. The s-ip and r-ip fields may or may not have the same value, depending on the network topology. For example, if the proxy is deployed as an explicit proxy, all of client's web requests are directed towards the proxy's IP address. In this case, s-ip of a transaction is the proxy's IP address, and r-ip is the original web server's IP address. If a proxy is deployed transparently inline, the s-ip field and the r-ip field may be identical.

Access logs are typically used to analyze and discover events that have taken place. The amount of information that may be derived from the access log depends on the number of fields in a given transaction that have been selected by the security team for access logging. Having detailed information about a transaction is important, but how such information is going to be leveraged is unknown when the access log is created. The following is an example list of fields that have been selected for access logging:

```
date time time-taken c-ip sc-status s-action sc-bytes \
cs-bytes cs-method cs-uri-scheme cs-uri-port cs-uri-path \
cs-uri-query cs-host rs-content-type \
cs-user-agent sc-filter-category s-ip r-ip
```

Most of the field identifiers are self-explanatory based on the prefix and the field name. Let's take a sample log entry based on this field selection list to illustrate how we can read the access log to extract useful information about a specific transaction:

```
2014-12-10 21:40:19 78 10.9.45.28 200 TCP_NC_MISS 1025 1916 GET http 80
/.element/ssi/www/breaking_news/3.0/banner.html ?s=25ea5t1a www.cnn.com
text/html "Mozilla/5.0 (Windows NT 6.1; WOW64) AppleWebKit/537.36
(KHTML, like Gecko) Chrome/39.0.2171.71 Safari/537.36"
News/Media 10.9.45.21 63.140.35.161
```

This log entry provides enough information to reconstruct what happened in this transaction. Based on *date* and *time*, we know that this transaction occurred on December 10, 2014, at 21:40:19. The total time taken to complete the transaction, provided by the *time-taken* field, was 78 milliseconds. This transaction was initiated from a client machine with IP address 10.9.45.28 based on the value of the *c-ip* field. From the value (TCP_NC_MISS) of the *s-action* field we can deduce that the proxy examined the server response and discovered that the origin server requested that the proxy not cache the returned content. This server-to-client data transfer totaled 1025 bytes, while client-to-server data transfer totaled 1916 bytes according to *sc-bytes* and *cs-bytes*, respectively. The next six fields—*cs-method, cs-uri-scheme, cs-uri-port, cs-uri-path, cs-uri-query*, and *cs-host*—together allow us to reconstruct the request URI, which in this case was

```
http://www.cnn.com/.element/ssi/www/breaking_news/3.0/
banner.html?s=25ea5t1a
```

The field *rs-content-type* tells us the MIME type of the requested content was "text/html". The browser that requested this page was the Chrome browser, as shown in the *cs-user-agent* field. The URI requested was categorized as "News/Media", as seen in *sc-filter-category*. The server IP was the proxy's IP address, which was 10.9.45.21, given by s-ip; the original content server's IP address was 63.140.35.161, given by the r-ip field.

Although this access log contains a lot of useful information if the objective is to track which user accessed what content at any given time, during a virus outbreak this log does not provide sufficient data to determine which devices may have retrieved malicious content and which servers may have been compromised. When a proxy and a dedicated virus scan appliance are deployed as a collaborative security solution and policies have been written to redirect specific content for scanning by the antivirus appliance, the scanning results can be recorded in the *x-virus-id* field, and the output can be written into a separate log file. Consider the following example policy:

```
1 <content>
2 virus_detected=yes access_log(main_log) access_log(virus_log)
3 access_log(main_log)
```

This example policy produces a "virus_log" file that contains virus scanning–related information, including the field *x-virus-id*. A sample virus log is shown here, which includes the virus identifier of the detected virus, and the URL where the infected content was downloaded:

```
# date time cs-host cs-uri-path rs-content-type s-ip x-virus-id
2014-12-10 21:40:19 www.cnn.com /.element/ssi/www/breaking_news/3.0/
banner.html text/html 63.140.35.161 trojan-virus-1
```

Logging all possible fields for each transaction will consume a considerable amount of CPU resources and memory, as well as disk space. The performance impact depends on the transaction volume being processed by the proxy. Information overload is problematic for security analysts who try to deduce attack vectors and identify victims of malware infection. The large volume of data could overwhelm the security analysts and cause distractions that obscure relevant evidence.

User Authentication

In the previous example, the defined policy indiscriminately disallows any access to web content that is classified as either "Adult Content" or "Gambling". Some websites are generally considered harmful or non-business-related but are acceptable or even essential for a specific group of employees. For example, if a website has been categorized as "Pornography" erroneously and is thus blocked by the proxy, an enterprise user can submit an IT service ticket requesting the website to be unblocked. Then it is up to the IT security team to manually review the website and override the policy by entering the website into a whitelist, if the user has made the correct claim. In this case, certain members of the IT staff should be exempt from the policy restrictions and be allowed to access the content and website that would be restricted otherwise. Similarly, a few employees may have special privileges and special status, and as part of performing their job duties they would be granted special permissions on the web. In the previous section, we wrote the policies that examine the content that is being accessed. In this section, we will design policies that focus on authenticating users and examining user permissions.

Imagine an enterprise that denies any access to web pages that offer hacking-related discussions and topics, possibly due to the elevated risk of downloading malicious content. However, the Engineering department is unable to do its job effectively without access to these sites for conducting threat research. The IT security team is tasked to create an exception for the Engineering department but also to warn of the potential risks before granting access to anyone from engineering. Let's assume that the networks for the Engineering department are physically separated from the networks for all other departments, and therefore the engineering networks are assigned an IP prefix 192.168.1.0/24. The policy now looks like this:

```
1 <proxy> url.category="Hacking"
2 client.address =192.168.1.0/24 exception(coach) allow
  access_log(main_log)
3 deny access_log(main_log)
```

Because this policy layer describes specifically how the proxy should handle sites that contain material related to "Hacking", every rule within this policy layer is applicable only if the given URL category is "Hacking". Therefore, line ① contains the layer guard `url.category="Hacking"`. The rule on line ② states that any client coming from network 192.168.1.0/24 should be presented with a coaching page warning the user about the danger of visiting such websites and that the transaction is logged but access permission is granted. For everyone else, the access is denied, and the request is logged (line ③).

This policy solution has two main limitations. For example, assume Alice is an employee from the Engineering department. The first limitation is that the policy rule on line ② restricts Alice to be physically connected to the engineering network if she wants to access "Hacking" sites, even when Alice is onsite and in the building. For example, she will not be able to do her research work if she mainly uses her laptop computer and she is in the lunchroom, which is connected to the corporate WiFi network. This is because the corporate WiFi network will have an IP address prefix that is different from that of the engineering network, which will cause the policy to block Alice's computer while she is on the corporate WiFi.

The second limitation is that the proxy cannot log user information regardless of whether the transaction is permitted. Enterprise networks typically deploy DHCP to assign dynamic IP addresses to attached devices. Although DHCP attempts to assign the same IP address to the same device each time, there is no definitive correlation between an IP address and its user. Clearly we need a better mechanism to identify the users.

Authentication is the process of verifying a user against their claimed identity, by challenging the user to present credentials or confidential information that only that user possesses. Authorization refers to the permissions and rights that have been granted to a user, which allow that user to perform actions and retrieve content within the confines of defined policies. A proxy performs user authentication by challenging the user for their username and password through a *captive portal*. With a captive portal, a proxy presents a login page and asks the user to enter their login credentials each time the user opens the web browser and tries to connect to a website, if that user has not been authenticated previously. We call this authentication method "local authentication" if the proxy keeps a database of usernames and passwords on the proxy appliance. User-entered credentials are matched against the proxy's local authentication database. For example, suppose an enterprise is providing a guest WiFi network for visitors. Every visitor is required to obtain a temporary username and password from the front desk in order to log into the guest WiFi. The following policy is written to deny any unauthenticated access:

```
1 <proxy>
2 authenticated=no deny
```

If the authentication fails, the condition `authenticated=no` remains true, subsequent requests are denied, and the proxy continues to present the user with the captive portal login page. Consider the following policy:

```
1 <proxy>
2 authenticate(local_realm) authenticate.mode(ip) refresh_time(300)
3
4 <proxy>
5 authenticated=no deny
6 allow
```

An *authentication realm* is a group of network resources that allow the proxy to query and authenticate a user. In this example, `local_realm` indicates that the authentication credentials are stored locally on the proxy. The authentication mode indicates that the IP address of the device is cached so that every connection with the same source IP address will be authenticated. This cached IP address is called a *surrogate credential* because this IP address will serve as the user's credentials and the proxy will challenge the user less frequently. We do not want to keep this cache indefinitely; otherwise, after this guest has left the building, another guest may have come in and pick up the same IP address, which would then bypass the authentication mechanism. We determine that 15 minutes of inactivity is a reasonable assumption that the user has logged out and is necessary to re-challenge the user, and so the `refresh_time(300)` policy property is written.

In the previous example, the local authentication realm provided a user challenge mechanism, but additional information, such as a user's job title, department, or geographic location, was missing. A *Lightweight Directory Access Protocol* (LDAP) can be used to store user information with additional attributes in a hierarchical manner. An example LDAP entry that describes user "John Smith" in the Engineering department looks like the following:

```
dn: uid=John,ou=Engineering,cn=thecompany,dc=com
objectClass: inetOrgPerson
uid: jsmith
sn: Smith
givenName: John
cn: john.smith
organizationUnit: Engineering
```

```
displayName: John Smith
uidNumber: 10000
gidNumber: 5000
userPassword: js1234
```

An LDAP entry consists of a number of attribute-value pairs. The dn attribute stands for *distinguished name* and is a unique attribute that is mandatory to position this entry in the LDAP database. There are a number of fields in the dn attribute: the uid field stands for *user id*; the ou field stands for *organizational unit*; and the cn field stands for *common name*. The last dc field, *domain component*, typically defines what kind of organization the company is, following the Internet domain convention, such as .com for a commercial organization or .gov for government. In this example, uid=John specifies the person, who is part of the Engineering department given by ou=Engineering, which is part of a company, thecompany.

The next field, objectClass, defines the list of attributes necessary to describe this entry. The inetOrgPerson object class holds information about people and contains attributes such as name, uid for *unique identifier*, gid for *group identifier*, and user password. Other object classes have a different set of required fields, but we are interested only in inetOrgPerson for the purpose of user authentication.

In order to communicate and retrieve user information from the LDAP server, the client must *bind* with the server. This step requires the client to authenticate with the LDAP server, and the LDAP server will authorize the client based on access privilege. The detailed user information is communicated back to the client when access is granted. In the context of proxy authentication, the proxy is the LDAP client, and the LDAP server can be an on-box or external server hosting the LDAP database.

LDAP defines an organization layout for storing information; however, it does not dictate how the client utilizes this information. As part of integrating LDAP authentication with the proxy for the purpose of authentication and retrieving group information, the policy must instruct the proxy on which attributes to use when matching username information and user group conditions. In other words, a policy instructs the proxy to match a user-provided username against givenName "John", uid "jsmith", or cn "john.smith". Similarly, a policy decides if the user-supplied group information is matched against gidNumber "5000" or organizationUnit "Engineering". The username needs to be globally unique for the purpose of authentication. For Windows Active Directory, the attribute sAMAccountName is used because it specifies the Windows login name. For LDAP it is possible to use the cn attribute or another custom attribute as long as the value is unique. Similarly, the group name can be any attribute value as long as it is uniquely identifiable.

Returning to the first example at the beginning of the section, this time the company has revised the policy to leverage LDAP information instead of relying on the physical location (or IP prefix) to define accessibility. Assume the authentication realm is called "LDAP_Realm". The stored username is retrieved from the cn attribute, and the stored group value is retrieved from the organizationUnit attribute. The following example shows the enhanced policies. An additional rule ⑥ states that any employee who attempts to access sports-related content during working hours from 9 a.m. to 5 p.m. is denied and logged.

```
1 <proxy>
2 authenticate(LDAP_Realm) ldap.user_attribute("cn")
    ldap.group_attribute("organizationUnit")
3
4 <proxy>
5 authenticated=no deny access_log(unauthorized_log)
6 url.category="Sports" time=0900..1700 deny access_log(main_log)
7 url.category="Hacking" group="Engineering" exception(coach) allow
    access_log(main_log)
8 url.category="Hacking" deny access_log(main_log)
```

With this policy, an unsuccessfully authenticated user will trigger the condition authenticated=no to be evaluated to *true* and the proxy denies the access. But if the user logs in correctly, then the value of the organizationUnit is retrieved as the group name that can be referenced in other policy rules. Notice that the authentication rule is contained in a separate policy layer. Recall that policy execution in each layer results in exactly one decision; putting the authentication rule together with all the other access rules will not work. The following policy is written incorrectly:

```
1 <proxy>
2 authenticate(LDAP_Realm)
3 url.category="Sports" time=0900..1700 deny access_log(main_log)
4 url.category="Hacking" group="Engineering" exception(coach) allow
    access_log(main_log)
5 url.category="Hacking" deny access_log(main_log)
```

In this case, policy execution will never reach the rules between line ③ and line ⑤. The reason is because for every new transaction, the authentication rule on line ② is executed unconditionally, thus causing the layer to exit once that rule completes.

Suppose Bob, the CEO of the company, is a baseball fan. He complains to the IT department that he is unable to check the scores of his favorite teams during the day. In addition, World Cup 2014 begins on 6/12/2014 and ends on 7/13/2014. During this time, the company decides to open up the sports websites. The new policy is then updated to reflect these changes. Notice that we use the ¡ notation to indicate the negation of a condition. The rule on line ⑤ denies access to any sports websites, unless it is Bob or for the duration of the World Cup games.

```
1 <proxy>
2 authenticate(LDAP_Realm)
3
4 <proxy>
5 url.category="Sports" user=!Bob date=!WorldCup2014 time=0900..1700
    deny access_log(log1)
6 url.category="Hacking" group="Engineering" exception(coach) allow
    access_log(main_log)
7 url.category="Hacking" deny access_log(main_log)
8
9 define condition WorldCup2014
10 date = 20140612..20140713
11 end
```

This policy is actually flawed. The policy rule on line ⑦ is not conditioned on any authentication group. Because the URL category can be determined based on the first HTTP request, the URL category-related policies are executed before authentication-related policies. This means that the rule on line ⑦ is always evaluated before the rule on line ②. Furthermore, the access log will not contain any user information because user authentication did not take place. A policy property called `force_authenticate` was designed to overcome this issue and instructs the proxy to perform the authentication procedure regardless of whether the transaction would be allowed or denied:

```
1 <proxy>
2 force_authenticate(LDAP_Realm)
```

With this new policy, user authentication always takes place in the early stages of a transaction, and the access log will contain the user information even if the transaction is denied.

An LDAP entry can store any arbitrary information. For example, the IT department may sometimes need to lock out a selected number of employees, and this can be done easily by adding the following rules to lock out users John and Bob:

```
1 <proxy>
2 authenticate(LDAP_Realm)
3
4 <proxy>
5 condition=black_list deny
6 allow
7
8 define condition black_list
```

```
 9 user=Bob
10 user=John
11 end
```

Alternatively, the company's LDAP server can be configured with a special attribute called `userLockout` in the user LDAP entry, and this attribute can be referenced in the following policy:

```
1 <proxy>
2 authenticate(LDAP_Realm)
3
4 <proxy>
5 ldap.attribute.userLockout=1 deny
6 allow
```

Using the new LDAP attribute, this policy can lock out a user by simply changing the attribute value in the user entry on the LDAP server. The policy rules remain unchanged, and the proxy automatically picks up the change in the lockout policy at runtime during the user authentication process.

LDAP was designed as a protocol to provide access to directory information services, and because LDAP can store and maintain user authentication information, it was later adopted as an authentication method. For this reason, LDAP is not considered as a secure authentication mechanism unless it operates over a secure transport layer such as SSL or TLS. Other types of authentication servers, such as Kerberos and RADIUS servers, can also be deployed with a proxy.

Kerberos is an authentication protocol that was designed to avoid sending user passwords over an unsecured network. The username is transmitted from the proxy to the authentication server (AS) in plain text. Both the proxy and the AS generate secret keys using the same cipher suite configured on the server. These secret keys, one in the hands of the proxy and the other in the hands of the AS, are used to symmetrically decrypt subsequent messages. If the secret keys do not match, the proxy is unable to decrypt the message given by the AS, and the authentication process fails; otherwise, the proxy decrypts the first message from the AS to find a timed ticket, called a *Ticket-Granting-Ticket* (TGT). The authentication process completes when the proxy successfully decrypts the TGT message. This ticket will be used in all subsequent proxy-to-AS communications. It is desirable to combine Kerberos and LDAP to take advantage of Kerberos' strong authentication architecture and LDAP's wealth of user information.

RADIUS stands for *Remote Authentication Dial In User Service* and provides full Authentication, Authorization, and Accounting (AAA) for user management. A user does not directly communicate with the RADIUS server; instead, a separate network entity called the Network Access Server (NAS) acts as the RADIUS client. As the name suggests, RADIUS was originally designed to provide authentication for remote dial-up users. When a user first establishes the network connection, the router challenges the user to authenticate. This router is the NAS. It takes the user-provided username and password, communicates with the RADIUS server, and either allows or denies subsequent network access by this user.

Safe Content Retrieval

One of the main goals of a secure proxy is to protect users from malicious content. In Chapter 5 we discuss URL categorization and content rating algorithms, which a proxy leverages to prevent users from reaching risky websites and compromised servers. Prevention is a great practice, and although these algorithms strive to be accurate in identifying sources of malicious content, perfect solutions that completely isolate users from malware do not exist. Well-devised malware requires only a few victims to spread its infection on a broad scale. The security posture is to assume such an infection has already taken place on the network, and continuous detection is the key to stop its propagation. Performing a thorough malware scan is computationally intensive, especially on an inline proxy, and thus is not a scalable solution. Mid-size and large enterprises implement security practices that include installing virus-scan solutions on the endpoints such as workstations and laptops, but they lack coverage on mobile devices. Also, not all users are diligent when it comes to keeping up with and applying the latest software updates.

Due to these factors and to mitigate threats at the enterprise level, a common approach is to acquire and deploy a dedicated virus- and malware-scanning appliance on the network; this is then combined with the proxy to form a single solution to find users that are prone to problematic content, and to stop malicious content from entering the network. The proxy operates inline and the antivirus appliance is attached to the proxy in a spoke configuration, as shown in Figure 3-12.

Corporate-wide security policies that have been designed on the proxy decide which content will be transferred to the antivirus (AV) appliance for scanning. The proxy communicates with the AV appliance over the Internet Content Adaptation Protocol (ICAP). ICAP operates with a request followed by a response model, similar to HTTP. ICAP allows an ICAP client to send HTTP messages to an ICAP server, which may then perform various transformations or specific processing, called *adaptations*, on those received messages. One possible adaptation is a virus- and malware-scanning service.

ICAP allows for HTTP *request modification* (or the *REQMOD* mode) and HTTP *response modification* (or the *RESPMOD* mode). In REQMOD mode, the ICAP client sends the ICAP server an HTTP request. The ICAP server can modify the HTTP request and send back the modified request to the ICAP client, or the ICAP server can return an HTTP response. It is possible for the ICAP server to return an error. In RESPMOD mode, the ICAP client sends the ICAP server an HTTP response. The ICAP server can send back either a modified response or an error. In the context of ICAP operation, the proxy acts as the ICAP client, and the AV appliance acts as the ICAP server when servicing a user transaction. For example, when the proxy sends content that was retrieved from a website to the AV appliance over ICAP in RESPMOD mode, the AV appliance may detect a virus embedded in the content. In this case, the AV appliance returns a modified response containing a simple page that warns the user about the website.

The following policy configures the proxy to send all HTTP content to the AV appliance over ICAP for analysis before it is given to the client. This is done via response modification. By default, the ICAP server listens for service requests on TCP port 1344.

```
1 <content>
2 response.icap_service(antivirus_service_1)
```

The content layer indicates that these rules apply to the server response instead of the client request, as in the case with the `<proxy>` layer. The fundamental difference lies in the policy execution checkpoint. Rules in the `<content>` layer are not evaluated or executed until a server response becomes available. The service `antivirus_service_1` is already configured to perform response modification on any content that is passed to an AV appliance that is reachable at a certain IP address and port. The configuration of `antivirus _ service _ 1` is vendor specific and typically contains the following information:

```
ICAP service:
Name: antivirus_service_1
ICAP version: 1.0
Service URL: icap://10.9.4.1/
Connection timeout: 60
Port: 1344
ICAP method: response modification
```

The name is a unique string that identifies this service. The ICAP version is 1.0 at the time of this writing and is the only version supported. Recall that ICAP is very similar to the HTTP protocol, and it uses the same URL construct except for the protocol part, which is `icap` instead of `http`. The service URL is the request URL issued by the ICAP client (proxy) to the ICAP server (AV appliance). The port is the TCP port on which the ICAP server listens for service requests and is TCP port 1344 by default. The ICAP method defines whether this service processes the user request or the server response. Notice in this policy rule that there is no explicit action that defines how to respond when a virus is detected. What the AV appliance returns over ICAP is either the modified HTTP response or a success status stating that the content is safe to pass on to the client. For example, when the AV appliance declares the content is virus-free, the ICAP response from the AV appliance is

```
ICAP/1.0 204 No Content
```

The proxy sends the content back to the client verbatim upon receiving the 204 status from the AV appliance. However, if a virus has been detected, then the HTTP response is modified and is encapsulated inside the ICAP response with status code 200:

```
ICAP/1.0 200 OK
Date: Mon, 08 Dec 2014 11:16:10 GMT
Connection: close
X-Virus-ID: "Conficker"
ISTag: "E13Td2EFG"
Encapsulated: res-hdr=0, res-body=200

HTTP/1.1 403 Forbidden
Date: Mon, 08 Dec 2014 11:16:00 GMT
Content-Length: 75
Content-Type: text/html
The requested content contains a virus, it has been notified and removed
```

In this case, this exact HTTP response is presented to the client in place of the original content, which is a customized error page containing a simple warning string. The virus ID detected by the ICAP server is returned by the X-Virus-ID header, which can be applied to the proxy policy condition virus-detected. Suppose the IT security team needs to track any activity of the notorious Conficker virus that has gone rampant. In addition to blocking and warning the user that this virus has been detected, this information needs to be sent to the security team for further analysis. The following policy is added to send an e-mail to IT_redalert@company.com:

```
<content>
virus-detected=yes virus-id="Conficker"
  notify_email("IT_redalert@company.com", "conficker found")
```

A keen reader may find this e-mail action to be too specific to one virus type and lacking sufficient information to describe fully what the situation is. A policy rule may contain variables for runtime substitutions, which describe properties of a transaction. For example, it will be useful that the e-mail contains the client's username, IP address, and the accessed URL. This information is readily available in a given transaction and can be easily included as part of the e-mail content:

```
notify_email("IT_redalert@company.com", "virus found", \
  "$(user) accessed URL $(url) that contains a virus $(virus_name)")
```

In this example, we use a single \ to indicate line continuation. The third parameter of the `notify_email` action comprises the e-mail body. A named variable enclosed in `$(variable_name)` is called a *substitution*; these variables are replaced by the corresponding values extracted from the transaction. This policy creates a more complete e-mail notification that contains the username, the actual URL, and information about the identified virus, from which a virus scan report can be generated.

Safe content is more than just blocking viruses. The ICAP response modification we have introduced is a form of *content transformation* that performs content insertion, removal, and modification. Thus far, the discussions on content transformation have focused on virus removal. In other cases, the removed content can be a JavaScript or Microsoft ActiveX plug-in. These active elements are embedded inside regular HTML pages and can automatically trigger browser actions without user interaction.

Suppose a new threat has been found that uses a Java applet to run the malicious content. The IT security team has decided to block Java applets from web pages while allowing all static content to pass through to reduce the chance of infection. A `deny` action stops a user from accessing a web page completely, and thus is not a viable solution here. Furthermore, a critical application that runs on its own website, `mycompany.com`, may need to use a Java applet. The aforementioned security objective can be achieved with the following content transformation policy:

```
1 <proxy>
2 url.domain=!mycompany.com action.strip_java_applets(yes)
3
4 define active_content strip_applets_and_indicate
5       tag_replace applet <<EOT
6             <b>java applet removed</b>
7       EOT
8 end
9
10 define action strip_java_applets
11       transform strip_applets_and_indicate
12 end
```

In this policy, two definitions are used. From line ④ to line ⑧, the definition on `active_content` applies to an HTML page where any HTML tag enclosed by `<applet></applet>` is replaced by the replacement string `<b>java applet removed</b>`. Because the page fits into an HTML format, the replacement is also formatted as HTML. The proxy simply performs a search-and-replace operation on all appearances of said tag. The string `<<EOT` marks the end-of-term and tells the policy compiler where the replacement ends. The second definition from lines ⑩ to ⑫ defines the action. This is a transformation action with only one action defined. In a more general case, there may be multiple actions, in which

case the action definition is the list of all the actions to be executed on the same transaction. The policy rule on line ② has the condition !mycompany.com to make the internal domain an exception to this rule; otherwise, all the Java applets are replaced with a single bolded string.

Note that an action is different from a property. An action defines a process to modify the original content; a property does not change the content but modifies the proxy behavior for a transaction. For example, deny terminates the current transaction, and therefore it is called a property. A transformation modifies the user-requested web page and presents the modified page to the user. Therefore, a transformation is called an action. Other possible actions include modifying the HTTP headers or performing a URL rewrite.

SSL Proxy

Regardless of how thoroughly security policies are designed, expressed, and implemented in an enterprise, these policies provide zero value unless they can be enforced effectively against all possible traffic types on the enterprise networks. SSL/TLS-encrypted traffic circumvents many security defenses unless these secure tunnels can be "cracked" open. A proxy that is capable of terminating an SSL connection and decrypting the payload is called an *SSL Proxy*. In Blue Coat ProxySG, the SSL proxy is one of a number of proxies that make up the ProxySG appliance solution.

An SSL session is comprised of two phases: SSL negotiation and encrypted data transfer. During the negotiation phase, communication takes place in plain text to exchange certificates and encryption settings. Once the two sides are in agreement, the subsequent communication exchange is encrypted. A very common application of SSL is HTTPS, which wraps an HTTP connection inside the SSL, encrypting both client requests and server responses. For a secure web transaction, the client and server communicate via HTTP, except that the HTTP protocol exchanges are carried over encrypted SSL messages.

The SSL proxy can either *tunnel* or *intercept* an SSL session. Recall that *intercept* refers to the procedure of terminating a client connection followed by establishing a server-side connection on behalf of the client. In the context of an SSL proxy, SSL interception refers to decrypting the client-side connection data, possibly modifying the data, and then transferring the resulting data to the server-side SSL connection. In SSL tunneling, the decrypted data from the client side is unmodified, re-encrypted according to what was negotiated on the server-side SSL session, and then transmitted over the server-side SSL connection. In other words, the client data is unmodified when it reaches the server over an SSL tunnel.

TLS (or Transport Layer Security) is based on SSL version 3.0 and was designed as an upgrade to version 3.0; however, TLS 1.0, TLS 1.1, and SSL v3.0 do not have interoperability. SSL v3.0 deployment is still prevalent at the time of this writing. In this section, we will use the terms SSL and TLS interchangeably unless the protocol version is explicitly stated. In late 2014, an SSL vulnerability codenamed "POODLE" was discovered. This vulnerability targets any SSL v3.0 implementation and allows it to modify the SSL payload. Applications that run on SSL v3.0 will be susceptible to this vulnerability.

The solution to POODLE is simple: do not use SSL v3.0, and use TLS 1.0 and later instead. However, this "simple" solution is difficult to implement in practice. The security team needs to identify all of the applications that may be using SSL, and either turn off SSL v3.0 manually or apply a security patch that disallows the use of SSL v3.0 on these servers. For some custom applications, these efforts may involve an engineering team creating and testing a security patch to ensure that these applications no longer use SSL v3.0. In addition, the security team needs to send out security advisories to all employees to disable SSL v3.0 on their browsers, whether Internet Explorer, Chrome, Firefox, or another browser. Still, employees may not fully understand what the security vulnerability entails and what the implications are, and they may put off this task until it is forgotten, leaving these workstations vulnerable to POODLE attacks and compromising business-critical applications.

The SSL proxy solves this problem by detecting possible use of SSL v3.0 during the negotiation phase. The security department can create a policy on their SSL proxy to issue a warning and display a solution page when an application attempts to negotiate a secure session using SSL v3.0, followed by the SSL proxy resetting such a connection:

```
1 <ssl>
2 client.connection.negotiated_ssl_version=SSLV3
  exception(warning_POODLE)
```

In this example, the `warning _ POODLE` exception page contains information about how to disable SSL v3.0 on a browser. Because a user is never able to make the SSL connection without turning off SSL v3.0, this is a much better solution than a security advisory e-mail. Because the SSL negotiation is in plain text, there is no need to decrypt the SSL content to detect the SSL version.

When an employee connects to a social network through an SSL session such as HTTPS, the secure proxy is typically given directives to intercept such a session to check for compliance against corporate policies. However, an enterprise-secure proxy is rarely instructed to intercept an employee's financial transactions due to privacy laws. The following policy reflects the preceding discussion:

```
1 <ssl-intercept>
2 category=!"Financial Services" ssl.forward_proxy(https)
```

The SSL intercept layer contains rules that are specific to making the SSL interception decision. The rule on line ② defines that an SSL connection is intercepted only if its category is not "Financial Services". The property `ssl.foward _ proxy` transfers ownership of this transaction from an SSL proxy to the HTTPS proxy, where the HTTPS-specific conditions can be observed, and properties can be set.

So how does the SSL proxy know the category of a connection when the URL in an HTTPS transaction is not visible until after the SSL interception has taken place and the category is necessary to decide whether the SSL proxy will intercept the connection? It turns out that the URL is not the only information available to categorize a website. In this example policy, a general categorization condition called `category` is used instead of a `url.category` condition. The former retrieves a category by any means necessary, while the latter relies on the URL and nothing else. In this case, the category can be derived from the server certificate's Common Name (CN), observable in plain text during SSL negotiation. For example, the CN in Wells Fargo bank's certificate is `www.wellsfargo.com`. This CN can be matched against the URL categorization database and is determined to be "Financial Services". The CN inside Facebook's certificate is `*.facebook.com` and it is categorized as "Social Network".

Reverse Proxy Deployment

Consider an example where a company is developing a new web-oriented service for its customers. The web service is tested on an internal web server with a hostname `service1.internal.mycompany.com` and an internal private IP address 192.168.1.100. This new web service is developed by multiple teams using different programming languages: Java, JavaScript, Perl, and so on. This company will face two immediate deployment challenges when the time comes to take the service and go live.

The first challenge is that the service will have been developed and tested using an internal hostname. Because the backend code is written by multiple teams, there is the possibility that this internal hostname may be hardcoded in some piece of code or scripts. The task of finding the hardcoded names, replacing those entries, and performing revalidation could be overwhelming and error prone.

The second challenge is about security. Although the web service will have been launched, however, performing security analysis and penetration testing on the new web service will be ongoing while the service evolves. For this reason, the web server that is hosting the new web service will remain completely hidden from external entities and will be visible only within the internal company networks. In other words, service requests originating from the Internet will not reach the new web server directly. A secure proxy that is deployed in the reverse proxy mode can solve these deployment issues.

First, let us assume the new web service has the external-facing URL `https://service.mycompany.com`, and `service.mycompany.com` is registered in the public DNS and is accessible from the Internet. The server hosting `service1` `.mycompany.com` can be reached via `http://service1.internal.mycompany` `.com`, but `service1.mycompany.com` is registered only in the internal DNS servers. The secure proxy is deployed as a reverse proxy inside the DMZ as shown in Figure 6-1.

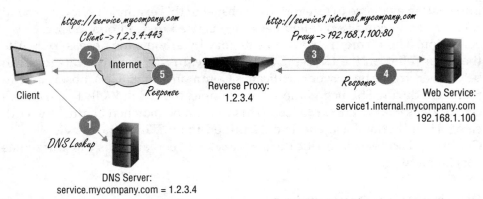

Figure 6-1:   Launching a New Web Service with Reverse Proxy

The client request to `https://service.mycompany.com` first reaches the reverse proxy. The proxy enables client access to the web service by performing *URL rewrite* and *request forwarding*. Upon receiving the client request, the proxy must first correctly determine that `service.mycompany.com` maps to `service1.internal` `.mycompany.com`. Therefore, after intercepting the client request, the proxy will reissue that request to the right internal server; this is known as request forwarding. All URL references to `service.mycompany.com` must be changed to `service1.internal.mycompany.com`, and all relative references must be set to this internal URL; this is known as URL write. In addition, a forwarding policy rule that specifies the URL mapping must be set in the proxy:

```
<forward>
service.name=web_service forward(service1.internal.mycompany.com)
```

In this policy rule, a `forward` layer specifies that this rule is evaluated when the proxy is making an upstream connection. In this example, we assume that the proxy is already configured to process `web_service` requests that are destined for IP address 1.2.3.4 over TCP port 443. Therefore, all connections intended to reach `https://service.mycompany.com` are forwarded to the internal web server that is located at IP address 192.168.1.100 on TCP port 80 for HTTP. From the internal web server perspective, all requests are relative to the URL `service1.internal.mycompany.com`. Therefore, a URL rewrite policy must be defined in the proxy:

```
1 define url_rewrite service1_url_rewrite
2 rewrite_url_prefix "https://service.mycompany.com"
    "http://service1.internal.mycompany.com"
3 end
4
5 define action service1_rewrite
6 rewrite(url, "https://service.mycompany.com/(.*)",
    "http://service1.internal.mycompany.com/$(1)")
7 transform service1_url_rewrite
8 end
9
10 <proxy>
11 service.name=web_service action.service1_rewrite(yes)
12
13 <forward>
14 service.name=web_service forward(service1.internal.mycompany.com)
```

The definition from lines ⑤ to ⑧ consists of two actions. The first action is the URL rewrite, and the second action defines a transformation. As stated earlier, a transformation modifies the content of the server response. Referring to Figure 6-1, the URL rewrite action on line ⑥ modifies the client request from step ② to step ③, while the transform action on line ⑦ modifies the server response from step ④ to step ⑤. The transformation performed by `rewrite_ url _ prefix` is to replace all occurrences of the original URL that are found inside an HTML page to the new URL. For example, take an HTML page such as this:

```
<html><title>login page</title>
<body>
<script src="http://service1.internal.mycompany.com/scripts/util.js">
<p>Login to the service.
</body></html>
```

After the transformation is complete, the revised HTML page is as follows:

```
<html><title>login page</title>
<body>
<script src="https://service.mycompany.com/scripts/util.js">
<p>Login to the service.
</body></html>
```

The process of rewriting both the request URL and the server response is called *two-way URL rewrite*. This type of transformation is necessary because it is inevitable that some web developers will leave absolute URLs inside the web page content, as shown in this example. Not all web developers will conform to the rules of using relative paths such as `<script src="/scripts/util.js">`. The time and effort involved in identifying all occurrences of absolute paths and URL references may be too significant to be feasible. A reverse proxy with content transformation capability offers a viable solution to handle such types of deployment problems.

URL rewrite has other useful applications outside of reverse proxy deployment. For example, suppose a secure proxy is deployed in an elementary school, and the students are learning to search for information on the Internet. However, the school is concerned that students may stumble upon inappropriate search results. We can implement a *safe search* action that performs a URL rewrite that utilizes the "SafeSearch" functionality offered by the Google search engine to alleviate this problem:

```
1 <proxy>
2 url.host.substring=google action.google_safesearch(yes)
3
4 define action google_safesearch
5 rewrite(url, "(.*)", "$(1)&safe=on")
6 end
```

For a Google search, appending the search request with `&safe=on` turns on the safe search feature, which filters out explicit search terms such as "nude" or "porn". In this example, a reverse proxy also performs SSL offloading. A reverse proxy handles SSL decryption at step ② and encryption at step ⑤. All communication between the reverse proxy and the internal web server is in plain HTTP. This eases the load on the web server.

In addition to offloading computationally intensive workloads from a web server, this reverse proxy example demonstrates another important protection that a secure proxy offers: the reverse proxy shields the real web server from being directly accessible by users and sanitizes application requests, including malicious ones, from harming an application. This protection capability is the essence of what is known as a *web application firewall* (WAF). For example, through special crafting of an application's input parameter, a hacker can break the application server's access control and retrieve restricted data.

According to the Open Web Application Security Project (OWASP), the top ten most critical web application security risks for 2013 were injection, broken authentication and session management, cross-site scripting, insecure direct object references, security misconfiguration, sensitive data exposure, missing function level access control, cross-site request forgery, using components with known vulnerabilities, and un-validated redirects and forwards. A secure proxy performs many protective functions as a WAF—with one of the important tasks being identifying known attacks against various applications—and shields applications and application servers from those known vulnerabilities even when those servers have not been patched. Because a secure proxy has in-depth knowledge of an application, the proxy can sanitize user input and application parameters before transferring an application request to the server. This prevents hackers from injecting manipulated data into an application, which causes that application to execute unintended or restricted commands such as creating new user accounts with administrative privileges for the hackers.

DNS Proxy

When a client makes a request for a network service or a network resource, it begins the transaction by first issuing a DNS query that tries to resolve a server name or a URL into an IP address. Deploying a DNS proxy provides the opportunity to analyze the type of resource or service that a client is asking for and prevents such an attempt as early as possible if a policy violation is detected. For example, suppose a company wants to block all access to pornographic websites, which we already know can be achieved by denying access based on the URL category, which is expressed in policy by the condition `url.category`. Alternatively, we can completely stop a client from initiating a TCP connection by intercepting the DNS query and responding to the client with a DNS error:

```
1 <DNS-Proxy>
2 dns.request.category=Pornography dns.respond(refused)
```

A client browser accessing a pornographic website will not succeed due to a name resolution error. Depending on a DNS proxy to block offending client requests is not a reliable method. First, if the client's DNS traffic traverses a path that is not covered by the proxy, then the DNS proxy does not have the opportunity to process any of the client's DNS queries. Second, the user can bypass this policy by directly entering the IP address of the pornographic website. It is for these reasons that such a DNS-based security policy cannot be reliably enforced. Also, DNS proxy cannot selectively block specific content on a web server. For example, if a server is hosting both `www.somestore.com/adult-books` and `www.somestore.com/comic-books`, in this case, the DNS proxy can be configured to block the entire `www.somestore.com` site, but not `www.somestore.com/adult-books` only.

Another use of a DNS proxy is to provision split DNS capability. Split DNS refers to the use of different DNS databases based on the requester's IP address. Suppose a company's internal hostnames are stored in the DNS server 10.9.1.53, while all the other DNS queries are forwarded to a public-domain DNS server located at 67.14.210.250. Internal clients are assigned IP addresses from the prefix

10.9.0.0/16. The following policy will forward DNS queries to a specific DNS server based on where the clients are located:

```
1 <DNS-Proxy>
2 client.address=10.9.0.0/16 dns.forward(10.9.1.53)
3 dns.forward(67.14.210.250)
```

The rule on line ② forwards DNS queries to 10.9.1.53 only if the client address has the internal address prefix, while DNS requests from all other clients are forwarded to the public DNS server 67.14.210.250.

Data Loss Prevention

Another aspect of enforcing safe content policies is to prevent the exfiltration of company secrets to external entities. Confidential information may be leaked by employees, whether intentionally or unintentionally, and the damage incurred on the company can be the same in either case. Data loss prevention (DLP) is also known as data leak prevention. The main objective of DLP is to protect sensitive data according to centrally defined policies from leaving an organization's internal network or an organization-controlled device. The sensitive data may be stored on mass storage media (known as *data at rest*), transmitted over the network (known as *data in motion*), and accessed by users on the end systems (known as *data in use*).

The first action taken by a DLP solution is to identify sensitive data that is mandated by central policies for protection; this stage is commonly known as the *content discovery phase*. Identifying at-rest data entails scanning the hard drives on file servers and on end systems to detect protected content. Identifying in-motion data means performing runtime scanning and analysis of network traffic for sensitive information. Identifying in-use data means scanning the endpoint system memory for sensitive material. Regardless of the location where the data may be present, content discovery demands content analysis techniques that effectively identify protected material. Examples of content analysis techniques include pattern-based matching algorithms (for example, for identifying Social Security numbers or credit card numbers), generating a fingerprint for an entire file for exact matching, or creating hashes for specific parts of a file for partial matching.

The second action taken by a DLP solution is to enforce data protection. Possible actions associated with protecting at-rest data include removal of sensitive data from the endpoint, in-place encryption of protected data, quarantine of the data by relocation, or modification of access rights. Protecting in-use data is achieved through security capabilities that are implemented as extensions to the operating system (OS) that powers the endpoint. In-use data protection requires constant monitoring of data movement within the OS, between the OS and the applications, and among the applications. For example, sensitive data may be prohibited from being shared between applications, and in this case, the copy-and-paste feature may be disabled for such data.

A DLP solution can be implemented as either an endpoint solution or a network-based solution. Content-based analysis is computationally intensive, as Chapter 5 illustrates in the section "Dynamic Webpage Content Rating." Not all endpoints have the computing power or resources to perform content analysis, which also impacts the end user experience. A good example is that although the endpoint antivirus software is always active, it does not perform virus scanning constantly because its scanning activities impact system performance significantly. An endpoint DLP must perform constant validation as data is accessed by applications. Because an endpoint DLP solution is designed and implemented for specific operating systems, a DLP solution may not exist for some types of endpoints. In addition, an endpoint DLP solution must prevent sensitive data from leaving the system, for example, by preventing protected data from being copied onto a USB drive.

Chapter 4 describes the various methods employed by malware to infiltrate an endpoint. The attacking malware then "phones home" by establishing connections to its command and control (C2) centers to receive further instructions. Oftentimes the C2 server commands the malware to exfiltrate data from the compromised host. Some of these C2 channels are also encrypted. Five key points can be made from the preceding discussion.

First, deploying a network-based DLP solution can provide better coverage across a broad array of endpoints of varying types. The protection is centralized, and the computation-intensive tasks are offloaded to one or more dedicated DLP appliances.

Second, DLP solutions offer limited value to an enterprise when deployed as standalone solutions. Similar to the situation with antivirus solutions, static pattern-based antivirus solutions are useful in combating existing known viruses and malware, but antivirus solutions must be deployed with real-time URL categorization and web content analysis systems to defend against zero-day attacks. DLP solutions afford an additional layer of protection when they are deployed with a secure proxy, especially when the proxy is capable of decrypting SSL/TLS-encrypted traffic. In addition, a secure proxy can act as an extension of the DLP by enforcing data protection because a secure proxy can remove content from a connection or terminate a connection abruptly.

Third, at the time of this writing, existing DLP solutions are more effective at protecting sensitive data from involuntary leakage due to erroneous implementation of security policies or simply bad practices of designed processes. However, current DLP solutions are mostly ineffective against exfiltrations that are initiated by malicious actors that have successfully attacked and gained access to a protected network.

Fourth, to improve the rate of successful enforcement, implementing DLP solutions must include a combination of both endpoint-based and network-based solutions. An endpoint solution is still necessary to protect data on devices that are mobile, such as laptop computers, and these devices can leave the physical perimeter of an enterprise network, although possibly at the expense of the end-user experience.

Last, centrally managed and administered policies dictate the integration of the DLP solution with a corporate-wide Document Rights Management (DRM) system, or in general, an Information Rights Management (IRM) system. Sensitive documents and data are registered with an IRM, and permissions and rights are defined and managed centrally. Having a DLP solution installed on an endpoint implies the presence of an active agent that communicates with the IRM. In other words, DLP can be considered as a critical subsystem of the overall IRM defense infrastructure.

A DLP appliance can be deployed with a secure proxy using the ICAP protocol, similar to the deployment between a secure proxy and an antivirus appliance. The most common layered defense that involves DLP is its integration with the e-mail system.

E-mail Filtering

For many organizations, e-mail is an indispensable communication tool and is used heavily for file transfer to both internal and external recipients. E-mail can represent a large part of a company's outbound traffic. An e-mail may contain extremely sensitive information both in the content and in its attachment. The e-mail system is also utilized heavily by scammers and spammers to sell illicit products and services or to swindle people out of their money. Phishing e-mails are still one of the most effective first-stage infiltration channels for black hats to penetrate an organization.

Over the years, e-mail filtering has evolved its focus from spamming e-mails to the detection and removal of phishing e-mails as an important security measure. E-mail can be misused by employees to transmit sensitive or confidential information such as competitive analysis, company financial records, employee data, and customer records to external entities or destinations, which is in violation of company policies and represents serious data breaches. Outbound e-mails may also contain inappropriate material that can create legal liability resulting in damaged reputations and financial losses. Therefore, outbound e-mails must be scrutinized for data exfiltration and be validated against compliance policies to mitigate potential risks. With the aid of a DLP solution, an offending e-mail may be blocked entirely by the proxy, followed by the proxy redirecting that e-mail to the legal or HR department for review. The proxy may remove the offending content or attachment before forwarding the e-mail to a mail server. The proxy can also return the e-mail to the user and advise the user to encrypt the e-mail before transmission, if the DLP engine informs the proxy that it has detected the presence of sensitive information.

Examining inbound e-mail focuses on scanning the e-mail attachment for known viruses and malwares. Modern e-mail readers have a built-in capability to display e-mail that is created in HTML format. The e-mail message body is scanned for the presence of URLs. Each URL is analyzed to determine if the URL points to a malware delivery server, if the URL contains an IP address that is a part of a known botnet, or if previous analysis history indicates the URL is risky. Chapter 5 discusses URL analysis techniques in detail. Any automatic download of content as a result of the presence of an iframe in an HTML e-mail must be prevented. Chapter 4 discusses drive-by downloads and the dangers of invisible iframes that can trigger the automatic downloading and execution of malicious code.

A Primer on SMTP

The primary protocol used in e-mail communication is the Simple Mail Transfer Protocol (SMTP), which transfers e-mail from one mail system to another until it has reached the recipient's e-mail server. The intermediate network nodes that participate in routing e-mails are called *mail transfer agents* (MTAs). The first system that receives the e-mail from a client's e-mail agent is called a *mail submission agent* (MSA). For example, the SMTP server configured in the Microsoft Outlook client software is the IP address of an MSA. Figure 6-2 illustrates a simplified e-mail route when a user's e-mail agent is configured to use the Gmail SMTP server for e-mail submission.

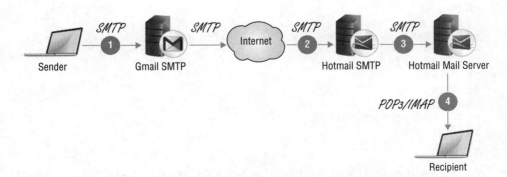

Figure 6-2: A Simplified View of an E-mail Route

In this case, the Gmail SMTP server is the MSA for the client. The client communicates with the MSA using the SMTP protocol. Based on the destination domain name, in this case `hotmail.com`, the Gmail SMTP server discovers the Hotmail SMTP server through DNS and forwards this e-mail to the identified mail server. The DNS Mail Exchanger (or MX) record contains the fully qualified domain name (FQDN) of the mail server for a given domain, and the DNS Address (or A) record contains the IP address of that mail server. This e-mail is then stored in the Hotmail internal e-mail server, waiting for the recipient to retrieve it. The e-mail is transferred using the SMTP protocol from stage ① to stage ③, and depending on the type of mail server hosting the recipient's e-mails, step ④ may be using a mail delivery protocol such as Post Office Protocol (POP3) or Microsoft Exchange protocol. The mail system that delivers the e-mail to the recipient is called a mail delivery agent (MDA). The MDA communicates with the MTA using SMTP but communicates with the recipient's e-mail agent using a mail delivery protocol. In this section, we are primarily concerned with the SMTP protocol.

The SMTP protocol is a server-talk-first protocol. Upon successful TCP establishment with the client-initiated connection request, the server sends its own hostname along with a `220` response to the client first. The client starts communication by sending a "hello message" (or `HELO`) with its own hostname and then waits for the server to respond. The server responds with `250 Ok` if it accepts this host. The string "Ok" that follows the response code `250` can be anything; what is important is the actual response code. Most SMTP servers today support the `EHLO`, or `Extended HELO`, message. `EHLO` works the same way as `HELO`, except that the server responding to an `EHLO` will include a list of options that are supported by this SMTP server. Each option is appended to the multi-line `250` response from the server, as shown in Figure 6-3.

As shown in Figure 6-3, an SMTP server responds to `EHLO` with eight options:

```
250-smtp.example.org
250-PIPELINING
250-SIZE 10240000
250-VRFY
250-ETRN
250-STARTTLS
250-ENHANCEDSTATUSCODES
250-8BITMIME
250 DNS
```

A line with a dash followed by the 3-digit response code indicates that there are more lines to follow. The first line always contains the domain name of the SMTP server, and subsequent lines list all the supported SMTP options. The meanings and syntax of these SMTP options are outside the scope of this book.

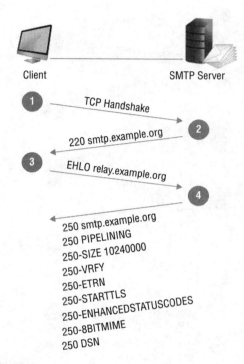

Figure 6-3: SMTP EHLO Exchange

Once the initial SMTP negotiation is complete, the client starts to transmit the e-mail message. The SMTP protocol exchange contains three parts: sender information, recipient information, and message data. Figure 6-4 summarizes this mail exchange process. Steps ① and ② represent the initial client's mail transfer request and the server's acceptance response. Step ⑤ provides e-mail sender information, and step ⑥ provides e-mail recipient information. Steps ⑨ to ⑫ involve the actual e-mail transfer from the client to the mail server (or the MSA).

An SMTP transaction occurs in plain text. There are two ways to secure an SMTP connection: SMTPS or STARTTLS. In SMTPS, the TCP handshake is followed by the SSL/TLS handshake before the first 220 response is sent from the SMTP server. This ensures that the entire SMTP communication is encrypted, as shown in Figure 6-5.

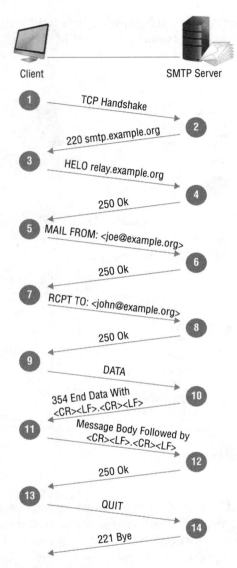

Figure 6-4: An Example SMTP Exchange

Another way of encrypting an SMTP connection is through the use of the STARTTLS option. A server that supports STARTTLS will advertise this option via a 250 response after a client's EHLO, as shown in Figure 6-3. When a client is notified of the STARTTLS option, it can initiate a secured session thereafter by sending a STARTTLS message to the server. The TLS negotiation ensues when the server acknowledges the agreement to the STARTTLS option by returning a 220 Ok response to the client, as shown in Figure 6-6.

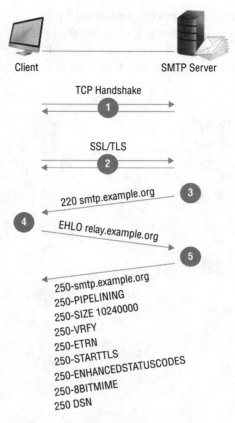

Figure 6-5: Securing SMTP Exchange with SMTPS

Many popular e-mail servers enforce encrypted SMTP messages. For example, Google Mail (Gmail) does not support plain-text SMTP; instead, it enforces SMTP over STARTTLS and SMTPS methods. Google uses Message Submission port 587 to handle SMTP over STARTTLS and rejects connections that do not use STARTTLS, as shown in the following example output:

```
MAIL FROM:<john.smith@gmail.com>
530 5.7.0 Must issue a STARTTLS command first. \
 dk5sm6776268pbc.61 - gsmtp
```

A typical e-mail message consists of text, HTML-formatted text, and attachments (text or binary). The e-mail message body is structured in the standard *Multi-purpose Internet Mail Extension* (MIME) format. The MIME format is designed to extend an e-mail into carrying more than just ASCII text. An e-mail is typically broken up into multiple parts including an HTML version and an ASCII version of the message. The content type for the message body is defined as "multipart/mixed" and each part is delimited by `boundary=`. The e-mail client looks for the delimiter and presents the multipart e-mail to the user based on the e-mail client's settings. Figure 6-7 shows an example e-mail message that can be presented in an e-mail client either as a plain-text message or in HTML format.

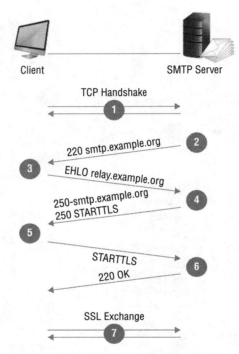

Figure 6-6: Securing SMTP Exchange with STARTTLS

In the example shown in Figure 6-7, the content type of the message is `multipart/alternative`, which indicates these are multiple parts with each part being one alternative of the same message. It is common to see this format where the e-mail message contains two alternatives—plain text and HTML format—and each part is described by its own content type. The boundary delimiter can be any ASCII string up to 70 characters long and is typically a randomly generated string to avoid collision with the actual e-mail content. The delimiters between different parts begin with the "--" marker followed by the boundary delimiting string. The final delimiter is denoted by enclosing the boundary string in two "--" markers, as shown Figure 6-7. The blank space between the `MIME-Version` and the first delimiter is called the *preamble,* while the space after the final delimiter is called the *epilogue.* The preamble and epilogue sections are typically blank spaces and are ignored by the e-mail client.

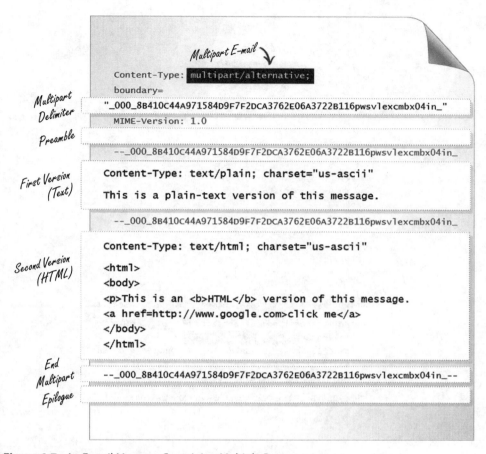

Multipart E-mail

Content-Type: `multipart/alternative;`
boundary=

Multipart Delimiter

`"_000_8B410C44A971584D9F7F2DCA3762E06A3722B116pwsvlexcmbx04in_"`

Preamble

MIME-Version: 1.0

`--_000_8B410C44A971584D9F7F2DCA3762E06A3722B116pwsvlexcmbx04in_`

First Version (Text)

Content-Type: "text/plain; charset="us-ascii"

This is a plain-text version of this message.

`--_000_8B410C44A971584D9F7F2DCA3762E06A3722B116pwsvlexcmbx04in_`

Second Version (HTML)

Content-Type: text/html; charset="us-ascii"

```
<html>
<body>
<p>This is an <b>HTML</b> version of this message.
<a href=http://www.google.com>click me</a>
</body>
</html>
```

End Multipart

`--_000_8B410C44A971584D9F7F2DCA3762E06A3722B116pwsvlexcmbx04in_--`

Epilogue

Figure 6-7: An E-mail Message Containing Multiple Parts

An e-mail attachment is basically another part of the message, except in this case it is an addition to the message, not an alternative. The content type `multipart/mixed` identifies an attachment, as shown in Figure 6-8.

The `mixed` keyword indicates that both parts are to be presented to the client instead of being alternatives to one another. The attachment contains additional information in its header. In this example, the attachment is a text file, and so the attachment has the `text/plain` content type. With a binary attachment, the content type can be `image/jpeg` for an image attachment, or `application/octet-stream` for a generic binary file, such as an executable system file. The `Content-Disposition` field has the value `attachment` followed by the filename. The `Content-Transfer-Encoding` field tells the e-mail client how to decode the attachment. A single e-mail can contain nested multi-part messages. Figure 6-9 illustrates an e-mail that contains two attachments.

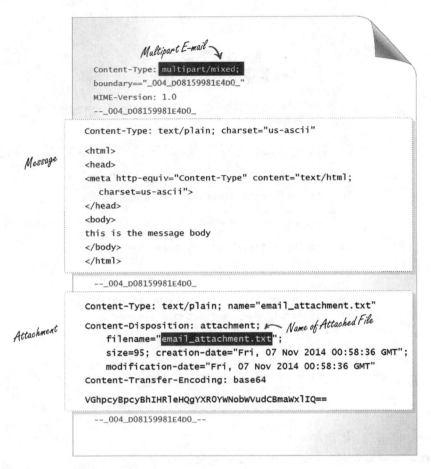

Figure 6-8: An E-mail with an Attachment

In this example, the first level indicates that this is a `multipart/mixed` e-mail that has two attachments. The first attachment is a plain-text file, while the second attachment is a Microsoft spreadsheet. We have changed the data to AAAA for illustration purposes; real data should be base64-encoded, as indicated by the `Content-Transfer-Encoding` field. In the message body, there is the second level of a nested multipart section with a different boundary delimiter.

So far we have assumed that the `Content-Type` field gives accurate information about the true format and nature of the attachment. A malicious sender can easily fabricate the file type by giving it a fake file extension and content type to bypass a naïve filtering mechanism that trusts such information blindly. Modern antivirus software solves this problem by examining the data and searches for known magic patterns that are associated with the various file types. For example, on the Unix system, a utility called `file` performs such content verification by checking for magic patterns and outputs the true type as shown here:

```
$ file --mime-type 1.txt
```

```
1.txt: application/pdf

$ file 1.txt
1.txt: PDF document, version 1.4
```

Content-Type: multipart/mixed;boundary="_005_D0815DC21E4D:
MIME-Version: 1.0
--_005_D0815DC21E4D3_

Content-Type: multipart/alternative;boundary="_000_D0815DC21E4D3_"
--_000_D0815DC21E4D3_

Content-Type: text/plain; charset="us-ascii"   *Text Message*
This is plain text message.

--_000_D0815DC21E4D3_

Message Body

Content-Type: text/html; charset="us-ascii"   *HTML Message*

```
<html>
<head>
<meta http-equiv="Content-Type" content="text/html;
    charset=us-ascii">
</head>
<body>This is HTML message</body>
</html>
```

--_000_D0815DC21E4D3_--

--_005_D0815DC21E4D3_--

Content-Type: text/plain; name="email_attachment.txt"

Content-Description: email_attachment.txt

Attachment 1

Content-Disposition: attachment;
    filename="email_attachment.txt"; size=95;
    creation-date="Fri, 07 Nov 2014 01:16:21 GMT";
    modification-date="Fri, 07 Nov 2014 01:16:21 GMT"

Content-Transfer-Encoding: base64

VGhpcyBpcyBhIHRleHQgYXR0YWNobWVudCBmaWxlIQ==

--_005_D0815DC21E4D3_--

Content-Type: application/vnd.openxmlformats-
    officedocument.spreadsheetml.sheet; name="test.xlsx"

Content-Description: test.xlsx

Attachment 2

Content-Disposition: attachment; filename="test.xlsx";
    creation-date="Fri, 07 Nov 2014 01:16:21 GMT";
    modification-date="Fri, 07 Nov 2014 01:16:21 GMT"

Content-Transfer-Encoding: base64

AAAAAAAAAAAAAAAAAAAAAAAAAAAAAAAAAAAAAAAAAAAAAAAAAA

--_005_D0815DC21E4D3_--

Figure 6-9: An E-mail with Multiple Attachments

In this example, `1.txt` was a PDF file renamed to hide its true identity. The `file` utility works by checking a magic file, which is written as a set of rules to classify the file format based on type signatures. An example of a PDF magic file is shown here:

```
#---------------------------------------------------------
# $File: pdf,v 1.6 2009/09/19 16:28:11 christos Exp $
# pdf:  file(1) magic for Portable Document Format
#

0    string      %PDF-       PDF document
!:mime  application/pdf
>5   byte        x           \b, version %c
>7   byte        x           \b.%c
```

The details of the magic rules can be found in the Unix man page: "man magic". We use PDF as an example. The rule contains two levels, indicated by the presence of a ">" symbol at the beginning of the line. The first level checks for the string `%PDF-` at offset 0:

```
0    string      %PDF-       PDF document
```

When the first-level rule matches, the `file` utility executes all rules on the second level to get more information. In this case, a single byte at offset 5 and offset 7 returns the PDF version of this file. Note that the second line that starts with ! is not used for pattern matching but is used to determine the MIME type should a match be successful.

```
>5   byte        x           \b, version %c
>7   byte        x           \b.%c
```

An MTA or a malware detection device needs to discover the correct MIME type of the attachment and should not rely on the "Content-Type" field or the file extension, as a malicious sender can easily create deceptions to circumvent the MTA.

E-mail Filtering Techniques

The goals of the e-mail filtering system are to prevent restricted information from leaving an organization and to block phishing e-mails from entering the network through the e-mail system. Integrating a DLP solution with the MTA can be an effective solution to filter outbound e-mails. Because e-mails are temporarily stored on the MTA, executing DLP scan operations does not require absolute real-time performance.

Many of the traditional e-mail filtering techniques are still relevant today. For example, the IP address of a system that is delivering incoming e-mails is verified against an IP address blacklist, and if the e-mails from that IP are found to be on the list, then they are marked as suspicious and are candidates for removal. An IP address that passes the blacklist check is then verified against a *DNS-based blackhole list* (DNSBL) or an *open relay database block list* (ORDBL) that contains a list of e-mail servers that are known or suspected to transmit spam or malicious e-mails. Similarly, the e-mail address of the sender is validated against a blacklist. The domain name of the sender's e-mail address is checked for validity, and so is the reply-to domain.

Scanning e-mail contents by a DLP solution implies there is a set of rules and policies that are defined in the DLP engine, and these rules are executed during the scanning process. These rules contain patterns, keywords, and regular expressions that classify sensitive data in the message body. In addition to searching for patterns, the DLP engine has the ability to perform semantic analysis on the content. For example, because a driver's license number is a piece of sensitive information, after discovering what appears to be a driver's license number, the DLP engine will search for a string that appears to be a birthday or an expiration date. This *contextual* scan and correlation reduces false positive classifications. Finally, associated with every DLP policy is an associated action that can instruct either the MTA or the proxy to drop the e-mail, modify the e-mail content and then deliver the e-mail, quarantine the e-mail and send notification to the legal or HR department, or permit the delivery of the original e-mail.

When an e-mail contains an HTML version of the message and the e-mail client is configured to display such an HTML version of a message, the message body should be scanned and processed in a similar fashion as for a web page to mitigate security threats. Therefore, an effective e-mail security system is one that is fully integrated with other security solutions, such as an antivirus system, web analysis, and a secure proxy, in addition to working in concert with a DLP solution. For example, if a security vulnerability is discovered in PDF documents, an organization may respond to such a threat by prohibiting any PDF documents that are attached to e-mails:

```
1 <proxy> service.name=SMTP
2 smtp.attachment.mime_type="application/pdf"
  action.remove_attachment(yes)
3 smtp.attachment.true_type="application/pdf"
  action.remove_attachment(yes)
4
5 define action remove_attachment
6 mime_remove(attachment, "PDF attachment is not safe, \
              removed by policy")
7 end
```

This policy layer applies to only the SMTP service, and rules on lines ② and ③ remove any attachment that either has the "application/pdf" MIME type or is detected to be an "application/pdf" true file type. The action is defined to completely remove the attachment. The e-mail that is delivered to the client will not contain a PDF attachment. Instead, a plain-text file containing the warning message "PDF attachment is not safe, removed by policy" is created to notify the recipient.

Summary

In this chapter, we have presented various security scenarios and offered policy implementation strategies on how to solve those challenges. While we examined the design logic behind these policies in detail, it should be apparent that these scenarios offer a small representation of the security landscape and are meant to explain how a secure proxy intercepts and processes a transaction through the policy system. The security engineer can dictate the desired security goals through a given policy language. Therefore, the level of sophistication of the policy engine and the expressiveness of the policy language reflect the capabilities of the proxy appliance and how well the proxy can enforce complex security policies. Insights gained from these examples that have been written in a real-world policy language should serve as useful litmus tests when selecting a secure proxy solution.

The Art of Application Classification

Application classification refers to the real-time identification of traffic flows as being part of a specific protocol or application. Timely and accurate classification of network traffic is commonly known as *network visibility*. Network visibility is the fundamental first step that enables network administrators and security specialists to write and implement meaningful security and traffic engineering policies, for example, "block Netflix traffic during work hours".

A *classifier* refers to a system or device that examines traffic in real-time and produces one or many matching classification results. A *pure classifier* performs the classification task only and produces a report. A classifier used in network security typically takes the result and performs one or more actions on the traffic flow. The action can be as simple as "allow" or "deny", or more complex, as in "logging user action and reducing the user's bandwidth usage". From a security standpoint, it is vital to perform the desired enforcement action as early as possible. For example, the classifier should conclude that a user is uploading files to Dropbox using as few packets as possible in order to avoid leakage of confidential information. In this case, the policy on the classification result, "Dropbox Upload", may include the actions, "Log the user who is uploading to Dropbox", and "Terminate the upload".

A classifier needs information that sufficiently describes each application in order for the classifier to make the proper decision. This information, known as an *application signature*, is the unique pattern that distinguishes one application from another. The signature may be bit patterns or ASCII patterns; for example, "GET" and "SIP" are visible ASCII characters that are found in the HTTP and SIP protocol payloads, respectively. Another type of signature is based on the behavior that an application exhibits on a network. The signature type determines the algorithms that are applied in making the classification decision. Some classification techniques identify an application category, such as P2P category, rather than a specific application.

In this chapter we will describe the signature types and structures and the associated classification techniques and algorithms. We will use the terms *classification engine* and *classifier* interchangeably throughout this chapter.

A Brief History of Classification Technology

Firewalls could be considered as the first classification devices that enforce security policies at a network's ingress and egress points. Legacy firewalls were confined to using the L4 packet header, specifically the port number information to identify both protocols and applications. The Internet Assigned Numbers Authority, or IANA, assigns port numbers to specific applications and services. Legitimate protocols and applications operate in conformance with these port designations. Even today, firewalls continue to perform port-based classification and are ubiquitous in network infrastructures. In essence, a firewall makes the classification decision on the first packet with very small computing overhead, as the port number resides on a known location in the packet, as shown in Figure 7-1. For ease of discussion, any extra headers such as VLAN or GRE or variable-length options are assumed to be absent from the packets. The classification process is simple and efficient. Instead of classifying packet by packet, a stateful firewall will classify a connection using the first packet, and then create and keep a connection state that includes the classification result. Future packets that belong to a known connection in the connection state table require a simple lookup for the classification ID.

Port-based classification is efficient and the process is deterministic when applications conform to the specifications. Unfortunately, many applications do not abide by the rules. For example, peer-to-peer (P2P) applications try to evade firewalls by using ephemeral ports. Other applications, especially malicious types, try to evade firewalls by communicating over well-defined ports. A plethora of web-based applications emerged with the explosive growth of Web 2.0. Instead of one-way information download, the web has become interactive. As such, a simple port-based classification engine would naïvely treat all traffic running on port 80 as simply HTTP protocol traffic, thus rendering the firewall ineffective because it could not, for example, distinguish the application activity of "Playing Farmville on Facebook" from "Reading a post on Facebook".

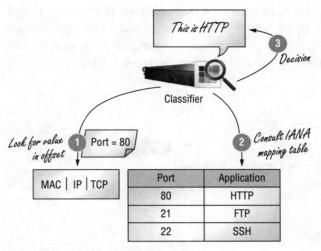

Figure 7-1: Port-Based Classification

Firewalls with Deep Packet Inspection (DPI) capability began examining the packet payload and searching for known patterns to identify protocols and applications. Payload-based classifiers make decisions slightly later in the flow lifecycle than port-based classifiers. For example, the HTTP classification engine typically searches for a string such as "GET /* HTTP/1" where * denotes any string. This information is not available until the TCP three-way handshake is complete. Therefore, the earliest time this flow can be classified as HTTP is on the fourth packet. Even with the fourth packet, as TCP is a stream-based protocol, the first HTTP GET request may be truncated into two packets, with one packet containing the "GET /" string and the other containing the "* HTTP/1" string. In this case the classifier needs to accumulate enough packets to make the classification decision. As L4 information is readily available in the payload-based classifier, a firewall with DPI also performs port-based classifications as part of the payload detection. With this hybrid approach, a flow on a standard port can be classified on the first packet, and the classification may change as more payload data becomes available. With applications that run on non-standard ports, the classifier will make the classification decision only after enough payload data becomes available.

The DPI classifier requires unique knowledge about the set of applications to be classified in order to know what to look for inside the payload. This knowledge can come from either a published specification or a signature database. Before we discuss how signatures are generated, let's first look at the structure of a payload-based classifier, as shown in Figure 7-2, assuming the signatures are already available. A payload-based classifier device can be generally broken up into the following operations: packet intake, flow association, classifications, and optionally actions to be applied to the outgoing packets. Some devices deploy the classifier entirely for visibility or retrospective analysis. For these types of devices, packets are retrieved for analysis but do not need to be transmitted after processing. Other devices may perform one or more actions, as specified by the enforcement policies on each packet before its transmission.

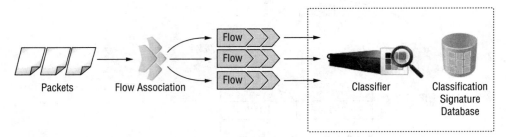

Packets   Flow Association   Classifier   Classification
                                                                                    Signature
                                                                                    Database

Figure 7-2: DPI-Based Classification

Flow construction consists of separating flows based on combined L3 and L4 information. A flow is represented by a 5-tuple: L4 protocol type, source IP address, source port, destination IP address, and destination port. In the case of TCP connections, the directionality of a connection is defined by the packet that contains the "SYN" flag, and directionality is maintained as a part of the flow state. Many classifiers can greatly improve the classification accuracy if the directionality is known.

At the completion of flow construction, a packet that matches an existing flow is accumulated with other packets until a certain amount of payload data becomes available, at which point the combined payload is dissected to look for specific patterns based on the set of known classification signatures. In the next section, we will examine signature-based classification engines in detail.

Signature-Based Pattern Matching Classification

The classification signature database is a collection of patterns that contain enough data to confidently classify a flow and to map the flow to a specific application as illustrated in Figure 7-3. An efficient pattern matching algorithm is critical to the performance of the real-time classification engine for pattern-based application signatures.

The classification engine needs to iterate through all the applications known to the classification engine and matches the collected payload against the set of application signatures. The value of the classification engine is in the number of applications it is capable of identifying. The pattern matching time grows in proportion with the number of applications. A classifier that simply iterates through all the signatures and performs pattern matching against each signature one at time is inefficient. Furthermore, many of the signatures may have overlapping patterns. Scanning the input for the same pattern repeatedly is an inefficient use of resources and increases the matching time unnecessarily.

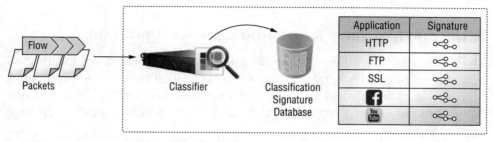

Figure 7-3: Iterative Signature Matching

Consider a naïve classification implementation that contains the following application signatures: Battlefield and Battle.net. The former is a network war game while the latter is a game server that hosts multiple popular strategy games. The example classification code is presented in pseudo-code format:

```
if data == "battle" OR data == "stella" ) then
    return BATTLEFIELD
else
    return UNKNOWN
endif


if data == "battle" then
    return BATTLE.NET
else
    return UNKNOWN
endif
```

The term "battle" is present in both signatures. A naïve classification implementation performs the exact same match on the term "battle" twice per flow, which is inefficient. Moreover, the performance of the classifier depends on the average number of classification signatures it needs to compare against before reaching a decision. We can make a few observations from this simple example. First, the quality of the signatures for both applications is poor. The most desirable signature is one that contains unique terms that are distinct from all other signatures; in other words, the fewer overlapping terms there are in a signature, the better quality the signature has. Second, the matching order is significant, and this is a symptom of the poor quality. In other words, if the classifier compares the input against the signature for Battle.net first, then it will reach a definitive result if the input string is "battle", without the need to check for "Battlefield". Third, it is desirable to have the ability to compare the input string against multiple signatures in parallel as a filter mechanism to create a candidate signature set that is a subset of the entire database for comparison when additional terms become available from the input.

Extracting Matching Terms: Aho-Corasick Algorithm

The *Aho-Corasick algorithm* is a simple and efficient algorithm for locating all occurrences of a finite number of patterns, also called terms, in a text sample. The Aho-Corasick algorithm constructs a finite-state machine (FSM) or finite automaton out of the given terms, and this pattern-matching machine is then used to locate these terms in an input string.

Consider a set of terms {"ACE", "FACE", "ACT", "SOFA", "SOS"}. We will use these terms to illustrate the step-by-step construction of an Aho-Corasick data structure. As with any finite automaton, each node represents a state. The Aho-Corasick FSM begins with a single root node 0 as the starting state, as shown in Figure 7-4. The terms are

Figure 7-4: Start State

represented in capital letters for ease of discussion. Oftentimes packet payloads are normalized, for example, into all capital letters, before feeding the data into the classifier.

The operation of the Aho-Corasick matching FSM is governed by three functions: the *goto* function, the *failure* function, and the *output* function. The transition from one state to another is dictated by the *goto* and *failure* functions. Every node has a *goto* function marked by a solid arrow and a *failure* function marked by a dashed arrow. An absence of a dashed arrow indicates the node has a default *failure* function that points back to the initial state 0. A node contains an *output* function denoted by a solid-colored node if a term has been matched.

The first term is "ACE", which will produce three nodes or states as shown in Figure 7-5. The *goto* function maps a state and an input into another state. In this example, the *goto* function maps the start state 0 and the input character "A" into state 1. The *goto* function maps state 1 and the input character "C" into state 2, and so on. State 3 contains an *output* function that produces "ACE", which indicates a match with "ACE" is found at state 3.

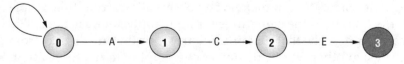

Figure 7-5: FSM for the Term "ACE"

The next term to be inserted into the FSM is "FACE". Construction of a new term always starts from the root node. Because "F" is not in any of the available state transitions out of the root node, a new node is created as shown in Figure 7-6. The main difference between Figure 7-5 and Figure 7-6 is the presence of explicit *failure* functions for states 5, 6, and 7. Part of the Aho-Corasick FSM construction is to define the *failure* function at each node.

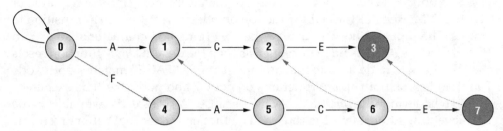

Figure 7-6: FSM after Inserting the Term "FACE"

The *goto* function can indicate a failure if the *goto* function cannot map a given input at a specific state into another state. For example, in Figure 7-5, if during input parsing at state 1 the input character is "H", the *goto* function reports a failure, and at that point the *failure* function is executed. The *failure* function causes a transition from one state to another. In this case, the lack of a dashed arrow implies state 1 does not have an explicit *failure* function. So the default *failure* function is executed, causing the FSM to return to starting state 0. In Figure 7-5, none of the nodes contains an explicit *failure* function, which implies the default *failure* function will take effect upon a matching failure, which will reset the FSM.

The FSM, as shown in Figure 7-6, has an explicit *failure* function defined at state 5, which maps state 5 into state 1 when the next input character does not map into state 6. The state which the *failure* function maps into, called the *failure node*, is derived by removing the first level transition "F" and looking for everything else up to the current node. In this example, the failure node for state 5 is derived by removing "F", which is state 1, a single "A"; thus, state 5 maps to state 1. On state 6, the failure node is derived by removing "F" from "FAC", which is "AC"; thus, state 6 maps to state 2. In other words, the construction of the *failure* function looks for the longest string match in the current Aho-Corasick tree, from the start state, using the new term obtained by removing the first character from the just inserted term ("FACE"), one at a time, until every node (4, 5, 6, 7) that leads to the end of the currently inserted term has been visited. Notice that on state 6, the path leading from the root node to the current state consists of three transitions with the characters "F", "A", and "C". The possible failure nodes are "AC" or "C". Even if hypothetically there is a single-character term "C", which leads from the root node to another state, the failure function of state 6 is still state 2, because the term "AC" is longer than this hypothetical term "C". With this rule, after a term has been inserted, one and only one *failure* function will be created on every state leading to the last state of this term. This example illustrates that the *failure* function is important to keep the FSM running without the need for rechecking all possible permutations of the matched string.

For a matching example, input sample "FACT" will traverse the FSM from node 0, 4, 5 to node 6. When input "T" does not match the next transition character "E", the FSM executes the *failure* function on node 6, resulting in a transition to state 2. The input is checked against the next transition character at state 2. In this case, again, there is no match, but this time the default *failure* function resets the FSM back to node 0. Note that an input sample "FACE" matches both node 7 and node 3, so both *output* functions on node 7 and node 3 will be executed.

The next term for insertion is "ACT". Because "A" is already available as the first level transition, state 1 is reused. The first character that differs from the existing path is the letter "T", so state 8 is created to form a new transition branch as shown in Figure 7-7. By removing one character at a time from the beginning of this term, neither "CT" nor "T" can be found in the current FSM. Hence, no failure node can be traced from the newly created node 8.

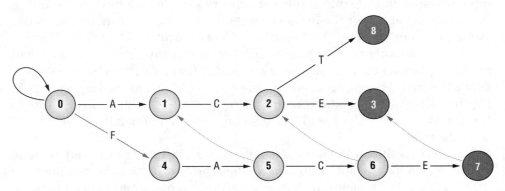

Figure 7-7: FSM after Inserting the Term "ACT"

Continuing the same insertion process with "SOFA" and "SOS", we will eventually arrive at the FSM as shown in Figure 7-8. Each of the solid-colored nodes denotes a positive pattern match, and in the context of application classification, a pattern match implies the input contains a term (or pattern) that is part of one or more application signatures.

For illustration purposes, we assume that signatures for Facebook and FaceTime both require the term "FACE"; as such, the output function (that is extended for application classification) at node 7 contains a table that lists the applications that are interested in this term, which are Facebook and FaceTime, as shown in Figure 7-9. The term alone may not be descriptive enough for the classification engine. Therefore, additional information, such as the byte offset in the input string where the term is found, may be recorded as part of the output of the FSM.

The byte offset serves as an additional matching criterion. In this example, the term "FACE" is part of the signature for FaceTime only if the term is located at byte offset 0 in the input string, but if the term is located between byte offset 10 and 20 inclusive, then it is part of the signature for Facebook.

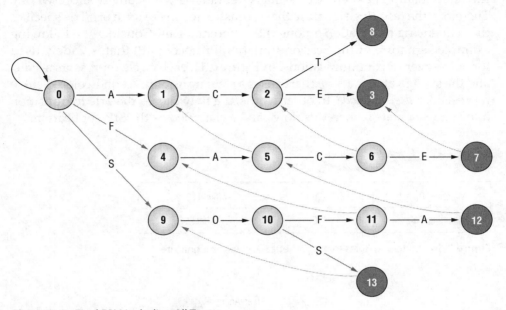

Figure 7-8: Final FSM Including All Terms

| Facebook | offset [10, 20] |
| FaceTime | offset 0 |

Figure 7-9: Output from a Pattern Match

An application signature typically contains multiple terms. For illustration purposes, we created a hypothetical application signature for Facebook, which contains the term "FACE" between offset 10 and 20 and the term "SOS" at offset 25. A signature such as this can be represented as a list of matching rules, as shown in Figure 7-10. All of the rules must match in order for a byte stream to be classified as Facebook using the hypothetical Facebook signature. In this case, the term "FACE" needs to match between the byte offset 10 and 20, and the term "SOS" must appear at byte offset 25 in the input stream.

Prefix-Tree Signature Representation

The quality of classification is greatly affected by how a signature is represented and utilized by a classifier. Instead of representing classification signatures using tables of static matching rules, recent research has shown that a *Prefix Tree* or simply *Trie* can be leveraged to implement signatures effectively. A Trie acts as an FSM similar to the Aho-Corasick FSM. In a Trie, the terms of a signature are arranged in chronological order, not with absolute offset. In other words, the relationship between two terms is defined by who-comes-before-whom. Therefore, the resulting signature that is constructed in the form of a Trie specifies the sequencing association among the different terms. Consider the following example signature of the Session Initiation Protocol (SIP) that is widely used for voice-over IP communications. In Figure 7-11, each circle represents a state, and the string value is a *term* that causes a state transition. A solid-colored circle represents a *decision node*. In other words, if a flow causes the Trie to transition into state 3 or state 5, then this flow can be classified as the SIP application.

Hypothetical Signature for "Facebook"

Matching Rule 1	"FACE"	offset [10, 20]
Matching Rule 2	"SOS"	offset 25

Figure 7-10: Matching Rules for Hypothetical Facebook Signature

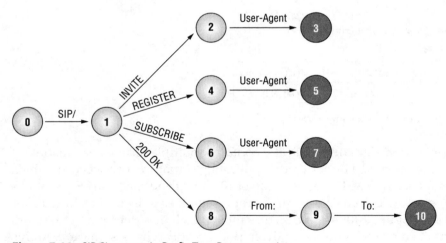

Figure 7-11: SIP Signature in Prefix Tree Representation

It is important to note that a Trie describes the entire application signature, while the Aho-Corasick FSM describes how a term can be matched against the input data stream. A decision point made on the Aho-Corasick FSM extracts a term that corresponds to a transition on the Trie. Let's now look closely at how the application signature is used by the classifier, assuming that this is the only application signature available to the classifier. The classifier parses the incoming stream of bytes and attempts to find matching patterns in its Aho-Corasick FSM. For illustration purposes, we are only showing a partial Aho-Corasick FSM and its relationship to the SIP signature. Recall that an Aho-Corasick FSM transitions on each input character while parsing the incoming data stream, and a decision node corresponds to a matching term that can possibly make a transition in the signature Trie FSM, as illustrated in Figure 7-12. The data stream is *classified* only if the classifier reaches a decision node in its signature Trie FSM. When the pattern "SIP/" is recognized by the Aho-Corasick FSM, the current state in the SIP signature Trie FSM advances its state to 1. At this point, the signature is interested only in four possible transitions out of the current state: "INVITE", "REGISTER", "SUBSCRIBE", and "200 OK". That is, if the next matching term is "FROM:" at the current state, even though this is a term of interest to SIP, that term is ignored, and the state remains in state 1. This flow is classified as SIP only if the current data stream causes the Trie FSM to reach any of the decision nodes: 3, 5, 7, or 10.

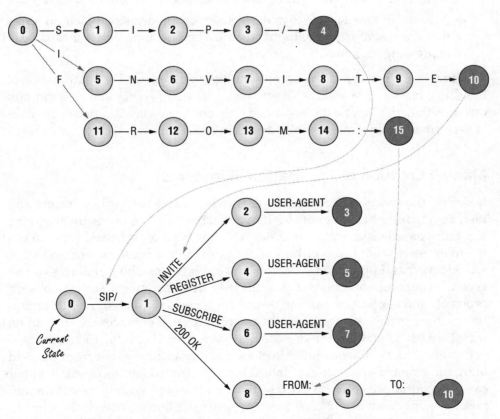

Figure 7-12: Relationship between Aho-Corasick FSM and the Prefix Tree-Based Signature

A closer look at the SIP signature Trie reveals that a number of enhancements may be necessary in the Trie representation:

- The absolute offset is omitted from the signature. In the earlier Facebook-versus-FaceTime example, the classifier required both the term and its offset in the input stream to classify the application. In this SIP signature, the absolute offset is replaced by the order among the terms. However, an absolute offset may still be necessary for classifying some applications. For example, the "GET" keyword in HTTP is useful only when it is found at the beginning of the payload (offset=0). This extra constraint can be detected during term extraction and be added to the signature as a criterion so that a state transition occurs only if a term matches at the desired offset.

- The Trie FSM is a syntactical parser and thus lacks representation of cross-correlation among different flows. For example, in the input stream, the data that follows the "FROM:" keyword may provide IP address information that may be useful to classify a subsequent flow. A signature that is structured as a Trie is incapable of expressing semantics of its terms.

- A classifier may be able to make a classification decision based on terms that are absent from the input stream. The Trie approach is incapable of expressing such matching criteria.

In practice, a Trie typically contains multiple signatures. The combination of the Aho-Corasick FSM and the Trie-based signature FSM provides an important optimization: the input data is scanned only once, and classification evaluation is performed against multiple signatures in parallel.

Manual Creation of Application Signatures

Defining the terms and constructing the signatures using these terms and then aggregating these signatures into a database are the prerequisites to the signature-based classification engines. The first type of signature creation is a manual process that involves human data analysts or protocol engineers. For well-defined and published protocols and applications, the signatures can be generated out of specifications such as the IETF RFC documents. For unpublished protocols and applications, the analysts or engineers must analyze the application exchanges using packet captures and then reverse-engineer the application signature based on both the protocol payloads and the protocol's operational behaviors. A data analyst may collect the packet captures either from the field or by running the application of interest in a controlled environment. In either case, the signature creation process requires manual sample collection and possibly applying a priori knowledge or heuristics in the analysis. Figure 7-13 provides an overview of this signature mining process.

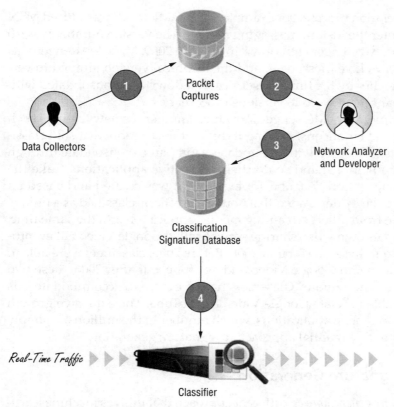

Figure 7-13: Overview of Signature Mining Process

The biggest problem with the packet capture-based reverse-engineering approach to creating an application signature is the lack of application feature functional coverage. For a more complete coverage, one must enumerate all of the possible menu options, generate traffic for each of the menu items, and then track the data flow and produce a signature for that specific feature accordingly. Not only is this method not scalable, but sometimes it is impossible to enumerate all possible features without specific data as feature input. For example, some business and legal applications grant access to certain features only when the user has a sufficient privilege level.

In addition, recent Internet trends are constantly challenging the effectiveness of the manual approach. Encrypted traffic is growing exponentially. One of the major challenges for pattern-based signature generation lies in the fundamental requirement to look into the payload. SSL encryption scrambles the payload data and renders this technique ineffective. Signature generation and traffic classification are impossible without visibility into the encrypted payload. The use of an SSL proxy to decrypt the traffic may be one way to overcome this challenge. Rapid updates to applications and protocols amplify the scalability issue facing the manual generation process. For example, in 1999 Microsoft introduced MSN Messenger to enter the instant messaging market. The version number was 9.0 by the time MSN Messenger shut down in 2012. In 2009, MSN Messenger was renamed Windows Live Messenger, and the technical version jumped to version 14.0 and was 16.4 by the time the service shut down and consolidated with Skype. This meant there were 16 versions in 13 years.

During this time, MSN Messenger introduced numerous new features such as voice, video, and emoticons, making it difficult for vendors that sold classification products to keep up with the updates. Companies consolidate through mergers and acquisitions, and so do their respective applications. Take the video sharing application YouTube, for example. It was created and based on Flash, but its popularity demanded that YouTube traffic be classified as a unique application aside from other "streaming media" applications. At the same time, Google launched its own video sharing service called Google Video but eventually decided to purchase YouTube in 2006. Before 2006, classifiers were able to separately identify both Google Video and YouTube, but after 2006, these two services became synonymous. Classifiers had to evolve to accommodate this change and be able to relate Google Video to YouTube. The explosive growth in web-based and mobile applications, which number in the millions, is simply overwhelming for any manual approach to signature generation.

Automatic Signature Generation

Automatic signature generation is a different approach that utilizes machine learning and data mining techniques to produce and constantly update application signatures. In a paper published in 2013 titled "SANTaClass: A Self Adaptive Network Traffic Classification System", Alok Tongaonkar and his fellow researchers proposed a method to automatically generate application signatures from what they called *invariant patterns,* also known as *common terms,* which are patterns that remain the same from flow to flow. The classification system defined in their proposal contained two main components: the *Automatic Signature Generator* and the *Real-Time Classifier,* as shown in Figure 7-14. We will describe their classification system and the proposed automatic signature generation method in this section. The Real-Time Classifier is based on the Aho-Corasick algorithm and the Trie and has been described in detail in the previous sections in this chapter.

The *Automatic Signature Generator* (ASG) contains three main components: the *Machine Learning* (ML) system, the *Signature Generator* (SG), and the *data collectors.* The ML system constantly collects and accumulates real-world traffic from one or more data collectors and performs necessary extraction of common terms from related flows. The SG takes inputs from the ML system and produces and refines signatures, eventually storing new signatures in the database. A real-time classification system is deployed in the critical traffic path to classify the traffic based on signatures produced by the ASG system. The goal of this ASG system is to constantly evolve and refine the signatures so that the classifier will produce better results over time and new applications can be discovered without human intervention. However, in practice a human inspector or analyst is generally required for the following reasons:

- The ML system employs probability algorithms to group flows into clusters as if these flows were generated from the same application. The clustering methods serve as a pre-selection or filtering process that will subsequently enable an analyst to fine-tune the algorithms to achieve the necessary accuracy.

- An analyst can modify an automatically generated signature by either inserting or removing terms according to heuristics or a priori knowledge to improve classification accuracy. Such a practice is particularly true for custom applications.

- The ML and signature generator system may be able to automatically generate a signature and accurately match the traffic against it, but the signature lacks a meaningful name. One of the biggest challenges of automatically mining and generating application signatures is the problem of associating the signature with its proper application name. For example, the signature generator may have created a signature to uniquely identify Skype traffic, but the classifier may not know the application is Skype.

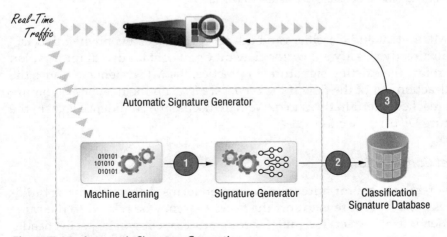

Figure 7-14: Automatic Signature Generation

A practical signature generation system therefore puts a human inspector in the loop, as shown in Figure 7-15. Notice that in this diagram, a few extra elements were added. First, the ASG now contains an extra element called the *distiller*. The distiller compares a new signature against the existing ones to check for redundancies and merge with and refine another signature. Details of the distiller will be discussed in a later section. Another interesting observation is that the signature generation path involving the human inspectors is not in the critical path. That is, the ASG system can run without human intervention, but the human inspector can retrieve and overwrite the resultant signatures by directly modifying the signature database. The work of the inspector should be performed out-of-path, denoted by 3.1 and 3.2, and not become a bottleneck in the system.

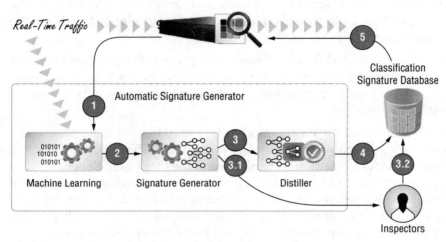

Figure 7-15: Automatic Signature Generation with Distiller

The ML system and classifier can both accept packets. Even when the classifier can already classify a flow, the flow may still contain useful information to help refine the existing signature. In practice, the ML system continues the data extraction out of the flow if the *confidence level* on the matched signature has not reached a certain threshold. We will discuss the confidence level in the "Signature Distiller" section.

Flow Set Construction

The first requirement for mining the common terms that are the basic building blocks of a signature is to sort the flows that may be related to the same application into a flow set. The initial sorting process relies on L4 packet header information. Because an application can utilize different L4 service ports and different applications may communicate over the same port, the quality of the signature depends on how accurately related flows are collected into the same flow set while unrelated flows are excluded from that set.

The majority of applications issue DNS queries before initiating connections to the intended destinations. Therefore, one way to correlate related flows is by leveraging the information obtained from the DNS exchange, such as the domain name and its associated IP addresses. Flows that are destined to the IP addresses corresponding to the same domain name are grouped together as one application. This DNS-based grouping approach makes the assumption that a domain name predominantly hosts one main application. This assumption is ineffective for web-based applications. For example, the Facebook social media site and Facebook games are all hosted under the domain name Facebook.com. However, grouping all traffic going to Facebook.com will not produce any quality signatures for the various Facebook games.

In light of the constraint just mentioned, a possible solution to solving this problem is to combine DNS information with *data clustering* techniques that we will describe in detail later in this chapter. We recognize that the same domain name can be used to host multiple applications, but each application should exhibit different network behavior. Take YouTube, for example. Traffic flows that are part of the YouTube website-browsing activities exhibit distinct network behavior that differs from traffic flows that are streaming YouTube videos in terms of packet sizes and inter-packet time gaps. Applying data clustering techniques using packet sizes and inter-packet gaps will yield two distinct data clusters, and this information can be used to further divide flows into two sub-flow sets, even when those flows are going to the same domain. In fact, the data clustering technique can help identify different actions being activated within an application. Thus, the resulting signatures can provide immense insight into the structure and the inner workings of an application.

Another challenge with the DNS-based grouping method is the requirement that the signature generator have visibility to all DNS traffic. The generator may not capture all DNS exchanges that take place on the network. L4 port information is utilized to group flows that have destination IP addresses that are not found in any of the preceding DNS queries. Because flows from multiple applications can run over the same port, the data clustering technique is again utilized to separate those flows into different sub-flow sets.

The resulting flow sets obtained from the procedures just mentioned may need to satisfy a number of constraints to ensure each flow set is a good representation of the corresponding application. The *server diversity constraint* is a measure of the number of different destination IP addresses that exist in a flow set. This measurement is an indicator of whether the flows in the set belong to traffic going to a specific server hosting a service. The *number of flows per destination IP address* limits the effect of one node on the signature. Beyond the threshold, the additional flows are excluded from the set. The *total number of flows in a flow set* ensures sufficient traffic payloads are available to generate the signatures.

These constraints not only act as flow selection parameters but also dictate where the data collectors can be deployed. Imagine the data collector is deployed inside an enterprise network. A small or medium-sized enterprise may have only a few static public IPv4 addresses. The presence of a NAT device at the enterprise network perimeter means connections that are initiated from within the enterprise will be mapped to one or two public IP addresses as the source IP address. Consequently, the server IP address is also limited to a few values. For example, before an enterprise user initiates a connection to Google Drive, a DNS query is issued for Google.com, which will solicit only a few IP addresses due to Google's global load balancing algorithm, which resolves the query based on the physical location of the source IP of the DNS query issuer. Whether Google.com resolves to one or two IP addresses also depends on the workload at each of its servers at the query time. Therefore, as this example illustrates, server diversity must be an adjustable parameter. As it turns out in practice, the data collectors are best deployed in the ISP networks to be effective in gathering the necessary data while meeting the constraints for the automatic signature generator.

Extraction of Common Terms

An important aspect of automatic signature generation is the extraction and selection of common terms from a vast collection of traffic flows. The common terms are extracted by pair-wise comparison between all the flows in the

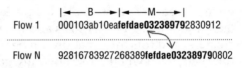

Figure 7-16: Extracting Common Terms

flow set obtained from the flow-set construction phase. A pair-wise comparison involves taking two flows and attempting to extract any common substrings such as that shown in Figure 7-16.

To perform a pair-wise comparison between flow 1 and flow n, we start from the first byte of flow 1 (B = 0), take the first M bytes on flow 1, and compare it against the entire payload of flow n. M starts with a minimum comparison size, typically 4, and increments until M reaches the end of flow 1. When M reaches the end of flow 1, the process starts over, skipping the first B bytes, and increments B by 1. M again starts with the minimum size of 4 and increments until the end of the flow.

```
for B in (0, sizeof(flow1) − 4)
    for M in (4, sizeof(flow1)-B)
        str = flow1's data of size M at offset B
        if str is found in flow n; then
            record str as a candidate term
        end if
    end for
end for
```

Each pair-wise comparison therefore requires $O(m^2)$ operations, where m is the average payload size in the flow set. Because every flow in the flow set will need to be compared to every other flow, there are another $O(n^2)$ operations. Combining these two sets of operations results in a total of $O(n^2m^2)$ operations. Even with a moderately large number of flows in the low thousands, the number of substring comparison operations is in the order of 10^{10}, which is an impractical solution to implement for real-world operations. Clearly something has to be done to reduce this complexity. The law of diminishing returns applies to the common term extraction problem. It is possible and thus desirable to partition the flow set into multiple smaller subsets and perform pair-wise comparisons within each subset. This way, the number of operations is divided by the square of the number of subsets, denoted by F. The resultant complexity is therefore $O\left(\dfrac{n^2m^2}{F^2}\right)$, which is much more manageable. The common terms that have been discovered in these flow subsets are then aggregated into a combined term set, and it is then subjected to additional selection criteria as follows:

- Short terms such as "\r\n" or "OK" produce little value but add noise and degrade the quality of the signature. The researchers of the SANTaClass proposal found four characters to be an acceptable threshold. Any term that is less than four characters long is therefore removed from the final set of terms.

- Some strings, such as specific date, time, or numeric values that may not be related to a protocol or application, are removed from the flow set. In practice, this selection method is challenging to automate because the strings may need to be examined in the context of the surrounding terms before they are eliminated. Also, it is difficult to assess the relevancy of a string when the protocol or application is unknown. This step is best executed by manual inspection.

- Two terms that are substrings of each other are combined. For example, consider the terms "HTTP" and "HTTP/". The presence of both terms is simply the result of automatic term extraction, but having both terms does not provide any value. When a substring is detected, the term with the higher probability is accepted, or the longer term is accepted if their probabilities are the same.

- High-frequency terms are kept and low-frequency terms are removed. The frequency of a term is derived from the percentage of the occurrences of the term over the total number of sampled flows. Two thresholds are defined: high and low. Any term whose term frequency is above the high threshold is accepted, while any term whose term frequency is below the low threshold is rejected. Empirical values for the high and low thresholds are found to be around 80 percent and 15 percent, respectively. Any term with a frequency between these thresholds is subject to the mutual-exclusion detection that will be described shortly.

- Mutually exclusive terms are kept in the final terms set. Using the term frequency threshold may sometimes omit terms that are important, but applies only to certain application variants. An example is that different HTTP methods such as "GET", "POST", and "PUT" may not occur frequently enough individually, but collectively produce a high enough frequency above the acceptance threshold. These terms are collected and used to produce different paths in the same application signature. A set of terms is considered mutually exclusive when these terms belonging to the same flow set do not appear in the same payload. Suppose that we have a 100-flow sample, where every flow contains one of "GET", "POST", or "PUT", and where "GET" appears in 50 flows, "PUT" appears in 25, and "POST" appears in 18. If the frequency threshold is set at 80 percent, then none of these terms can be accepted as they all have a term frequency under the threshold. However, we know that in any given flow, if "GET" appears as a term, then "POST" will not be present because these operations are mutually exclusive and cannot co-exist in a single HTTP request. Similarly, if "PUT" appears in the flow, then "GET" cannot be found in that same flow. We can also compute the combined term frequency of "GET", "POST", and "PUT" as (50%+25%+18%=93%), which is above the acceptance frequency threshold of 80 percent. Based on this information, we can conclude that these three terms are mutually exclusive and may be relevant for inclusion in the final terms set.

A prefix tree is then generated using the terms from the final set, which constitutes a signature for the application.

Signature Distiller

The signature generator produces common terms that are present among all of the flows that are considered to be the same application under the flow set construction process. This is a somewhat narrow view, and the distiller module attempts to mitigate this problem by looking at the freshly generated signature in a global context. Specifically, a distiller performs the following actions after obtaining a new signature:

- Eliminates redundant signatures and optimizes the signature trie. Flows from an application may be sorted into different flow sets, for example, because the same application can run on multiple ports. In these cases, a partial signature of an application can exist in the signature database while the newly acquired signature represents another aspect of the same application. The distiller compares the newly created signature to all of the signatures in the current database and searches for similarities. Two signatures that resemble one another will be combined into one. In the context of the prefix tree FSM representation, combining signatures is about modifying the FSM such that branches with the same state transitions that are triggered by the same input are merged, and additional new branches may be created at a given state as part of the merge.

■ Assigns a confidence score to each signature. Every signature will be assigned a confidence score at its creation time. The more flows that have been applied in the signature generation process, the higher the confidence is given to the resulting signature. Therefore, the confidence score may be used to measure whether the signature requires additional refinement. The confidence score also serves as the tie-breaker in the case where a flow matches multiple signatures. The confidence score can be computed based on multiple criteria such as path length, transition probabilities, and term relevance. The path length refers to the number of terms in a single "path" in the signature that leads to the decision node. A longer path length generally indicates a better signature quality. A simplified version of the SIP signature is shown in Figure 7-17 for illustration purposes. The decision nodes 3 and 6 are assigned a path length criterion of 4 and 5, respectively. These values are computed from a number of nodes leading up to this decision.

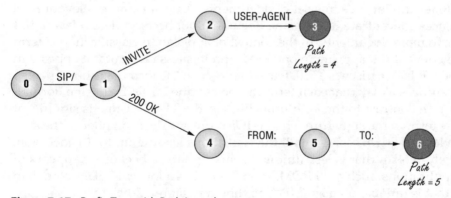

Figure 7-17: Prefix Tree with Path Length

The transition probabilities refer to the probability that a flow will take a specific path in the FSM given that it can be classified as that application. Transition paths that have higher combined probabilities are given higher confidence scores. For illustration purposes, we created an artificial path with the term "OTHER", as shown in Figure 7-18. The transition probability applies only when there are multiple transition branches out of a state. When there is a single branch, there is a single outcome; as a result, the transition probability is 100 percent and therefore omitted. The transition probability for a path is computed at the decision node and is calculated as the product of all of the transition probabilities leading up to this decision.

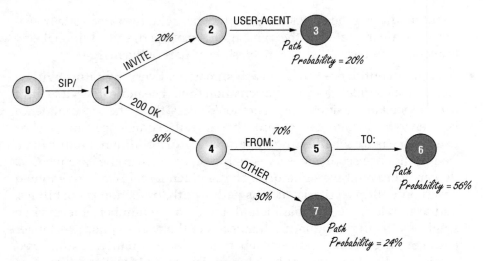

Figure 7-18: Prefix Tree with Path Probability

Last but not least, the term relevance is calculated using the Term Frequency-Inverse Document Frequency (TF-IDF) value. TF-IDF is the metric used to compute term relevance to a set of documents. A term is more relevant if its occurrences concentrate in the same document but becomes less relevant if it appears in more documents. In the context of application classification, a term is more relevant if it appears in one FSM, and it is less relevant if it appears in multiple FSMs. We discuss TF-IDF in Chapter 5, so the formula is not repeated here. It suffices to say that each term can be assigned a TF-IDF value normalized to 1. In contrast to the path probabilities, the TF-IDF value is significant on every term in the signature. The TF-IDF score at a decision node is the sum of individual TF-IDF scores on all the transitions leading up to this decision. Intuitively, a term that is less unique to this signature because it appears in other applications, such as "FROM:" and "TO:", has a lower TF-IDF score than a term that is unique, such as "SIP/", as shown in Figure 7-19.

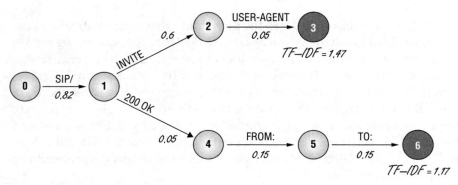

Figure 7-19: Prefix Tree with TF-IDF

The automatic signature generator is a complex system that is typically constructed using a computing cluster. Unlike inline traffic processing devices such as firewalls, both the signature generation and distillation processes are performed offline, not in real-time, because real-time packets are captured and stored. Therefore, accuracy of signature generation is more important than processing performance.

Considerations

An automatic signature generation system can dramatically reduce the amount of human intervention required to collect, analyze, and produce quality signatures. However, there are drawbacks and issues that demand continued research in this technology domain to improve the algorithms. For example, one of the issues is *data overfitting*. The signature generated on one network infrastructure may work very well when classifying traffic on that same network but may work poorly on a different infrastructure. The training set may contain terms specific to a network infrastructure on which the samples are taken. A generic algorithm does not have the intelligence to filter out these terms. The effect of data overfitting becomes even more prevalent in statistical learning machines, as we will discuss in the next section.

The use of automatic signature generation does not solve the problem when it comes to encrypted traffic. Because the system relies on its ability to sniff out common terms among flows, encrypted data completely evades this technique. There may be some useful information that can be extracted from the initial certificate exchanges, but there will be little value to the signature generator after the encrypted sessions have been fully established and the data is encrypted thereafter.

Putting the data collector at the ISP backbones will require the generator to sanitize and remove private information such as usernames, IP addresses, and e-mail addresses before applying the signature generation algorithms. These pieces of information must be transformed into generic token terms such as "IP-Address" and "Email-Address", meaning it is important to know a term is an e-mail address but the exact e-mail address is not important.

An automatic generator does not have the ability to interpret semantics of data that is embedded in the payload, which can serve as an important term. For example, without knowing the actual FTP protocol, an automatic generator may not be able to recognize the IP address of the data channel, which is embedded in the payload in an obscure format that looks like "192,168,1,100,23,15". On the other hand, this IP address information can be easily identified by an experienced protocol engineer.

In a connection, the traffic patterns from client to server can be distinctly different from the traffic patterns going in the opposite direction. Terms that appear in one direction are most likely different from those appearing in the opposite direction. Likewise, the behavioral features constructed from the client-to-server traffic may not apply to its server-to-client exchange. Therefore, application signatures should be generated separately in the training phase. In the classification phase, the traffic collector should separate each connection into two directions before submitting the packets to the classifier. A naïve classifier may perform classification on the first n bytes, without a separate signature for each direction. In this case, asymmetric routing can affect the classification results, because there is no guarantee that the classifier has access to packets that traverse different network paths.

Machine Learning–Based Classification Technique

Pattern- or signature-based classification is either not applicable or ineffective in classifying. Examples include encrypted traffic and traffic flows with short payloads such as interactive applications, mobile applications, or applications with payloads that do not contain sufficient invariant patterns.

Machine Learning (ML) is an interdisciplinary field that combines statistics, data mining, and artificial intelligence, a *learning-by-example* technique where the system learns and evolves for the better as more data becomes available. In the previous section, we introduced machine learning as a tool to categorize flows and generate signatures for the classification engines. In this section, we will take a closer look at different machine learning techniques, specifically clustering and statistical analysis, to aid and refine traffic classification.

There are two main types of machine learning, namely, supervised and unsupervised. In the context of the application classification problem domain, supervised machine learning provides the learning machine with a collection of traffic flows, known as the *training data set,* and these traffic flows have been given proper classifications. The learning machine executes against the training set and refines its algorithms to reach the predefined results, in this case, arriving at the same known classifications. The automatic signature generator discussed in the previous section is a form of supervised machine learning system, where the flow set constructor creates the classification on which subsequent machine learning is based.

Unsupervised machine learning attempts to derive the structure and *features* in the data set without a priori knowledge of what this data represents. In other words, traffic flows that exhibit a similar structure or contain similar features are grouped together by the unsupervised machine learning as potentially belonging to the same application. However, for the result to make sense to a security engineer, the clusters of flows need to be labeled. Unsupervised machine learning is unable to assign meaningful labels or application names to these clusters. It is unlikely that any machine learning technique can be completely free of any human intervention, as we demonstrated earlier.

The set of *features* to be extracted for analysis is critical in both supervised and unsupervised machine learning. We use probability to describe features used in a machine learning algorithm. In the context of traffic classification, the probabilities of these features allow us to answer the following question: If we observe feature X and feature Y on a given flow, which one, out of all possible classification categories, is the most likely? Let us review some basic probability concepts here:

- Random Variable—In statistical analysis, a *random variable* is defined as a function that produces a real value out of a sample space. Take "dice tossing" as an example. We know that a die produces six outcomes, so the random variable takes on a value between 1 and 6. In the context of traffic classification, we can describe a feature using a random variable. The outcome of the feature will affect the classification result on given test data. For example, we can say that the "average packet length" is a feature that affects the classification outcome, and this feature is a random variable with possible values between 1 and 1500.

- Probability Distribution Function—The probability distribution function describes the random variable by assigning observations to the corresponding likelihoods of an outcome. Using the "dice tossing" example, the probability distribution of this random variable, D, can be defined as

$$p(D) = \frac{1}{6}$$

That is, every value of the die has an equal probability of $1/6$. Let us now assume that this is a loaded die such that it has a higher chance to land on 6. In this case, the probability distribution of D can be expressed as

$$p(D) = \begin{cases} 0.5, & d = 6 \\ 0.1, & d = 1,2,3,4,5 \end{cases}$$

As a convention, we use the capital letter to represent a random variable and its corresponding lowercase letter to represent an instance of the random variable.

The *parameter* λ of a probability distribution function can be used to define a specific distribution behavior such as in the loaded die example. Suppose we define λ to represent the probability of the die landing on 6. In this case, the distribution can be represented as

$$p(D) = \begin{cases} \lambda, & d = 6 \\ \dfrac{1-\lambda}{5}, & d = 1,2,3,4,5 \end{cases}$$

Knowing the probability distribution function, we can easily describe the severity of the tainted die using the parameter. For example, we can say that a mildly loaded die has a small λ, while a heavily loaded die has a larger λ value.

- Conditional Probability—A conditional probability describes the event given that another event has occurred. Typically, the "given" clause is written using the vertical bar, such as $p(X \mid event)$. For example, say that someone is playing a game of tossing a die and he wins $1 every time he rolls an even number. Assuming we already know that he wins $1, this rules out any chance of an odd-numbered outcome. The conditional probability of tossing a die based on this new information is

$$p(D \mid win) = \begin{cases} \lambda, & d = 6 \\ \dfrac{1-\lambda}{2}, & d = 2, 4 \end{cases}$$

Now, instead of six possible outcomes, the extra information reduces the possible number of outcomes to three; therefore, the conditional probability is modified to reflect that.

Feature Selection

A *feature* is defined as a certain trait of the traffic that can be retrieved and analyzed by a machine learning system. One example of a feature is the average packet length. If we can group together flows with a similar average packet length, we may be able to deduce that a flow that fits this profile is likely to be a certain type of application or traffic, for example, a file download or an instant messaging application. The set of features to be extracted depends on what the classifier needs to achieve. Selecting the right features for classification is an important step for supervised machine learning. Some machine learning algorithms are robust to the presence of irrelevant features, while other algorithms have less tolerance for noise in the feature set. A feature is considered relevant if it contributes to the quality of the classification results. A feature can have strong or weak relevance. With a *strongly relevant feature*, the lack of this feature reduces the accuracy of the classifier. With a *weakly relevant feature*, removing that feature may or may not impact the quality of the classifier, depending on what other features it combines with in the classifier. The *optimal feature set* contains all strongly relevant features and some weakly relevant features and may even contain irrelevant features. However, the optimal feature set produces the best-quality classification results.

Based on empirical studies, behavior features such as inter-packet gaps, average packet length, packet length variants, flow durations, TCP PUSH flag, and initial advertised TCP window size have served as relevant and important features. There is no definitive process to derive a behavioral feature. However, once potential features have been created, various methods exist to assist the selection of features based on their relevance and weight of contribution towards the classification results. One of these methods is the *wrapper approach*. The wrapper approach creates a decision tree that is comprised of all permutations of the feature sets. By using a supervised machine learning algorithm, also known as an *induction algorithm* in this context, the wrapper approach finds the feature set with the highest evaluation metric that was produced by the induction algorithm. An example of such an algorithm is the Naïve Bayes method, which will be introduced in a later section. The wrapper approach treats the induction algorithm as a black box. It uses only the evaluation metric that the induction algorithm produces and reapplies the same evaluation to different permutations of the feature sets to discover the optimal feature set.

The wrapper approach organizes all different possible (feature set) states in a way that each state is connected to another state that has one feature deleted or added. A state is represented by a vector of binary bits, with each bit representing a feature. For example, suppose there are three features in the feature selection, a state can be represented by a bit set (1,0,0): where a 1 indicates that a feature is present and a 0 indicates that the feature is absent. This state will be connected to other states with one and only one feature being different, namely, (0,0,0), (1,0,1), and (1,1,0). Each state represents a feature set that is a permutation of the selected features, and we will call each state a *feature set permutation* for ease of discussion. The result is an interconnected state diagram, referred to as the *search space* and illustrated in Figure 7-20. The size of the search space for n features is $O(2^n)$.

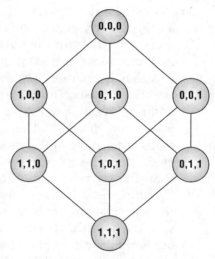

Figure 7-20: Wrapper Method for Subset Feature Selection

The evaluation metric is a numeric quantity that measures the quality of the classifier. The evaluation metric for each feature set permutation can be obtained through an accuracy estimation method called *k-fold cross-validation*. As a feature set permutation is created by either adding or removing features, a test set is necessary to measure the result of the learning machine executed with that feature set permutation. Because an explicit test set is not available for each feature set permutation, the original training set is utilized to create a hypothetical test set for validation. The entire training data set is randomly divided into k equal partitions with k-fold cross-validation method. Out of k partitions, one partition is used as test data, the other k-1 partitions are used as training data, and the result of the learning machine executed with that feature set permutation is recorded. The motivation to split all of the training data into *k* partitions is to mitigate the effect of *data overfitting*, a problem where the learning machine models too closely to the training set and loses sight of the generality of the system. This process is repeated *k* times until each partition has served as a test data set. The average of all of the recorded results is used as the evaluation metric for that (feature set) state of the search space.

Because the wrapper approach produces a search space, finding the optimal feature set becomes a searching problem. The search algorithm defines the initial state and the termination condition: How do we know that we have reached the state that has the highest accuracy? Notice that the search space is typically much larger than this illustration. A search space with 40 features contains 2^{40} states, or about one trillion states. It requires a structured approach to decide, while traversing and evaluating each state, when to terminate further searches. This is the goal of the search algorithm. We describe two search methods here:

- The *Hill-Climbing Search*, also known as the greedy search or steepest ascent, starts from the initial state and computes the evaluation metric of each of its children. The child with the best evaluation metric is selected as the next node, and the search continues from that child. The algorithm stops when none of the child nodes evaluate to be a better feature set than the current node. The Hill-Climbing Search is not an exhaustive search algorithm because it may stop at a node that is locally optimal but is not the most optimal set in the entire search space. We will look at an example using a much smaller search space that contains three features as illustrated in Figure 7-21. The number below the feature bitmap

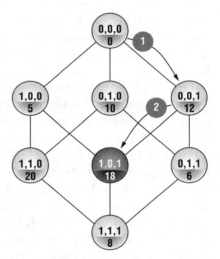

Figure 7-21: Wrapper Method with Hill-Climbing Search

represents the evaluation metric of each feature set.

By inspection, the best feature set is (1,1,0), which has an evaluation metric of 20, the highest amongst all states in the search space. Applying the Hill-Climbing Search algorithm, we can see that the first step it takes is towards (0,0,1), which has the best evaluation metric among all children of the initial state (0,0,0). On iteration 2, it is found that (1,0,1) has an evaluation metric that is better than the others, and hence the search moves on to (1,0,1). At this point, none of its children has a better evaluation metric than itself, the search algorithm stops, and (1,0,1) is declared to be the most optimal feature set. The "local comparison" property of the Hill-Climbing algorithm does not guarantee that an optimal solution can be reached in the entire search space. However, because the number of evaluation computations is small, this algorithm is very efficient when applied to large search spaces.

▪ The *Best-First Search* selects the most promising state generated so far that has not already been expanded, that is, its children have not been traversed. The operation defines two lists: OPEN and CLOSED. When the search algorithm first begins, the OPEN list contains just the initial state, while the CLOSED list is initially empty. The process then picks the best state out of the OPEN list, which is (0,0,0) in the first iteration, and adds this state to the CLOSED list. Every child from this node is then evaluated and added to the OPEN list. On the next iteration, the best node is picked from the OPEN list, and all of its children are evaluated and added to the OPEN list. This node from the previous iteration is moved to the CLOSED list, and if it has the best evaluation metric seen so far, then the node is marked as the candidate node. This is an exhaustive search that, if allowed to continue, will visit every single node in the search space. A reasonable approach is to terminate the search when the evaluation metric has reached a certain confidence level.

Using this example and referring again to Figure 7-21, we start with the OPEN list containing just the initial node (0,0,0):

```
OPEN: (0,0,0)
BEST: none
```

Step 1 evaluates all of its children and moves the completed node to the CLOSED list. When a node is moved into the CLOSED list, it compares against the current BEST and replaces it if the new state is better. All of the children are added to the OPEN list and sorted according to the evaluation metric from the best to the worst:

```
OPEN: (0,0,1) (0,1,0) (1,0,0)
CLOSED: (0,0,0)
BEST: (0,0,0)
```

Because (0,0,1) has the best evaluation metric, this node is moved to the CLOSED list, and all the children of (0,0,1) are evaluated and moved to the OPEN list, if they are not already there. They are again sorted according to their evaluation metrics. Because (0,0,1) is better than the current BEST node, the BEST candidate is replaced:

```
OPEN: (1,0,1) (0,1,0) (0,1,1) (1,0,0)
CLOSED: (0,0,0) (0,0,1)
BEST: (0,0,1)
```

The next step traverses to node (1,0,1), which is first in line. The search algorithm examines its children (1,0,0) and (1,1,1). In this case, (1,0,0) is already in the OPEN list, so only (1,1,1) needs to be evaluated and moved to the OPEN list. Again, (1,0,1) replaces (0,0,1) as the current best node:

```
OPEN:   (0,1,0)  (1,1,1)  (0,1,1)  (1,0,0)
CLOSED: (0,0,0)  (0,0,1)  (1,0,1)
BEST:   (1,0,1)
```

The next node to visit is (0,1,0), which has an unevaluated child (1,1,0). This new node is evaluated and added to the OPEN list. Because the current node (0,1,0) has a lower evaluation metric than the current BEST, it is simply added to the CLOSED list:

```
OPEN:   (1,1,0)  (1,1,1)  (0,1,1)  (1,0,0)
CLOSED: (0,0,0)  (0,0,1)  (1,0,1)  (0,1,0)
BEST:   (1,0,1)
```

The next node from the OPEN list is then (1,1,0). There is no child that needs to be evaluated, and because (1,1,0) has a better evaluation metric than the current best, it replaces the current BEST node:

```
OPEN:   (1,1,1)  (0,1,1)  (1,0,0)
CLOSED: (0,0,0)  (0,0,1)  (1,0,1)  (0,1,0)  (1,1,0)
BEST:   (1,1,0)
```

The process continues until there are no more search nodes on the OPEN list, which means that every single node has been evaluated and accounted for. A Best-First Search algorithm typically chooses a threshold on which the algorithm stops.

The Best-First Search algorithm is considered more thorough, although not necessarily the better fit for feature selection. Choosing the search algorithm for a machine learning model should take into consideration the *bias-variance dilemma*. The *bias* stems from erroneous assumptions in the machine learning algorithm, while *variance* comes from sensitivity to small fluctuations in the training set. A network on which packet traces are collected creates a *bias* in the data set that is localized to that network. In the attempt to use the data to create a general application signature, the supervised training machine typically tolerates small data variations. These are conflicting criteria; a machine learning system should readjust its parameters based on the results to reach a balance between *bias* and *variance*.

Supervised Machine Learning Algorithms

A supervised learning machine relies on the availability of labeled training data to create a mapping from a set of features to a corresponding output. In the context of classification, the features are packet or flow behaviors. The output is the classification result. The learning machine derives a mapping function from the data to the output so that the classifier can use this mapping function to predict classification results. In this section, we will look at the Naïve Bayes method.

Naïve Bayes Method

The *Naïve Bayes method* applies Baye's theorem to independent features. The *Naïve* part refers to its assumption that every feature considered in the machine learning system is independent of one another. Andrew Moore and Denis Zuev provided the early work on applying the Naïve Bayes method to traffic behavior feature sets to classify traffic into a discrete set of categories. The set of features includes flow duration, TCP port, packet inter-arrival time (IAT), packet size, effective bandwidth, and Fourier Transform on packet IAT.

In Chapter 5, we describe how Baye's theorem, in its simplest form, can be represented using the following formula:

$$P(A|B) = \frac{P(B|A) * P(A)}{P(B)}$$

where *P(A|B)* is the conditional probability of event A occurring given that event B has occurred, and *P(A)* and *P(B)* are the probability of event A occurring and the probability of event B occurring, respectively. To apply this theorem in the context of a classifier, our goal is to *find the probability of a flow belonging to category C given the set of features* $F_1, F_2, \ldots, F_n$, denoted by

$$P(C | F_1, F_2, \ldots, F_n)$$

The theorem therefore indicates that this probability can be evaluated using the following formula:

$$P(C | F_1, F_2, \ldots, F_n) = \frac{P(C) * P(F_1, F_2, \ldots, F_n | C)}{P(F_1, F_2, \ldots, F_n)}$$

In other words, we need to first evaluate *P(C)*, the probability of a category C, independent of any conditions; then evaluate $P(F_1, F_2, \ldots, F_n)$, the probability of a feature set, independent of any conditions; and finally evaluate $P(F_1, F_2, \ldots, F_n | C)$, the conditional probability of a feature set given that a category C is observed. The joint probabilities $P(F_1, F_2, \ldots, F_n | C)$ and $P(F_1, F_2, \ldots, F_n)$ can be computed with the independence assumption by taking the product of individual conditional probability of each feature from the feature set. The following formula applies to the conditional probabilities:

$$P(F_1, F_2, \ldots, F_n | C) = P(F_1 | C) * P(F_2 | C) * \cdots * P(F_n | C) = \prod_{i=1}^{n} P(F_i | C)$$

Similarly, the probability of a feature set without condition can be computed by multiplying the probability of each feature from the feature set:

$$P(F_1, F_2, \ldots, F_n) = P(F_1) * P(F_2) * \ldots * P(F_n) = \prod_{i=1}^{n} P(F_i)$$

The Naïve Bayes machine learning system therefore independently evaluates a feature to derive the conditional probability distribution based on a given classification result. The training data therefore needs to have prior knowledge of which category it should belong to, typically achieved by a DPI classifier, in order to calculate the conditional probabilities.

The simplest form of Naïve Bayes assumes a Gaussian distribution, or normal distribution, of a feature variable. While collecting the data, the *mean* and *variance* of each feature are collected, and this feature is assumed to have a Gaussian distribution. This assumption simplifies the calculation of the conditional probabilities, but may not be accurate in practice. Taking packet size, for example, if the average packet size of the data set on *Web Category* is 500 bytes with 25 bytes variance, the probability distribution function is shown in Figure 7-22.

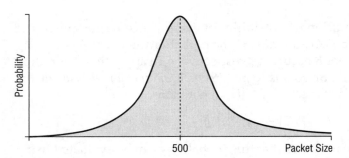

Figure 7-22: Gaussian Distribution

This distribution implies that with 500 bytes being the mean, traffic belonging to the Web Category is unlikely to generate packets that have a packet size that is small, such as 64 bytes. In practice, the distribution can be multi-modal. This means that more than one *peak* can be found in the probability distribution function, as shown in Figure 7-23.

Now, in order to classify an application, say Facebook, we need to first collect a set of training data from the Facebook application. Each of the training flows needs to be marked as Facebook so that the system knows what to expect. These flows are used to generalize the probability distribution function of the feature: $P(X|Facebook)$, where X is the feature we are studying. Assuming that we are only using three features—packet length, inter-packet gap, and flow duration—the Naïve Bayes system can be illustrated in Figure 7-24.

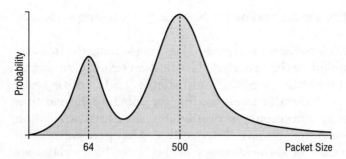

Figure 7-23: Multi-modal Distribution

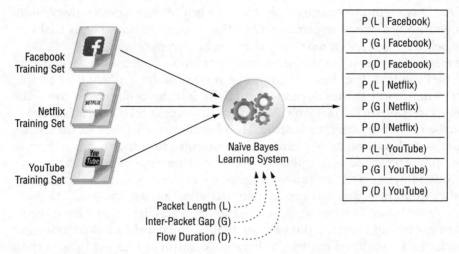

Figure 7-24: Naïve Bayes Learning System

Given the training data, we can easily derive the individual probability distributions for $P(L)$, $P(G)$, $P(D)$, $P(Facebook)$, $P(Netflix)$, and $P(YouTube)$. The challenge now is to calculate the joint probability distribution of L, G, and D given that an application is Facebook, denoted as $P(L,G,D|Facebook)$. Recall that our goal is to find the probability that an application is Facebook given the set of feature values, L, G, and D, which is found with Baye's Theorem using the following formula:

$$P(Facebook| L,G,D) = \frac{P(Facebook) * P(L,G,D \mid Facebook)}{P(L,G,D)}$$

This is where the feature independence assumption comes to our rescue. The probability theory states that for independent variables, the joint probability distribution is the product of the probability distribution of each individual random variable. Therefore,

$$P(L,G,D| Facebook) = P(L| Facebook) * P(G| Facebook) * P(D | Facebook)$$

These are the distributions evaluated by the Naïve Bayes learning system as shown in Figure 7-24.

Because the Naïve Bayes classifier is a supervised learning system, the training data needs to be accompanied by the expected classification result. One way to obtain the classification information for the training data set is to utilize a reliable DPI classifier to classify the traffic while feeding the data into the learning machine. This approach may sound counter-intuitive, but it is a feasible solution given the availability of classifiers both commercially and in open source. The problem with this approach is that the accuracy of the Naïve Bayes classifier depends on the accuracy of the DPI comparator. Another way is to run the said applications in a controlled environment and feed the known data into the classifier. This method is more labor-intensive but offers more accuracy than the previous approach. The problem with this approach, however, is that the feature behavior generated manually may not be diverse enough.

One factor that can affect the performance of Naïve Bayes is the *skewed data bias*. When the training data set contains more data for a particular traffic category than another, the decision boundary will become biased towards the dominant feature. This is unavoidable in real-world traffic, which is most likely to be predominantly web traffic. The classifier, due to the fact that there are more samples towards web traffic than samples for other types of applications, may prefer the web category over the other applications. A variant of the Naïve Bayes classifier, called *Complement Naïve Bayes*, uses all training data other than the requested application to derive the *complement* of the conditional probability. For example, using the previous diagram where three different groups of training data are available, the conditional probability $P(L|Facebook)$ is computed not by the Facebook training data but by all other training data sets. In this particular example, the data from Netflix and YouTube is used to derive the complement of conditional probability distribution, or mathematically $1 - P(L|Facebook)$. In a real-world learning system where the number of applications is much larger than three, as in our example, the *Complement Naïve Bayes* variant usually achieves better results, especially on training sets where one or two applications dominate.

Unsupervised Machine Learning Algorithms

An unsupervised learning machine is presented with data without knowing the structure of the data and what it represents. Just like a supervised learning machine, the goal of an unsupervised machine is to create a mapping function between data and classification results. Without knowing the "correct answer" up front, an unsupervised machine refines and readjusts its mapping function based on additional data iteratively until no further improvement can be made. In this section, we present two unsupervised learning machines: Expectation-Maximization and K-Means.

Expectation-Maximization

With unsupervised learning, we are given a set of data with unknown properties. To create a classifier out of the unknown data, we are now faced with two conflicting requirements: we need to know the classification of each data entry in order to create a model for the feature set, but we also need the model to classify the data entry, as the learning is unsupervised.

The basic concept of the Expectation-Maximization (EM) algorithm is to estimate the accuracy of the current assumption against the data sample and iteratively refine this assumption based on new data samples, all without a priori knowledge of the data. The operation of the EM algorithm begins with an initial assumption on the probability distribution functions of the features. Taking in a manageable set of data entries at a time, the algorithm estimates the likelihood of observing the current data set on all possible classification results. A data set that is more likely to occur in the context of a classification result is given a higher *weight* value. This weight is applied to the current data set, essentially putting more emphasis on the data set that is more likely to occur. With the weighted data set, new estimations of the probability distribution function parameters are derived, and the process repeats itself.

This process iterates repeatedly until the parameters of the estimated probability distribution functions converge. By convergence we mean that the difference between a new estimation of the parameters and the old estimation is below a certain threshold. The converged parameters are the desired parameters that describe the probability distribution of the feature set. For example, a binary feature such as the existence of a TCP PUSH flag has a value of either 1 or 0. The probability distribution of this feature can be described using the *Bernoulli* distribution, with the probability of having the "TCP PUSH flag is set" being the only parameter describing how the TCP PUSH flag is distributed. Let us hypothetically treat the TCP PUSH flag as an important feature to classify an application as interactive, but we do not know if 30 percent of the packet having the PUSH flag set is good enough to make that decision or not. So we start with a rough assumption that if an application is interactive, then 30 percent of the packets have the PUSH flag set, and if an application is not interactive, then 60 percent of the packets have the PUSH flag set. The values 30 percent and 60 percent are the *estimation* of the parameter. Mathematically, a parameter is denoted by θ, and an estimation of a parameter is denoted by $\hat{\theta}$. In addition, an estimated parameter corresponding to an interactive application is denoted as $\hat{\theta}_I$, while an estimated parameter corresponding to a non-interactive application is denoted as $\hat{\theta}_N$. With these definitions we can describe the initial estimations mathematically as follows:

$$\hat{\theta}_I(0) = 0.3$$

$$\hat{\theta}_N(0) = 0.6$$

The parenthesized value 0 in this case refers to the iteration count, which is zero when the EM first starts. The system first retrieves a finite number of samples on each iteration. In this example, assume we take five flows at a time. At this point, the system has no knowledge of whether a flow belongs to the interactive category or not. However, we can use the previously established estimations to derive the probability of these flows being categorized as interactive or not. This is the *Expectation step*. The Expectation step takes sampled data and computes the likelihoods of the set of five flow samples being either interactive or non-interactive given the current estimates.

For simplicity, we assume that each flow contains exactly ten packets. For every packet, the presence of the PUSH flag is denoted by 1, while an absence is denoted by 0. The first flow collected can look something like the following stream of binary values: `1000010110`. Given the estimation that the probability of an interactive flow containing a PUSH flag is 0.3, we can compute the probability that a flow produces these packets given that it is an interactive flow. The first bit 1 has the probability of 0.3, the second bit 0 has the probability of 0.7, and so on. The conditional probability of observing this particular series of PUSH flag values on a flow given it is an interactive application, denoted as I, is therefore

$$p(flow1|I) = 0.3 * 0.7 * 0.7 * 0.7 * 0.7 * 0.3 * 0.7 * 0.3 * 0.3 * 0.7 = 0.000953$$

Similarly, the conditional probability of observing this particular series of PUSH flag values on this flow given it is a non-interactive application, denoted as N, can be computed as follows:

$$p(flow1|N) = 0.6 * 0.4 * 0.4 * 0.4 * 0.4 * 0.6 * 0.4 * 0.6 * 0.6 * 0.4 = 0.000531$$

The Expectation step uses the probability of each outcome to compute the *weight* of the current training data, normalized among all possible outcomes. Because there are only two possible outcomes, interactive or non-interactive, the weights can be derived using the previous conditional probabilities:

$$w(flow1|I) = \frac{0.000953}{(0.000953 + 0.000531)} = 0.64$$

$$w(flow1|N) = \frac{0.000531}{(0.000953 + 0.000531)} = 0.36$$

The probability of a flow is used to compute the *weight* of this flow. A higher weight means that the data is more relevant in re-evaluating our new estimation. The current flow "flow1" contains four packets with a PUSH flag and six packets without a PUSH flag. Applying the weight to the current data stream `1000010110` yields `0.64*4=2.56` occurrences of a PUSH flag and `0.64*6=3.84` occurrences of a packet without a PUSH flag on an interactive application. Similarly, the weight for a non-interactive application on this sample flow is 0.36; hence, the weighted occurrence of packets with PUSH flags is `0.36*4=1.44`, and the weighted occurrence of packets without PUSH flags is `0.36*6=2.16`. By repeating this process on all five flows, we can derive the following table of weighted occurrences based on the current estimation, as shown in Figure 7-25.

Samples	Weight Table		Weighted Occurrences of 1 and 0	
	Interactive	Non-Interactive	Interactive	Non-Interactive
1000010110	0.64	0.36	2.56, 3.84	1.44, 2.16
0111111111	0.003	0.997	0.027, 0.003	8.97, 0.997
1010101010	0.34	0.66	1.7, 1.7	3.3, 3.3
0010101000	0.86	0.14	0.027, 0.003	8.97, 0.997
0100100000	0.96	0.04	1.7, 1.7	3.3, 3.3
Sum of Weighted Samples			8.787, 19.243	14.21, 7.757

Figure 7-25: Table of Weighted Occurrences

The results of all the weighted samples are accumulated to produce the cumulative weighted samples, and these values are used as a basis to create a new estimation of the parameters. The *Maximization step* takes this "Sum of weighted samples" as input and computes the new estimation. Recall that in our example, the TCP PUSH flag feature is a Bernoulli distribution. Our current goal in the *Maximization* step is to produce $\hat{\theta}_I(1)$ so that this estimate can be used as a basis in the *Expectation* step of iteration 1. In this particular case, a new estimate can be easily computed. The conditional probability of observing a PUSH flag being set on an application can be computed using the sum of weighted samples with the PUSH flag set, divided by the sum of all weighted samples. Mathematically, the new estimate can be found using the following equations:

$$\hat{\theta}_I(1) = \frac{8.787}{8.787 + 19.243} = 0.313$$

$$\hat{\theta}_N(1) = \frac{14.21}{14.21 + 7.757} = 0.647$$

The process then repeats until the estimated parameters converge. In other words, if $\hat{\theta}_I(n) - \hat{\theta}_I(n-1)$ is smaller than a threshold, say 0.001, then the algorithm converges. The final values of $\hat{\theta}_I$ and $\hat{\theta}_N$ are the best estimates of the parameters.

The EM algorithm works on multiple features that exhibit different probabilistic behaviors. The EM system designer must define the desired features and make intelligent decisions about what probability distribution function best describes each feature. The process that analyzes the data stream and estimates the parameter of a statistical model is called the *Maximum Likelihood Estimation*, or MLE.

In this example, we have used the simple binary distribution to describe our feature. Practical features can be *Gaussian, Poisson,* or *Binomial* distributed. The calculation based on the current data set is different for each probability distribution. For example, let's assume that the feature *packet length* is a Gaussian distribution with two parameters: mean μ and variance σ. The data collected from the sample is therefore a vector of a packet length such as {40, 40, 40, 150, 268, 352, 60, 492, 40, 40}. Just like the PUSH flag example, we can calculate the probability of a data stream with this series of packet lengths by applying the probability distribution function using the current parameter values. Assuming that the current mean and variance are 120 and 30, respectively, on the interactive application, the probability of obtaining a packet with length x can be computed using the Gaussian formula:

$$f(x,\mu,\sigma) = \frac{1}{\sigma\sqrt{2\pi}} e^{-\frac{(x-\mu)^2}{2\sigma^2}}$$

Applying the values $x = 40$, $\mu = 250$ and $\sigma = 30$, the probability of obtaining a 40-byte packet is 0.000378. This formula is applied to every packet on the data stream with a different x value. The product of ten probability values is the conditional probability of this data stream, given that the packets are from an interactive application. This product will be used as the basis to compute the weight, as in the previous PUSH flag example. By changing the probability distribution function and its corresponding parameters, we can apply the same principle as shown earlier with the binary feature and extend that to a complex distribution function such as the Gaussian distribution.

The performance of the EM algorithm depends on the initial assumptions and estimations. The algorithm strives to find the optimal parameters that fit the distribution property it was initially given. If the EM was given a bad distribution model to begin with, the result will be incorrect as well.

K-Means Clustering

K-Means clustering is a method that attempts to identify clusters or groupings in a data set, such that each data point belongs in a cluster that it is closest to. The distance is measured between the data point and the center of the cluster. In other words, K-Means clustering is a method to group similar data samples into a finite set of clusters or groups. The K-Means clustering concept is best explained using a well-known example of calculating T-shirt sizes and making T-shirts that can fit an entire population. Let's assume a T-shirt company has gathered statistical data on the heights and weights of a population. The results of the statistics are shown in Figure 7-26.

Because the T-shirt company cannot economically make a shirt for every size, it will use these statistics to create three different sizes: small, medium, and large, as shown in Figure 7-27.

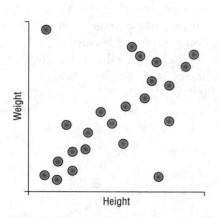

Figure 7-26: Weight and Height Sample Statistics

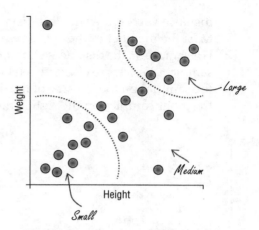

Figure 7-27: Partitioning the Weight and Height Sample Statistics

This is the basic idea of K-Means clustering, which is typically applied to an n-dimensional space where n is the number of features to consider, and the sample space is divided into k clusters. The goal of the K-Means algorithm is to draw the boundaries, as shown in Figure 7-27. The algorithm is an iterative approach and consists of the following steps:

1. Pick initial states. The algorithm starts with k initial *centroids* for each cluster. A centroid is defined as the geometric center of a cluster C_k. To compute the centroid, the average value along each dimension is computed among all the samples, and the resultant vector is the centroid. A Euclidean distance is the length of the line connecting from point A to point B in an N-dimensional space, which can be computed using the following formula:

$$D(\hat{P},\hat{Q}) = \sqrt{(q_1 - p_1)^2 + (q_2 - p_2)^2 + \cdots + (q_n - p_n)^2}$$

    where p_n is the nth dimension of point P. The initial position of a centroid is arbitrary; the following steps will iteratively adjust its centroid based on real samples until no further changes can be made. For illustration purposes, we assume that there will be two clusters, and there are a total of 14 samples, with each sample denoted as S_i. Each sample contains two features, which means that the cluster is a two-dimensional plane. The initial centroids $c1$ and $c2$ are chosen to split up the space into left and right spaces, as shown in Figure 7-28.

2. Compute cluster membership based on the Euclidean distance vector. For each sample, K-Means calculate the Euclidean distance from the position of the sample to every centroid that results in a distance vector. Within this

distance vector, the smallest distance is selected, and this sample is said to be the member of the cluster whose Euclidean distance is the smallest. For sample S_1, the distances D_1 and D_2 are computed, and because $D_1 < D_2$, sample S_1 belongs to cluster 1, as shown in Figure 7-29. At the end of Step 2, the samples on the left side of the dotted line belong to cluster 1, while all the other samples on the right side belong to cluster 2.

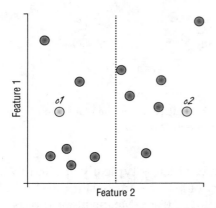

Figure 7-28: Separating the Sample Space Using Centroids

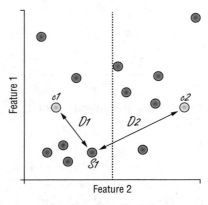

Figure 7-29: Cluster Membership Based on Euclidean Distance Vector

3. Adjust cluster centroid. After the membership has been determined, a new centroid is computed based on all samples within the same cluster. This new centroid is a point inside the existing cluster where its value at dimension n is the average of dimension n of all samples that belong to this cluster. The new centroids are used as the new basis for distance vector calculation, as shown in Figure 7-30.

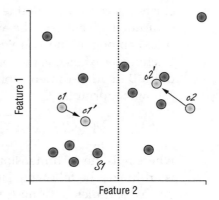

Figure 7-30: Cluster Centroid Adjustments

4. Iterate until convergence. After the new centroids are calculated, the cluster memberships are reset for all of the samples. The algorithm returns to Step 2 and repeats until no further changes to the location of the centroids can be made. At this point, the centroids are said to have *converged*.

The K-Means clustering algorithm always produces clusters of the same shape. An application that exhibits a strong cluster in one feature may have diverse behavior in another. Simple K-Means that consider both features may not properly capture the cluster of this application. Therefore, the K-Means cluster is typically used as a first step or refinement step to classification problems.

Classifier Performance Evaluation

The performance or the accuracy of a classifier is evaluated against a number of metrics: *False Negatives, False Positives, True Positives,* and *True Negatives.* Figures 7-31 through 7-34 illustrate the difference between these metrics:

- False Negatives (FN)—Traffic that should be X but is incorrectly classified as not belonging to X.

- False Positives (FP)—Traffic that should not be X but is incorrectly classified as belonging to X.

- True Positives (TP)—Traffic that should be X and is correctly classified as belonging to X.

- True Negatives (TN)—Traffic that should not be X and is correctly classified as not belonging to X.

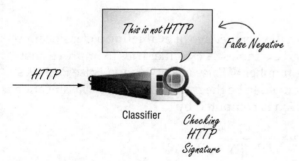

Figure 7-31:   False Negative

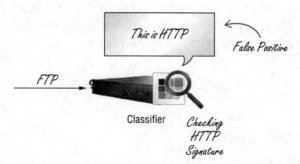

Figure 7-32: False Positive

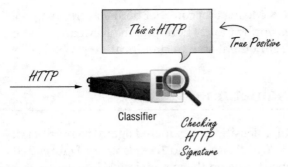

Figure 7-33: True Positive

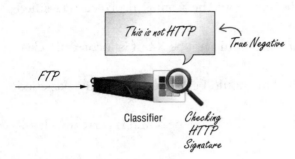

Figure 7-34: True Negative

The metrics are evaluated from the perspective of evaluating a classification X, which is HTTP in the illustrated examples. A classifier tries to improve on its True Positives while reducing the number of False Negatives and False Positives.

The *accuracy* of a classifier is defined to be the fraction of correct classification results over all of the results, which is computed by

$$Accuracy = \frac{TP+TN}{TP+TN+FP+FN}$$

Ironically, the accuracy metric does not accurately reflect the performance of a classifier. For example, suppose that we are interested in classifying SIP traffic out of 1,000,000 flows. There are only 1,000 flows that are truly SIP traffic. A classifier does not recognize any SIP traffic so always returns *false* with respect to SIP traffic classification. The evaluation metrics are shown here:

True Positive = 0

True Negative = 999,000

False Positive = 0

False Negative = 1,000

The accuracy of this "classifier" is computed as

$$Accuracy = \frac{TP+TN}{TP+TN+FP+FN} = \frac{999000}{1000000} = 99.9\%$$

and appears to be an extremely "accurate" classifier. However, this "classifier" does not provide any value regarding SIP traffic classification. In light of this deficiency in accuracy, two other evaluation metrics are used: *recall* and *precision*. Recall and precision emphasize how much the classifier gets right, while ignoring what it did not get wrong. This translates to putting emphasis on the TP value while ignoring the TN value. The formal definitions of *recall* and *precision* are as follows:

- Recall is the percentage of members of class X correctly classified as belonging to class X, as illustrated in Figure 7-35. It measures the sensitivity of the classifier by computing the percentage of the correct items that are classified.

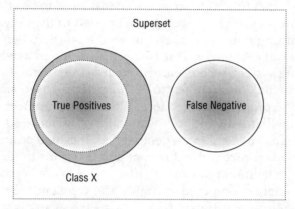

Figure 7-35: Recall

Recall can be defined mathematically using the following formula:

$$Recall = \frac{TP}{TP + FN}$$

- Precision is the percentage of those instances that truly have class X, among all those classified as class X, as illustrated in Figure 7-36. It measures the relevant accuracy of the classifier by computing the percentage of the classified items that are correct.

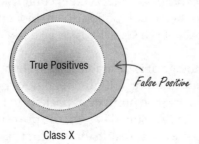

Figure 7-36: Precision

Precision can be defined mathematically using the following formula:

$$Precision = \frac{TP}{TP + FP}$$

Naturally, *recall* and *precision* are opposing values. As *recall* increases, *precision* decreases. A classification design strives to achieve a balance between recall and precision.

Machine learning relies heavily on the training data set to generalize application behavior. A system can sometimes try too hard to fit their model, resulting in a model that *overfits* the training data. We use the bias error and variance error to evaluate the degree of overfit. A system that has a very high bias is considered to be *underfit,* while a system that has high variance is considered to be *overfit.*

A system that overfits can perform very well when applied to the network environment on which training data was taken but works poorly when the system is moved and deployed elsewhere. This is especially true in a behavioral-based machine learning system, where features such as inter-arrival time or packet length are used as the dominant features. For pattern-based signatures, it may be possible that a properly defined term filter can eliminate terms that are site-specific, which will greatly reduce the amount of variance so that the generated application signatures are more generalized. It is also desirable to obtain samples from various sources or at different points in time to reduce the number of redundant behavioral patterns. Traffic patterns are typically very different during office hours compared to nights and weekends. So collecting data from multiple sources at different times is a good way to diversify the samples. Machine learning systems are statistical in nature. It may not be realistic to expect the model to fit every environment; however, a system should contain tunable parameters that will fit the model to the particular network environment the system is deployed in.

In traffic classification, more information typically results in better classification results. However, more information infers that a classifier needs to collect more packets on a given flow to reach a classification decision. The problem with requiring more packets on a flow is twofold: first, on systems that require a classification decision to perform a flow-based policy action such as a QoS device, an early classification result is essential so that packets consume the allocated bandwidth instead of adhering to the default policy due to indecision. On a security device where every leaked packet is a security risk, an early decision is of fundamental importance.

Second, accumulating packets requires storage. It is desirable for a system with limited resources that is performing classification on a high-speed network to minimize memory footprint per flow. Reducing the number of packets to reach a classification decision is a desirable criterion. As stated earlier, the port-based classification approach can obtain the classification results on the first packet. The DPI-based classification typically looks at only the first N-bytes payload of the packets. The machine learning system depends completely on the features selected. Some features, such as flow duration, require a flow to be completed before a decision can be made and therefore are useful only when analyzing an application retrospectively. A security engineer may prefer one type of system to another, depending on the objectives of traffic classification.

Proxy versus Classifier

As detailed in Chapter 1, a proxy is designed to intercept traffic and to communicate with the end points of the original connection according to defined security policies. Therefore, a proxy must have intrinsic knowledge of the protocol that is used in that communication. Metaphorically, the proxy needs to know how to "speak the language". On the other hand, a classification engine wants to know "what language is spoken". In addition, the proxy must not only be capable of "speaking the language" but must also assume the identity of one speaker while speaking to the other, and vice versa.

We covered the proxy architecture in the section titled "The Proxy Architecture" of Chapter 1. That architecture diagram, shown again here as Figure 7-37, illustrates that the proxy has an embedded classifier. This classifier appears to be a hybrid of a port-based and DPI-based classifier. The security policy in the proxy dictates that the proxy must act on the first packet; otherwise, the proxy cannot masquerade as the end point. This is because the proxy would be detected as a "third-party" if the proxy "did not initiate the conversation". This basic operating requirement forces the proxy to first act as a port-based classifier.

By definition, the proxy examines the payload packet by packet, which enables the proxy to function as a DPI-based classifier. As the proxy continues to classify the proxied traffic, the proxy verifies whether its original classification is accurate. In the language analogy, as the proxy continues to speak, it verifies if it is indeed speaking the correct language as expected by the other party. As soon as the proxy detects its original classification is incorrect, the proxy performs a *protocol handoff* that essentially transfers the connection to another proxy that is designed to process that application. Still using the language analogy, the proxy "switches the language" as soon as it detects what it has spoken to the other party is not the right language. Sometimes the proxy realizes the correct language is not one it is capable of speaking; at that point the proxy terminates the connection, breaks the application, and possibly exposes its presence.

As the proxy architecture illustrates, a typical commercial proxy appliance has a limited number of application proxies operating within itself. Twenty application proxies operating in a typical commercial proxy appliance is already a high number. This number is a tiny fraction when compared with a typical commercial application classification appliance that enforces QoS-centric policies, which can classify between 2,000 and 5,000 applications. Developing a comprehensive proxy for a specific application requires many months of intensive protocol analysis and development time. For a complex application, the proxy may take years to perfect. For an application that operates over an encryption protocol, the task of developing a proxy is extremely difficult if not impossible. Having a proxy for every application is simply not feasible with today's technology.

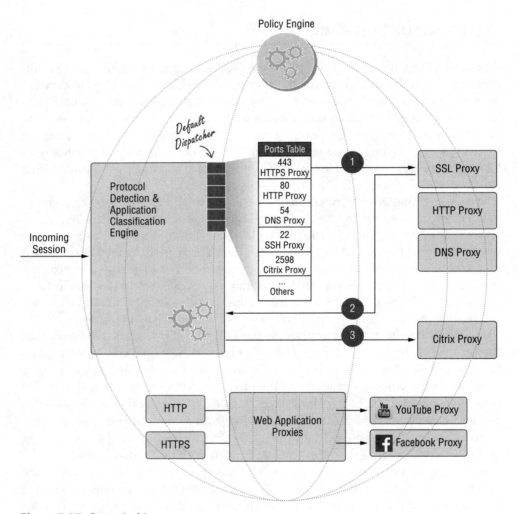

Figure 7-37: Proxy Architecture

Consider an example security policy that states "Block Dropbox Upload". This will require the proxy to examine a connection from the very beginning, simply because the first payload could be a portion of a file that is being uploaded to Dropbox. Therefore, if the first packet offers any indication the flow may come from a Dropbox application, the proxy must terminate and intercept the connection at the first packet. Two observations can be made from this scenario:

- Because the proxy begins with a port-based classifier, if the first packet has a destination port or IP address that is not known to be used by Dropbox, then that connection may circumvent the proxy. The only viable solution to solving this proxy-avoidance problem is for the proxy to intercept each and every connection. There are quite a few issues associated with this "shotgun" approach. First, performance and scalability become significant requirements for the proxy. We have observed in several large school districts that there are typically 120,000 users during the day, generating 200,000 connections per second, 6 million active connections at any given moment, and 18 million web requests per day, and running close to 1,000 applications that include web-based, mobile, and traditional applications. Second, intercepting connections from applications that the proxy does not have any knowledge to handle as a proxy will cause an application to misbehave, operate incorrectly, or stop functioning completely. Consequently, the proxy cannot be transparent if it keeps "breaking applications" and causing user uproars.

- The *first-packet interception* requirement prevents a proxy from employing a machine learning-based classifier. Most practical machine learning algorithms that are utilized for classification solutions require sample features that translate into multiple packet collections. Packets received during the classification phase are "leaked" and are very likely to violate strict security policies.

Enforcing QoS policies can be difficult even in a dedicated network visibility appliance. Suppose a hypothetical network management requirement is to restrict the bandwidth usage of Dropbox download activities. Because Dropbox traffic is encrypted and assuming the classifier is a learning machine-based classifier having *inter-packet arrival time* and *average packet size* as the algorithm features, ten seconds worth of traffic is collected as the sample to be extracted for classification. During this ten-second interval, all of those packets in the sample are transmitted using a default QoS policy. This default QoS policy must not be too restrictive or else it may negatively impact an application that is granted high bandwidth with certain timing guarantees. On the other hand, if the application turns out to be one that must be restricted in bandwidth usage, that application would enjoy ten seconds of unlimited utilization of valuable network resources before the application is properly classified. On a high-speed 10G network, ten seconds worth of traffic can be significant, although the actual volume depends on the application in question. In addition, on a large network that provides services to thousands of users who may favor the Dropbox application, the aggregate bandwidth consumption caused by the ten-second classification delay can be significant enough to render the QoS policies useless.

The industry has desired and attempted for years to combine the dedicated proxy appliance with a dedicated application classification appliance into a single-box solution, which could possess the abilities to specify and enforce both strict security policies and QoS-centric traffic engineering policies. However, the technical challenges illustrated in the previous discussion, compounded by the SSL interception challenges, have prevented the successful construction of such a commercially viable super appliance to date.

Summary

Traffic classification is a challenging problem, and classification technology is far from mature. The increasing emphasis on data encryption obfuscates the information a classifier needs to make classification decisions. The explosive growth in web-based and mobile applications amplifies the difficulties facing designers of classification algorithms. Classification technology should be implemented according to intended objectives. For example, a classification system that is used primarily for retrospective analysis prefers accuracy and a breadth of application coverage and can be more tolerant of classification delay. On the other hand, using a hybrid set of classification techniques to implement comprehensive security policies will prefer early classification decisions and real-time performance but may accept a signature database with a smaller set of applications. A classifier may be deployed in a network environment that needs to see and analyze every packet, while others may respect individual privacy and not track any private and personal information. A versatile solution has its compromise, and each solution may excel at solving one aspect of the classification problem at hand; however, it is still up to the practitioner to make the final decision on which combination of technologies can best serve the objectives while meeting performance expectations. The adoption rate of hybrid solutions that combine multiple classifiers, which may include both signature based classifiers and learning machines, continues to grow as the Internet continues to evolve with an increase in application complexity.

CHAPTER 8

Retrospective Analysis

An *advanced persistent threat* (APT) is a targeted attack that is stealthy and can maintain its presence in victimized systems for months if not years without detection. Infiltration by APT typically begins with a prolonged campaign against a specific target. The "advanced" aspect of APT does not necessarily imply the attack is based on advanced technology but rather that the attack deploys a combination of methods, ranging from traditional techniques to custom code while launching the assault. The attackers have complete situational awareness and are adaptive when it comes to altering attack approaches. As APTs are typically launched by well-funded and well-organized entities, the attack objectives are focused and specific, such as acquiring military or commercial intelligence or inflicting some type of damage. Therefore, the "persistent" aspect of APT comes from the fact that the attack will not stop until the successful infiltration and the intended objectives have been achieved.

Because APTs are not traditional threats, they cannot be treated as traditional threats, and the traditional security mechanisms are ineffective at detecting and defending against them. For example, with all of the known APTs that have been uncovered, none has ever triggered an IDS system. The lack of visible symptoms does not imply that security compromises do not exist or that exfiltration of sensitive data is not already underway. Therefore, planning, designing, implementing, and refining detection solutions is just as important and mandatory as the continued deployment of proactive preventive solutions. Solving the APT problem is about detection because APT can enter the network as legitimate traffic. APT traffic behaves like regular legitimate traffic, and therefore the focus should be on the detection and prevention of outbound data, that is, on data exfiltration, and this is one of the main objectives of deploying secure proxies.

Performing effective APT analysis depends on both the quality and the quantity of the data collected about the network that is under examination. Data collection can be comprised of logs from applications and services and full network traffic captures that contain each and every packet for all connections and flows. The collected data must be managed and indexed because one of the most important tasks of the analysis process is for a security analyst to conduct various queries against the stored data, followed by correlating the answers to discover suspicious patterns. Because the analysis is performed against offline data, it is performed on events that have already taken place. As such, *retrospective analysis* interrogates and scrutinizes events back in time to uncover the beginning of an APT attack and then, from that point in time, trace forward to divulge the attack in its entirety and expose the extent of the damage.

In this chapter, we will focus our discussions on data management that facilitates retrospective analysis.

Data Acquisition

A retrospective analysis system works with data that was collected in the past. From that data, the system should be able to observe the occurrences of certain network events, obtain detailed information about the occurrences, retrieve additional events that are related to those occurrences, and finally draw conclusions based on the compiled information. The functionalities of the retrospective analysis system require the design of the system to facilitate in the following aspects:

- *Data acquisition*—The acquired data should cover all occurrences of all network events within the time period specified by the retrospective analysis system. The acquired data should contain enough detailed information to elaborate the network events. For example, the collected data may list the source and destination IP addresses of a connection. Or, if a file download is included in an HTTP connection, the collected data may contain the type of the file, the file size, or even the actual file.

- *Data organization*—The acquired data should be organized in such a way that it is easy to manage, process, and retrieve. In particular, the retrospective analysis system needs to query the data containing detailed information about the network events and expect rapid responses with results that are linked to those events. In certain cases, those results are the abstracted records from the collected raw data, and we may also need to retrieve the original raw data together with the result records. The data organization also includes storage of the data.

With those specific design requirements in mind, in this section, we will cover collecting and indexing the data with concrete examples showing how that data is made available to a retrospective analysis system.

Logs and Retrospective Analysis

Network appliances and hosts generate logs to record network statistics, events, and resolutions. From the logs, we can get information on what happened in the network and reactions to those events. In the following example, we list two sample logs. The first line is a firewall or IDS log, in which the type of intrusion is recorded along with its source and target. The second line is a proxy log, which records much richer information, like the date and time of the event, the browser type, the destination URL, and, most importantly, the action (that is, policy enforcement) on the traffic flow.

Sample Network Logs

```
1   UDP Snork attack from 10.1.1.1 to 192.168.2.10 on interface outside
2   2014-12-01 00:49:13 2 192.168.2.10 - - policy_denied PROXIED
"News/Media" -   403 TCP_DENIED GET - http www.cnn.com 80 / - -
"Mozilla/5.0 (Windows NT 6.1; WOW64) AppleWebKit/537.36 (KHTML, like
Gecko) Chrome/39.0.2171.95 Safari/537.36" 192.168.2.10 760 1662 -
"CNN" "none"
```

Generally speaking, the entire spectrum of logs can be categorized into four types. *Security logs* record system security events. They cover all incidents that are related to system intrusion, attacks, malware or viruses, data loss or leaks, and other types of security breaches. For example, on some Linux systems, the security logs are stored at /var/log/secure, where the user log ins and authentication-based resource access events are recorded.

Operational logs cover a wide range of logs that are generated while the appliance or software is in operation. The operational logs provide real-time information to the system operators on the events that are happening or the status of the appliance or software. While there are many good examples of operational logs, we refer you to the sample proxy log in the previous example. It is a proxy access log generated to report a policy in action.

Debug logs are designed by developers to gather internal information on the system and software. There is usually a performance cost when debug logs are enabled due to the sheer volume of logs generated. Therefore, in most cases, the debug logs are disabled in a production environment, but they can be enabled on demand.

Compliance logs provide measures to IT auditors to evaluate IT compliance such as Payment Card Industry (PCI), Health Insurance Portability and Accountability Act (HIPAA), and Federal Information Security Management Act (FISMA). Although there is a certain overlap between compliance logs and security logs, the compliance logs are recorded exclusively for compliance regulations and mandates.

Log Formats

Different appliances and devices may generate logs according to different syntax. In order to parse, search, and analyze the various formats of logs, we need to understand how and in what syntax the events are recorded. There are several commonly adopted log formats.

The *NCSA Common Log Format* (CLF) is a standardized log format that is easy to understand. NCSA stands for National Center for Supercomputing Applications and CLF originated from the NCSA httpd project. The CLF writes log entries in the format of "host user-identifier username date:time request status-code bytes". For example, a CLF log entry may look like the following code, where the host is `192.168.2.2`, and the user-identifier is not available and is replaced with the "-" mark. The log also shows the following information: the username is `jdoe`, the `GET` request to `/book/images/cover.gif` occurred at `12:10:17` on `December 31, 2014` Pacific Time, the HTTP request was successful with status code `200`, and the total bytes downloaded were `350`.

Sample NCSA CLF Log

```
192.168.2.2 - jdoe [31/Dec/2014:12:10:17 -0800]
"GET /book/images/cover.gif HTTP/1.0" 200 350
```

Although CLF logs are lightweight and easy to parse, they are quite simple and may not contain all the detailed information we need to record. This gives rise to logs with extended formats. *Extended Log File Format* (ELFF) is a web server log format proposed by W3C and used by Microsoft Internet Information Server (IIS). This format contains two types of basic elements, *directive* and *entry*, and each line can be of either type. The *directive lines* start with the # character and define general information like version, fields of data recorded, software name, start and end time, and so on. The *entry lines* elaborate the details of an HTTP transaction through a sequence of *fields*. The *fields* can specify information like the time of the transaction, bytes transferred, client/server IP addresses, HTTP status code, and so on.

The following example "Sample W3C ELFF Log" shows a sample piece of a W3C ELFF log. In the *entry* line, it records the client IP address, date and time, HTTP client-to-server method (`GET`), URI of the download resource, server return code (`200`), bytes downloaded, client-to-server (browser) referrer link, HTTP version, total time taken to serve the request, and user-agent of the client. The client username is also a field in the *entry*, but the software cannot provide such information, so "-" is used as a placeholder. The previous proxy access log is also an example of an ELFF log. The details of the proxy access log and its fields can be found in Chapter 6.

Sample W3C ELFF Log

```
#Version: 1.0
#Software: SampleLogger
#Fields:  c-ip cs-username date time cs-method cs-uri sc-status bytes
cs(Referrer)  cs-version time-taken cs(User-Agent)
192.168.2.2 - 2014-12-31 12:10:17 GET /book/images/cover.gif 200 350
"http://192.168.1.100/author/pub/secbook.html" HTTP/1.0 200 "Mozilla/5.0
(Windows NT 6.1; WOW64; rv:26.0) Gecko/20100101 Firefox/26.0"
```

The Apache log format is adopted by the widely used Apache HTTP Server and other related projects in the Apache Software Foundation. Apache logs can be of either the Apache Common Format or the Apache Combined Format, which resemble the CLF and the ELFF, respectively. However, the Apache log format has its unique field directives. For example, it uses %a to represent the client IP address, %s to represent the status code, and so on. If we want to use the Apache Combined Log format to record the W3C ELFF log entry previously listed, the log format and entry will look like this:

Sample Apache Combined Format Log

```
#Log Format:  %a %l %t %m %U %s %b %{Referrer}i %H %T %{User-Agent}i
192.168.2.2 - [31/Dec/2014:12:10:17] GET /book/images/cover.gif 200 350
"http://192.168.1.100/author/pub/secbook.html" HTTP/1.0 200 "Mozilla/5.0
(Windows NT 6.1; WOW64; rv:26.0) Gecko/20100101 Firefox/26.0"
```

Other log formats are available, including the Unix syslog format, the XML-based Intrusion Detection Message Exchange Format (IDMEF), and the key-value based ArcSight Common Event Format (CEF). Formatted logs are easy to parse because they can be structured by columns. However, not all logs are well formatted. For the unstructured logs, it is important to make sure the retrospective analysis system is capable of extracting useful information out of them. (Later in this chapter, we will discuss ways to index and search unstructured data.) In addition, not all logs consist of human-readable ASCII characters (for example, the binary format Windows Event Log). For those logs, we need to process the entries and organize them in a format that is convenient to index and search.

Log Management and Analysis

Given the various formats and sources of logs, it is important to centrally manage and analyze the logs. Such a log management and analysis system is a critical piece in a retrospective analysis system, and it should have the following two properties. First, the log management and analysis system should be able to parse the logs of different formats. Second, the system should be able to correlate the log entries in different logs and help to analyze certain network security incidents.

We give an example in Figure 8-1 to show how we can use a log management and analysis system to study APT. Suppose that a corporate network is protected by a proxy. All Internet traffic goes through the proxy, and all intranet traffic bypasses the proxy. Inside the corporate network, a source code server is running an installation of Apache Subversion (SVN) that contains the core intellectual property assets of the corporation, and only certain personnel in the corporation have access to the source code server and checkout (download) source code with their login credentials. The log management and analysis system is deployed on the corporate network, and it can receive logs from both the proxy and the source code server. The proxy log can be configured to use the ELFF format, and the Subversion on the source code server adopts the Apache log format by default. Figure 8-1 depicts the network architecture of the corporate network, and "Sample Log Configuration" lists the sample log configurations on the proxy and the source code server.

Sample Log Configuration

```
#Version: 1.0
#Software: Proxy
#Fields: date time time-taken c-ip cs-username cs-auth-group
x-exception-id sc-filter-result cs-categories cs(Referer)  sc-status
s-action cs-method rs(Content-Type) cs-uri-scheme cs-host cs-uri-port
cs-uri-path cs-uri-query cs-uri-extension cs(User-Agent) s-ip sc-bytes
cs-bytes x-virus-id x-vendor-application-name
x-vendor-application-operation

#SVN Log Format: %{%Y-%m-%d %T}t %u %h repo:%{SVN-REPOS-NAME}e
%{SVN-ACTION}e (%B Bytes in %T Sec)
```

Suppose on the first day of 2015, the corporation found its source code of ProjectY was leaked on Internet. The IT security investigator first studies the proxy access logs and searches for possible threads that may suggest a bulk file transfer. Using the log management and analysis system, the proxy access logs can be sorted by the cs-bytes field, which specifies amount of data uploaded. Unfortunately, the IT security investigator is not able to find any suspicious transactions that could suggest a source code exfiltration event.

In the next step, the log management and analysis system queries the Subversion logs to list all users that have access to ProjectY and have checked out a copy of the source code. To satisfy the search, the SVN log entries should contain the string repo:ProjectY checkout-or-export. The search results provide a list of IP addresses on which copies of the source code exist, as well as the time when the code was first checked out. This list of IP addresses is a potential leakage point, and all transactions from those IP addresses may contain the actual source code exfiltration events. However, it is still not possible to examine each of the suspect transactions due to their vast number of entries. Instead, it is necessary to shortlist the IP suspect list. In this example, the list of suspect IP addresses contains `192.168.2.23` and `192.168.2.10`.

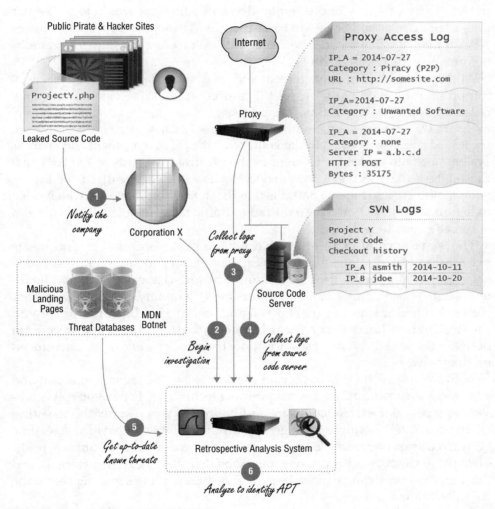

Figure 8-1: Analyzing Log Files for APT

Knowing that the corporation could be a victim of APT, the log management and analysis system goes back to the proxy access logs and tries to find traits of malware download. There are two ways to perform the search. If there is a list of known MDN server IP addresses or landing page URLs, then such a list can be applied to the access log to search if any transaction has `s-ip`, `cs(Referer)`, or `cs-uri-path` in that list. Alternatively, it is also possible to search on `cs-categories` and list all transactions that fall into suspicious categories, for example, Adult, Malicious Sources, Botnet, Phishing, Scam, Spam, Piracy, and so on. In this example, it is found that one IP address (`192.168.2.10`) that has a copy of `ProjectY` source code visited some website in the Piracy category and downloaded some file that was categorized as Potentially Unwanted Software from that site. This could be the first sign of APT, or malware download. The date of that event was more than four months before it was discovered (2014-07-27).

At this stage, the log management and analysis system has three pieces of important information: the suspect IP address (`192.168.2.10`) that has a copy of leaked source code, the timestamp T1 (`2014-07-27 18:21:11`) when potential malware was downloaded, and the timestamp T2 (`2014-10-20 11:20:11`) when the leaked source code was checked out. What the log management and analysis system needs to do next is to identify the exfiltration events in the APT that caused the actual leakage of source code. However, as we have discussed earlier, what makes APT so hard to detect is that the data exfiltrations are well hidden in legitimate transactions: the exfiltration traffic takes up a small volume and is spread over a long period of time.

There are several techniques to filter the proxy access logs and locate exfiltration transactions. First, it is only necessary to search in the transactions that happened after T2. Second, the low-risk categories can be filtered out. Those categories include Business/Economy, Financial Services, News/Media, Search Engine/Portal, and so on. Third, transactions with the destination hosts that appear before and after T1 can be filtered out because those persistent destination hosts are not likely to be introduced by the malware.

With the rest of the transactions in the access log, the log management and analysis system can apply some data-mining techniques. For example, it is possible to separate the transactions by destination hosts and study the statistical characteristic (for example, average and variance of upload payload size, time between transactions, and so on) of transactions to the same destination hosts. Then the destination hosts can be grouped by their statistical characteristic, and the abnormal ones can be picked out. Those abnormal ones may represent the APT destination servers.

One approach to grouping is to use the K-Means clustering algorithm that we introduced in Chapter 7. While we do not plan to dive deep into data-mining techniques, the idea here is that certain tools are available to process and analyze the logs and locate the exfiltration events. The following log listing shows the sample log entries that contain events of source code checkout, potential malware download, and APT exfiltration.

Sample Logs Showing APT (Actual Malnet IP/URLs Omitted)

```
#SVN log showing source code checkout
2014-10-11 09:00:39 asmith 192.168.2.23 repo:ProjectY checkout-or-export
/r1978 depth=infinity (645217532 Bytes in 188 Sec)
2014-10-20 11:20:11 jdoe 192.168.2.10 repo:ProjectY checkout-or-export
/r2048 depth=infinity (675876251 Bytes in 198 Sec)


#Proxy log showing potential malware download from suspicious category
2014-07-27 18:21:08 10448 192.168.2.10 - - - PROXIED "Piracy/Copyright
Concerns;Peer-to-Peer (P2P)" http://somesite.com/  302 TCP_NC_MISS GET
 text/html;%20charset=UTF-8 http somesite.com 80 /wp-
content/themes/current/video_search.php ?query=lucy php "Mozilla/5.0
(Windows NT 6.1; WOW64) AppleWebKit/537.36 (KHTML, like Gecko)
Chrome/39.0.2171.95 Safari/537.36" 192.168.2.1 389 640 - "none" "none"
2014-07-27 18:21:11 164 192.168.2.10 - - - PROXIED "Potentially Unwanted
Software" http://somesite.com/  200 TCP_MISS GET application/
octet-stream
http files4.file-mirror.info 80 /download/1084396/dl
?bc=1084396&pid=16275&brand=somesite.com&country=US&cb=1354937941&zTmp=1
 - "Mozilla/5.0 (Windows NT 6.1; WOW64) AppleWebKit/537.36 (KHTML,
like Gecko) Chrome/39.0.2171.95 Safari/537.36" 192.168.2.1 684891 478
 - "none" "none"


#Proxy log showing potential APT exfiltration events
2014-12-21 01:05:26 1201 192.168.2.10 - - - PROXIED "none"
http://a.b.c.d/upload.htm?FILEDST=/public/
200 TCP_NC_MISS POST text/plain http a.b.c.d 80 /upload - -
"Mozilla/5.0 (Windows NT 6.1; WOW64) AppleWebKit/537.36
(KHTML, like Gecko) Chrome/39.0.2171.95 Safari/537.36"
 192.168.2.1 207 35175 - "none" "none"
2014-12-24 02:23:02 3550 192.168.2.10 - - - PROXIED "none"
http://a.b.c.d/upload.htm?FILEDST=/public/
200 TCP_NC_MISS POST text/plain http a.b.c.d 80 /upload - -
"Mozilla/5.0 (Windows NT 6.1; WOW64) AppleWebKit/537.36
(KHTML, like Gecko) Chrome/39.0.2171.95 Safari/537.36"
192.168.2.1 207 71368 - "none" "none"
```

Packet Captures

Capturing network traffic is another important step in designing and implementing a retrospective analysis system. The general goal of data capture is to obtain a complete view of the network traffic so that the retrospective analysis system never misses a network event when analyzing traffic captures.

Capture Points

In order to capture all the events in the entire network, it is important to know what the capture devices are, and what they are capable of capturing, so that we can put them in the right places.

An *Ethernet hub,* albeit an old-fashioned network device, is a perfect example of a network capture device at the physical layer in the OSI network model. The hub connects multiple Ethernet devices together using a shared bus. Internally, the hub sends out traffic it receives on one port to all the ports so that every device on the hub sees all of the traffic within the hub. For example, say there are three devices on the hub, A, B, and C. If device A wants to send a packet to B, this packet is repeated by the hub on all three ports. Normally, C will not take the packet because the *network interface controller* (NIC) finds that the destination MAC address in the packet is not its own MAC address, and the packet is dropped silently. However, we can configure the NIC on C to operate in *promiscuous* (or promisc) *mode* so that the NIC accepts and potentially records all packets it sees, even if the packets are not destined to it.

The type of networking in the hub is also called *collision domain* because each Ethernet device on the hub can transmit at the same time and cause collisions. While the hub is very inefficient due to collisions, it is a very useful traffic capturing point. In the previous sample-logs example, device C can be used as a capturing device to observe communication between A and B.

Switches solve the collision problem by associating the MAC address with the physical switch ports. In particular, based on the destination MAC address of a packet, the switch only sends the packet to a specific port that this MAC address is associated with. To learn the MAC address and port association, the switch observes the source MAC address on packets from the ports and keeps a lookup table to record the association. If the switch cannot find the packet's destination MAC in its lookup table, it needs to flood once in order to find at which port that particular destination MAC address is located. Unlike a hub, a switch does not repeat packets, and thus, it is not possible to monitor all network traffic by listening on a port. However, most modern switches are manufactured with port mirroring capabilities. With *port mirroring,* the switch can be configured to send a duplicated copy of packets that are received on certain ports to a common mirrored port. The mirrored port is sometimes called a SPAN port, from the Cisco terminology Switch Port for Analysis. The switch can be utilized as a capture point when we place a capturing device on the SPAN port.

Routers are network layer devices that send packets to their destinations in an interconnected network. Unlike switches that mostly work with MAC addresses, routers are more concerned with IP addresses. Some routers are equipped with port mirroring functions so that they can be used as capture points. Other routers have built-in packet capture features and can hold a limited volume of captured packets. In addition, routers have logs to record network incidents. For example, Cisco routers can be configured to perform network traffic filtering based on IP access control lists (ACLs). Logs can record network access events (either allow or deny) that match the configured access control entries (ACEs).

Other network devices can also work as capture points. Those devices can process and capture network traffic at different layers. For example, a *proxy* is often able to perform packet capture while processing at layer 3 and below. Meanwhile, it can also generate logs to record policy enforcement events that are valuable to network forensic analysis. In addition, specially designed inline deployed packet-processing appliances are capable of either capturing packets or calculating and generating network statistic reports. Blue Coat's PacketShaper product is an example. It can monitor and process network traffic, generate records for each of the network flows, and present reports on the collected records. We will visit the possible record formats in the next section.

Capture Formats

Different capture devices collect different formats of captures to record network events. Depending on the capture points and the capture devices, the commonly used capture formats are introduced in this section.

Packet capture (.pcap) is probably the most widely adopted format of network traffic capture. A variety of monitoring software exists on different operating systems that is capable of taking packet captures, including the popular open source tools tcpdump and Wireshark. The underlying engine that handles the actual capturing in those two tools is libpcap, or its Windows port WinPcap. The libpcap library enables the software built on top of it to access the packets from the NIC directly. The grabbed packets can be displayed or stored to a file, usually with the extension .pcap or .dmp.

What libpcap captures are the actual packets that are seen on the wire. This means that the captured packets are raw Ethernet frames that contain both the Ethernet headers and the IP headers and payload. When using tcpdump and Wireshark to capture packets, a timestamp recording when the packet is captured is also added. Because libpcap and tcpdump record the full packet, the sheer size of the capture file makes it difficult, if not impractical, to load and analyze the packet capture using tools like Wireshark. To limit the capture size, it is possible to apply the Berkeley Packet Filter (BPF) during the capturing process. For example, the BFP syntax supports different qualifiers like port, portrange, host, src, dst, tcp, udp, and so on. The expression `tcp dst port 80` will instruct libpcap to only capture TCP traffic that is destined for port 80, and `ip src 10.2.2.200` will limit the captured traffic to only that which originated from IP 10.2.2.200. The capture tool tcpdump also supports a capturing limit based on packet count (-c option), capture file size (-C option), and time duration (-G option). In addition, it can save the capture into multiple files (-W option).

Another consideration when performing packet capture is the size of individual packets. In some commercial ISP networks, it is prohibited to record and analyze capture with full packet length due to privacy and other regulations. In such cases, it is possible to use the snaplen (-s option) argument in tcpdump to limit the captured frame size. Because libpcap records the raw Ethernet frame, a 20-byte Ethernet header length is counted in the snaplen.

NetFlow is a network traffic record format initially introduced and implemented by Cisco on its routers and switches. Compared with packet capture, a NetFlow record provides more compact and concise information to characterize a flow; for example, NetFlow records the most useful tuple <srcaddr, dstaddr, srcport, dstport, proto> but ignores the actual data payload of the flow.

Many devices can generate NetFlow records. Besides routers and switches from major vendors, other inline-deployed traffic-processing appliances such as Blue Coat PacketShaper can also emit NetFlow records while managing network traffic. NetFlow has ten versions, with the most popular being version 5. Versions 8 and 9 have also been widely adopted. Figure 8-2 contains a sample of NetFlow Version 5 records showing the <srcaddr, dstaddr, srcport, dstport, proto> tuple together with start time, duration, packet count, and byte count of the flows monitored.

Date flow start	Duration	Proto	Src IP Addr:Port	Dst IP Addr:Port	Packets	Bytes
2014-12-04 18:21:26.588	300.000	UDP	2.5.33.93:55192 ->	6.9.37.97:8205	1	180
2014-12-04 18:21:26.588	300.000	UDP	2.5.8.96:53443 ->	6.9.12.100:8205	1	180
2014-12-04 18:21:26.588	300.000	UDP	2.5.35.232:53 ->	6.9.39.236:50011	1	72
2014-12-04 18:26:11.577	15.011	TCP	6.9.28.213:80 ->	2.5.24.209:6500	16	20256
2014-12-04 18:26:11.577	15.011	TCP	2.5.24.209:6500 ->	6.9.28.213:80	14	728
2014-12-04 18:26:26.588	0.000	UDP	6.9.42.178:53 ->	2.5.38.174:11572	1	164
2014-12-04 18:26:26.539	0.049	UDP	2.5.38.174:11572 ->	6.9.42.178:53	1	60
2014-12-04 18:26:11.579	15.012	TCP	6.9.42.48:80 ->	2.5.38.44:3525	28	1456
2014-12-04 18:26:11.579	15.012	TCP	2.5.38.44:3525 ->	6.9.42.48:80	27	36874

Figure 8-2: Sample NetFlow Records

To collect NetFlow records, various vendors have their own proprietary implementations, often as a part of the network monitoring module. On the open source side, nfdump (http://nfdump.sourceforge.net/) is a free software suite that includes NetFlow capturing, displaying, and processing modules. The nfdump software is also capable of receiving NetFlow records from multiple sources. Although NetFlow was originally designed to facilitate network usage billing, its records can also be utilized for security analytics. In the example shown in Figure 8-2, the NetFlow record clearly lists the contact time and duration of a flow between two distinct IP addresses and ports and the aggregated size of all packets in the flow. If one of the IP addresses belongs to one of the C2 servers in a malnet, then the NetFlow records provide statistical information about the communication on the C2 channels.

It is worth noting that NetFlow may not be enabled by default on appliances that are capable of generating NetFlow records. There are two reasons for this. First, NetFlow generation requires a lot of computation resources on the appliances themselves, and there is a trade-off between packet processing and NetFlow record generation. Second, emitting NetFlow records consumes network bandwidth. When the flow count in the network is large, the NetFlow records volume increases proportionally with the number of flows. In addition, when the flows are short-lived, more NetFlow records are burst in a short period of time to report the start and stop of the flows, and this can cause a surge in NetFlow bandwidth usage as well.

Internet Protocol Flow Information Export (IPFIX) that is based on NetFlow Version 9 is an IETF-defined protocol. The advantages of IPFIX over older versions of NetFlow are its extensibility and flexibility, for example, its integration with IPv6 to emit IPv6 flow records, support of vendor-specific definitions of the records, and user selection of the flow keys in the records. In addition, IPFIX also tries to define a unified metering, exporting, and collection architecture in network monitoring. As a proposed standard, IPFIX is supported by mainstream networking appliances from major vendors.

Capture a Large Volume of Data

Different networks and appliances generate and collect data at various speeds. To capture the data without any loss, a retrospective analysis system should be able to handle captured data at the highest speed that is possible on the network, which is the line speed. In a typical enterprise network, that speed is 10Gbps. The retrospective analysis system should be designed to capture packets at 10Gbps speed.

Capturing a packet consists of two steps. First, the NIC receives a packet and makes it available for storage. Second, a packet-recording program takes the packet and writes it somewhere on the storage device. In the example of a Linux host, the second step can be done in either kernel space or user space. If it happens in kernel space, the packet-recording program needs to take the packets directly from the NIC driver and dump them on the storage device. In such a case, we need to implement the packet-recording program and build it into a custom kernel. If this happens in user space, it is critical to make sure the packets are transferred to the memory both quickly and efficiently. A popular approach is with direct NIC access, in which the specially designed NIC drivers store the received packets in some pre-allocated memory space that can be directly accessed by user space programs without needing to copy the packets from kernel to user space.

The particular challenge for the packet-recording program is the speed of the storage I/O subsystem. In 2014, the storage controller on mainstream servers was SAS (Serial Attached SCSI), with a rate of 6Gbps. Apparently, that rate is smaller than the input rate of 10Gbps. In this regard, in order to fully capture 10Gbps traffic, multiple instances of the packet-recording program need to be running at the same time. Fortunately, modern Ethernet NIC adapters are equipped with advanced features like receive-side scaling (RSS). With RSS, the packets received by the NIC are distributed into multiple hardware receive queues. To improve packet processing performance, each receive queue can be assigned to a unique interrupt that is affiliated with a separate CPU core. Therefore, it is possible to run a packet-recording program simultaneously on different CPU cores and write packets to different storage devices. With the help of direct NIC access and RSS, we can write a user space program to achieve high-speed packet capture.

There are other issues to consider in packet capture, one being the storage layout. Well-structured storage helps to locate and retrieve packets efficiently. Because RSS distributes packets based on the hashing of the IP addresses, it is possible to store the packets based on the IP address and port. In such a case, the storage is structured with multiple top-level directories representing IP addresses, and in each directory, there are subdirectories for different ports to store the raw packets. Alternatively, packets can also be stored based on time so that the directories can be structured by day, hour, and minute. No matter what directory layout is chosen to store the packets, each of the raw packets should be clearly identified, for example, with a unique packet ID. In that case, when the retrospective analysis system needs to retrieve a single packet, it can first locate the directory in which the packet is stored and then retrieve it from that directory by the unique packet ID.

Another issue is packet processing. Although the goal of packet capture is to receive and store the packets at line speed, it is still necessary to perform certain types of processing on the packets. One type of processing is to add an ID to the packets for efficient retrieval. Another example is to timestamp the packets and record when they were received. Such time stamping needs to be quite accurate, and as a matter of fact, there are a few off-the-shelf timestamping cards that can append a timestamp to the end of the packet while receiving it. If the timestamps are unique, they can even be used as packet IDs. An important packet processing application is to index the packets. Indexing allows the retrospective analysis system to quickly search the packet capture and respond to a user query regarding what happened in the captured traffic. We will explain in detail how to efficiently index packet captures in the next section.

Data Indexing and Query

With the terabytes, if not petabytes, of data collected, the first question to ask is how to organize that data so that it is possible to easily look up and retrieve a relevant piece of data. For that purpose, it is necessary to index the data, and such indexing should be able to resolve queries on the data effectively and efficiently.

Most database administrators or users are familiar with the term index. A database *index* is a data structure designed to sort multiple database entries on certain fields so that searching for a record based on the field value in the index is much faster than linear traversal on the records. The index data structure also holds pointers to the actual records for fast retrieval. However, maintaining such an index structure requires additional storage spaces, either in memory or on disk.

B-tree Index

B-tree is a binary search tree (BST) based data structure that is widely implemented in database systems for indexing records, which allows for efficient operations such as record insertion, deletion, and searching. B-trees are balanced search trees, which is a unique property that requires all of the leaf nodes to be at the same depth level from the root. The height of a B-tree with n nodes is $O(\log n)$ (a later section will provide a more precise value), which means a query takes $O(\log n)$ comparisons in the worst case to determine if an entry is in the tree. As with any BST, each node contains a key that is compared with a search key when a query is issued into the B-tree. When applying a B-tree indexing algorithm for implementing retrospective analysis, examples of a key can be a packet arrival timestamp, a timestamp of an event occurrence, a policy enforcement action code, or the hash value of a predefined log string.

Each tree node also contains a *pointer* for locating the associated file (such as a packet capture) or record (such as a NetFlow record or a line of a proxy log). For example, the pointer can be a file pointer in the file system or an offset within a file such as a record offset within a raw packet capture file. We will use the term *key* to refer to the (key, pointer) pair in a B-tree node to simplify discussion.

What makes a B-tree different from a BST is that one B-tree node can contain multiple keys, and each B-tree node can have more than two children or sub-trees. Figure 8-3 shows an example B-tree. The root node has two keys and three children. These immediate children nodes each also have one to two keys, with two to three children. This example B-tree has 20 nodes with a depth of three levels. In contrast, a regular BST can only hold up to eight nodes with the same depth.

For each non-leaf node, its keys are sorted in increasing order. In the example in Figure 8-3, node E and node G each have three keys, and these keys are sorted by their increasing value. The keys within an internal node separate the children nodes. For an internal node with a single key, such as node C, the key values of the child node G (10, 11, 12) to the left of this node C must have values no greater than the key in node C, while the key values of the child node H (14) to the right of node C must have values no less than the key in node C. Node D has two keys with values 20 and 30, and these two keys separate three children nodes. The left child of key 20 is node I, and the right child is node J. The key values in node I (17, 18) must be less than 20, while the key values in node J (22, 25) must be greater than 20 but less than 30. The key values in node K (40, 60) must be greater than 30.

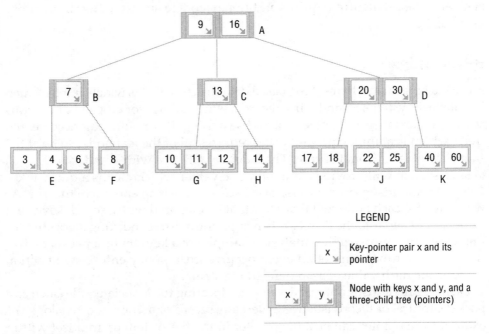

Figure 8-3: A Simple B-tree

Each B-tree has a minimum degree t, which is greater than or equal to 2. The minimum degree specifies how many keys a node can hold. For an internal node, it can have a minimum of $(t–1)$ keys and a maximum of $(2t–1)$ keys. For each B-tree node of x keys, there are $(x+1)$ children. Therefore, for a B-tree of minimum t degrees, the number of children an internal node can have is between t and $2t$. In the example given in Figure 8-3, its minimum degree is 2. For an internal node, the minimum number of children is two, and the maximum number of children is four. Because the number of children is two, three, or four, such a B-tree is also called a *2-3-4* tree. A B-tree with a minimum degree of t, at level h, can hold up to $(2t)^h$ keys. That is to say, if we have over 1 billion keys, we can use a B-tree with a minimum degree of 500 and tree depth of three levels to include all of these keys. In practice, large B-trees usually have minimum degrees between 25 and 1,000.

B-tree Search

In the context of retrospective analysis, imagine we have a NetFlow collector gathering NetFlow records from various sources. A B-tree is used to index the flow records. In each node the key value is an integer value that represents the flow duration in seconds, and the pointer points to the actual NetFlow record on disk for retrieval. Searching for a specific flow record in a B-tree is illustrated in Figure 8-4.

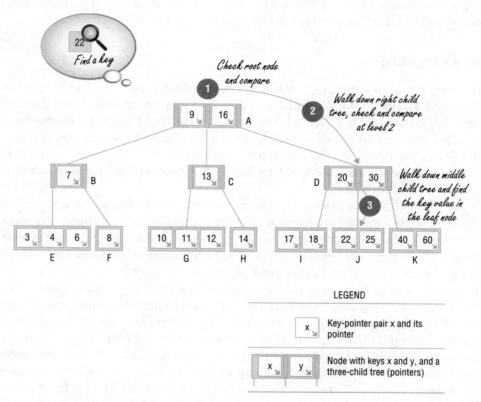

Figure 8-4: Performing a Search in a B-tree

The B-tree shown in Figure 8-4 has 11 nodes (A to K) with 20 keys distributed across three levels. The root node has two keys with values 9 and 16. It has three children or sub-trees. The key values in the root node separate the sub-trees according to the B-tree property. So, to locate the key value 22, the keys in the root node are compared with the search key 22. Because 22 is larger than 16, the search continues in the rightmost sub-tree. At node D, the search key is between key values 20 and 30, and therefore the middle sub-tree is visited next. Then the value 22 is found at leaf node J as its first key value.

The search algorithm can be implemented in a recursive manner. In the first step, we check all the keys in the node to see if the queried key value is present. If a matching key is found, then we return the node as the result. We terminate the search and return "not found" if the current node does not have any sub-trees. Otherwise, we choose the right sub-tree and continue the search in the same manner recursively. In general, for any B-tree of minimum degree t, because each node has at most $(2t-1)$ keys to compare, the cost is $O(t)$. Because there are at most $O(\log n)$ levels, or $O(\log_t n)$ if we factor in t, the overall time complexity of the B-tree search is $O(t \log_t n)$.

B-tree Insertion

Capturing and inserting new flow records into a retrospective analysis system is a common operation. We will illustrate a B-tree insertion example in this section. Suppose a newly collected flow has a five-second duration. The insertion process involves first finding the right location where the key can be inserted and, after the insertion, deciding if the updated tree needs to be restructured to maintain the balance and the B-tree property. Consider the insertion example shown in Figure 8-5.

First, a search is performed in the tree to find the leaf node where the key value 5 can be inserted. In this example, the right spot is the leftmost leaf node, a sub-tree of the node with key value 7 (②). Then a decision needs to be made on how to insert this new key. The leftmost leaf node already has three keys, which is a full node according to the B-tree property of a maximum $(2t-1 = 3)$ keys per node. This leaf node must be split in order to fit the new key. So the median key value 4 is removed, and the leaf node is divided to form two new nodes from each half, with one new node containing the key value 3 and the other containing the key value 6 (③). The removed median key is merged with the parent node, and the newly formed nodes are linked with the parent node (④). The node with key value 3 is attached to the left of key value 4, and the node with key value 6 is the new middle child node where key value 5 is inserted. The updated tree is balanced, and each node contains an appropriate number of keys.

This insertion example shows that the insertion algorithm performs two main operations. The first operation is finding the insertion location, which is essentially a B-tree search problem. The time complexity for this operation is $O(t \log_t n)$. The second operation is to split a full node into two non-full nodes. A full node has $(2t-1)$ keys, so the two new nodes have $(t-1)$ keys each after the split. Therefore, the split operation runs with $O(t)$ complexity. Combining the cost of the two operations, we find that the overall time complexity of B-tree insertion is $O(t \log_t n)$.

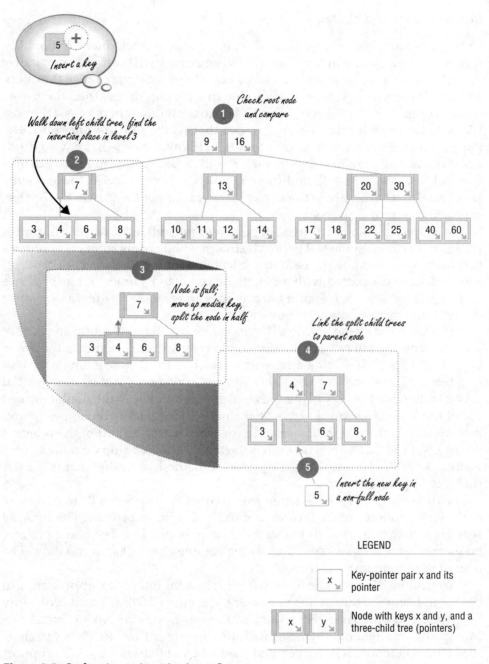

Figure 8-5: Performing an Insertion into a B-tree

Range Search and B⁺-tree

In the previous sections, we have shown the exact-match query or equality search using a B-tree index. The following search will return a particular record or several records with the same key. However, if we change the query to find all records that have a key value in a certain range, then the B-tree structure makes the search difficult because the matched keys are most likely to be scattered in different nodes that reside in different sub-trees. For example, if we want to search for all NetFlow records that have a duration between 10 and 30 seconds, then the matched results are in six different nodes (C, D, G, H, I, J), and there is no good way to access those results sequentially accordingly to the key value. A variant of the B-tree, the B⁺-tree, can facilitate range queries.

The B⁺-tree resembles a B-tree but possesses two unique features. First, all of the keys are stored at the leaf node. The internal nodes only store value separators that can determine the path to the leaf node during a search. Second, all leaf nodes are connected with a double-linked list to support range searches and sequential searches. Figure 8-6 provides an example B+-tree, a derivative of the B-tree that is shown in Figure 8-3.

Performing a range search on a B⁺-tree begins by first conducting an equality search using the lower bound value of the range. In this example, the lower bound is 10 (seconds). Doing an equality search in the B⁺-tree is similar to that in a B-tree. The search for key value 10 ends at node J. We start a sequential probe from node J by following the right sibling pointer in the double-linked list of the leaf nodes, until reaching the node that contains the upper bound key value, which is 30 in this case; in this way, we collect all of the relevant nodes J, K, L, M, N, O, and P as each is visited. The search stops at node Q after visiting key 30. The linear probing stops at the first key value that is greater than the upper bound.

The time complexity of the range search covering d keys in a B⁺-tree consists of the lower bound equality search and the cost of linear probing. The equality search takes $O(t \log_t n)$ steps to locate the lower bound key. The linear probing takes at most d comparisons, and so the complexity is $O(d)$, a constant. The overall time complexity is then $O(t \log_t n)$.

B-trees and B⁺-trees are the most widely adopted index approaches in both relational database management systems (RDBMS) and Not Only SQL (NoSQL) databases. For example, the most popular NoSQL database, MongoDB, implements B-tree as its indexing algorithm. RDBMS Oracle 8, IBM DB2, Microsoft SQL Server, and the NoSQL database CouchDB support B⁺-tree-based indices.

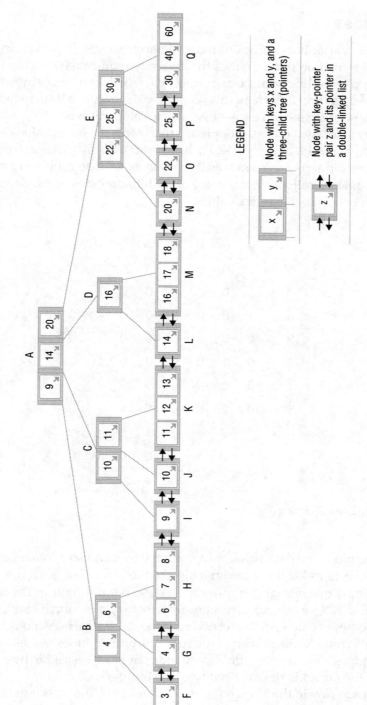

Figure 8-6: An Example B⁺-tree

Bitmap Index

B-tree and its variants are efficient indexing approaches. However, insertion or any other operation that modifies the tree may require rebalancing the tree to maintain certain important tree properties, which can be costly when the frequency of operation is high. In this section, we introduce a bitmap index that is efficient for both insertion (append) and search operations.

The *bitmap index* is an indexing approach that stores the index value as a set of bit sequences, as shown in Figure 8-7. Each column ($b^0, b^1, b^2, \ldots$) is a bitmap, and together these bitmaps are known as the *bitmap index*. The number of bitmaps in a bitmap index is called the *cardinality* of the bitmap index and is determined by the number of possible index values.

	Data	b^0	b^1	b^2	b^3	b^4	b^5	b^6	b^7
1	3	0	0	0	1	0	0	0	0
2	0	1	0	0	0	0	0	0	0
3	0	1	0	0	0	0	0	0	0
4	2	0	0	1	0	0	0	0	0
5	1	0	1	0	0	0	0	0	0
6	7	0	0	0	0	0	0	0	1
7	5	0	0	0	0	0	1	0	0
8	4	0	0	0	0	1	0	0	0
9	2	0	0	1	0	0	0	0	0
10	6	0	0	0	0	0	0	1	0

Figure 8-7: An Example Bitmap Index

In this example, the data values range from 0 to 7, and so a total of eight bitmaps are used to index the stored data in the bitmap index. Each row of data can choose only one bitmap to represent its data. For example, in the first row, the data value is 3, so bitmap b^3 is chosen by setting the fourth bit in the row as 1. For another example, in the second row, the data value is 0, and the chosen bitmap is b^0, which is the first bit of the row. The bitmap index is a set of binary arrays of equal size if we view the bitmap index by rows instead of by columns. The size of the arrays is the cardinality of the bitmap index.

Because each row in the bitmap index is a data entry, the insertion operation consists of creating a bit array with the cardinality as the array size, setting the bit value at the appropriate column, and then appending the array to the end of the existing bitmap index. The creation of a bit array can be done efficiently by the bit shifting and bitwise OR operation. For the example illustrated in Figure 8-7, we can use an 8-bit unsigned integer to present the bit array. To set bit x, we use `array |= 1 << x`. Bitmap indices are best for read-mostly and append-only data because appending a bitmap index is a simple and efficient operation.

An attribute of the stored data, which will serve as the index for later searching and retrieval operations, can be represented by a bitmap index. Example attributes of a network flow are the source and destination IP addresses, the source and destination ports, and the protocol type. So, for example, if the destination port will serve as the index to retrieval flows that match a specific destination port, then the destination ports and the associated flows can be represented by a bitmap index. In this case, the possible values range from 0 to 65535, and the cardinality of this bitmap index is 65536. If there are 1,000 rows (or flows) to be stored, then we can build a bitmap index that consists of 65,536 bitmaps with 1,000 rows in each column; that is, this bitmap index consists of 1,000 × 65,536 bits.

Bitmap Index Search

Searching for an exact match using a bitmap index is straightforward. Because each bitmap represents an attribute value, searching for records that have a particular value essentially involves listing the rows that have the "1" bit in that particular bitmap (or column) representing that value. For example, in the bitmap index given in Figure 8-7, to search for records with value 2 in the bitmap index, we first locate bitmap b^2. Then we find that two rows (row 4 and row 9) contain the value 1; therefore, those two rows are retrieved as the search result.

Range searches can also be done easily using a bitmap index. First, we need to identify all bitmaps that fall within the searched range. For example, if the range search is to find all records whose data value x is within the range $3 \leq x \leq 6$, we need to first select the bitmaps that represent this range. Because the possible data values within the range are 3, 4, 5, and 6, the selected bitmaps are b^3, b^4, b^5, and b^6. The range search means that any record that is marked in any one of these columns satisfies the search condition. Therefore, performing the range search involves executing the bitwise OR operations on the selected bitmaps to obtain a single resultant bitmap. The rows that have "1" bits in the resultant bitmap are the records that satisfy the range search.

Each bitmap index can be used to store one data attribute, and if the data has multiple attributes that will contribute to the searching criteria, then multiple bitmap indices, as many as the number of attributes, are necessary to index the stored data. For example, it is possible to store the source port of network flows in a single bitmap index; however, if flow selection depends on the values of both source and destination ports as search attributes, then two bitmap indices are necessary to manage the stored flow records. A range search on a single bitmap index is a *one-dimensional query*. We can perform a *multi-dimensional query* by combining the results of multiple one-dimensional queries, similar to performing a range query, as shown in Figure 8-8.

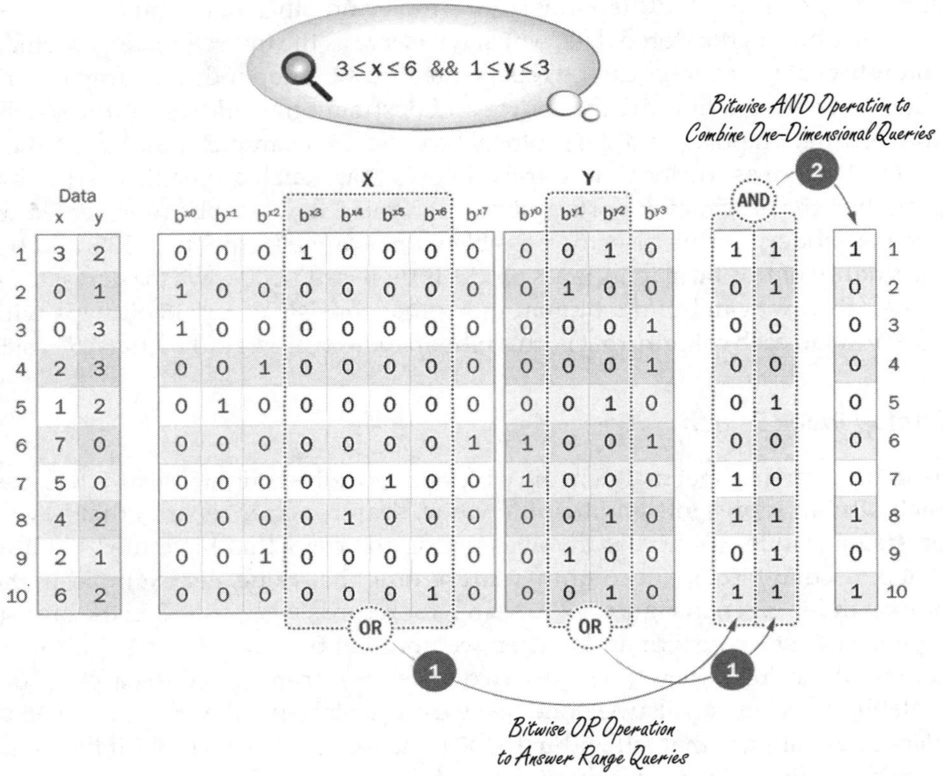

Figure 8-8: Two-Dimensional Query

In this example, we illustrate a range search on data that has two attributes X and Y. Each attribute is represented by a bitmap index. We are interested in finding the entries such that $3 \leq x \leq 6$ and $1 \leq y \leq 3$, where x and y are values of attribute X and Y, respectively. From the previous range search example, we know that the one-dimensional query on attribute X is the result of bitwise OR operations on bitmaps b^{x3}, b^{x4}, b^{x5}, and b^{x6}. Similarly, the one-dimensional query on attribute Y is the result of bitwise OR operations on bitmaps b^{y1} and b^{y6}. Finally, the two-dimensional range query is the bitwise AND operation on the two resulting bitmaps that are answers to the individual one-dimensional queries.

We will now show how to apply multi-dimensional searches using bitmap indices to solve real-world problems in the context of retrospective analysis.

As we discussed in previous sections, the large files of raw packet captures are stored on multiple hard drives, and we need to build a fast search system to quickly retrieve the desired data according to query conditions. For the sake of discussion, we limit the query fields to source and destination IPv4 addresses and associated ports. These are the attributes of the data managed through the bitmap indices. Each packet has a unique packet ID (similar to the row number in the simple bitmap index example shown previously). As shown in Figure 8-9, there exists a packet record file that associates each packet ID with an actual packet capture file holding the raw packet data and the offset value, specifying the location of that raw packet within the capture file. For example, as shown in Figure 8-9, the packet record file can locate *packet 301* in the file named *ad.pcap* at offset *0x5a46*. Packet 301 can be retrieved quickly with such detailed information.

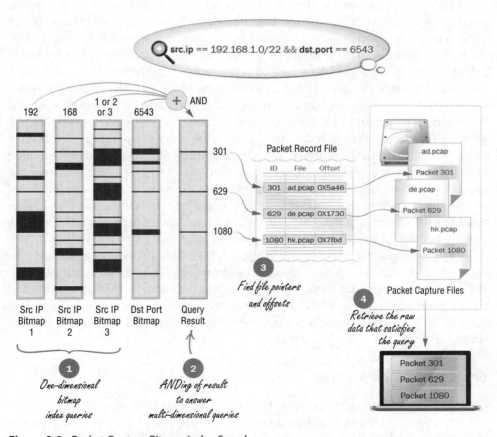

Figure 8-9: Packet Capture Bitmap Index Search

We first build the bitmap indices to serve the query. Because the query may contain four different attributes (source and destination IP and ports), we need to build multiple bitmap indices. As we have mentioned, the port attribute can be represented using a bitmap index of cardinality of 65536, and we need two different bitmap indices each for the source and destination ports. For the IP address attribute, it is difficult to store them in a single bitmap index because the IP address has four octets. Instead, we construct four bitmap indices for the IP address attribute: one bitmap index for each byte in the IP address. Because for an IPv4 address, each byte in the address can have a maximum value of 255, the cardinality of the IP address bitmap index is 256. Together, we have $4+4+1+1=10$ bitmap indices to index the packets in the capture files.

Figure 8-9 shows the query process to search for packets that have source IP range 192.168.1.0/22 and destination port 6543. The source IP range can translate to the bitmap query as "value of IP first byte is 192, value of IP second byte is 168, value of IP third byte is 1 or 2 or 3 (this is because the prefix is /22, the upper 6 bits is 0, and the lower 2 bits can be 1 or 2 or 3), and value of IP fourth byte is ANY." It means for the IP address attribute that exact-match queries need to be performed on the first two bitmap indices, the third bitmap index requires a range search, and no query is needed on the fourth bitmap index. As shown in the figure, in the IP first byte bitmap index, the bitmap for value 192 is selected. We use a black line to represent "1" in the bitmap and a black box to represent a block of "1"s. The thicker the black box, the larger the block of "1"s. Similarly, we select a bitmap for value 168 from the IP address second byte bitmap index and 5432 from the destination port bitmap index. For the IP address third byte bitmap index, we perform bitwise OR operations to obtain a bitmap containing range search results. Each of the bitmaps selected or generated is an answer to a one-dimensional query (shown as step 1), and to answer the original multi-dimensional query, we combine the results of one-dimensional queries by doing bitwise AND operations on the bitmaps (shown as step 2). The final result is a bitmap that has only three "1"s. The rows of those "1" entries are the packet ID that satisfy the query.

In this example, the IDs are 301, 629, and 1080. To retrieve those packets, the retrospective analysis system locates the entries in the packet record file with the returned packet IDs from the search (shown as step 3). With the extracted file pointers and offset values of those packets from the packet record file, it is possible to fetch the raw packets from the actual packet capture files and process them for display (shown as step 4).

Bitmap Index Compression

One drawback of bitmap indices is the large amount of storage they require. In the previous example, a single packet entry is represented in ten bitmap indices in different cardinalities. The eight IP address bitmap indices have 256 columns each, and the two port bitmaps each have 65,536 columns. Together, for a single packet entry, that is 133,120 bits, or more than 16KB, which is a huge overhead. Compressed bitmap indices bring more space efficiency while maintaining the fast bitwise operation properties that the basic bitmap indices have to offer.

To compress a bitmap index, the most common approach is run-length encoding. The key concept of run-length encoding is to use a single data value and a count number to represent consecutively repeated occurrences of the data value. For example, to compress the string "WWWWAAWWAAAAAAWWBBBB", we can apply run-length encoding to compress it as "W4A2W2A7W2B4". The number represents the repeated times the preceding letter occurs in the original string, where in sequence, W repeats 4 times, A repeats 2 times, W repeats 2 times, and so on. However, this simple run-length encoding approach is not the appropriate method to compress a bitmap index because if we want to perform bitwise operations on two compressed bitmap indices, we will need to first un-compress them, run bitwise operations, and compress the resulting bitmap index. Clearly, this is not the desired solution.

Word-Aligned Hybrid (WAH) coding is a run-length encoding algorithm that makes it possible to logically operate on compressed bitmap indices. In particular, when using WAH coding, the result of logical operations on two compressed bitmap indices is exactly the same as performing the same operations on the uncompressed bitmap indices followed by compressing the result. Therefore, searching the compressed bitmap indices generates the same results as searching in the uncompressed bitmap indices.

We use the IP address bitmap index as an example to show how WAH coding works. The IP address bitmap index contains 256 bits for each byte in the IP address. In the example, the first byte of the IP address is 192, so the 193rd bit in that row of the bitmap index is 1 and the remaining 255 bits are 0. As shown in Figure 8-10, the 256 bits are represented as "192*0, 1*1, 63*0", sequentially showing the value of each bit.

256 bits	192*0, 1*1, 63*0								
31-bit words	31*0	31*0	31*0	31*0	31*0	31*0	6*0,1*1,24*0	31*0	8*0
Literal HEX	00000000	00000000	00000000	00000000	00000000	00000000	01000000	00000000	00000000
WAH HEX	80000006						01000000	00000000	00000000

Figure 8-10: WAH Bitmap Index Compression

Suppose we use an x86 32-bit system to process the bitmap index. In Intel's x86 architecture, each word is 32 bits long. To apply WAH coding, we first divide the 256 bits into nine words, in which only the lower 31 bits are used and the unused bits are filled by 0s. In this example, the first 6 words are all 0, the 7th word has 6 zeros, and then 1 one, followed by another 24 zeros. The 8th word is also 0. The 9th word only has 8 bits, all of which are 0, and the word itself is also 0. Those nine words can be written as 4-byte hexadecimal numbers; this is called the literal representation of the bitmap index.

The key piece of the WAH algorithm is to count words that consist of repeated bits and compress them as a *fill word*. In the example, all the bits in the first 6 words are 0, so we can compress them as a single fill word that has a count of 6. The fill word has three parts. The most significant bit is the indicator bit, and it is always 1. The second-most significant bit is the fill bit showing the repeated bit value, which is 0 in this example. The remaining 30 bits record the fill length (repeated word count), which is 6 in the example. Therefore, the first 6 words can be compressed as a hexadecimal number 80000006 where 8 means it is a 0-filled *fill word*.

In addition to a fill word, WAH coding also has a *literal word*. A literal word has 0 in the most significant bit, and the literal word is the same as the literal hexadecimal representation of the 31-bit word. In this example, the 7th word contains a bit of 1 and 30 bits of 0, so it cannot be compressed. WAH coding treats that word as a *literal word*, which can be written as a hexadecimal number 01000000. The 8th word is all zeros, and it is also a *literal word* because no repeating words can be compressed with it. Finally, the last word is called an *active word*; although its literal value is 0, it actually has only 8 bits of zeros. This *active word* is specially treated (shown as an asterisk superscript in the example) and we need to store it separately. This is because in WAH implementation, each compressed bitmap index is contained in a structure (class) in which the active word itself, its literal value, and bit count are member variables. As shown in the example, WAH coding compresses the original 8-word (256-bit) bitmap index into 4 words—a compression ratio of 2. This ratio is even larger when we compress the 65,536-bit port bitmap index: 2,048 words into 4 words.

WAH coding defines a set of functions to perform logical operations (for example, AND, OR, XOR, and so on) on the WAH compressed bitmap index. The key properties of the logical operations are two-fold. First, the resulting bitmap index from the logical operations on multiple WAH compressed bitmap indices is the same as running the same logical operations on the uncompressed bitmap indices, and compresses the resulting bitmap index using WAH coding. This property means that WAH compressed bitmap indices can fully represent and replace basic bitmap indices. Second, the logical operation complexity of WAH compressed bitmap indices is linear to the total size of the input. Because the compression ratio for some basic bitmap indices (for example, the port bitmap index) is so high, the operations on compressed bitmap indices can be much faster.

There are many other bitmap index compression schemes, for example, Byte-aligned Bitmap Code (BBC), Compressed Adaptive Index (COMPAX), Enhanced WAH (EWAH), Roaring bitmaps, and so on. Besides the application of indexing large packet captures in a retrospective analysis system, bitmap indexing is widely used by major RDBMS vendors like Oracle and IBM, as well as distributed data storage like Apache Hive.

Inverted File Index

Both B-tree indexing and bitmap indexing require pre-processing on the raw data. For example, when using B-tree to index packet captures, this requires that the source IP address string of the packet be hashed into a number, create a B-tree node with that number as a key, and insert that node in the B-tree. When using a bitmap index, we need to divide the IP address into 4 bytes, create a bit array for each of the bytes, append it to the bitmap index, and compress it.

As an alternative to the aforementioned two indexing methods, there is a demand for a lightweight pre-processing indexing approach. When applying such an approach, each packet can be represented as plain text that contains metadata of the packet without a payload, for example, the source and destination IP addresses and ports as text. Such representation is similar to NetFlow, but at the granularity of packet level. Creating and saving metadata is one action per packet, as opposed to multiple actions for the source IP and port, destination IP and port, and protocol field for a single packet when using B-tree or bitmap indexing. Figure 8-11 shows sample metadata of packet captures.

Document ID	Packet Metadata
1	sip:192.168.1.2 sport:34762 dip:74.125.239.100 dport:80 proto:tcp
2	sip:192.168.2.5 sport:52941 dip:83.145.2.171 dport:6543 proto:udp
3	sip:74.125.239.100 sport:80 dip:192.168.1.2 dport:34762 proto:tcp
4	sip:83.145.2.171 sport:6543 dip:192.168.2.5 dport:52941 proto:udp
5	sip:192.168.1.2 sport:50143 dip:192.168.2.5 dport:22 proto:tcp

Figure 8-11: Example Packet Metadata in Documents

In addition, not every form of collected network data is well structured. In some cases, logs from certain network appliances are unstructured in nature; it is not easy to parse these logs, create fields, and index them. Furthermore, even if all the logs the retrospective analysis system collects are well formatted, the formats can be different. Instead of creating indices for each format of the log and performing the same query in each index, it would be much more efficient to create a single index for all logs so that without querying on multiple indices, a single query on a single index is sufficient.

Inverted File

When the index is built to search on text among a collection of text files (documents), the prevailing approach is inverted file indexing. An inverted file, also known as a *posting file*, contains lists of pointers to every occurrence of each *term* (unique word) in the documents. The list is called an *inverted list* or *posting list*. Each pointer (*posting*) in the inverted list records the documents in which the term appears.

In Figure 8-11, we have packet metadata saved in five documents. For now, let us assume there is only one piece of packet metadata in each document; we will relax this assumption later. Each document is uniquely identified by a document ID, from which it is possible to locate the actual packet capture file containing the raw packets that are present in the document. Also, in the packet metadata, we list only the <sip, sport, dip, dport, proto> tuple to show how to create an inverted file. An additional metadata field can be included and indexed using the same method. In Figure 8-12, we list the documents with their document IDs on the right and their contents (packet metadata) on the left.

Term	Inverted List (Document ID)
sip:192.168.1.2	1 → 5
sport:34762	1
dip:74.125.239.100	1
dport:80	1
proto:tcp	1 → 3 → 5
sip:192.168.2.5	2
sport:52941	2
dip:83.145.2.171	2
dport:6543	2
proto:udp	2 → 4
sip:74.125.239.100	3
sport:80	3
dip:192.168.1.2	3
dport:34762	3
sip:83.145.2.171	4
sport:6543	4
dip:192.168.2.5	4 → 5
dport:52941	4
sport:50143	5
dport:22	5

Figure 8-12: Inverted File for Metadata

To create an inverted file from the packet metadata, we first extract the terms. Let us define a term in the metadata as *type:value*. For example, `sip:192.168.1.2` is a term, and `proto:tcp` is another term. The reason we create terms in such a way is for the convenience of making a query. We will explain this later when we discuss queries. With the extraction of terms, each document can be viewed as a collection of terms, and the same term can appear in different documents. For example, the term `sip:192.168.1.2` appears in both documents 1 and 5.

The way to construct an inverted file in this example is to create a list of document IDs for each of the terms. For example, Figure 8-12 shows that the term `sip:192.168.1.2` has two postings, 1 and 5, in the inverted list because the term appears in documents 1 and 5. The inverted list can be implemented using a linked list. The requirement here is that the postings be sorted in monotonically increasing order based on document ID. The inverted file is created by repeatedly adding the terms and their postings. The terms themselves can be hashed so that they are easy to look up. When we have a new term and posting to add, we first look up the term, and if the term is present, we append the posting to the inverted list of the term. If not, we append the term to the inverted file and create an inverted list with the document ID as the first posting. In this way, as long as the documents are processed in the order of their ID, it is guaranteed that the postings in the inverted lists will be sorted accordingly.

Inverted File Index Query

Because the inverted list already contains all occurrences of the term, in order to find which documents contain a particular term, it is possible to walk through the postings in the term's inverted list and simply return the postings. For example, to perform the query and obtain all documents containing the term `sip==192.168.1.2`, we walk through the inverted list of this term and return each posting; in this example, the IDs are 1 and 5. Inverted file indexing is also very efficient at performing logical queries combining multiple terms.

With the inverted file shown in Figure 8.12, let us look at an example of the logical AND query `sip==192.168.1.2 && proto==tcp`. To perform this query, we first locate the inverted list of the two terms. To answer the logical AND query of the two terms is to find the common postings in the two inverted lists—in other words, the intersection of the two linked lists. In this example, because the inverted lists are short, we can quickly tell that the common postings in the two inverted lists are 1 and 5. For longer lists, it is possible to apply the following simple algorithm to find the common postings.

Algorithm for Finding Common Postings in Two Inverted Lists

```
Find_Common_Posting(L1, L2)   { // L1 and L2 point to head of
                                // two inverted lists
1   result = < >;
```

```
 2   while (L1 != NULL && L2 != NULL) {
 3       if Doc_ID(L1) == Doc_ID(L2) {
 4           result.add(L1);
 5           L1++; L2++;
 6       } else if (Doc_ID(L1 < Doc_ID(L2)) {
 7           L1++;
 8       else
 9           L2++;
10   }
11   return result;
}
```

Similarly, other inverted list algorithms can be designed to realize different logical queries on the terms. For example, a logical OR query on the terms is to find the union of postings in their inverted lists. We now revisit the extraction of the terms to answer why we choose to represent the packet metadata's source IP field as a single term `sip:192.168.1.2` instead of `sip` and `192.168.1.2`. First, `sip` is a common word in all packet metadata; indexing such a common word alone does not help to make a query easier. The term `192.168.1.2` is merely an IP address, and it can be either a source IP or a destination IP. If we were to create separate terms for `sip` and `192.168.1.2`, we would not even be able to perform queries like `sip==192.168.1.2`. To fully take advantage of inverted file indexing, it is best that the logical operands be the terms that are comprised of meaning components.

Inverted File Compression

In order to help explain the example given in the previous section on inverted file creation and query, we made an assumption that every document contains exactly one piece of packet metadata. This assumption helps us represent the postings as document IDs. However, in reality, a much more efficient way to save packet metadata is to put multiple entries of the metadata into a single document, with one piece of metadata in each row. Such a document usually maps to a packet capture file so that the raw packets are saved in the packet capture file and their metadata is stored in a single document. In that case, a posting may contain two parts: the document ID and the offset (for example, the row number) of the metadata in the document. To differentiate those two parts, we denote < > as the list of document IDs, and [] as the list of offsets within the same document.

Suppose we have a term with an inverted list like the following: < 88[25,28,30,45,90,100], 95[1002,1045,1120], 130[99876,99902,99954], 150[2,7,12,15,19,25] >. To store such a list as plain text, it is clear that larger numbers require more storage than smaller ones. For example, offsets 99876, 99902, and 99954 need five characters each to store, while offsets 2, 7, and 12 require only one or two characters each. Because the property of the inverted list is that the postings are sorted in strictly increasing order, it is possible to compress the listing by only recoding the gaps between them. For example, the postings `<88, 95, 130, 150>` can be compressed as `<88, 7, 35, 20>`, the offset list of `[25,28,30,45,90,100]` can be compressed as `[25,3,2,15,45,10]`, and the offset list `[99876,99902,99954]` will become `[99876,26,52]`. As this example shows, it takes less space to store the compressed lists.

It is further possible to apply advanced coding schemes (for example, γ code or δ code) and encode the (gap) numbers on the lists to various-length code words because the code words are even more space-efficient than strings or integers. The detailed encoding and decoding algorithms can be found in the following books: *Introduction to Information Retrieval* (Cambridge University Press, 2008) and *Managing Gigabytes: Compressing and Indexing Documents and Images* (Morgan Kaufmann, 1999).

Besides indexing packet metadata, inverted file indexing is best known as the core technology for search engines in free text searches. The search engines use this approach to index millions of documents so that they can quickly return a list of documents containing certain queried keywords. Inverted file indexing is also a key piece in Apache Solr and its offspring, Elasticsearch, which is used as the underlying platform to index pcap files by the open source network capturing and indexing system, Moloch (`https://github.com/aol/moloch`).

Performance of a Retrospective Analysis System

With the design methodology and specific algorithm discussed in the previous section, we now focus on putting the ingredients together and building a retrospective analysis system for enterprise network security. In particular, we are interested in showing what resources it takes to run such a system and what its capacity is.

Suppose the retrospective analysis system is designed to record and analyze full packet captures. We choose full packet capture as an example to show how the sheer volume of data impacts the performance of the system. Let us consider the scenario where *one week* of network traffic is captured on an enterprise network of 250 users. The IT security personnel of the enterprise are aware of a live malnet campaign that was first uncovered two days before, and they have a list of 100 malicious URLs that are landing pages of the malnet. With the retrospective analysis system, the IT security personnel want to issue a query to list *all users that have visited those URLs within the past two days* because those users are potentially compromised.

Index Sizes

We use *WAH compressed bitmap indexing* as an example to calculate the amount of resources a retrospective analysis system needs to support the query stated in the last paragraph. Please note that the following calculations are from theoretical values based on the properties of the approaches and algorithm; we present them to give an estimate or guideline. The actual resource usage may vary depending on the final implementation.

There are three elements in the query: *user, time,* and *URL.*

- *User* can be represented by an IP address. For example, in certain LDAP deployments, it is possible to associate a user with an IP address. As we have shown in the example in the bitmap index section, an IPv4 address can be implemented using four bitmap indices with the cardinality of 256 each to represent its 4 bytes.

- *Time* is the timestamp when the packet is recorded. Because the retrospective analysis system in this example is designed to capture one week of traffic, we can use a 7-column bitmap to record the day of the week, a 24-column bitmap to record the hour of the day, and a 3,600-column bitmap to record the second of the hour. Another 1,000-column bitmap can be added to show the millisecond-level granularity of the packet capture time. Together, they comprise four bitmaps.

- *URL* is a string of text, and a bitmap is not a natural representation of strings. To convert a URL into a number and store it in a bitmap, we can use hash functions. In Chapter 5, we hash a category string into numbers and check if they are present in a bloom filter. The idea here is similar, but instead of using multiple hash functions together, we use only a single hash function to hash the URL to an integer, say, less than 65,536. Those 65,536 values can form a bitmap. However, given the vast number of URLs, it is very likely that multiple URLs are hashed into the same value.

    To resolve the hash collision, we use another layer of hashing with a different hash function. The second layer of hashing is another bitmap. Still, there can be collisions. A third layer of hashing can be added, or we can store the URLs in a link list. Because the number of colliding elements after two layers of different hashing is limited, it is not time consuming to linearly traverse the link list. We call this type of hashing the *hash bucket* method, where each hash bucket is a bit in the bitmap. Therefore, for the URL element, we use two bitmaps.

Although not a part of the query, there are still some hidden elements. Those hidden elements frequently appear in queries, and we want to index them as well. They include the destination IP address (4 bitmaps), source and destination ports (2 bitmaps), IP protocol number (1 bitmap), and packet length (1 bitmap). In addition, we might want to record the classification results based on the systems we designed in Chapter 7. Although this information may not be available at the time of packet capture, we can nonetheless add the classification of the flow to each packet the flow contains. Such classification results can be represented with a 10,000-column bitmap, which maps to 10,000 different classified applications.

Adding up all the indexing elements together, we get a total of 19 (4+4+2+4+2+1+1+1) bitmaps with various column counts. We also need to know the row counts, which is the number of packet records within the one-week time frame. According to research conducted by a team at Cisco in 2014 (*Cisco Visual Networking Index: Forecast and Methodology, 2013–2018*), an average business user generates 4 to 10GB of Internet and WAN traffic per month. Taking 8GB as an estimate, the retrospective analysis system sitting on a 250-user enterprise network can capture 500GB per week. If the packets are an average of 1KB in size, then the 500GB, one-week traffic capture will contain 500 million packets.

Now we need to compress the bitmaps using WAH coding so that we can estimate how much space we need to accommodate those bitmaps. In all of the bitmaps, for each row, there is only one bit that is 1, and all the rest are zero; that is to say, the bitmaps are really sparse. A property of WAH coding is that for sparse bitmaps, the maximum size of a compressed bitmap index is about $2N$ words, where N is the number of rows in the bitmap. For a 64-bit system, the size of a word is 8 bytes, and in a 32-bit system, a word requires 4 bytes. To calculate the overall size of the compressed bitmap indices, we multiply the terms together to obtain the size $s = 500\text{M} \times 2 \times 8 \text{ bytes} \times 19 \approx 152\text{GB}$.

That is a large index! Even if we apply a more advanced and space-efficient compression algorithm like EWAH or COMPAX, the index size is still tens of gigabytes. Loading the whole index in memory imposes a strong requirement on the physical memory size of a retrospective analysis system. In this regard, the compressed indices should be divided into smaller chunks and saved on storage devices. The indices can then be loaded when performing a query.

This is actually a natural choice for a retrospective analysis system. As the packets are being recorded, the retrospective analysis system also tries to index them along the way. The separator of the index chunks can be time; for example, every 15 minutes worth of packets are indexed in a single compressed index so that there will be 4 indices every hour, and the one-week traffic will create 672 indices. Because the packet counts (bitmap rows) are smaller in each index, the size of each index is smaller. In addition, the indices of day and hour in the original bitmaps are now removed, which makes the index size still smaller. Finally, when performing queries on time, we can first locate which of the 672 indices fall into the time range, and we load each of the indices to conduct the query. Assume the regular business traffic runs to 12 hours per day, 5 days a week; the busy hour packet count in 15 minutes is roughly 2 million (500 million/5/12/4). Using the aforementioned approach, the size of the index is now $s = 2\text{M} \times 2 \times 8 \text{ bytes} \times 17 \approx 544\text{MB}$, which is a much more realistic memory requirement.

Index Building Overhead

Packet attributes like IP addresses, port numbers, IP protocol number, length, and so on, are well-defined header values and are stored in a pre-defined offset in a packet. When a packet is read into memory, reading those values from the packet and setting the corresponding bit in the bitmap does not cost many CPU cycles. Instead, saving the packets as well as the index to the storage device involves many I/O operations.

Because there are about 2 million packets per 15 minutes and the packet size is about 1KB, the average rate at which the data is captured is about $2\text{M} \times 1,000$ bytes $/ (15 \times 60$ seconds$) \approx 2.2\text{MB/s}$. Even when we add the size of bitmaps created from the packets, the total amount of data to be saved is much less than the write speed of a regular 7,200-rpm SATA hard drive, which can write at the rate of 100 to 150MB/s. That is to say, it is possible to perform real-time indexing and packet saving while capturing.

Query Response Delay

To serve a query, the retrospective analysis system has to first locate and load the index into memory, then run logical operations on the bitmap, and finally load the query results. The query response delay is the sum of all delays incurred in the aforementioned steps. In the example query we gave in an earlier section, the query time frame is the past two days, which covers 192 out of a total of 672 indices. To obtain the sum of all delays, we calculate the delays on 1 index and multiply that by 192 in the end.

We first take a look at the time complexity of the logical operations on WAH compressed bitmaps. A 2006 paper by Wu et al. called "Optimizing bitmap indices with efficient compression" (ACM Trans. on Database Systems, 2006) offers detailed analytical results from performing general bitwise operations. For two bitmaps x and y of m_x and m_y words, respectively, the time complexity of generic bitwise operations between the two bitmaps is $O(m_x + m_y)$. In particular, for a sparse bitmap, the cost of overall bitwise operations is upper-bounded by $C(m_x + m_y)$, where C is a constant decoding and compressing cost for a WAH word.

As shown in the previous section, the query is constructed as a single-row bitmap. To create a range query of range span l, the logical operations are done on l bitmaps of the same size, which is Clm_x in total. We also showed that a single-row sparse bitmap can be compressed into four words, and the total logical cost Clm_x can be bounded by $4Cl$. When performing a search, the query is actually the logical operation between the single-row query bitmap and a compressed bitmap index of N rows. Because of the maximum size of a compressed index $2N$ word, the total cost is roughly $C(4l + 2N)$. Given $2N$ is far greater than $4l$, the total cost of logical operations in the query is $2CN$. We know that in the example, the N value for each index is around 2 million. That makes the total operation count $8C$ million. An Intel quad-core 3.3GHz i5 CPU, which is found on many mid-range business desktops, can do about 83,000 million instructions per second (MIPS). Because the cost value of C is far lower than 10,000 CPU instructions, performing the logical operations to conduct a search on a bitmap requires far less than a second time to complete.

Locating which of the 192 indices are to be looked up to serve the query is a relatively light operation. We can use bitmap or B+-tree to provide the time-based query that finds those indices. Even if we do linear traversing on those 672 indices, it does not cost many CPU cycles. However, loading those indices into memory does cost I/O operations. A mainstream 7,200-rpm hard drive can do a random read at around 150MB/s. Loading a 544MB index from a hard drive takes around 3.6 seconds.

In the final step, when the packets that satisfy the query are identified, they need to be loaded into memory so that they can be displayed and examined by IT security personnel. Regardless of how and where the packets are stored, the time cost for reading those packets depends on the total size of the packets and the read speed of the hard drive. Note that the average size of a packet is 1KB, which is less than the normal 4KB read per I/O operation. That is to say, when reading 1KB packets one at a time, the speed of the hard drive is about one-quarter of the speed when reading a large chunk of a file. Because in the example query, the packets from malicious landing pages are retrieved, the number of those packets cannot be huge. Let us suppose there are 10,000 packets, which contribute to a total size of 10MB. Loading 10MB of packets that are 1KB each from a 7,200-rpm hard drive costs about 0.3 second (10MB/(150MBps/4)).

Adding the three delay components together, we can see that the time used to operate on the bitmap is really negligible, and the bottleneck of the search speed is from the I/O operations. In this example, to load the 192 indices from the hard drive costs about 10 minutes, which is about the total time needed to complete the query. Note that in our calculations, we use the maximum or upper-bound values for many variables, so the results roughly represent the worst-case scenario.

The aforementioned analysis clearly indicates that the bottleneck of the query speed is the disk I/O operation. In order to speed up the query, it is possible to use hard drives that have a higher average IOPS (input/output operations per second) value. For example, the 7,200-rpm SATA drive we used in the example has fewer than 100 IOPS. The 10,000-rpm SATA or SAS drive can perform up to 150 IOPS, while a 15,000-rpm SAS hard drive can go up to 200 IOPS. That is to say, we can save up to half of the query time by using a higher-IOPS hard drive.

It is possible to further increase the IOPS by deploying a RAID storage system. However, in the RAID system, a disk-write operation may require many disk operations that act as a penalty to the overall system IOPS. In this regard, the overall IOPS in a RAID system is not the aggregate IOPS of all the drives. For example, in a RAID 5 deployment, we can use an array of 25 7,200-rpm hard drives to achieve the total IOPS of 1,000. At the cost of more storage, we can bring down the query response time quite significantly.

Using a solid state drive (SSD) is another way to increase query speed. A consumer-grade SATA SSD can now support up to 85,000 IOPS, and a performance-oriented PCIe interface-based SSD can easily support more than 200,000 IOPS. That is a huge improvement over the 7,200-rpm hard drive that we used in the example. The major drawbacks of SSD are the high cost and lack of long-term reliability.

Scalability

The scalability obstacles to a retrospective analysis system come from two challenges. The first challenge is the complexity of the query. In our example, to perform time range queries on packages with certain URLs, we use 19 bitmaps to index the packet captures. If the query becomes more complex with more variables—for example, vlan ID—we need to extract more information from the raw packet while processing it and to create additional bitmap indices for the added variables. Although performing logical operations on the added bitmap indices may not cause a noticeable slowdown in query response, loading and storing the indices can greatly impact performance because as we have shown in the aforementioned calculations, the query response time is proportional to the number of bitmaps that fall within the query range.

The second challenge comes from the scale of the input data rate. In the example, we positioned the retrospective analysis system in an enterprise of 250 users that each generated 8GB of data per month. That equals about 18Mbps of traffic. If we were to put the system on the enterprise intranet where the traffic was flowing at a line rate 1Gbps, the volume of data to be indexed would be more than 50 times as large. And if the storage period were extended from one week to one month, that would be another 4 times more data, which would take the total amount of data from the initial 500GB to 100TB. The data volume would surge to a petabyte if the system were placed on a 10Gbps link.

The solutions to address the scalability challenges include the following three aspects:

- *Fast I/O*. From the analysis, we know that the speed of the I/O is the bottleneck in performing the query. In addition, if the incoming data rate or packet capture rate is greater than the overall disk-write rate, the captured packet cannot be dumped to the storage and we will accumulate more and more packets in memory. As a consequence, we will end up with a situation where no more packets can be captured and recorded. If we can improve the disk I/O speed (IOPS) through either RAID or SSD, the retrospective analysis system can both process the incoming data and serve the queries more quickly.

- *Index size*. The example we have shown uses a WAH compressed bitmap to index the collected packets. Although the compressed bitmap is significantly smaller than the raw bitmap, it is still not the optimal compression solution. We have also shown that the cost to operate on the indices while performing the queries is negligible when compared with the cost to read and store the indices. This suggests space-efficient indexing is the key to scalability.

- *Parallelization*. In the example given at the beginning of this section, we divide the time into 15-minute intervals and index packets within those intervals. We perform searches sequentially on each of the indices to produce the results. When this approach is applied to search in a packet capture of daunting size (say, 1PB capture on a 10Gbps link), it is impractical if not implausible. However, because all bitmap indices are independent of each other, we can parallel the search (logical operations) on different indices at the same time and aggregate the results together when the searches are completed.

  If the indices are not independent (for example, B-tree), it is possible to replicate the indices and have several search tasks running on different replicas simultaneously. The parallel tasks can be running on the same machine as different processes or threads, or they can be scaled to run on different machines. The parallelization can be implemented with an existing big data framework, for example, MapReduce and NoSQL technologies. Parallelization is critical to the horizontal scalability of the retrospective analysis system.

Notes on Building a Retrospective Analysis System

Given the huge amount of data collected and the complexity of indexing and querying on the data, it is not practical (if at all feasible) to store and process all of the data on a single machine. In other words, the demands of scalability require that the retrospective analysis system be designed in such a manner that tasks can be distributed and completed in parallel. In this section, we discuss the parallel data processing paradigm of MapReduce and show a sample retrospective analysis application under the MapReduce framework. We also introduce some off-the-shelf products with MapReduce ingredients that can be used to build a retrospective analysis system.

MapReduce and Hadoop

MapReduce is a data processing paradigm. The goal of MapReduce is to process large volumes of data in a parallel and distributed way and to obtain useful aggregated results. MapReduce contains two functions: `Map()` and `Reduce()`. Both functions come from the study of functional programming, where `Map()`

is used to transform (map) a list of values to another list of values, and Reduce() is used to condense (reduce) the mapped list of values into a single value. To explain the basic concepts of Map() and Reduce(), we give an example in real life.

Suppose there is a basket of fruit containing apples, oranges, and grapefruits, and you want to make a glass of juice out of them so that you can enjoy a blend of fruits. However, you cannot make a glass of juice directly from the whole fruits, because the blender can only work with small chunks of fruit. Fortunately, it is possible to use a knife to cut the fruits into slices. By cutting up the fruits, instead of whole apples, oranges, and grapefruits, you now have apple slices, orange slices, and grapefruit slices. With a different form of the original fruits, that is, in slices, not whole fruits from the basket, the blender can now be used to work on those slices and create a blended juice.

Now, let us view the original fruit basket as a list of values (apples, oranges, grapefruits), and the knife as a Map() function. What the Map() function does is to prepare (or transform) the list of values into another list of values (apple slices, orange slices, grapefruit slices). Similarly, the blender is the Reduce() function. It condenses the mapped list of values into a single value, which is the glass of juice.

Let us go back to the world of computing and look at a sample problem. The problem is to calculate the sum of squares of a given array of integers. Every programmer can write the solution quickly, similar to the following small code snippet. While this piece of code works well when the input array is relatively small, it does not scale when there are millions, if not billions, of integers in the array. In such a scenario, the desired approach is to distribute the computing task to multiple processing tasks and compute in parallel.

Sample Code Snippet to Get Sum of Squares

```
sum_of_squares(a)  { // a is an array of integers
1   int result = 0, i = 0;
2   for (i = 0; i < a.length; i++) {
3       result += a[i] * a[i];
4   }
5   return result;
}
```

Sample Code for MapReduce to Get Sum of Squares

```
Map(fn, a) {
1   for (int i = 0; i < a.length; i++) {
2       a[i] = fn(a[i]);
3   }
}

Reduce(fn, a, val) {
4   int   result = val;
5   for (int i = 0; i < a.length; i++) {
```

```
6      result = fn(result, a[i]);
7   }
8   return result;
}

square(v) {
9   return (v * v);
}

summation(s, val) {
10 return (s + val);
}

//Map process
Map(square, a);
//Reduce process
Reduce(summation, a, 0);
```

To revisit the sum of squares problem and apply the concepts of MapReduce, we divide the problem into two sub-problems. First, we obtain the list of squares values from the input list of integers. Then, we calculate the sum of the elements in the list of squares values. The first sub-problem can be solved by the Map() function, in which we create a new list and map each of the original values in the input array of integers to its squares values in the new list. The second sub-problem requires the Reduce() function, which works on a list of squares values and computes their sum.

To further generalize the two functions, Map() can be written as a framework, and the concrete implementation of how the mapping works can be a parameter of the Map() function. In the sample code, one of the input parameters of Map() is a function pointer fn(), and the actual implementation of fn() is to get the squares values (the square() function). Similarly, Reduce() can also take a function pointer with the actual implementation being the summation of all values in the input list (the summation() function). The Map() function takes the input array a and maps each of the array elements in place to a different value through the square() function. In this way, the mapped array is still a, but with a whole new list of values. The Reduce() function takes the mapped array and reduces the elements to a single value through the summation() function.

This framework can also be applied to solve other problems as long as those problems require performing some operations on each of the elements of the array. In addition, in the sum of squares example, the Map() function is not concerned with the order in which the input array is processed, nor is the Reduce() function concerned with the order of the elements for summation. In this regard, it is possible to divide the input array into two sub-arrays with half of the integers and assign two CPU cores to run the Map() function in parallel. In this way, the Map() function can be performed twice as quickly.

MapReduce for Parallel Processing

In the "sum of squares" example, we have shown that it is possible to divide the map process to two different processing tasks and assign these tasks to different CPUs. In this section, we generalize the concept and discuss the MapReduce framework for parallel processing.

We continue with the fruit and juice example to explain the concept of parallel processing in MapReduce. As we discussed earlier, the `Map()` function is the knife, and the `Reduce()` function is the blender. To parallel `Map()` and `Reduce()`, we need multiple knives and blenders. Suppose there are many baskets of fruit, with each containing apples, oranges, and grapefruits. The goal is to create bottles of a single fruit juice—for example, apple juice, orange juice, and grapefruit juice—from the whole fruits. In operation, we first parallel the cutting process by using multiple knives to slice the fruits into apple slices, orange slices, and grapefruit slices. For each of the fruit baskets, we use the same knife to cut all of the fruits, just as we did in the previous example. In this case, with the same knife, we have created different fruit slices. In order to create single fruit juices, we need to group all the slices from all the baskets by their fruit. After the grouping, we have a pile of apple slices, one of orange slices, and one of grapefruit slices. To create the juices, we use three different blenders, one for each fruit. The blenders take the fruit slices and output the bottles of juice.

In this example, each basket is the input of each `Map()` function. To represent the fruits in the basket, we can use a list of `<key, value>` pairs, for example, (`<a, apple>`, `<o, orange>`, `<g, grapefruit>`). The output of the `Map()` function is another list of `<key, value>` pairs, and we denote it as (`<a', apple slices>`, `<o', orange slices>`, `<g', grapefruit slices>`). Therefore, the parallel `Map()` function maps a list of `<key, value>` pairs to another list of `<key, value>` pairs.

The next step is to shuffle the `Map()` output and group the shuffled output for the `Reduce()` function. In this example, the shuffling and grouping are done by merging the `<key, value>` pairs that have the same key. Note that by merging the `<key, value>` pairs, we have `<key, value-list>` pairs, where the value-list is the aggregation of all values that share the same key. In this example, the value-lists are all fruit slices of the same type. Finally, each `Reduce()` function takes the `<key, value-list>` as input and reduces it into a single value, and the parallel `Reduce()` functions reduce the `<key, value-list>` pairs into a list of values, which are the bottles of single-fruit juice. In summary, the parallel MapReduce framework converts a list of `<key, value>` pairs into a list of values.

There are two aspects to note in the parallel MapReduce framework. First, the key to link `Map()` and `Reduce()` functions is the shuffle step. To abstract the shuffle step, we can view it as a processor-matching problem. The outputs of the `Map()` function are M`<key, value>` pairs with N unique keys. If we have N processors to process each of the N unique keys, we need to match each of the

M<key, value> pairs to a processor based on its key. Then, in the reduce process, N processors run the Reduce() function (also called the *reducer*) in parallel to create a list of output values. If we have fewer than N processors to run Reduce(), we need a *partition function* to associate a given key to a *reducer*. The partition function should consider balancing the load among reducers.

The second aspect is the input to the Map() function. The design of the Map() function is to use multiple processors, or even multiple machines to process all input data and generate M<key, value> pairs. Such a design requires that the input data be distributed, which suggests that there should be no dependency among the data that is processed on different processors. Similar to the *partition function*, the distribution to the Map() function should also take load balancing into consideration.

We now take a real-word application as an example to describe how to use the MapReduce framework in retrospective analysis. Suppose the retrospective analysis system is designed to analyze proxy logs. The particular application is to process the logs and show the counts of all policy enforcement actions on each of the users (IP addresses).

Recall that in the previous sections, we introduced the ELFF log format for proxy logs. In such logs, at each line of policy enforcement action, there is an IP address (for example, 192.168.1.2) and the applied policy results (for example, policy_denied). To process each line of the log, we need to extract the *IP address* and *policy* fields from the log. The input data is then collected from proxy logs that are millions of lines long. Because the log entries are independent of each other, it is possible to truncate the logs and divide them into smaller log files that are of similar size. Each of the log files is fed into the Map() function, which extracts the two fields of interest from the log entry and forms the <IP address, policy> pair.

In the MapReduce framework, the *IP address* is the key and *policy* is the value. The *partition function* groups the list of pairs by IP address and transforms the <IP address, policy> list into <IP address, policy-list>. To assign the <IP address, policy-list> to the reducers, the partition function can hash the IP address into N values, where N is the number of reducers. Finally, the Reduce() function can process the *policy-list* and count the occurrences of each policy.

Hadoop

The most popular open source implementation of the parallel MapReduce framework is Apache Hadoop. A typical deployment of Hadoop consists of a cluster of commodity servers. One server works as a *master* node, which distributes, schedules, and parallelizes the other machines, which are known as *worker nodes*. For a MapReduce task, a *JobTracker* process runs on the *master* node, and each worker node runs a *TaskTracker*. When the client application submits a MapReduce job—which includes the Map(), Reduce(), and partition functions (also called the *combine function* in Hadoop)—the *master* node, based on the amount of resources the Hadoop cluster has, distributes the Map and Reduce tasks to the worker nodes and monitors the job status.

The distribution of tasks is to assign which nodes run Map tasks (*mapper*) and which nodes run Reduce tasks (*reducer*). This process usually starts with the input data being split, where each split is usually 16MB to 64MB in size. The split data is fed into each of the *mapper* nodes. As we explained previously, the Map task is to map a list of `<key, value>` pairs into another `<key, value>` list. In Hadoop, the output of the mapped `<key, value>` list is stored in memory, and the *combine function* is invoked periodically to process the `<key, value>` list into `<key, value-list>`. After the Map task is done, the TaskTracker notifies the JobTracker. When all TaskTrackers on the mappers are finished, the JobTracker will start the TaskTrackers in the reducers. When the TaskTrackers in all reducers report the completion of Reduce tasks, the whole MapReduce task is completed and the JobTracker can take another MapReduce task from the client application.

Another important use of the JobTracker is to monitor the status of each TaskTracker. If any of the TaskTrackers crash, the JobTracker will restart another worker node with the same task. That is to say, if the crashed TaskTracker is in a mapper, the restarted worker node will rerun the Map task from the very beginning with the same split of data as the crashed mapper, and if a reducer crashes, a new reducer will rerun the entire Reduce task with the same `<key, value-list>` assigned to the crashed reducer.

Another core piece of Hadoop is the Hadoop Distributed File System (HDFS). Each of the files stored in HDFS is made up of blocks. The metadata describing what blocks a file has is stored in the *NameNode*, a similar concept to the *master node* in MapReduce. A secondary NameNode can be configured as a hot standby. The actual storage of the blocks is on the *DataNodes*, which are the counterparts of *worker nodes*. A file is usually replicated multiple times (the default is three times) and stored distributively on the DataNodes. The file metadata also keeps track of which blocks are stored on which DataNodes. Therefore, when a client application, say, the sample log processing application in the previous section, wants to read a file, it needs to communicate with the NameNode first to obtain the metadata.

Such a request is done via the Hadoop client API, and the request to the NameNode contains the block index of the data to be read. The NameNode returns which of the DataNodes contains a copy of the requested block so that the client application can contact the DataNode directly to obtain that block. To write a file to HDFS, the client application needs to write the file to all DataNodes. The NameNode will assign one of the replicas as a primary copy and the rest as secondary copies. Although the copies of files are pushed from the client application directly to all the DataNodes, the files are held in a buffer. In order to complete the write process, the client application needs to talk with the DataNode that has the primary copy and send the "commit" request to write the data from the buffer to the actual storage devices. The primary DataNode then orders the actual write of file blocks among all the DataNodes. HDFS and MapReduce tasks are often tied together, where the input splits of data to the *mappers* are from HDFS, and the outputs from the *reducers* are individual files that are written back to HDFS.

Building around the Hadoop cores (MapReduce and HDFS) are the related projects and products that together create the Hadoop ecosystem. The other components include HBase (the Hadoop database), Pig (MapReduce task converter), Hive (a SQL-like query language), Mahout (data modeling and analytics toolset), Storm (real-time data stream processing), Zookeeper (high availability through redundancy), and so on. Architecting the retrospective analysis system can well leverage the available modules in the Hadoop ecosystem.

Open Source Data Storage and Management Solution

In previous sections, we introduced and analyzed several indexing approaches and algorithms that are very efficient for managing the huge amount of data collected in a retrospective analysis system. As a matter of fact, those approaches and algorithms are available in many off-the-shelf data storage and management solutions. A good example of such a system is known as a relational database management system (RDBMS). The most typical RDBMS products that are widely deployed include Oracle database, MySQL, Microsoft SQL Server, and PostgreSQL. Such an RDBMS might fit perfectly with enterprise or other applications; however, it is not the best solution to store and manage data in a retrospective analysis system.

Why a Traditional RDBMS Falls Short

A traditional RDBMS and a retrospective analysis system are designed around different goals, and the way they operate is not quite the same. The reasons why a traditional RDBMS is not a proper solution for a retrospective analysis system can be categorized as follows:

- An RDBMS is designed to do frequent addition, modification, editing, and removal of data. An RDBMS also has a complex design to keep track of data changes to ensure the integrity of the data. However, a retrospective analysis system does not require many of these operations. A retrospective analysis system mostly writes data for storage and reads data for analysis. Only in very rare cases, if at all, does a retrospective analysis system need to modify or remove the data from storage.

- An RDBMS is intended to manage data of a uniformed format because it operates with predefined schemas. However, a retrospective analysis system collects, stores, and analyzes structured and unstructured data of various formats, and the unstructured data may be hard to describe with schemas. In this regard, an RDBMS is not able to manage all types of data required by a retrospective analysis system.

- Typically, when inserting a data entry into an RDBMS, we need to make such an entry by providing the values in the fields the entry requires. To extract those values from raw data, we need to do some processing on its raw format. In this regard, an RDBMS manages the extracted relations in data, not the actual data. However, a retrospective analysis system requires both a fast query on the data and retrieval of the data in its original raw format, which an RDBMS cannot offer.

- An RDBMS does not scale well in performance because it mainly focuses on data relations (for example, multiple tables) and management (for example, transaction processing). However, a retrospective analysis system needs to handle gigabytes, if not petabytes, of data that may be stored and processed on different machines. Therefore, scalability is key to a retrospective analysis system.

NoSQL and Search Engines

Because an RDBMS is not appropriate for building a retrospective analysis system, we are interested in finding alternative solutions that fit the requirements of a retrospective analysis system.

Not Only SQL or Not using SQL (NoSQL) database technologies have emerged to address the performance and scalability challenges in the presence of large volumes of data. There are a variety of data models in NoSQL so that it can process structured, semi-structured, and unstructured data on a large scale. Unlike the SQL query language in RDBMS, NoSQL provides an object-oriented API to manipulate data, and it is easy to integrate with other applications. The major types of NoSQL include the following:

- *Key-value store* is the simplest form of NoSQL. It stores the data in the format of `<key, value>` pairs. Because of its simplicity, it is a popular solution in embedded systems. Well-known key-value store databases include Redis and DynamoDB.

- *Document store* does not work on schemas so that each database record can have a different format (for example, a different number of columns with various numbers of values). Internally, it implements a document structure to hold the keys, and the database operations are around the documents. The most notable NoSQL document store is MongoDB, which is the most popular NoSQL database.

- *Wide-column store* organizes data by columns instead of rows. Because the size and number of columns are dynamic, wide-column store shows great scalability. Wide-column store is also schema-free, and it can be viewed as a two-dimensional key-value store database. Examples of this type of NoSQL database are Cassandra and HBase.

- *Graph database* is designed to store the type of data that shows strong connectivity properties among the records. Such connectivity can include network links, social connections, and so on. Typical graph database implementations include Neo4j and Titan.

A search engine is a tool to search and retrieve data. By strict definition, search engines are not NoSQL databases because they do not consider data storage as much as NoSQL databases do. Search engines can be high performing and scalable with the help of powerful, efficient, and accurate search algorithms; however, what sets search engines apart is their ability to perform searches based on relevance. For example, think about the *TF-IDF* algorithm we discuss in Chapter 5; the results of the search can be ranked by the *TF-IDF* score to show relevance. Such abilities possessed by search engines in terms of information retrieval cannot be found in NoSQL databases. Popular search engine solutions include open source projects like Lucene, Apache Solr, Elasticsearch, and commercial products like Splunk.

NoSQL and Hadoop

Hadoop MapReduce and NoSQL are two related techniques in the realm of big data. As a matter of fact, they can co-exist in a single product. For example, the most popular NoSQL database, MongoDB, internally has a single-thread implementation of MapReduce. Using its MapReduce commands, it is possible to query on a large volume of data in the database, process the query responses in parallel, and condense them into aggregated results. For another example, the default database in Hadoop is HBase, which is the wide-column store NoSQL database, and it has a well-defined API to use Hadoop MapReduce. In addition, it is also possible to integrate other NoSQL databases that are not based on Hadoop with the MapReduce framework. One such example is Cassandra, which is a NoSQL data store that is best used for web analytics. The Cassandra project has provided a set of utilities to input data from Cassandra to MapReduce, and then retrieve output from MapReduce and save it back to Cassandra.

Choosing which type of MapReduce and NoSQL integration to use is based on the specific design consideration of the retrospective analysis system, because different NoSQL technologies have their own unique characteristics. For example, Cassandra is efficient at database replication but less efficient when there is more than one index. MongoDB is relatively easy to deploy and has simpler internal commands to perform MapReduce tasks that otherwise can take a lot of coding work with Hadoop. However, MongoDB also takes a longer time to process the MapReduce tasks than a distributed Hadoop deployment.

Summary

Victims of an APT typically discover the breach because an organization's confidential information has been made available to the public or has been exposed to the hacker community. The public disclosure comes with both humiliation and detrimental effects to the business. Because APT is stealthy, targeted, and difficult to detect using traditional security defense mechanisms, retrospective analysis is an important method in the detection of APTs. Petabytes of logs and packet captures are the essential elements in a retrospective system. Efficient indexing and storage management of such large volumes of data allows for flexible and fast queries to be issued by security analysts, a fundamental step in discovering the suspicious patterns that will eventually lead to the uncovering of an implanted APT.

CHAPTER 9

Mobile Security

The Apple iOS and Google Android mobile operating systems have revolution-ized the mobile device market, as evidenced by the amazing market growth in the mobile phone industry. Millions of mobile applications have been developed to serve just about any purpose or need imaginable. These devices have changed our social behavior and influenced the way we do business in this new mobile computing era.

Mobile devices and smartphones provide ubiquitous and convenient access to information and services. Major news networks, entertainment content, social networks, blogs, and tweets are only a click away. Mobile device–specific applications have been built to enable access to corporate email systems, web mail systems, online banking, online shopping, prescription services, and point of sale (POS) systems, which are as comprehensive as traditional in-person services but consume only a fraction of the time to complete. The computing power and feature sets of these mobile devices are evolving rapidly and are becoming comparable to those of desktop and laptop computers. A popular prediction is these mobile devices will replace desktop and laptop computers in the not-so-distant future. These new-generation mobile devices are more than just gadgets for entertainment and making phone calls.

The always-on, anywhere, and anytime computing paradigm trades security for convenience. "Bring your own device" (BYOD) refers to the situation where an employee's personal mobile device has become an integral part of their corporate computing experience. This is a symptom of users adopting new technology and then forcing corporate IT departments to adapt. Unfortunately, in many situations the IT department yields to user demands and the new technology is integrated into the corporate IT system with little or no assessment of security impacts. The lack of consideration for security raises the risk of compliance violations and jeopardizes an enterprise due to possible theft of intellectual property and leakage of corporate secrets as a result of malware intrusion.

In this chapter, we will examine the various real threats that are targeting mobile devices, analyze the challenges of securing mobile devices, and propose a network-centric view towards solving some of these mobile security problems.

Mobile Device Management, or Lack Thereof

In today's corporate environments, the boundary between private and corporate use of mobile devices and smartphones is blurring. Most employees prefer to purchase these mobile devices on their own to ensure mobile number permanency even when they change employers. These personal devices are utilized to access corporate information. The main challenges of the BYOD problem are that corporate access policies must not interfere with privacy while still complying with applicable regulations, corporate access policies must not restrict private use, privately installed applications that are disqualified by corporate policies must be restricted from accessing corporate data, and some applications may be permitted to access corporate data depending on the current device location.

The main goals of mobile device management (MDM) include remote management of the mobile device, centralized provisioning of policies and configurations, monitoring of user activities, and retrieval of log files from the device. Remote management of a mobile device, or over-the-air (OTA) device management, utilizes cellular or WiFi networks to administer the device and to perform tasks such troubleshooting, locking the device, or completely wiping the device of all data if it is lost or stolen.

MDM is driven by the need to manage employees' personal devices that are utilized for enterprise-related productivity tasks. Therefore, the enterprise IT defines access and security policies centrally, identifies and permits the installation of certain applications, creates standardized device configurations, and then remotely distributes these settings to all registered devices. However, although MDM infrastructure and technology are on the path to standardization, the current implementations and architectures vary from vendor to vendor.

A commonality in the MDM architecture is the server-client model where the server component is managed by the enterprise and the mobile device is required to install MDM client software. One of the biggest hurdles of MDM adoption is the involuntary installation of a piece of software that the employer can use to track the employee's activities. An employee is highly likely to disable the software on a personal device when possible, which defeats the purpose of having MDM. When the employee cannot tamper with the client MDM software, they will simply not use that device for job-related activities, or they will carry two mobile devices: one that is issued by the employer for work and one that is purchased personally for everything else.

If MDM is truly meant to provide both convenience for the employee and intellectual property protection for the employer with increased employee productivity, then MDM has yet to succeed. First, carrying multiple devices is an inconvenience, and working with monitoring software on a device creates resentment and arouses suspicion. Second, although wiping a device remotely if it is reported lost can presumably be achieved with little effort, this protection can easily be bypassed if the stolen device is intentionally disconnected from the cellular network by removing its subscriber identity module (SIM) card, and by disabling the device's WiFi feature to isolate the device from any network.

According to the National Institute of Standards and Technology (NIST), the security objectives of a mobile device must include *integrity, confidentiality,* and *availability*. Integrity, or more specifically data integrity, refers to the ability to detect when data tampering occurs in transmission or in storage and to guarantee the accuracy and consistency of the original data. Confidentiality requires the ability to define rights and restrictions on data in transmission or in storage and to prevent unauthorized access. Availability refers to the ability to provide reliable access to data at all times.

However, the server-client model of MDM architecture is not free of vulnerabilities and is susceptible to threats just like any other networked infrastructure. Data integrity and confidentiality are outside the responsibilities of existing MDM solutions and are made possible only when the underlying mobile operating systems provide the necessary system-level support. For example, the underlying mobile OS must offer encryption application program interfaces (APIs) so that a document reader (in the form of a mobile application) can encrypt and decrypt a document from a mobile device's data storage. With the increased size of storage on mobile devices (128GB or more), it is possible to store a large part of, if not the entire, corporate employee contact database on a mobile device. As a matter of fact, mobile users tend to download and carry more data on their mobile devices than they actually need. Such behavior is allowed to ensure undisrupted productivity when network connectivity is lost. However, this practice also results in a huge risk of data loss or even data theft if the mobile device is lost.

Another example of MDM vulnerability is that a mobile e-mail client must utilize an encrypted connection to the mail server in order to secure the mail exchange. This communication channel is not supervised by the MDM solution. Many existing enterprise networks do not implement restricted access to corporate IT services. For example, many enterprises allow e-mail access through the web, which allows a mobile device such as an iPhone to connect to the corporate Microsoft Exchange Mail server using the built-in iOS mail application, without the need to connect through a virtual private network (VPN). An e-mail attachment containing confidential information such as a financial report can be shared with another application on the same device and can cause a potential leakage of that information. These activities are not monitored, protected, or supervised by existing MDM solutions.

Current MDM solutions do not prevent managed mobile devices from using untrusted wireless networks. When using untrusted networks, man-in-the-middle (MITM) attacks can be launched by intercepting or even modifying communications from a mobile device, which can also include the communications between MDM agents on managed mobile devices and remote MDM servers. Such a MITM attack is clearly a violation of the integrity and confidentiality objectives of an organization.

In addition, MDM solutions do not prohibit managed mobile devices from accessing untrusted contents. In such a scenario, a managed mobile device can install applications created by unknown parties or from an untrusted alternative application store or marketplace. Attacks through malicious mobile applications are most common, and with a high success rate, and pose the biggest security threats to a mobile device and its owner.

Furthermore, existing MDM solutions do not protect managed mobile devices from malware or malnets. For example, a mobile device can scan a Quick Response (QR) code that may lead to a malicious landing page and eventually to the download and installation of malware. Current MDM solutions cannot address device interactions with other external systems. Attacks are known to occur via USB cable when a device is connected to a desktop computer to synchronize and back up data from the device. Hackers can leverage the installed malware to monitor and log user activities or even keystrokes on the infected mobile device in order to intercept corporate credentials and passwords. When the compromised mobile device connects back to the corporate network, the entire network is exposed to a potential advanced persistent threat (APT) attack.

Because of the aforementioned security protection limitations, existing MDM solutions cannot fulfill the security objectives as defined by NIST for mobile devices. Mobile devices that are managed by existing MDM solutions, and which are permitted on corporate networks, continue to be one of the weakest points in the enterprise security domain. The inability of MDMs to fully protect managed mobile devices partially comes from their ineffective security model, which lacks an understanding of enterprise security objectives and requirements. An MDM is designed to protect the security of a physical device. It is a passive security approach that does not proactively prevent a hacker from attacking the managed mobile device, but reactively relies on remotely wiping the data off the device after some security violations have occurred. In the event of a device breach, the data-erasing mechanism may fail because the MDM server needs to communicate with the MDM agent on the device to perform the erase operation, and the mobile device may be turned off, thus losing network connectivity, after it is compromised.

Finally, an MDM imposes restrictions on what users can do with a managed mobile device. In the era of BYOD that is now expanding into what is called "bring your own network" (BYON), when mobile devices are no longer provided by corporations, MDM becomes an unattractive option.

Mobile Applications and Their Impact on Security

The evolution of mobile security demands a better approach to protecting enterprise information stored on mobile devices. This gives rise to Mobile Application Management (MAM). Unlike MDM, MAM focuses on mobile applications that have access to corporate networks and data on a device. By ensuring that only trusted applications from the enterprise application store can be installed on mobile devices, MAM can isolate untrusted applications from accessing corporate resources. However, MAM solutions provide little or no protection for either the mobile devices or the corporate data stored on the devices.

The core of enterprise mobile security is enterprise data security. The particular problem to address is how to implement fine-grained policies to device data management in order to achieve access control and confidentiality. For example, the goal is to limit the amount of data that can be stored on the device and make encryption mandatory to both minimize the chance of data theft and reduce potential damage in the case of a security breach of the mobile device. The solution to this data security problem requires multilayered approaches that include mobile device management, application management, data encryption, policy enforcement, network access control, malware detection and prevention, and so on.

A close examination of the mobile application landscape reveals some undeniable trends. For example, each mobile application is designed to access a specific service, and many of these services are cloud-based. Also, a vast number of mobile applications access a service directly through the mobile OS networking layer by means of custom protocols, instead of using a traditional web browser or the HTTP protocol. Therefore, solving the BYOD challenge in a corporate environment demands a thorough understanding of the mobile applications and their users. Deep knowledge of mobile applications enables better decision-making for security, performance, network optimization, and risk management. Visibility into mobile applications enables detailed logging and reporting for compliance. From the mobile network operator (MNO) perspective, accurate identification of mobile applications is mandatory in enforcing a service level agreement (SLA).

There are almost as many mobile applications as there are publishers. Unlike the traditional desktop software market where the publishers are typically well-known and established companies with trustworthy reputations, most mobile developers have unknown reputations, and many may publish just a single application and then disappear permanently. The sea of apps, in the millions, makes mobile users less concerned about the presumed identity of an individual developer and the developer's reputation.

In theory, users must scrutinize the pedigree of any mobile application to be installed on their device. However, the distribution channels of these mobile applications, namely, the Apple App Store and Google Play, make these applications available to end users very quickly from publication to installation. This rapid acceptance changes mobile users' perception about the criticality of a publisher's reputation and the intent behind a mobile app. Even when the developers are not nefarious characters, many of them are not seasoned programmers and are not versed in security. Some simply have little or no regard for security. As such, applications created by these types of developers are prone to attacks and can be easily exploited and turned into malicious actors.

Mobile app marketplaces do not necessarily concentrate on vetting these mobile applications from a security perspective, although each makes a diligent effort at conducting a rudimentary security review, identifying malicious applications, and ensuring the timely removal of those bad apps. The pricing of mobile apps—where many cost a few dollars or less and others are ad-sponsored and therefore free—is another factor that affects a user's judgment in selecting and allowing apps to be installed on their device.

The availability of a large number of apps raises the curiosity of end users and entices them to experiment with as many apps as possible. As quickly as their fingers can point and swipe, mobile users install the free applications, often without heeding the security warnings that appear during app installation. For example, although Android implements a privilege separation model, where a sandbox isolates application execution such that the application's data is protected within the sandbox from unauthorized access, the user may unintentionally grant a malicious app *Signature/System* permission, thus allowing the malicious app to circumvent this protection model.

Security Threats and Hazards in Mobile Computing

The different types of connectivity available on mobile devices—including Bluetooth, 3G and 4G, and WiFi access—combined with the physical mobility attribute, have broadened the attack vectors of these mobile devices compared to desktop systems. The protection options for mobile devices are limited today for various reasons.

First, there is a general lack of antivirus and anti-malware software that is specifically designed for mobile devices. This is mainly due to the large diversity in both mobile operating systems and hardware platforms. The makeup of the device platform, such as the processor selection, the system-on-chip (SoC) design, the memory, the persistent storage, and the battery, varies from vendor to vendor and thus increases the complexity and scalability of providing uniform software for each device type.

Second, the underlying mobile OS or platform may restrict the capability of the antivirus software. For example, because Apple iOS is a closed proprietary mobile OS, third-party vendors cannot modify the kernel or provide system libraries for the OS. Because each application that executes in the iOS is shielded from other running applications, a virus scanner running as an application will not be able to access system files and look for a virus infection. Therefore, Apple must grant special privileges to antivirus scan applications. However, in the past Apple rejected a well-known antivirus software vendor in its bid to produce a version of its product for iOS-powered devices. Even for an open system such as Android, running an antivirus scan can overheat the CPU and drain the battery rapidly because virus scanning is a complex operation.

Third, although mobile security research is an active area with commercial support from the industry, mobile security is still in the early stages, and commercial solutions that stem from these research activities are still far from fruition. This is partly due to the OS design, whether Android or iOS, with the goal of luring application developers to build as many applications as is humanly imaginable, and as fast as is humanly possible, to expand the mobile application landscape. The more apps there are, the faster and more solidified the market adoption of the mobile OS—and the mobile devices that are powered by these mobile operating systems—will become.

Finally, most end users have neither the technical knowledge to comprehend the possible security threats nor any interest in acquiring such knowledge even as the media have increased their coverage of cyber-attacks; as such, the demand for mobile security products is limited at best.

In the following sections, we list some of the more severe security issues challenging mobile operating systems.

Cross-Origin Vulnerability

From the very beginning, mobile operating systems were designed for usability and interaction, and security was an afterthought. At the core of this security challenge is the lack of security-related support at the OS level. Consequently, one of the most severe security problems is cross-origin vulnerability.

WebView is the most utilized software on mobile devices today, and it is the biggest attack surface because just about every mobile app uses the WebView APIs to access the Internet. Both iOS and Android adopted the WebView class, which enables a mobile application to incorporate basic browser functionality. They embedded these capabilities inside a mobile app, which enables the app to interact with the web and web contents as a basic browser. However, the same-origin security policy enforcement and protection that restrict content from one website from accessing and interfering with content retrieved out of a different website are missing from the mobile operating systems. On a mobile device, one app can interact with other apps or requesting services that are running on the same device to enhance its functionality. An example is the iOS mail reader, which can launch an appropriate app and send an attachment to that app for processing. The same-origin policy is not available in the inter-app communication channels in the mobile operating systems, which allows attackers to launch mobile cross-site request forgery (CSRF) attacks and cross-site scripting attacks.

The root of the problem lies in the underlying implementation of the app-to-app communication channels inside iOS and Android. The inter-app communication channels include the Android *intent* channel, the *URL scheme* for both iOS and Android, and the utility component (or class), such as WebView. Fundamentally, the messages that are exchanged within these channels do not contain any origin information. The intent channel is Android-specific and allows one app to activate the activities of another app or activate a background service. Similarly, the URL scheme allows one app to use a URL to launch another app or service.

Without origin-crossing protection in the mobile operating systems, a malicious app can essentially activate another app with arbitrary parameters, retrieve the contents of the other app, and ultimately manipulate the other app to steal credentials or other confidential data. Because this cross-origin vulnerability exists in both iOS and Android, the fixes must be applied to the underlying operating systems. Fixing this vulnerability will take time due to the need to change the underlying OS design, which can cause massive app compatibility issues. In addition, applying the necessary patches across all vendors is a daunting task, which leaves many existing devices vulnerable.

Near Field Communication

Near Field Communication (NFC) technology is increasingly designed into mobile devices. NFC allows mobile devices that are in close proximity to pair and communicate with each other. Examples of NFC being used include in-store payment transactions, exchange of contact information, and device configuration. The first commercial use of NFC in Apple iPhone 6, followed by its adoption in Android-based mobile devices, will demand mutual device authentication as an essential step, a technology that is immature today. Apple has restricted the use of the NFC chip to Apple Pay and has not made NFC available to third-party developers. A user's fingerprint is more than just a passcode to unlock the phone and is now associated with the built-in mobile payment system.

The proliferation of NFC will go beyond the payment and POS system. However, as with any new technology, attacks on NFC will begin to surface, and protecting the mobile device from unintentional NFC communication will become mandatory. Malicious NFC tags that contain URLs can cause the device to process a URL and land at a malicious website, resulting in attacks such as drive-by downloads. Unless protected, peer-to-peer interactions with other NFC-enabled systems can potentially cause involuntary retrieval and installation of malicious apps, in addition to potentially leaking information to malevolent devices.

Application Signing Transparency

Android apps in Google Play are digitally signed using self-signed certificates. The identity and information offered in self-signed certificates can be fabricated to anything the signer intends. Based on a study conducted in April 2014, out of the 97 percent of apps that are free in Google Play, which represent over 980,000 apps, 97 percent of those free apps have self-signed certificates. If a reputable and legitimate key is stolen, Google Play will not have an effective mechanism in place to revoke the key.

Library Integrity and SSL Verification Challenges

Android is a popular mobile OS platform, having close to 80 percent of the market share, and it has some unique security challenges of its own. Because Android applications are developed using the Java programming language, various tools are available to decompile and repackage an application. Attackers have attached malicious payloads or injected malicious code into legitimate apps and then repackaged the modified applications for redistribution to infect unsuspecting users. Similar attacks have been applied to third-party libraries as well.

The first type of modification is to remove license protection from the third-party library. Another type of attack involves creating a new library that occupies the same namespace, essentially masquerading as its legitimate counterpart. Many capabilities on Android devices are provided by third-party libraries, and free apps that are sponsored by advertisers include ad-libraries. The abundance and availability of third-party libraries means that an Android-based mobile app has a higher chance of embedding in it a third-party library that may be rogue, and which may exhibit unwanted activity such as collecting information on user behaviors and analyzing and exporting users' private data.

Studies done by a security vendor have shown that over 40 percent of sampled Android apps were not properly programmed with the SSL library. These programming errors include lack of or improper server certificate validation and lack of server hostname verification against CA-issued certificates, resulting in Android apps being susceptible to MITM attacks even when SSL/TLS has been enabled in the transaction. Many of these same apps are also found to ignore SSL errors.

Ad Fraud

Ad fraud and malvertising are two prevalent problems on the Android platform. Malvertising refers to the injection of malicious advertisements into the advertising networks and contaminating syndicate contents. Malvertising is made possible due to the practice of *ad arbitration*. Ad arbitration refers to the process of buying and selling advertisements, which results in an undesirable situation where a website cannot guarantee the origin and the integrity of an advertisement that is displayed on its web pages.

Those ad-sponsored "free" Android apps must link with ad libraries so that advertisement content can be fetched from the ad servers and then displayed to the end user. These apps are prone to attacks that turn the mobile device into a bot that then stealthily clicks ads without displaying the ads to the user and without user consent, thus fraudulently generating revenue for the ad publishers. These stealthy ad downloads can also retrieve malvertising content and subject the device to further hacking.

Research Results and Proposed Solutions

In this section, we provide an overview of some of the representative solutions and frameworks that have been proposed to address mobile device security problems.

An ontology-based semantic firewall focuses on protecting the privacy of a user's identity and data. The data set that requires protection is gathered first. Then the explicit knowledge of data access patterns by mobile applications is expressed using the *OWL Web Ontology Language*. The predefined security policies are represented in the *Semantic Web Rule Language*. In this proposed semantic firewall, once the ontologies have been populated and when a request is being made, the firewall consults the description logic reasoning module to perform the inferences according to the configured policy rules. The result of the inference is a binary action of *permitted* or *forbidden*. If the request is permitted, then the firewall provides the requested data and subsequently logs the transaction.

The purpose of an *application lockbox* is to protect a sensitive application and its data by means of an encrypted application volume. The sensitive application, its data, and the memory swap file during execution all reside inside the sandbox and are cryptographically protected. The proposed design is comprised of two cooperating components: the on-box limited trusted computing platform (TCP) and the off-box policy decisions and trust modeling component. The off-box decision component determines the access control and is enforced by the on-box TCP. The communication taking place between the on-box TCP and the off-box decision module is secure. The main security goal of the application lockbox in this proposal is to protect the sensitive application and its data in cases where the physical device has been compromised.

The bare metal hypervisor, also known as the Type-1 hypervisor approach, assumes that the built-in mobile OS, the pre-installed applications, and third-party applications installed by the user are all untrusted. The bare metal hypervisor is the only trusted component in the mobile execution environment that has direct access to the physical hardware. Running on top of this trusted hypervisor are the built-in mobile OS and its applications, and the trusted mobile OS running trusted applications. In this model, the hypervisor isolates the trusted systems from the untrusted systems of the mobile device ecosystem. The open source L^4 Android project offers another virtual machine approach by means of developing a microkernel that can run multiple virtual machines (VMs) to achieve isolation.

Intrusion detection systems that are specific to mobile devices and smartphones use an on-device lightweight agent to gather intelligence followed by off-box analysis to detect anomalous behaviors. Various solutions take this approach and differ in the types of data that are gathered, the context in which the data is interpreted, and the types of analysis that are performed. For example, in the knowledge-based temporal abstraction method, time-stamped primitive parameters and events are collected. The context interprets a primitive parameter to form an abstract parameter. For example, CPU usage is a primitive parameter, user-activity is the context, and interpreting a high CPU utilization when the user is inactive indicates an abnormal system state. The user-activity context maps the value of the primitive parameter, for example, 30 percent CPU utilization, to a value of HIGH for an abstract parameter CPU-state. Then, patterns are formed for anomalous analysis.

In the cloud-based antivirus solution, the mobile agent sends files to a cloud service, where multiple antivirus engines, each running inside a VM, will perform simultaneous scanning on those files. Another behavior-based detection framework takes on the crowd-sourcing strategy. The agent application tracks the API calls of each application and sends the log into the cloud, where logs from other users are combined for analysis and detection of malware.

The iOS and Android mobile OS come with a built-in virtual private network (VPN) solution. In particular, the iOS VPN solution has been designed with the enterprise in mind. The Apple mobile device management (MDM) infrastructure allows an IT manager to provision a specific device profile into an iOS device remotely. The MDM device profile enables the VPN on-demand feature in iOS, where access to certain domains or IP addresses will activate the VPN service automatically, thus providing a seamless method to access the enterprise networks securely. The VPN technology is also deployed to bridge mobile phones to cloud-based security services. In this case, all traffic that originates from the mobile device is directed into the cloud where security services such as virus and malware detection, data leak prevention, and phishing attack detection are performed.

The VPN-based solution deserves some extra discussion because the technology is adopted by enterprises as well as by cloud service vendors. Because enterprises and cloud vendors have deployed iOS VPN solutions in practice, we will focus our discussion on iOS. The network component of the VPN client inside iOS is based on an early version of the open source *Racoon* software. The specific version of Racoon adopted in iOS, as verified in iOS version 4.0, has limited configurability, and due to what appear to be software bugs, it cannot process certain configuration parameters sent by the VPN server correctly. As such, the VPN on-demand feature is not as configurable as intended. In addition, iOS does not have the ability to establish multiple active VPN tunnels simultaneously. The end result is problematic because the iOS device cannot connect to multiple services—such as to the enterprise network, a third-party cloud service, and services on a home network—at the same time.

Even if multiple VPN channels can be established at the same time, the split-DNS support is missing. Without split-DNS it is difficult to perform DNS name resolution for local domain names (for the iOS device side, for example, these are home network nodes), the internal domain names (the enterprise or cloud internal nodes), and external domain names (all other nodes that reside outside the enterprise, cloud, and home networks) when multiple VPN tunnels are active.

The problem is that when the VPN connection is established, if the VPN server sends the DNS server information to the iOS device, this provided DNS server will be used for internal domain name resolution as well as for all other name resolutions. For example, consider the situation where an enterprise user with an iPad is connected to an enterprise WiFi network. When that enterprise user needs to access a cloud-based service, the iPad connects to the cloud over VPN. As soon as the iPad connects to the cloud, the cloud sends back a DNS server as part of the VPN configuration. At this point, the internal enterprise resources are no longer accessible by hostname (such as "mail.internal.bluecoat.com") simply because the DNS server that is given by the cloud does not contain any entries for the internal resources. Although each internal resource may still be accessible by specifying the actual IP addresses, it is still problematic because IP addresses can change constantly when DHCP is used for address assignment.

Enhancements made to Android since the introduction of version 4.2 include multiple user accounts and restricted profiles. The concept behind multiple user accounts is to designate one user as the owner while all other accounts enjoy the same privileges as the owner account without user management capability. The restricted profile accounts cannot manage users and cannot install apps on the device. These enhancements toward user data isolation are on the right path to a more secure system, but they fall short in both design and implementation. The design deficiencies not only fail to offer isolation protection for the user, user-initiated apps, and user data, but they may also allow secondary users to launch privilege escalation attacks within the system. The evolution towards execution separation and data isolation must leverage mobile processor hardware capability such as the TrustZone extension offered by ARM (Advanced RISC Machines), which is specifically designed for security and offers physical partition of system resources into a secure world and a normal world.

Techniques for malicious app detection include *dynamic analysis* and *static analysis*. Dynamic runtime analysis observes an app's runtime execution behavior, by means of *sandboxing* and *system call interposition*. With sandboxing, a mobile app is executed inside a VM and emulator and uses the *fuzzing* technique that injects different input to induce runtime behaviors for analysis. The fuzzing technique can also be applied to probe app vulnerability. Dynamic analysis includes an external component that monitors and records network activities generated by the app. Static analysis is identical to the reverse engineering process and mostly performs code analysis through call graphs and data dependency graphs. In system call interposition, an analysis module attaches to a running app and monitors the app's interaction with the system by intercepting and analyzing the system calls made by the app.

Infrastructure-Centric Mobile Security Solution

Device-based security solutions are segmented and are mostly research-based solutions with little commercial exposure. As a result, the adoption of a specific solution remains in the context of academic research with some endorsement from the industry. In other words, mobile security solutions are still in their infancy. The problem is particularly thorny given the issues of mobile OS and hardware platform diversity, which are driving research on combining cloud-based protection with a lightweight on-device agent.

An infrastructure-based protection solution solves the mobile end-point problems of lack of computing power (although mobile platforms are advancing on this front), lack of a mature antivirus and anti-malware scanner software on each platform, and fast depletion of battery power. Mobile security must be a collaborative effort among mobile service providers and mobile network operators, with mobile users being willing to offer cooperation and permit inspection. The mobile network must be made programmable so that the network can evolve according to ever-changing security needs.

Furthermore, in today's networks, there exist *middle-boxes* or *proxies* that enable in-network protection—such as data leak prevention (DLP), web filtering, and antivirus—to be applied to traffic crossing the boundary between the corporate network and the Internet. Because mobile applications and devices face some of the same attack vectors as their desktop counterparts, the lack of protection from security proxies on cellular data networks exposes these mobile devices to attacks on a massive scale.

Towards the Seamless Integration of WiFi and Cellular Networks

WiFi and cellular networks are two complementary types of wireless access networks. Although the cellular network data rate has increased drastically over the last decade with the help of advanced radio technologies, it still cannot match the growth of data-hungry devices, such as smartphones and tablets. As a consequence, mobile network operators (MNOs) are under constant pressure from limited licensed spectrums for cellular use. In addition, poor indoor cellular coverage forces the MNOs to explore alternative connectivity solutions to deliver better network services. Integrating WiFi with cellular networks not only extends the coverage of MNOs' networks but also reduces congestion on cellular network backbones. As a matter of fact, WiFi and cellular network integration has become the industry trend. Figure 9-1 shows a sample WiFi and cellular inter-networking solution under the 3GPP framework.

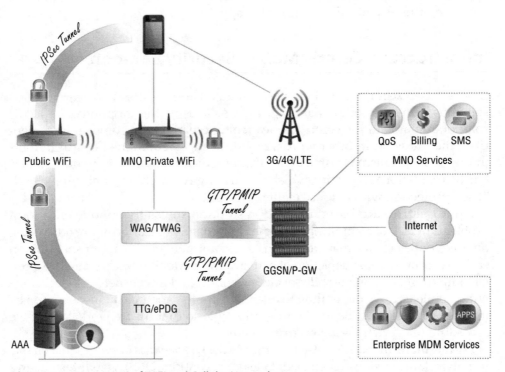

Figure 9-1: Integration of WiFi and Cellular Networks

In such implementations, the user equipment (UE) can choose to connect to either cellular networks (for example, 3G, 4G, or LTE) or WiFi networks. Like the current cellular network structure, the cellular towers are connected (through the radio access network) to the Gateway GPRS Support Node (GGSN) in 2G/3G architecture or the Packet Data Network Gateway (P-GW) in 4G/LTE architecture. The GGSN/P-GW has access to both the Internet and the MNO's own service network where the core MNO services, including QoS, billing, and SMS, are provided. For WiFi access, the UE has the option to use the MNO's own private WiFi service or the public WiFi in the event that the MNO's WiFi network is not available. In the former case, because the WiFi access point (AP) is operated and owned by the MNO, the UE can view it as a trusted WiFi service and therefore no encryption is required. When an MNO's private WiFi AP receives traffic from the UE, the AP needs to tunnel the IP traffic using the cellular standards and send it to the GGSN/P-GW. Such tunneling is performed at the wireless access gateway (WAG) in 2G/3G architecture or the trusted wireless access gateway (TWAG) in 4G/LTE architecture.

The protocols that use tunneling, such as the GPRS Tunneling Protocol (GTP) and Proxy Mobile IP (PMIP), provide IP mobility so that the UE can roam seamlessly between access networks. Using a public WiFi is the most complicated scenario because it requires that the UE establish a secure tunnel connection between itself and the MNO's network through the untrusted public WiFi network. The MNO network module for handling the secure tunnel is called the Tunnel Termination Gateway (TTG) in 2G/3G architecture or the Evolved Packet Data Gateway (ePDG) in 4G/LTE architecture. Usually, the secure tunnel is an IPsec tunnel initiated by the UE using the credentials that can be authenticated by the AAA server in the MNO's network. The TTG/ePDG not only decrypts the IPSec tunnel from the UE but also encapsulates the decrypted IP traffic using GTP or PMIP and forwards it to the GGSN/P-GW to support mobility. It can be seen that regardless of the wireless access network the UE uses, the UE can roam freely and securely reach the Internet and, hence, the enterprise MDM services through the MNO's core cellular network.

With this integration, a wireless enterprise user can roam freely between WiFi networks and cellular networks without losing connectivity to the enterprise MDM services. The user can choose to connect to both networks at the same time to aggregate the wireless network bandwidth. The user's privacy is also better protected because the MNO can steer the user's traffic so that only business-related traffic is directed to the enterprise network. Meanwhile, the MNO can offload some traffic from the cellular network to the WiFi network while maintaining the same level of MNO core services. WiFi and cellular network integration makes it possible to fully realize enterprise MDM goals.

Security in the Network

The network-centric solution, shown in Figure 9-2, becomes much more feasible due to the continuous drive to integrate WiFi and cellular networks, with seamless roaming between these two technologies.

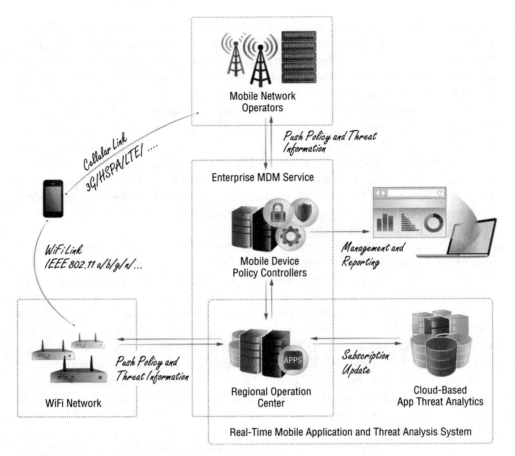

Figure 9-2 labels: Mobile Network Operators; *Push Policy and Threat Information*; Enterprise MDM Service; *Cellular Link 3G/HSPA/LTE/* ....; Mobile Device Policy Controllers; *Management and Reporting*; *WiFi Link IEEE 802.11 a/b/g/n/* ...; *Push Policy and Threat Information*; *Subscription Update*; WiFi Network; Regional Operation Center; APPS; Cloud-Based App Threat Analytics; Real-Time Mobile Application and Threat Analysis System

Figure 9-2: Network-Based Mobile Device Protection

In the network-centric mobile security solution, the mobile device is under the protection of both the WiFi and the cellular networks. Mobile application classification is performed in the network. When the mobile device connects to the wireless access point (AP), the WiFi AP extracts a small amount of packet data and payload bytes and submits the information to an on-box classifier. The on-box classifier tries to classify the traffic against its application cache; if that is not present, then it sends the information to the regional operation center (ROC). The ROC classifies the traffic and then pulls the associated application threat attributes from a cloud-based analytics service. The classified application and its attributes are then examined against a set of policies defined by the enterprise, and the corresponding policies are provisioned into the WiFi AP for enforcement. The WiFi AP installs and enforces the new security policies accordingly. Newly analyzed information is then recorded and submitted to a cloud-based analytics service to propagate to other ROCs. Similar operations are performed on the cellular networks.

Summary

There are now well over a million unique mobile applications in Google Play and the Apple App Store combined, and the growth of those app marketplaces shows no sign of slowing down. Unlike traditional computing systems, implementing adequate end-point security solutions in mobile devices is impractical with the current designs of mobile operating systems and under the constraints defined by the hardware platform. Mobile security is under active research, and viable solutions are still under development. Infrastructure-centric security solutions combined with cloud-based defense are important practical strategies in combating the ever-evolving and highly adaptive threats in the wild.

Application identification and behavior profiling are key to implementing intelligent, fine-grained, and policy-based control on mobile applications. Enterprises and government agencies must pay close attention to this mobile security problem. Mobile service providers and operators must understand the importance of security and privacy, begin the construction of infrastructure-centric mobile security solutions as a mandatory service, and proactively offer these new services to mobile users to gain their trust and cooperation.

Bibliography

Aho, Alfred V., and Margaret J. Corasick. 1975. "Efficient string matching: An aid to bibliographic search." *Commun. ACM*, 18(6) (June 1975): pp. 333–340.

Albright, David, Paul Brannan, and Christina Walrond. 2010. .ISIS Reports: "Did Stuxnet Take Out 1,000 Centrifuges at the Natanz Enrichment Plant? Preliminary Assessment." In `http://isis-online.org/isis-reports/detail/did-stuxnet-take-out-1000-centrifuges-at-the-natanz-enrichment-plant/`.

Arzt, S., S. Rasthofer, C. Fritz, E. Bodden, A. Bartel, J. Klein, Y. Le Traon, D. Octeau, and P. McDaniel. 2014. "FlowDroid: Precise Context, Flow, Field, Object-sensitive and Lifecycle-aware Taint Analysis for Android Apps." *SIGPLAN Not.* 49(6): pp. 259–269.

Bierma, M., E. Gustafson, J. Erickson, D. Fritz, and Y. R. Choe. 2014. "Andlantis: Large-scale Android Dynamic Analysis." In Proceedings of the Third Workshop on Mobile Security Technologies (MoST) 2014. San Jose, CA, USA.

Blasco, Jaime. 2014. "Scanbox: A Reconnaissance Framework Used with Watering Hole Attacks." In `https://www.alienvault.com/open-threat-exchange/blog/scanbox-a-reconnaissance-framework-used-on-watering-hole-attacks`.

Blue Coat Systems. 2014. "One-day Wonders: How Malware Hides Among the Internet's Short-Lived Websites." In `https://www.bluecoat.com/security-report-one-day-wonders`.

Bos, Herbert. "Shelia: A client-side honeypot for attack detection." In `http://www.cs.vu.nl/~herbertb/misc/shelia/`.

Boutin, Jean-Ian. 2013. "Targeted information stealing attacks in South Asia use email, signed binaries." In `http://www.welivesecurity.com/2013/05/16/targeted-threat-pakistan-india/`.

Burguera, Iker, Urko Zurutuza, and Simin Nadjm-Tehrani. 2011. "Crowdroid: Behavior-based malware detection system for Android." In Proceedings of the 1st ACM workshop on Security and privacy in smartphones and mobile devices (SPSM) 2011. ACM, New York, NY, USA, pp. 15–26.

Chen, Xiaobo and Dan Caselden. 2013. "New IE Zero-Day Found in Watering Hole Attack." In `http://www.fireeye.com/blog/technical/2013/11/new-ie-zero-day-found-in-watering-hole-attack.html`.

Cisco Systems (2014). Cisco Visual Networking Index: Forecast and Methodology, pp. 2013–2018.

Cooijmans, T., J. de Ruiter, and E. Poll. 2014. "Analysis of Secure Key Storage Solutions on Android." In Proceedings of the 4th ACM Workshop on Security and Privacy in Smartphones and Mobile Devices (SPSM) 2014. ACM, New York, NY, USA, pp. 11–20.

Crussell, J., R. Stevens, and H. Chen. 2014. "MAdFraud: Investigating ad fraud in android applications." In Proceedings of the 12th annual international conference on Mobile systems, applications, and services (MobiSys) 2014. ACM, New York, NY, USA, pp. 123–134.

Curtsinger, Charlie, Benjamin Livshits, Benjamin Zorn, and Christian Seifert. 2011. "ZOZZLE: Fast and Precise In-Browser JavaScript Malware Detection." In Proceedings of the 20th USENIX Conference on Security Symposium, pp. 33–48.

Dabrowski, A., K. Krombholz, J. Ullrich, and E. R. Weippl. 2014. "QR Inception: Barcode-in-Barcode Attacks." In Proceedings of the 4th ACM Workshop on Security and Privacy in Smartphones and Mobile Devices (SPSM) 2014. ACM, New York, NY, USA, pp. 3–10.

Dinaburg, Artem, Paul Royal, Monirul Sharif, and Wenke Lee. 2008. "Ether: Malware analysis via hardware virtualization extensions." In Proceedings of the 15th ACM conference on Computer and communications security, pp. 51–62.

The Economist. 2010. "War in the fifth domain: Are the mouse and keyboard the new weapons of conflict?" In `http://www.economist.com/node/16478792`.

Fahl, S., S. Dechand, H. Perl, F. Fischer, J. Smrcek, and M. Smith. 2014. "Hey, NSA: Stay Away from my Market! Future Proofing App Markets against Powerful Attackers." In Proceedings of the 2014 ACM SIGSAC Conference on Computer and Communications Security (CCS) 2014. ACM, New York, NY, USA, pp. 1143–1155.

Farshchi, Jamil. 2010. "Statistical-Based Intrusion Detection." In `http://www.symantec.com/connect/articles/statistical-based-intrusion-detection`.

Feng, Y., S. Anand, I. Dillig, and A. Aiken. 2014. "Apposcopy: Semantics-based detection of Android malware through static analysis." In Proceedings of the 22nd ACM SIGSOFT International Symposium on Foundations of Software Engineering (FSE) 2014. ACM, New York, NY, USA, pp. 576–587.

Fewer, Stephen. "Reflective DLL Injection." In `https://github.com/stephenfewer/ReflectiveDLLInjection`.

Fisher, D. H., M. J. Pazzani, and P. Langley (eds.). 1991. *Concept Formation: Knowledge and Experience in Unsupervised Learning.* San Francisco: Morgan Kaufmann.

Fisher, Dennis. 2012. "Final Report on DigiNotar Hack Shows Total Compromise of CA Servers." In `http://threatpost.com/final-report-diginotar-hack-shows-total-compromise-ca-servers-103112/77170`.

Frantzen, Swa. 2011. "DigiNotar breach – the story so far." In `https://isc.sans.edu/diary/DigiNotar+breach+-+the+story+so+far/11500`.

Fusco, F., M. Stoecklin, and M. Vlachos. 2010. "NET-FLi: On-the-fly Compression, Archiving and Indexing of Streaming Network Traffic," *VLDB End.* 3(2): pp. 1382–1393.

Ge, X., H. Vijayakumar, and T. Jaeger. 2014. "Sprobes: Enforcing Kernel Code Integrity on the TrustZone Architecture." In Proceedings of the Third Workshop on Mobile Security Technologies (MoST) 2014. San Jose, CA, USA.

Global Research & Analysis Team, Kaspersky Lab. 2013. "Winnti. More than just a game." In `http://securelist.com/analysis/internal-threats-reports/37029/winnti-more-than-just-a-game/`.

Goodin, Dan. 2012. "SHA1 crypto algorithm underpinning Internet security could fall by 2018." In `http://arstechnica.com/security/2012/10/sha1-crypto-algorithm-could-fall-by-2018/`.

Gorla, A., I. Tavecchia, F. Gross, and A. Zeller. 2014. "Checking App Behavior Against App Descriptions." In Proceedings of the 36th International Conference on Software Engineering (ICSE) 2014. ACM, New York, NY, USA, pp. 1025–1035.

Green, Matthew. 2012. "The Internet is broken: could we please fix it?" In `http://blog.cryptographyengineering.com/2012/02/how-to-fix-internet.html`.

Grier, C., L. Ballard, J. Caballero, N. Chachra, C. J. Dietrich, K. Levchenko, P. Mavrommatis, et al. 2012. "Manufacturing Compromise: The Emergence of Exploit-as-a-Service." In Proceedings of the ACM conference on Computer and communications security, pp. 821–832.

Gudeth, Kevin, Matthew Pirretti, Katrin Hoeper, and Ron Buskey. 2011. "Delivering secure applications on commercial mobile devices: The case for bare metal hypervisors." In Proceedings of the 1st ACM workshop on Security and privacy in smartphones and mobile devices (SPSM) 2011. ACM, New York, NY, USA, pp. 33–38.

Gummeson, J. J., B. Priyantha, D. Ganesan, D. Thrasher, and P. Zhang. 2013. "EnGarde: Protecting the mobile phone from malicious NFC interactions." In Proceedings of the 11th annual international conference on Mobile systems, applications, and services (MobiSys) 2013. ACM, New York, NY, USA, pp. 445–458.

Hu, W., D. Octeau, P. D. McDaniel, and P. Liu. 2014. "Duet: Library integrity verification for android applications." In Proceedings of the 2014 ACM conference on Security and privacy in wireless and mobile networks (WiSec) 2014. ACM, New York, NY, USA, pp. 141–152.

Hunt, Galen, and Doug Brubacher. 1999. "Detours: Binary Interception of Win32 Functions." In Proceedings of the 3rd USENIX Windows NT Symposium.

Invernizzi, Luca, S. Benvenuti, M. Cova, P. M. Comparetti, C. Kruegel, and G. Vigna. 2012. "EvilSeed: A guided approach to finding malicious web pages." In Proceedings of the 2012 IEEE Symposium on Security and Privacy, pp. 428–442.

Invernizzi, Luca, L. Invernizzi, S. Benvenuti, P. M. Comparetti, M. Cova, C. Kruegel, and G. Vigna. 2014. "Nazca: Detecting Malware Distribution in Large-Scale Networks." In Proceedings of the Network and Distributed System Security Symposium (NDSS).

Ho, Grant, Dan Boneh, Lucas Ballard, and Niels Provos. 2014. "Tick tock: Building browser red pills from timing side channels." In Proceedings of the 8th USENIX Workshop on Offensive Technologies (WOOT).

K, Abid Rahman. 2012. "K-Means Clustering – 1: Basic Understanding," `http://opencvpython.blogspot.com/2012/12/k-means-clustering-1-basic-understanding.html`.

Kapravelos, Alexandros, Marco Cova, Christopher Kruegel, and Giovanni Vigna. 2011. "Escape from monkey island: Evading high-interaction honeyclients." In Proceedings of Detection of Intrusions and Malware, and Vulnerability Assessment (DIMVA), pp. 124–143.

Kapravelos, Alexandros, Yan Shoshitaishvili, Marco Cova, Christopher Kruegel, and Giovanni Vigna. 2013. "Revolver: An Automated Approach to the Detection of Evasive Web-based Malware." In Proceedings of the 22nd USENIX Security Symposium, pp. 637–652.

Karagiannis, T., A. Broido, N. Brownlee, K. Claffy, and M. Faloutsos. 2004. "Is P2P dying or just hiding?" In Proceedings of the Global Telecommunications Conference, 2004 IEEE.

Kirat, Dhilung, Giovanni Vigna, and Christopher Kruegel. 2014. "BareCloud: Bare-metal analysis-based evasive malware detection." In Proceedings of the 23rd USENIX Security Symposium, pp. 287–301.

Kirk, Jeremy. 2013. "Hacking victim Bit8 blames SQL injection flaw." In `http://www.infoworld.com/article/2612962/intrusion-detection/hacking-victim-bit9-blames-sql-injection-flaw.html`.

Kohavi, R., and G. H. John. 1997. "Wrappers for Feature Subset Selection." *Artificial Intelligence*, 97(1–2) pp. 273–324.

Kolbitsch, Clemens, Benjamin Livshits, Ben Zorn, and Christian Seifert. 2012. "Rozzle: De-cloaking Internet Malware." In Proceedings of the Oakland Symposium on Security and Privacy (SP), 2012, pp. 443–457.

Krebs, Brian. 2013. "Security Firm Bit9 Hacked, Used to Spread Malware." In `http://krebsonsecurity.com/2013/02/security-firm-bit9-hacked-used-to-spread-malware/`.

Lange, Matthias, Steffen Liebergeld, Adam Lackorzynski, Alexander Warg, and Michael Peter. 2011. "L4Android: A generic operating system framework for secure smartphones." In Proceedings of the 1st ACM workshop on Security and privacy in smartphones and mobile devices (SPSM) 2011. ACM, New York, NY, USA, pp. 39–50.

Li, Qing. 2008. "A Novel Approach to Manage Asymmetric Traffic Flows for Secure Network Proxies." In Proceedings of the Network and Parallel Computing IFIP International Conference (NPC) 2008, Shanghai, China.

Li, Zhou, Sumayah Alrwais, Yinglian Xie, Fang Yu, and XiaoFeng Wang. 2013. "Finding the linchpins of the dark web: A study on topologically dedicated hosts on malicious web infrastructures." In Proceedings of the Symposium on Security and Privacy (SP) Conference, 2013, pp. 112–126.

Liang, S., A. W. Keep, M. Might, S. Lyde, T. Gilray, P. Aldous, and D. Van Horn. 2013. "Sound and precise malware analysis for android via pushdown reachability and entry-point saturation." In Proceedings of the Third ACM workshop on Security and privacy in smartphones and mobile devices (SPSM) 2013. ACM, New York, NY, USA, pp. 21–32.

Luo, Jim and Myong Kang. 2011. "Application Lockbox for Mobile Device Security." In Proceedings of the 2011 Eighth International Conference on Information Technology: New Generations (ITNG) 2011. IEEE Computer Society, Las Vegas, NV, USA, pp. 336–341.

Manning, Christopher D., Prabhakar Raghavan, and Hinrich Schütze. 2008. *Introduction to Information Retrieval.* Cambridge University Press.

McGregor, Anthony, Mark Hall, Perry Lorier, and James Brunskill. 2004. "Flow Clustering Using Machine Learning Techniques." In Proceedings of the 5th International Passive and Active Network Measurement International Workshop (PAM) 2004.

Mekky, Hesham, Ruben Torres, Zhi-Li Zhang, Sabyasachi Saha, and Antonio Nucci. 2014. "Detecting Malicious HTTP Redirections Using Trees of User Browsing Activity." In Proceedings of the 33rd IEEE International Conference on Computer Communications (INFOCOM), pp. 1159–1167.

Moran, Ned, Mike Scott, Sai Omkar Vashisht, and Thoufique Haq. 2013. "Operation Ephemeral Hydra: IE Zero-Day Linked to DeputyDog Uses Diskless Method." November 10, 2013. In `http://www.fireeye.com/blog/technical/cyber-exploits/2013/11/operation-ephemeral-hydra-ie-zero-day-linked-to-deputydog-uses-diskless-method.html`.

Morley, Patrick. 2013. "Bit9 and Our Customers' Security." In `https://blog.bit9.com/2013/02/08/bit9-and-our-customers-security/`.

Müller, Thomas, Benjamin Mack, and Mehmet Arziman. "Web Exploit Finder." In `http://www.xnos.org/security/web-exploit-finder.html`.

Nappa, Antonio, Zhaoyan Xu, Zubair Rafique, Juan Caballero, and Guofei Gu. 2014. "CyberProbe: Towards Internet-Scale Active Detection of Malicious Servers." In Proceedings of the 21st Annual Network and Distributed System Security Symposium (NDSS), San Diego, CA, USA, pp. 1–15.

Nazario, Jose. 2009. "PhoneyC: A Virtual Client Honeypot." In Proceedings of the 2nd USENIX conference on Large-scale exploits and emergent threats: botnets, spyware, worms, and more (LEET).

Ness, Jonathan. 2012. Microsoft Security Response Center, "Flame malware collision attack explained." In `http://blogs.technet.com/b/srd/archive/2012/06/06/` `more-information-about-the-digital-certificates-used-to-sign-the-` `flame-malware.aspx`.

Neuner, S., V. van der Veen, M. Lindorfer, M. Huber, G. Merzdovnik, M. Mulazzani, and E. Weippl. 2014. "Enter Sandbox: Android Sandbox Comparison." In Proceedings of the 3rd Workshop on Mobile Security Technologies (MoST) 2014. San Jose, CA, USA.

Nguyen, Thuy T.T., and Grenville Armitage. 2008. "A Survey of Techniques for Internet Traffic Classification Using Machine Learning." *IEEE Communications Surveys & Tutorials*, 10(4): pp. 56–76.

Oberheide, Jon, Kaushik Veeraraghavan, Evan Cooke, Jason Flinn, and Farnam Jahanian. 2008. "Virtualized in-cloud security services for mobile devices." In Proceedings of the First Workshop on Virtualization in Mobile Computing (MobiVirt) 2008. ACM, New York, NY, USA, pp. 31–35.

Rastogi, V., Y. Chen, and X. Jiang. 2013. "DroidChameleon: Evaluating Android anti-malware against transformation attacks." In Proceedings of the 8th ACM SIGSAC symposium on Information, computer and communications security (ASIA CCS) 2013. ACM, New York, NY, USA, pp. 329–334.

Ratazzi, P., Y. Aafer, A. Ahlawat, H. Hao, Y. Wang, and W. Du. 2014. "A Systematic Security Evaluation of Android's Multi-User Framework." In Proceedings of the Third Workshop on Mobile Security Technologies (MoST) 2014. San Jose, CA, USA.

Reich, Y., and S. Fenves. 1991. "The formation and use of abstract concepts in design." In D.Fisher, M.Pazzani, and P.Langley (eds.), *Concept Formation: Knowledge and Experience in Unsupervised Learning*. Morgan Kaufmann, San Mateo, CA, pp. 323–353.

Riden, Jamie. 2008. "How Fast-Flux Service Networks Work." In `http://www` `.honeynet.org/node/132`.

Rossow, Christian, Christian Dietrich, and Herbert Bos. 2013. "Large-scale analysis of malware downloaders." In Proceedings of the 9th international conference on Detection of Intrusions and Malware, and Vulnerability Assessment (DIMVA), pp. 42–61.

Russello, G., A. B. Jimenez, H. Naderi, and W. van der Mark. 2013. "FireDroid: Hardening security in almost-stock Android." In Proceedings of the 29th Annual Computer Security Applications Conference (ACSAC) 2013. ACM, New York, NY, USA, pp. 319–328.

Seifert, Christian and Ramon Steenson. 2008. "Capture-HPC Client Honeypot/ Honeyclient." In `https://projects.honeynet.org/capture-hpc`.

Shabtai, Asaf, Uri Kanonov, and Yuval Elovici. 2010. "Intrusion detection for mobile devices using the knowledge-based, temporal abstraction method." *J. Syst. Softw.* 83(8): pp. 1524–1537.

Soska, Kyle, and Nicolas Christin. 2014. "Automatically Detecting Vulnerable Websites Before They Turn Malicious." In Proceedings of the 23rd USENIX Security Symposium, 2014, pp. 625–640.

Sotirov, Alexander, Marc Stevens, Jacob Appelbaum, Arjen Lenstra, David Molnar, Dag Arne Osvik, and Benne de Weger. 2008. "MD5 considered harmful today: Creating a rogue CA certificate." In `http://www.win.tue.nl/hashclash/rogue-ca/`.

Stringhini, Gianluca, Christopher Kruegel, and Giovanni Vigna. 2013. "Shady paths: Leveraging surfing crowds to detect malicious web pages." In Proceedings of the ACM conference on Computer and communications security, pp. 133–144.

Tendulkar, V., and W. Enck. 2014. "An Application Package Configuration Approach to Mitigating Android SSL Vulnerabilities." In Proceedings of the 3rd Workshop on Mobile Security Technologies (MoST) 2014. San Jose, CA, USA.

Tongaonkar, Alok, Ram Keralapura, and Antonio Nucci. 2013. "SANTaClass: A Self Adaptive Network Traffic Classification System." In IFIP Networking 2013 Conference, Brooklyn, NY, USA, May 22–24, 2013, pp. 1–9.

Truong, H. T. T., E. Lagerspetz, P. Nurmi, A. J. Oliner, S. Tarkoma, N. Asokan, and S. Bhattacharya. 2014. "The company you keep: Mobile malware infection rates and inexpensive risk indicators." In Proceedings of the 23rd international conference on World wide web (WWW) 2014. ACM, New York, NY, USA, pp. 39–50.

Vadrevu, Phani, Babak Rahbarinia, Roberto Perdisci, Kang Li, and Manos Antonakakis. 2013. "Measuring and Detecting Malware Downloads in Live Network Traffic." In Proceedings of the 18th European Symposium on Research in Computer Security (ESORICS), pp. 556–573.

Vidas, T., J. Tan, J. Nahata, C. L. Tan, N. Christin, and P. Tague. 2014. "A5: Automated Analysis of Adversarial Android Applications." In Proceedings of the 4th ACM Workshop on Security and Privacy in Smartphones and Mobile Devices (SPSM) 2014. ACM, Scottsdale, AZ, USA, pp. 39–50.

Vidas, T., and N. Christin. 2014. "Evading android runtime analysis via sandbox detection." In Proceedings of the 9th ACM symposium on Information, computer and communications security (ASIA CCS) 2014. ACM, New York, NY, USA, pp. 447–458.

Vincent, Johann, Christine Porquet, Maroua Borsali, and Harold Leboulanger. 2011. "Privacy protection for smartphones: An ontology-based firewall." In *Information Security Theory and Practice: Security and Privacy of Mobile Devices in Wireless Communication*, Claudio A.Ardagna and JianyingZhou (eds.). Heidelberg: Springer, pp. 371–380.

Wang, Gang, Jack Stokes, Cormac Herley, and David Felstead. 2013. "Detecting Malicious Landing Pages in Malware Distribution Networks." In Proceedings of the 43rd Annual IEEE/IFIP International Conference on Dependable Systems and Networks (DSN), pp. 1–11.

Wang, R., L. Xing, X. Wang, and S. Chen. 2013. "Unauthorized origin crossing on mobile platforms: Threats and mitigation." In Proceedings of the 2013 ACM SIGSAC conference on Computer and communications security (CCS) 2013. ACM, New York, NY, USA, pp. 635–646.

Watkins, L., C. Corbett, B. Salazar, K. Fairbanks, and W. H. Robinson. 2013. "Using Network Traffic to Remotely Identify the Type of Applications Executing on Mobile Devices." In Proceedings of the 2nd Workshop on Mobile Security Technologies (MoST) 2013. San Francisco, CA, USA.

Wei, F., S. Roy, X. Ou, and Robby. 2014. "Amandroid: A Precise and General Inter-component Data Flow Analysis Framework for Security Vetting of Android Apps." In Proceedings of the 2014 ACM SIGSAC Conference on Computer and Communications Security (CCS) 2014. ACM, New York, NY, USA, pp. 1329–1341.

Werthmann, T., R. Hund, L. Davi, A. Sadeghi, and T. Holz. 2013. "PSiOS: Bring your own privacy and security to iOS devices." In Proceedings of the 8th ACM SIGSAC symposium on Information, computer and communications security (ASIA CCS) 2013. ACM, New York, NY, USA, pp. 13–24.

West, Andrew G., and Aziz Mohaisen. 2014. "Metadata-driven Threat Classification of Network Endpoints Appearing in Malware." In Proceedings of the 11th Conference on Detection of Intrusions and Malware and Vulnerability Assessment (DIMVA) 2014, LNCS 8550, Sven Deitrich (ed.), Egham, UK, pp. 152–171.

Witten, Ian H., Alistair Moffat, and Timothy C. Bell. 1999. *Managing Gigabytes: Compressing and Indexing Documents and Images*. Morgan Kaufmann.

Wu, K., E. Otoo, and A. Shoshani. 2006. Optimizing bitmap indices with efficient compression. *ACM Trans. on Database Systems*, 31: pp. 1–38.

Yang, W., J. Li, Y. Zhang, Y. Li, J. Shu, and D. Gu. 2014. "APKLancet: Tumor payload diagnosis and purification for android applications." In Proceedings of the 9th ACM symposium on Information, computer and communications security (ASIA CCS) 2014. ACM, New York, NY, USA, pp. 483–494.

Yang, Z., M. Yang, Y. Zhang, G. Gu, P. Ning, and X. S. Wang. 2013. "AppIntent: Analyzing sensitive data transmission in android for privacy leakage detection." In Proceedings of the 2013 ACM SIGSAC conference on Computer and communications security (CCS) 2013. ACM, New York, NY, USA, pp. 1043–1054.

Zarras, A., A. Kapravelos, G. Stringhini, T. Holz, C. Kruegel, and G. Vigna. 2014. "The Dark Alleys of Madison Avenue: Understanding Malicious Advertisements." In Proceedings of the 14th ACM SIGCOMM Internet Measurement Conference (IMC) 2014. ACM, Vancouver, BC, Canada, pp. 373–380.

Zhang, Junjie, Christian Seifert, Jack Stokes, and Wenke Lee. 2011. "ARROW: GenerAting SignatuRes to Detect DRive-By DOWnloads." In Proceedings of the 20th international conference on World Wide Web, pp. 187–196.

Zhang, M., Y. Duan, H. Yin, and Z. Zhao. 2014. "Semantics-Aware Android Malware Classification Using Weighted Contextual API Dependency Graphs." In Proceedings of the 2014 ACM SIGSAC Conference on Computer and Communications Security (CCS) 2014. ACM, New York, NY, USA, pp. 1105–1116.

Zheng, M., M. Sun, and J. C. S. Lui. 2014. "DroidRay: A security evaluation system for customized android firmwares." In Proceedings of the 9th ACM symposium on Information, computer and communications security (ASIA CCS) 2014. ACM, New York, NY, USA, pp. 471–482.

Zhongyang, Y., Z. Xin, B. Mao, and L. Xie. 2013. "DroidAlarm: An all-sided static analysis tool for Android privilege-escalation malware." In Proceedings of the 8th ACM SIGSAC symposium on Information, computer and communications security (ASIA CCS) 2013. ACM, New York, NY, USA, pp. 353–358.

Zhou, W., Y. Zhou, M. Grace, X. Jiang, and S. Zou. 2013. "Fast, scalable detection of Piggybacked mobile applications." In Proceedings of the third ACM conference on Data and application security and privacy (CODASPY) 2013. ACM, New York, NY, USA, pp. 185–196.

Zorz, Zeljka. 2012. "Trustwave revokes 'MitM' certificate, vows never to issue one again." In http://www.net-security.org/secworld.php?id=12369.

Index

A

AAA (Authentication, Authorization, and Accounting), 176

Abstract Syntax Tree (ASTs), Zozzle applying to content analysis, 140–142

access control
policy decisions and, 70
web access policies, 164–167

access logging
filtering access logs, 257
policies, 167–170

access points (APs), network security and, 314

ACEs (access control entries), 260

ACLs (access control lists), 260

actions, compared with properties, 181

ad arbitration, 308

ad fraud, 308

ad networks, malvertising attacks, 113–114

advanced persistent threats. *See* APTs (advanced persistent threats)

Advanced RISC Machines (ARM), solutions to mobile security, 311

Aho-Corasick algorithm
extracting matching terms, 208–211
Prefix Trees compared with, 212–214

AIC (application intelligence and control), firewall deficiencies and, 6

allow policy, vs. deny-all policy, 165

AND operations
bitmap searches and, 276
connecting policy conditions and properties, 163

Android apps. *See also* Google Android

application signing transparency, 307

library integrity and SSL verification challenges, 307

Android gadgets, 3–4

Android OS
mobile device market, 299
NFC (Near Field Communication) in mobile devices, 306–307
solutions to mobile security, 309–310
use of WebView class, 305–306

antivirus solutions
access logging policies, 169–170
cloud-based, 309
components of content analysis system, 138
embedded devices and, 4
end-point solutions, 121–122
implementing security policies, 90–91
mobile devices and, 304–305
safe content retrieval policies, 177

Apache log format, 255

Apache Mahout, sources of URL classifiers, 129

Apache Subversion (SVN), log management and analysis, 256

Apple iOS. *See* iOS

application classification
Aho-Corasick algorithm for extracting matching terms, 208–211
classifier performance evaluation, 243–247
comparing classifiers with proxies, 247–250
considerations in automatic signature generation, 225–226
EM (Expectation-Maximization) in unsupervised machine learning, 237–240
extracting common terms, 220–222

feature selection in machine learning, 228–232
flow set construction for term mining, 218–220
functions of signature distiller, 222–225
generating application signatures automatically, 216–218
generating application signatures manually, 214–216
history of classification techniques, 204–206
K-means clustering in unsupervised machine learning, 240–243
machine learning approach to, 226–228
Naïve Bayes method in feature selection, 233–236
overview, 203–204
prefix-tree signature representation, 211–214
signature-based pattern matching in, 206–208
summary, 247–250
supervised machine learning, 232–233
unsupervised machine learning, 236

application intelligence and control (AIC), firewall deficiencies and, 6

application lock boxes, mobile security solutions, 308

application proxies, components of secure proxies, 20

application signatures. *See also* signature-based pattern matching
defined, 203
generating automatically, 216–218
generating manually, 214–216
signature distiller and, 222–225

application signing transparency, 307